Saving Our Cities

Saving Our Cities

A Progressive Plan to Transform Urban America

William W. Goldsmith

Cornell University Press

Ithaca and London

Publication of this book was made possible, in part, by a grant from the Clarence S. Stein Institute for Urban and Landscape Studies, Cornell University. The publisher also gratefully acknowledges the support of the institute's director, Stephan Schmidt.

First published 2016 by Cornell University Press
Printed in the United States of America

Library of Congress Cataloging-in-Publication Data

Names: Goldsmith, William W., author.
Title: Saving our cities : a progressive plan to transform urban America / William W. Goldsmith.
Description: Ithaca : Cornell University Press, 2016. | Includes bibliographical references and index.
Identifiers: LCCN 2016015482 | ISBN 9781501704314 (cloth : alk. paper)
Subjects: LCSH: Urban policy—United States. | City planning—United States. | Sociology, Urban—United States.
Classification: LCC HT167 .G665 2016 | DDC 307.760973—dc23
LC record available at https://lccn.loc.gov/2016015482

Cornell University Press strives to use environmentally responsible suppliers and materials to the fullest extent possible in the publishing of its books. Such materials include vegetable-based, low-VOC inks and acid-free papers that are recycled, totally chlorine-free, or partly composed of nonwood fibers. For further information, visit our website at www.cornellpress.cornell.edu.

Cloth printing   10 9 8 7 6 5 4 3 2 1

In memory of Maggie—
teacher, editor, and companion extraordinaire

Contents

ACKNOWLEDGMENTS

The sources for this book are listed in great detail in the many endnotes, but special credit is due to a small number of indefatigable researcher/ activists whose persistent advocacy and clearheaded analyses have clarified things and helped hold our feet to the fire. More importantly, they have pushed the nation toward turning points in urban policy: on the drug war, Marc Mauer; on food and nutrition, Marion Nestle; on schools, Deborah Meier; and on city austerity and inequality, Peter Marcuse. On race, still the American dilemma, I owe much to June Thomas and to POCIG, the Planners of Color Interest Group.

Thanks to Cornell undergraduates in urban studies and graduate students in city and regional planning for many classroom discussions of the subjects in this book. Special thanks to students who helped as research assistants over a period of several years, often while working on master's theses: Anna Read, Amanda Hickey, Jennifer Pierce, Lauren Schunk, Anna Brawley, Aditi Sen, Cymone Bedford, Becky Gershon, Sam Scoppettone, Miran Jang, Amy Ellison, Vishwesh Viswanathan, Leah Coldham, Joy Chen, Kevin Waskells, and Joe Rukus; and to others writing closely related theses: Jonathan Welle-meyer, Nora Wright, and Lena Afridi.

Thanks to friends and colleagues who read the manuscript at one stage or another and provided generous comments: Pierre Clavel, Peter Wis-soker, Neil Hertz, Matthew Drennan, Paul Sawyer. In response to lec-tures, Marco Cremasci, Peter Marcuse, Rolf Pendall, and Bob Beauregard helped at crucial junctures. Thanks to editor Michael McGandy and two anonymous readers for the Cornell Press who provided extremely gener-ous suggestions that sharpened my arguments. Thanks also to Susan Specter, Susan Barnett, and Bethany Wasik at the press and copy editor Glenn Novak.

Thanks to Johanna Looye for arranging a talk for the National Under-ground Railroad Freedom Center in Cincinnati; Chris and Hazel Gunn, for hosting upstate URPE conversations; Ben Kohl, for so many friendly debates. Sudeshna Mitra, Kanishka Goonewardena, Brian Mier, and Sheryl-Ann Simpson variously collaborated and conspired to help, as have board members, staff, and prisoner-students of CPEP (the Cornell Prison Education Program).

I usually took the advice from all these helpful people, but not always, so the errors remain mine alone.

Looking Upstream

Go up the stream . . . to see who is pushing the people in.

TOM JOHNSON, MAYOR OF CLEVELAND, 1901–1909

America abuses its cities and their poorest suburbs, mistreating them like despised stepchildren, first to be blamed and last to be helped. Treated with negligence and even hostility, these places are deprived of resources and discouraged from using their own energies and ideas. Federal and state budgets, regulations, and programs, in line with the interests of corporations and privileged citizens, stand in the way of progressive reform. The failures weaken entire metropolitan areas, which nearly everywhere in America are tied closely to the fate of their central cities.

Policies in four areas—on austerity, schools, food, and drugs—have a great deal to do with urban affairs, yet they rarely enter into serious discussions of city or metropolitan well-being. Across a wide range of places, from small cities to giant metropolises, from central cities to sprawling suburbs, policies in these four areas have made things worse rather than better. Critics have pointed out the failures and posed sensible, feasible alternatives. They have spoken in opposition to counterproductive policies locally and nationally, and people are beginning to listen. As we move toward the turning point after a long downward trend of negative social change, this is a moment to be seized, to prepare to move upward. Each of these city/metropolitan issues has become a hot item on the national agenda. It makes sense now to tie them together, not as elements external to cities but as part of a new, more progressive urban agenda.

As I will show, many cities and a number of states have new programs under way to restrain or redirect policies that have exacerbated inequality, damaged schools, worsened nutrition, and created violence over drugs. Outspoken politicians propose far-reaching improvements that would aid cities. Well-armed advocacy groups offer support. My contention is that if cities, with federal and state assistance, were to take on these four interrelated problems, then positive movement would occur in traditional urban policy as well. The combination would assist cities and pump new energy in, to revitalize metropolitan areas. Empowered by new city-centered energy, the entire nation would prosper.

The rhetoric on traditional sorts of urban reform is often more promising than the practice, with calls for broad national policies that would narrow household income disparities and combat racial injustice, as well as demands for expansion of specific "urban" programs for housing and transportation, social services, inter-municipal coordination, and environmental protection. The most commonly regarded "urban" policies are place-based interventions such as urban renewal, redevelopment, and community development. But these have had limited influence on improving conditions in cities, often enough producing distributive effects that worsen inequalities.

Neither the broad reforms nor the more specific urban programs will help enough, as long as external forces keep dragging cities and poor suburbs down. Some things seem not to change: a century ago, Cleveland's Mayor Tom Johnson said that while it would be noble to rescue drowning people by pulling them out of the river, it might be more useful to stop others upstream from throwing them in.[1] Federal and state policies and corporate power operated upstream then as they do now. This book makes the case for radical improvement in four "upstream" policies. These policies are not typically regarded as urban policies, but they ought to be. In their present forms they damage cities; but they can be changed. Such changes, I argue, have the best potential for improving our cities.

The good news? Each of the policies is ripe for reform. These issues attract the bright lights of the media, as popular movements challenge austerity, struggle to improve schools, worry about food problems, and oppose the drug war and unwarranted imprisonment. Politicians position themselves from time to time not too far behind. So far, cities have seen only minor progress, but one can imagine an accelerating trend. Indeed, the daily newspapers, the evening broadcasts, NPR and other radio stations, weekly magazines, and websites are filled with news about the subjects dealt with in this book. Some of the news is miserably depressing, some filled with promise. No book can keep up. The events follow their own schedule. But this book shows how yesterday's events fit into recurring patterns and how they are interconnected. Even though the book necessarily discusses events from the past, the analysis is about the future. It will help guide those who make reforms.

I will treat austerity first, because it offers the most encompassing view of federal (and corporate) policy toward cities. Without a discussion of the ways Wall Street and its acolytes demand austerity policies, we can see neither the reasons for austerity nor the ways it harms cities. Schools next, because although "everyone knows" suburban schools are good and city schools are bad, careful consideration of the evidence leads to a more critical stance. Food, next, to clarify the key role of corporations and the effects on cities of unrestrained capitalism. Drugs last because even though the drug war is widely considered to be insane—direct, in your face, and violent in particular city neighborhoods—the best solutions appear sensible only after a broader analysis.

City-damaging policies in these areas are tightly interwoven, reinforced by municipal divisions that isolate cities from suburbs, making the damages seem natural. But they are neither natural nor necessary. Human decisions govern the policies and lay out the divisions. State governments *create* municipal boundaries, allocate resources, establish municipal governments, and assign responsibilities. In the formal language of scholars, the society "socially constructs" these divisions in a seemingly neutral, evenhanded way, offering advantages to some jurisdictions and heaping penalties on others. When cities fail under unfair pressure, they themselves receive blame. When suburbs prosper, they deserve the gain.

Authorities erect boundary lines that constrain legal, social, and even physical exchange, to keep city damages from spreading. The chief executive for Oakland County, a Detroit suburb with a population of 1.2 million, reelected for more than twenty years, likes high fences. He explained his approach in 2014: "What we're gonna do is turn Detroit into an Indian reservation, where we herd all the Indians into the city, build a fence around it, and then throw in the blankets and corn."[2] Perhaps reflecting similar values, suburban police just outside Hartford, Connecticut, have been known to illegally stop black and Latino families, city residents driving on the weekend to picnic in suburban public parks, turning them back, sending them home—where municipal services fail, schools don't teach, good food is scarce, and drug warriors attack, to choke the cities inside the suburban white noose.

Fortunately, political tipping points are within reach. Rather than disempowering and damaging cities, federal and state policies instead can empower and enhance them. It would be a stretch to say that austerity as a mode of national economic management has run its course, but in many ways austerians do find themselves on the defensive. The election of activist organizer Betsy Hodges as mayor of Minneapolis in 2013 and then the inauguration of Bill de Blasio as mayor and the triumph of the Working Families Party in the New York City Council elections in 2013 signaled the rise of popular anti-austerity sentiment and the spread of frustration with inequality. Public school ills remain, as everyone knows, but people call persistently for improvements, and big-city education experiments abound. Philadelphia, for example, with one of the nation's most troubled school districts, shows promise in its efforts with "restorative justice" to replace "zero tolerance" suspensions and self-reinforcing patterns of failure. Similar experiments occur elsewhere.[3] Rising health costs and nearly epidemic obesity have led to widespread interest in healthier foods and better nutrition, including improvements in food access for needy city residents. The futility of the drug war and the high costs of prison growth have become clearer to the public year by year.

In each of these four areas city advocates and researchers have produced enormous bodies of evidence calling for reform. Vast troves of annual survey data as well as solid statistical analyses come from public agencies such as the National Center for Education Statistics, the Bureau of Justice Statistics, and the Food and Nutrition Service. More information comes from fair-minded advocacy organizations as diverse as the American Society of Civil Engineers, the American Federation of Teachers, the Food Research and Action Center, and the Drug Policy Alliance. Still more comes from think tanks on the left, center, and right, from various state

and city research organizations, new local programs, investigative jour-
nalists, and the research reports, journal articles, and books written by
hundreds of individual researchers and research teams based for the most
part at colleges and universities. One of my main tasks is to condense and
stratify evidence and arguments from thousands of often overlapping and
sometimes-conflicting documents, so as to write this relatively short book.

Municipalities and Political Power

In the many localities across each metropolitan area, political power is
exercised in overlapping jurisdictions among municipal, state, and federal
authorities, with commercial and nongovernmental players participating
as they will. Federal and state agencies, judicial systems, municipal governments, school districts, and various public and quasi-public authorities
all run programs, spend, regulate, and tax. Businesses lobby, fund political campaigns, invest in development, and pay (or evade) local, state, and
federal taxes. Nongovernmental organizations enter the fray in various
ways. Residents, elected and appointed officers and boards, public employees from zoning officers to police officers, private businesses, and other
groups enjoy complex and frequently disputatious relationships. Against
the assumption that governments simply govern, political economists and
political scientists have struggled for decades if not centuries to clarify
questions about the relative autonomy of the state at all levels, to what
extent the rules may be fair, and the degree to which private power, posi-
tioning, and especially money matter.[4]

At the municipal level, these questions confront many independent
jurisdictions. For example, the San Francisco Bay Area, not including
outlying parts of the region that the U.S. Census considers part of the
Combined Metropolitan Area, includes fifty independent towns and cities,
about as many school districts, as well as county governments and authorities, such as the autonomous Golden Gate Bridge, Highway and Transportation District.

For the four problems dealt with in this book, at both the national and
the local level, the municipal mix of political power varies considerably.
In the case of austerity and the city, the roles of big government and big
business may be paramount, with localities entering less often as initiators,

or makers, and more often as recipients, or takers. What happens on Wall Street and at the Treasury, or for that matter in the global economy, likely influences municipal budgets much more than decisions taken at the municipal level. For these considerations the structure and performance of the economy matters a great deal, as do the many routes through which corporations influence policy, from the revolving door of personnel between business suites and top-level Washington offices, to the writing of tax policy, to the funding of congressional, senatorial, and presidential campaigns. Contrary to claims of interested parties (say, the U.S. Chamber of Commerce), no clear and uniform "business interest" exists. Nevertheless, at the municipal level, business influence can be overwhelming, as illustrated in cases of the fiscal collapses of New York City and Cleveland in the 1970s and Detroit in the 2010s.

The situation is quite the opposite in the case of schools, where the intensely local interests of residents most often drive policy. Frequently the force behind the *formation* of suburban jurisdictions is the desire for exclusive control over the schools that only the residents' children can attend. This parochial form of control has been sometimes challenged and at other times reinforced by federal political leaders, including at crucial junctures chief justices of the Supreme Court and presidents.

In the case of food and nutrition, although cities and some suburbs take very heavy hits, for the most part national concerns predominate. A small number of giant corporations take the lead, while federal agencies play subordinate but crucial parts. Mostly, "food policy" is absent, as food producers on farms and in factories work in their own interests to develop new "products" and advertise. In cities and poor minority suburbs, severe problems loom large with the marketing of junk foods in stores and restaurants and with school meal inadequacies.

Finally, the politics surrounding the drug war take on still another configuration, in some ways simpler. In the political power plays over the war on drugs, the victims—the cities themselves—exercise almost no influence. Nor do the impoverished, otherwise unemployed drug peddlers and drug users, themselves likely African American and Latino residents of cities and select suburbs. The beneficiaries include a very few minority drug kings and *narcotraficantes*. More importantly, beneficiaries include various parties who participate in the drug economy and in the war itself, as well as bystanders—from bankers laundering money to congressional representatives working to protect the nation's youth, religious zealots, and bigots. Anti-drug policy has for more than a century been promoted as a struggle against the "other," anti-Chinese, anti-immigrant, anti-black, and anti-brown. So, as we will see, improvements in drug policy, of enormous import to cities, will have to come about in complex interplay among many partially invested parties, public and private, corporate and citizen.

As my argument moves from one topic to the next, the relative importance of the federal government, private corporations, local governments, and resident preferences will wax and wane. But always they will play off one another, as money and influence find ways to respond, or not, to residents' grievances and the high costs of continuing with the status quo. As a preview, the next section ranges across the broad checkerboard and complex set of interests that constitute important elements of one large metropolitan area.

Magnificence and Misery

The large, multinucleated region known as the Bay Area, anchored by the three cities of San Francisco, Oakland, and San Jose, constitutes the nation's fifth-most-populous metropolis, with about 8.5 million inhabitants. Mayor Richard J. Daley once said of the third metropolis, Chicago, it is neither too high, in comparison with New York, nor too spread out, in comparison with Los Angeles. One can say of the Bay Area that it is neither too populous nor too small, so that its successes and problems may illustrate the experiences of many urbanized areas nationwide.

San Francisco and the Bay Area are admired for magnificent vistas, cool foggy mornings followed by brilliant sunshine, prodigious wealth, technological innovation, progressive politics, diverse cultures, delicious cuisine, and cutting-edge health care. Heading north or south along the Pacific coast's Highway 1, the traveler moves on roads that are among the most scenic in the nation.

The area displays stunning affluence, even by California movie standards. It includes Silicon Valley, where corporations, the Defense Department, and venture capitalists first boomed with investments that led to today's remarkable assemblage of high-technology virtuosi. With Stanford University and the University of California at Berkeley, the Bay Area enjoys two of the world's foremost centers for research and learning, themselves surrounded by 130 junior colleges, colleges, and other universities. Thriving immigrant and ethnic neighborhoods throughout the area invite residents and visitors alike to stroll, shop, and eat. The area's grocery stores offer abundant, eye-catching, and nutritious varieties of fresh foods grown in the Central Valley. Area hospitals provide excellent basic care and attend patients from around the world with the highest levels of advanced treatment. Some of the strongest antitobacco efforts in the nation came from medical researchers at the University of California at San Francisco. Tolerance for recreational drug use is high throughout the region, and programs for treatment and rehabilitation are among the most advanced anywhere.

Sadly, that same wealthy, vibrant, diverse, and tolerant Bay Area is also a place where schools fail and people of color and immigrants suffer discrimination and mistreatment. It is a place where impoverishment can mean malnutrition. It is a place where the authorities unevenly enforce counterproductive drug laws, abusing neighborhoods and destroying lives. The beautiful Bay Area is a place afflicted with inequality.

Even in that wealthy Bay Area, thousands of children drop out each year without finishing high school. For immigrants who work at high-end jobs, life in the Bay Area can be splendid. For many others, especially those who have "nonwhite" skins, or who arrive poor, with little formal education or weak skills in English, the only employments available pay low wages and may be illegal. Nutritional deficiencies abound among children, the elderly, and working-age adults who are ill or infirm. Drug arrests in the Bay Area (and in the rest of the state) filled so many jail cells with African Americans and Latinos that the Golden State prison system was aptly called the Golden Gulag.

Destined for lifetimes of failure, school dropouts burden themselves, their families, and their communities. In the Oakland school district, to take but one case, out of a sample consisting of thirty-two hundred high school students from ninth through twelfth grade, barely half, only 53 percent, graduated on schedule in 2010. Thirty-seven percent of the total dropped out of school altogether. Among African American, Filipino, and Latino students, not even half managed to graduate. In the wealthier San Francisco school district, just across the bay, things are not quite so bad, but still not good, with about 19 percent of the city's Latino and African American students dropping out before graduation.[5]

In Santa Clara County, at the southern end of Silicon Valley, immigrants constitute 36 percent of the population. Some of them are well off, working as engineers and scientists, for example. The majority of immigrants are poor, however, and they include economic and political refugees from Africa, Asia, and Latin America, many without documentation. Poor immigrants are frequently denied access to the judicial system, even when they are hit with indefinite and mandatory detention. Federal agencies like Immigration and Customs Enforcement, or ICE, have acted with vigor. From 2009 until early 2012, ICE deported more than sixty thousand immigrants from California alone, even though the vast majority of deportees, about 70 percent, had not been convicted of any crime other than a routine traffic or administrative violation.[6]

In San Francisco and nearby Marin County (one of the wealthiest counties in the nation), nearly 225,000 people depend on the San Francisco Food Bank to provide weekly groceries. About two in five of the households who receive this food include a working adult; almost one in five is homeless; and among children in the delivery area, one in five needs assistance to regularly meet nutritional needs.[7] Another group, Food Runners, sends more than two hundred volunteers to collect perishable excess from more than 250 restaurants, bakeries, groceries, and farmers' markets. They deliver more than fifteen tons of food each week, enough for five thousand meals daily.[8] A third group, Project Open Hand, had 125 volunteers in 2012 who operated each day in San Francisco, Oakland, and Alameda County outside Oakland to prepare and deliver food to thirty-three hundred people with HIV/AIDS or who are homebound or critically ill, as well as forty-one hundred seniors who get lunch at community centers.[9]

Following the 2008 recession, the Obama administration overcame strong opposition to help with three redistributive moves: expanding food stamp eligibility, extending unemployment insurance, and reducing payroll taxes. Despite these moves, which put food on the table for more people, the need for volunteer assistance rose. The Alameda County Community Food Bank faced a doubling of demand for emergency food assistance between 2008 and 2012, and demands on the San Francisco Food Bank increased nearly as much, by 70 percent.[10]

If problems with austerity, schooling, and nutrition erode the region's vitality gradually, the drug war attacks more suddenly. In a drug bust in the suburban city of Vallejo and other East Bay locations in April 2012, federal agents seized "about 45,000 Ecstasy pills, 4 pounds of crack cocaine, a half-pound of heroin," $200,000 in cash, and about $1 million in property. Agents arrested twenty-five people associated with Thizz Nation, a group apparently involved in more than two decades of robberies of pizza parlors and banks, drug sales, and killings. According to Vallejo police lieutenant Ken Weaver, the bust, four years in the making, put an end to "an explosion of rap music and rock cocaine." DEA officials said that "the streets of Vallejo [would] be a little safer this [2012] summer."[11]

Maybe rap music was the problem, but without rap, who's left to track, report, and record the "urban" experience? Maybe the streets got safer, but the Vallejo bust was just one skirmish in a war on drugs that the record shows has not worked. Drug busts just move the problem around, leading to little or no reduction in drug use, exacerbating violence rather than limiting it, and destroying residential communities and individual lives.

Beyond the Bay Area, throughout the country, systematic failures in schooling, nutrition, and drugs occur also in less affluent and smaller metropolitan areas. Inequalities are extreme, worsened by austerity policies. The central city and usually some inner suburbs in every metropolitan area with more than two hundred thousand residents are highly likely to carry these burdens. In one key sense, these are *national* problems: added together, metropolitan areas two hundred thousand or larger comprise more than four-fifths of the country's entire population.

The Vitality of Cities

Core-city vitality connects tightly with metropolitan achievement to promote national success, as scholars have long pointed out. In the nineteenth century the French sociologist Émile Durkheim used the term "organic solidarity" to explain how the metropolis, especially its densely populated center, promotes social cohesion and mutual interdependence, leading to innovation, economic growth, and political progress. Urban planners, economists, and sociologists today speak of positive externalities or neighborhood effects. This functioning of urban areas as incubators of success is borne out even by counts of Wikipedia entries showing big cities as the most likely birthplaces of notable persons.[12]

In the twentieth century, Jane Jacobs's book *The Economy of Cities* prompted a renewed focus on innovation as a crucial process for the metropolis. Jacobs showed how a nation's economic power originates in the complexity and diversity of its broadly defined cities. Were we to follow Jacobs, we would cast our most important votes for governments not at federal or state levels, but in each metropolis. Earlier, with her *Death and Life of Great American Cities*, Jacobs aimed attention even more locally, toward neighborhoods, to demand that city planners of the urban renewal era change their destructive ways, to protect architectural diversity and human vitality in dense but human-scaled and varied city neighborhoods. For this earlier work Jacobs was celebrated, and the force of her ideas helped stop the bulldozers, but not often enough. Putting her two arguments together, we again connect the health of the central city with the success of the metropolis and the nation.

Three very different recent general-audience books by leading scholars emphasize this city-metropolis connection, tying each city together with its metropolitan area, marking them jointly as sources of national well-being. Although each of these books either overstates or neglects key issues, each recognizes the city at the center of its metropolis as the key site for social and economic progress. *Rebel Cities*, by geographer David Harvey, argues that the economic and social health of urban areas has long served as the main force for national change. As in many publications since his pathbreaking *Social Justice and the City*, Harvey puts the focus on the contradictions that plague the metropolis, of the sorts highlighted by the Occupy movement's One Percent challenge to Wall Street in 2011. Following arguments by the French urban sociologist Henri Lefebvre, Harvey finds that cities contain not only the concentrated power of the productive economy but also the seeds of revolutionary politics. For Harvey, "revolutionary movements frequently if not always assume an urban dimension." The working class, although traditionally constituted in factories and other places where employees collectively confront machines and bosses, can also be constituted in neighborhoods. Neighbors, confronting common problems, can organize and protest.[13] When Harvey argues for Lefebvre's "right to the city," he expresses visions and pathways recognizing not merely the city, but also its linked metropolitan economic heft, which serves as the mainspring for the social and economic changes that would lead to a reconstructed and more equal society.[14]

Another book connecting city and metropolis, *The Metropolitan Revolution: How Cities and Metros Are Fixing Our Broken Politics and Fragile Economy*, displays a celebratory mood. Authors Bruce Katz, director of the Metropolitan Policy Program of the Brookings Institution, and Jennifer Bradley, a journalist, bubble with enthusiasm about early twenty-first-century metropolitan achievements already under way. In these "revolutions," modest compared to Harvey's notion of the right to the city, metropolitan power and emergent authority eclipse the inadequate budgets of federal agencies and the restricting laws of states. Federal and state agencies serve as obstacles "organized as a collection of hardened silos," mired in their "dysfunction." Katz and Bradley's listings of vibrant and innovative city-centered metropolitan initiatives contain vague items such as "economy shaping in New York City and Northeast Ohio, society building in Houston, and coalition building in Denver and Los Angeles," ignoring corporate tax-dodging and underestimating municipal subordination to state legislation. But their work supports the notions that cities are key to national prosperity and that they need to escape negative pressures from the outside.

The third book, *Triumph of the City: How Our Greatest Invention Makes Us Richer, Smarter, Greener, Healthier, and Happier*, by urban economist Edward Glaeser, expands from celebration to carnival. Aimed not at his usual audience of urban economists, but at more general readers, Glaeser's book authoritatively attacks antiurbanism and praises cities' strengths—pointing to their "high productivity, wealth, social mobility, innovation, mutual understanding and personal freedom and even environmental sustainability." For Glaeser, the city's triumph is "the key to human development in the 21st century."[15]

Despite their marked differences, these three books argue convincingly for the importance of city-centered metropolitan economies and societies. They correctly stress the intimate connection between metropolitan well-being, on the one hand, and both national and inner-city vitality and health, on the other. Each book, in its own way, however, is too optimistic about "revolutionary" change. Glaeser, who focuses narrowly on individual consumer preferences, technological change, and markets, uses the familiar framework of mainstream economic theory to disregard almost entirely the focused and often overwhelming power of corporate decisions and political influence. He offers a rich palette of colorful examples, evidence for the enormously productive advantages of city density, emphasizing repeatedly the point made so long ago by Durkheim, that "urban concentrations can have magical consequences." Yet Glaeser neglects the force of concentrated money as it influences not only which kinds of industrial and commercial complexes will develop, and where, but also how policies and politics empower suburbs to shortchange their cities.[16] Katz and Bradley cherry-pick their examples of metropolitan innovation and success, thus overestimating so-called revolutionary capacities and leaving aside any serious consideration of the deep problems of inequality that remain in even their most successful cities. Both these books—*Triumph* and *Metropolitan Revolution*—decry poverty and racial inequity, yet they offer no clues for dealing with them, other than to claim that all will benefit from urban success. As we will see, it is not so simple

In *Rebel Cities*, Harvey focuses on precisely those deep problems of inequality, and—unlike the other authors—he deals with flaws in the underlying economic and political structure. But in its focus on those structures, and despite its rich and evocative detail, the book leads one to underestimate the distance to be traveled to overcome those who resist changes in the way the society is structured. One of my purposes in this book is to suggest four ways in which cities can move in this progressive direction.

All three books connect cities with their metropolitan areas. They point to the potential for locally based productive and progressive change, and they recognize that cities are essential for national success. Two other books go one step further, documenting recent progressive changes in cities and metropolitan areas. Pierre Clavel's *Activists in City Hall* reports on the many ways that some city governments already redistribute resources and city services to assist the neediest residents.[17] His studies show that coalitions of neighborhood groups, civil rights advocates, and other progressives can make improvements when they seize municipal power by winning control of city council or by electing strong mayors. Clavel's heartening evidence comes from a wide variety of cities, including Cleveland, Hartford, Santa Monica, Berkeley, Burlington, Boston, and Chicago. In *Just Growth*, Chris Benner and Manuel Pastor spread the net more broadly, identifying seventeen metropolitan regions that were "getting it (more or less) right" consistently from 1980 until 2000. A dozen of those city-regions with populations exceeding two hundred thousand reduced inequality as they generated economic growth—Boston, Appleton (WI),

Cincinnati, Columbus, Kansas City, Minneapolis, Jacksonville, Nashville, Ocala, Colorado Springs, Fort Collins, Olympia, and Seattle. These two books also err in their optimism: neither focuses on the ways in which federal policy and corporate power put damaging pressure on cities.

In the examples found in these five books we have fair evidence suggesting that Bill de Blasio's election in New York City—even if his reforms fall victim to the power of big money on the right—is no fluke. Similarly, the recent elections of progressive mayors and city councils in Pittsburgh, Minneapolis, Phoenix, Philadelphia, and Richmond (CA) stand as testimony to the pressure for change. There exists a sense that things are not right and that failing cities and deeply troubled neighborhoods connect tightly to a national economic and political malaise. This is good news, this spreading recognition that to fix the nation, we need to fix our cities. But the examples of positive change are still few, the successes tentative and incomplete, and the challenge to external pressures insufficient. As Ada Colao, the radical activist elected mayor of Barcelona, said upon her election in 2015, "City governments are key to the democratic revolution," but "one city alone cannot solve all the problems we are facing . . . because today the economy does not have borders."[18]

Doughnuts and Checkerboards

Conventional definitions and descriptions of cities, suburbs, neighborhoods, and districts prove inadequate to the task of understanding extensive urbanized areas. These conventions are even more problematic for those who would design better policies or practice progressive politics. When one says *city*, does one mean only the municipality in the center, or the entire metropolis, or something in between? Are some suburbs "urban" but others not? What about suburban places designated "city" by state law? How do we comprehend giant metropolitan areas that have two or several distinct, large, and dense administrative or commercial centers—Washington-Baltimore, for example? How do we deal with the fact that some municipal boundary lines are drawn close in (making San Francisco home for less than 10 percent of the Bay Area's population) while others are drawn much farther out (making New York City home for 36 percent of its region's population)?

Answers to these questions come typically in the form of stylized urban geographies. In the classic depiction of urban America in the twentieth century, the metropolis was a doughnut, with black, poor people constrained to live in the center, and white, more prosperous people in the surrounding suburban circles. In the twenty-first century, while large concentrations of poor minority residents continue to live in central cities, increasing numbers of black, Latino, and Asian residents, often majorities of minorities, live in suburban rings. For example, whereas African Americans in the Washington, DC, area previously resided mainly in poor neighborhoods in the District, today the largest concentration resides in suburban Prince George's County, Maryland, itself two-thirds black, one of the country's many majority-black suburban areas. Elsewhere, center-city economic revivals lead to claims that cities are doing fine—one thinks of high rents and costly lifestyles in San Francisco or Manhattan or Seattle. Even in troubled Philadelphia boosters brag about the Center City's revival. The doughnut form no longer holds.[19]

How, then, does one make sense of metropolitan social and economic geography? Consider the extreme case of New York, a three-state area with more than 23 million inhabitants, with a core city of 8.5 million. To the immediate north, amid the great white wealth of the Westchester County suburbs, pockets of poverty exist, with concentrations of minority residents. Yonkers, in Westchester, is a sizable city with poor black and Latino residents. Several smaller suburban enclaves of racialized poverty exist, some along the wealthy east shore of the Hudson River. Other poor suburbs, some of them sizable cities themselves, lie to the west, in New Jersey, and neighborhoods of poverty sprawl to the east, dotting the landscapes of Long Island and Connecticut. Even inside New York City's boundaries, the layout defies easy summary. One startling contrast involves two congressional districts, each with about six hundred thousand people. The fourteenth, the Upper East Side of Manhattan, one of the nation's wealthiest, practically abuts the sixteenth, the South Bronx, the nation's very poorest. Two parts of the central city, they "are barely a mile apart, separated by a few gritty streets and a thin muddy stretch of water known as the Harlem River."[20] The upshot? Analysis requires close attention to boundary lines, across which neighborhood racial and income characteristics vary sharply as one moves from area to area inside cities or across lines from one suburban jurisdiction to another.

In some ways and in many places, of course, the old doughnut-like clarity of city-suburb division almost holds. In the city of Detroit, non-Hispanic whites make up not even 8 percent of the residents, while in many of the surrounding suburban communities nearly everyone is white. Inside Detroit, where the suburban executive would fence in his reservation, more than 38 percent of families have annual incomes under $25,000, but among suburban residents, less than 13 percent are that poor. The city is bankrupt, but not the suburbs. Yet even in the Detroit suburban rings, things are more complex. In the suburban city of Flint, for example, population one hundred thousand, just an hour outside Detroit, 43 percent of families have incomes below $25,000.

In many metropolitan areas the pattern is more like an emerging checkerboard, with distinct zones of great wealth and others of great poverty occurring in both center and periphery, and with the race or ethnicity of residents nearly always aligned with their incomes. Some zones are long established and fairly stable, others are the results of recent shifts in real estate markets. The gap separating the poor, minority South Bronx from the silk-stocking Upper East Side repeats itself endlessly, separating usually small neighborhoods along many suburban corridors throughout the nation. In Ferguson, Missouri, a white policeman shot and killed a black teenager in the summer of 2014. This Saint Louis suburb has a population of about twenty thousand, in one of the most highly segregated metropolitan areas in the nation. Ferguson was until recently nearly all white. In 2014, although some observers reported it as racially mixed, even integrated, it appears instead to be two-thirds on its way to becoming a nearly all-black municipality.[21] The protests and militaristic repression that followed the killing served to remind us all of the tensions involved when players make their moves across the metropolitan checkerboard.

In the Los Angeles metropolitan area, concentrated poverty occurs in a more spread-out, uneven fashion, with poor and minority residents located in central districts, but also in zones lying across the enormous urbanized sprawl. In the city of Los Angeles itself, most census tracts have relatively low portions of poor households, but a few tracts are markedly poor. Predominantly black or Latino neighborhoods lie concentrated in South Central (now officially South) Los Angeles, with more than a half million residents. The Eighth City Council district, with a 2010 population of 243,000, was 3.9 percent white, 41 percent Latino, and 50 percent African American. Beyond the Los Angeles city and county limits there are very poor black and Latino neighborhoods in wealthy Orange County and in the Riverside suburbs far to the east. The city of Riverside has 314,000 residents, half Latino, 34 percent white, 18 percent below the poverty line.[22] Riverside County has 2.3 million residents, nearly half Latino, 39 percent white, 16 percent below the poverty line.

Styles of City Planning

The excellent ideas and programs that city planners and other policy makers put forth for fixing cities vary tremendously, but rarely do they tackle the underlying damages resulting from austerity, school failures, nutritional deficits, or drug conflicts. Some city observers see a center-city revival under way, but as Nicholas Lemann suggests, what people see depends on what they look for.[23] Some planners emphasize the benefits of improved urban design, as they did in San Francisco when they zoned building heights to magnify the city's steep hills and vistas. Other ideas stress the promotion of justice, community solidarity, and improved distribution of opportunity, using devices such as development fees to fund affordable housing, as urged by scholars and activists who belong to organizations like Planners' Network. Some call for other methods to improve and expand housing and develop neighborhoods, as in HOPE VI teardowns and redesigns of public housing, funded by the federal Department of Housing and Urban Development. HUD's Choice Neighborhoods program focuses on the neighborhood scale, rather than just the housing stock, and it aims, in theory at least, at turning areas of concentrated poverty into sustainable, mixed-income neighborhoods with increased access to jobs and services. Still others stress the advantages of wholesale center-city gentrification based on the attraction of upper-middle-class residents, or on the constructive civic role played by groups of elite, artistic, "creative" residents. Many city leaders across the nation also plan for economic growth based on attracting high-technology entrepreneurs, hoping for their own Silicon Valley bubbles. And then there are those who promote subsidies to outside investors, or encourage high-rise developments and the increase of center-city populations through the offer of tax advantages.

Most of these programs are appropriate in one context or another, to serve one goal or another. Unfortunately, most operate with biases toward helping those firms, residents, and neighborhoods that are *least* in need.

And none has been capable of responding to the most serious of the difficulties that our cities encounter.

New approaches are required. Good proposals to lessen austerity, support schools, improve nutrition, and deal with drugs have been put on the table, some advocated by politically effective groups at the national level, many more subjects for localized experiments. Pressures on respected but cautious institutions, such as the National Academy of Sciences, and on an otherwise uncooperative, uncollaborative Congress, have resulted in remarkable reforms, for example, in drug and prison legislation. Better policies are already under consideration by many state legislatures, and they are being introduced by a growing number of cities. Even though these issues are national in scope, they are quintessentially urban. And although solutions will often begin with city action, the problems are directed at cities and most severe in cities. A quick review displays the challenges.

Austerity and Inequality

Serious national shortcomings bear on city viability, and they have recently risen in prominence. The United States has fallen rapidly behind, although no prominent Republican or Democratic politician will mention it. America is *not* number one. According to recent surveys, thirty-three of the world's thirty-five most economically advanced countries, all but Romania, have lower child-poverty rates than the United States. In the percentage of four-year-olds who attend preschool, the United States ranks twenty-eighth. For the proportion of young adults (ages twenty-five to thirty-four) who have a higher education, it ranks fourteenth. For infant mortality, the United States ranks forty-ninth. Only for military spending and incarceration do we rank as number one.[24] The nation has more weapons and more prisoners than any other country in the world, and it has the highest percentage of its population behind bars.

To begin walking the path to a better urban future, to institute better national policies for cities, we will have to confront three bedrock liabilities. First, America suffers from extreme inequalities. With its disruptions, the Occupy Wall Street movement got the country to pay attention to income disparities, but disparities persist despite editorial hand-wringing. In the presidential debates in the fall of 2012, with both candidates vowing support for the "middle class," there was no mention of severe inequality and poverty. Second, each of the nation's metropolitan areas suffers from deep fragmentation, a checkerboard superimposed on a doughnut, with neighborhoods of wealth often surrounded by poverty in the cities, and with places of poverty hemmed in by better-off suburbs. Rational and just governance requires that we overcome this fragmentation. Worse yet, the jurisdictional separations allow the haves to insulate themselves from the have-nots, helping people with authority and with resources to stay emotionally as well as politically and materially uninvolved in the problems. Class segregation has worsened sharply, as income groups sort into more homogeneous residential districts.[25] Finally, the nation suffers a history of racism. Despite recent declines, residential segregation remains intense in *every* large metropolis.

City Schools

In large cities across the country, profoundly weak school performance virtually guarantees shortcomings in job preparation and citizenship, shortcomings blamed either on children and families or on the cities themselves. In fact, the blame belongs to failed federal and state policies that combine with metropolitan structures to reward selfish parochialism.

School shortcomings perpetuate poverty, expand social welfare rolls, and help to create the world's largest prison system, putting huge stress on federal, state, and local budgets. These shortcomings divide neighborhoods one from another. They induce families with children to move to better school districts, if they can afford to. They help to produce neighborhoods of despair. School problems are complex, but one central cause is simple and direct—schools in cities operate separately and differently from schools in better-off surrounding suburban districts. Separate *is* unequal, and not only financially. Good schools require constant attention and nurture, but they get it only in favored districts. The disparate results, with failing schools in central cities, are staggeringly negative for millions of city children. Literally millions. Beyond those central cities, even including well-off suburbs, the costs in social disorder and lost productivity impose enormous burdens not only on each metropolis, but also on the nation.

Undoing school inequality requires broadening of tax bases from municipalities to county level and state level, as well as increased funding from states and federal agencies for teacher preparation and continuous

20 *Looking Upstream*

education. It requires payback for decades of accumulated debt owed to the children of poor and unschooled parents, and also great caution about the weakening of public schools in favor of privatization. Money shortages are profound, but they are far from the only problem. Inequalities of social class and race must be acknowledged and confronted with sensitivity and authority. If school success is to be broadened, then the multiplicity of school districts that most state constitutions permit in each metropolis cannot remain divided by race and class.

Politicians pay close attention to school issues as they debate matters in statehouses, the Congress, the White House, and especially in localities. Citizens eagerly await better solutions. As advocates point out, school improvements will contribute fundamentally to city well-being—and thus to national social and economic progress. Profound benefits will ensue from better programs and from reallocations of budgets. In the medium and longer term, even the budgetary payback will be powerfully positive. If we solve our school problems, the social and political payback will include more participation in politics, better relations between officials and communities, and reduced alienation and withdrawal.

Food/Nutrition/Health

At all levels of government, policy makers, often in response to food industry lobbying, have failed to establish sufficient programs to improve food availability and nutrition. Needy residents face shortcomings in pricing and provision of food, which abet growing problems of obesity and illness, putting further burdens on health services. These problems cause Americans to spend more on health care, thus denying many households the ability to spend adequately on other needs, inducing people who can least afford it to shoulder a larger burden of health costs. As with so many issues in the United States, darker skin color and poverty signal double jeopardy, and the aging of the nation's population adds another crucial dimension. It remains true, as a study for the secretary of health and human services reported in the 1980s, that "the health problems of cities such as New York, Baltimore, Cleveland, Detroit, and many others" are "increasingly the health problems of the elderly, African Americans, and Hispanics." As health-planning scholar Michael Greenberg writes, "poor, elderly, and minority communities in . . . America's cities . . . need help."[26]

Nationwide, ratios of African American to white mortality give only a tepid indication of the much worse conditions that prevail in big-city minority neighborhoods of poverty. The national ratios, which include not only the poor, but also well-off middle class, suburban members of both races, understate the urban problems. Even these underestimates put death rates from diabetes for African Americans more than twice as high (220 percent) as they are for white males, and twice as high (200 percent) for infant mortality and cirrhosis. For cancer, the black/white mortality ratio is 160 percent, and for heart diseases, 150 percent.[27] Health does not link to nutritional intake with precision, but the direction of causation is clear—food insufficiency harms health. Despite long-term improvements in city health rates, cities still rank far behind their suburbs, and until policies shift to take us beyond current health care reforms, the differences promise to grow.

Improvements in nutrition and health require balanced regulatory controls for food production, processing, and distribution so as to ensure provision to the poor and to underserved areas. Strengthened policies need to protect small producers, to guarantee food safety, and to improve nutritional intake. A good place to start is further improvements in the federally supported school lunch program, to supplement recent changes.[28] As the leading student of school lunch programs tells us, education on nutrition and health is key to the prevention of diet-related diseases but "woefully under-resourced in our schools." Federal school regulations have "made it difficult for teachers and schools to allocate time to teaching . . . healthy food habits."[29] The cutback in food stamp funding enacted by the Congress in 2014 after a multiyear delay moved decidedly in the wrong direction.

The Drug War / Incarceration

Federal drug policies destroy city neighborhoods. Drug-war proponents imagine an epic struggle against violence, addiction, and immorality, but in truth U.S. drug policies force police to focus their attack on poor city neighborhoods and their African American, Latino, and immigrant residents. Rather than stemming violence, the war provokes violence, while it yields virtually no reduction in rates of addiction. Research shows that contrary to virtually all depictions in the media, white and minority addiction rates are similar, and drug usage rates vary little by income or by place of residence. Yet the drug war makes targets of poor city people of color and their neighborhoods. When the Vallejo police lieutenant claimed that the bust would put an end to rap music, he perhaps revealed his biases. Militarization of police forces, massive arrests, and imprisonments drive down the economic potential of already poor neighborhoods, deprive households of support, and deprive children of their parents.

A few state governments, hoping to lessen their fiscal crises stemming from the Great Recession, have initially acted to shrink the prison industry by relaxing prohibitions, shortening prison terms, reducing felony indictments for nonviolent crimes, and even closing prisons. Marijuana legalization expands from state to state. The federal government has moved to reduce the most egregious racial unfairness in criminal penalties. Nevertheless, against logic and against overwhelming evidence, drug policies continue to punish cities and their poorest residents. As an attack organized by race, place, and class, the drug war hits its target—poor city neighborhoods.

The remedy for this disaster is straightforward: replace the drug war with appropriate public health programs, counseling, public persuasion, and sales restrictions. Good examples exist with management of the more widely abused and far more dangerous substances of tobacco and alcohol. Both are marketed legally by giant corporations, but taxed and regulated by the government. Drug-war cancellation would have profound and positive effects on foreign policy, as well. Public opinion has shifted in recent years as critics have intensified doubts about the efficacy of the drug war. We need to move this debate front and center to turn this malign element of urban policy into a chief candidate for reform.

Politics for Change

My proposals are straightforward and (I think) quite evidently sensible. The *politics* for the recommended and relatively simple technical changes, however, are exceedingly difficult. They grow only more difficult to the extent that the national conversation shifts away from fairness, decency, and caring, toward more abstract notions of budget balances, fiscal sustainability, and the ever more illegitimate entitlements that favor the wealthy and big business. This situation exposes biases that lie at the core of a corrupt political economy.[30]

City planners, neighborhood activists, housing reformers, campaigners for civil rights, immigrants' rights advocates, those fighting for women's rights, active urban environmentalists, and other city supporters get it. Many know of better options than to leave cities and poor suburban areas to wither. Cities can be treated as places of opportunity rather than places with problems. With strongly revived cities and suburbs, working as places that serve all their residents, metropolitan areas will be more likely to thrive, thus making the national economy more productive, the environment better protected, the citizenry better educated, and the society more reflective, sensitive, and humane.

At the surface, one wants to *insist* on support for the fundamentals when dealing with big-city problems. For a good urban policy, we need to demand sensible fiscal decisions, good schools for all, enough affordable nutritious food, and an end to the drug war. It is one thing for a policy wonk to point to the logic of the situation, and, alas, quite another to figure out how to overcome racial animus, build political coalitions, persuade state legislatures and the Congress, and resist the corrosive influence of corporate money. The government is neither a slave to business interests nor autonomous. Political leaders must forever compromise, just as they must select their issues carefully.

The present book notes the many reforms undertaken by cities or regions, but focuses on *restraints imposed from outside*, externally created damages that occur in four particular ways. Knowing more about these outside forces, progressives can establish footholds to push back. Cities can gain strength as they resist damaging outside forces, to stop problems from arriving like bodies floating down from upstream. Four particular opportunities—anti-austerity, education, food, and drugs—are the most likely candidates for early progress, as we seek *defensive* reform that will encourage still more change.

During the progressive era from the late nineteenth century up to World War I, and again from the New Deal into the 1970s, "urban liberalism" promoted what today are termed "radical" reforms, including "a tax policy based primarily upon the ability to pay," an inclusive voting franchise, economic regulation to aid the less well-off,[31] and other expansions of democracy in politics, social life, and the economy. Political control in each case shifted away from business elites, first starting with immigration-stimulated big-city machine politics and second starting with

Roosevelt's response to the Great Depression. "Urban politicians and voters [were] the mainstay of liberal causes."[32] As I will argue in this book,
troubled urban conditions today provide similar entry points for the formation of new coalitions. Changes in policy are not made by analysis, but
by organizing shifts in power. It is my hope that reformers can make use of
this information and analysis and that this book's arguments will influence
the design of policy.

1

CITIES AS POLITICAL TARGETS

Late in 2013 a monitor appointed by Michigan's conservative governor pushed the City of Detroit into the largest municipal bankruptcy in U.S. history. Detroit, once the nation's fourth-largest city, still lies at the center of the nation's eighth-largest metropolitan area, with nearly 5.5 million inhabitants. Many less prominent cities are unable to meet their payment obligations, although few attempt formal bankruptcy—either because of the stigma attached, or because half the states restrict or prohibit bankruptcy. From 2008 through 2013, thirteen municipalities did file for bankruptcy, as did about three times that number of local authorities, such as water districts. States sometimes impose monitors, as in Detroit, forcing elected city officials to surrender their authority.[1]

Austerity causes significant urban damage, directly and indirectly, as evidence I present in this and the following chapter shows. Austerians— especially those who make key decisions in banks, corporations, the federal administration, Congress, and the courts—sometimes have cities in mind as they make policy, but usually not. If they do make the connection, they may aim to punish cities. They surely do not regard fiscal and economic policy as part of "urban policy." Yet austerity policies do constitute "upstream" flows that can flood cities and swamp their options. Austerity thus needs to be incorporated into discussions and actions on "urban policy."

Thirty-eight years before the Detroit debacle, the focus was on New York. When, in October 1975, President Gerald Ford refused federal assistance, the city hovered on the brink of bankruptcy. The president did not actually say "drop dead," despite the headline in the *New York Daily News*, and that December the federal government did lend money.[2] Nevertheless, the headline framed what would become a powerful trend, as the government began to cut support for cities. Starting in the late 1970s, support began to fall, and it has fallen persistently since. Following the Great Recession of 2008, city finances dipped to truly ruinous levels. Four decades of decline takes a toll—by the summer of 2012, cities, counties, and authorities were bankrupt or nearly so in at least nine states—Alabama, Illinois, Michigan, New Jersey, New Hampshire, New York, Pennsylvania, Rhode Island, and especially California.[3]

Cities and Austerity

Two words—*city* and *urban*—that elsewhere carry positive meaning often express negative ideas in the United States. Elsewhere, city centers are celebrated as productive powerhouses and also for their pleasurable urbanity. City leadership serves as a stepping-stone to the office of president or prime minister, but not in the United States. The planner for the Bologna region in Italy, Alessandro Delpiano, told graduate students in the United States that they seemed not to grasp the context for one of his lectures. "I am European," he said, "and for Europeans *urban* is part of our DNA." Not so for Americans. The ugly term *urbanicity*, invented by American sociologists, carries a negative meaning. *Urban* used in a pejorative sense originally meant poor, despised, and immigrant. Now it means poor, despised, and African American or Latino. American city sentiments have long been dampened by rural skepticism, a Jeffersonian suspicion. The anthology by Morton and Lucia White, first published in 1962, is titled *The Intellectual versus the City*.[4]

A signal moment in twentieth-century urban austerity came with President Ford's refusal to New York. What can it mean when the headline says to drop dead? After all, metropolises with more than a quarter-million inhabitants account for well over 80 percent of the national population. The president did not intend to demean *all* these people. What we understood was, *central cities* drop dead. In the 1970s, city residents, disproportionately people of color, were regarded with special scorn, a negative counterweight to the celebrated white residents of suburbs, who had become the nation's prime electoral force, of particular importance for President Ford's Republican Party. Presumably the party did not feel threatened by the prospect of dead cities. Places with a high index of "urbanicity" were to be ignored.

Moving ahead forty years, to the second decade of the twenty-first century, one finds some central cities to have revived, and many "urban" problems to have spread to the suburbs. More than half of the *poor* people in the average American metropolis today live *not* in the city, but in surrounding suburbs. Some city centers have become so high-class and expensive as to be unlivable for middle-class households. Revivals in San Francisco, Seattle, Portland, and Boston, and in the boroughs of Manhattan and Brooklyn, for example, appear to have turned things completely around. Edward Glaeser sees New York City "rising as a financial phoenix," leading to a resurgence for its entire metropolis.[5] Is the United States transforming its city geography to become more like Europe, where highly valued central zones serve well-off people but push poorer people, including immigrants of color, to the periphery? Does the American city therefore escape the negative sense of "urban"?

The data say not. Despite a few powerful center-city revivals, most U.S. cities and many of their residents remain in deep trouble. Even the most revived cities live with profound difficulties. Philadelphia provides a good example. The fifth-largest city in the country, with a population just over 1.5 million, Philadelphia from 2000 to 2010 grew over the decade for the first time since 1950, with new investment and rising tax revenues. As the Center City Development Corporation reports: "The revival of Center City in the last 16 years demonstrates what is possible when business and civic leaders share a vision of a competitive and animated downtown while government provides the support and incentives that make success possible. We have moved from *dirty and dangerous* to *clean and safe*, from 40%

office vacancy . . . to a thriving mixed-use Avenue . . . from 4.5 million square feet of vacant, obsolete . . . space to 11,000 new housing units . . . from no outdoor cafes to 187."[6] Downtown is one thing, but all Philadelphia, quite another. Center City's CEO boasts that Philadelphia's job loss after 2008 was less severe than job loss in its region or in the nation, and "it went into recession later[,] fell less far and has rebounded faster."[7] He finds Philadelphia as a whole doing better than places like Phoenix and South Florida, or Detroit and Cleveland. Yet the economic downturn makes it doubly difficult to hide the fact that Philadelphia overall is *not* doing well. In November 2008, just a year and a half after publication of the celebratory Center City report, Mayor Michael Nutter acknowledged a $1 billion budgetary shortfall. The giant fiscal shortfall was new, but not the sharp contrasts between the exciting developments at the center and the despair in many neighborhoods. As one study reported in 2009: "At 25 percent [Philadelphia's] poverty rate is the highest among the ten largest U.S. cities, and its level of unemployment exceeds the national average. The city's education system is a shambles: 80 percent of its public elementary schools and 50 percent of its middle and high schools do not have a functioning library. The high-school dropout rate is the second highest among large U.S. cities."[8]

Philadelphia's situation may be among the worst, but its conditions are mirrored in many metropolitan centers, some of them worse off. Still, aside from the rare formal bankruptcy filing, cities' fiscal problems hardly register in the national consciousness. President Ford's purpose, four decades ago, was to reduce the net cost of public funding, above all to lessen the cost of support for the racialized urban poor. With surprisingly few exceptions, major neighborhoods in cities with more than one hundred thousand inhabitants, albeit now together with their poorest suburbs, still constitute a racialized, impoverished *urban* population. Across the nation, in the case of cities from Fresno to Denver, Tulsa to Minneapolis, Birmingham to Syracuse, most surrounding suburbs are getting by, but the central cities are not. Their worst problems show up dramatically, as I will show in later chapters, in sky-high rates of school failures, extensive nutritional deficiencies, and the violence of the drug war.

Austerity, defined as "enforced or extreme economy," was the 2010 Word of the Year for the Merriam-Webster dictionary. Recent attention suggests that austerity is new—in 2012, for example, the political commentator

Thomas Edsall published *The Age of Austerity*, and in 2013 the Keynesian, Nobel Prize–winning economist Paul Krugman referred to advocates as *austerians*. But the austerity push has long been building, with cities serving as key targets, and the word *austerity* was used in relation to cities as early as 1980.[9] Without using the word, James O'Connor wrote about austerity in the 1970s, noting that "although the state has socialized more and more capital costs, the social surplus (including profits) continues to be appropriated privately." When the public pays the costs but private firms get the profits, he made clear, this "creates a fiscal crisis, or 'structural gap,' between state expenditures and state revenues."[10]

Then, as now, points out political scientist Geoff Kennedy, austerity was imposed not to resolve the fiscal crisis, nor to aid financial institutions to recover their losses, nor to earmark funds for building social capital or offering services. To resolve the fiscal crisis, after all, we need new banking controls and small taxes on speculative transactions, as proposed long ago by Nobel Prize–winning economist James Tobin. Banks recovered their losses with the bailouts. But strong conservative opposition nixed increased funding for social capital. "Austerity is about opening up new areas of investment to enable finance capital to continue its expansion."[11] In Krugman's words, austerity is "about using deficit panic as an excuse to dismantle social programs."[12] As in the 1970s, the price is paid in unemployment, stagnant wages, cut services, and declining neighborhoods. This "incipient fiscal crisis" affects local governments nationwide, but it distinctively affects cities. As urban geographer Jamie Peck has written, we suffer an *urban* crisis because "cities have been hit especially hard by the housing slump and . . . mortgage foreclosures." He notes that "cities are disproportionately reliant on public services," and "they are 'home' to many of the preferred political targets of austerity programs—the 'undeserving' poor, minorities and marginalized populations, public-sector unions and 'bureaucratized' infrastructures."[13]

Seventy Years of Debates over Cities

Much twentieth-century U.S. city planning was antiurban in the sense that it mainly served establishment rather than majority needs, privileged rather than typical neighborhoods, and suburbs rather than city centers.

But for a time, some programs for cities were relatively progressive. Conflict and contradiction clutter the history.

Urban Liberalism

From the 1930s until the mid-1960s, and in some ways through the city-troubled 1970s, city planning, often backed by federal programs, provided support to central cities and many needy residents, even as suburbs won more. In boom years after World War II, economic growth provided the wherewithal for job expansion and federal aid to cities, enabling even residents close to the bottom of the urban ladder to climb up at least a rung or two. Many achievements of that era still stood in 2008 not only as higher family incomes for a very broad middle class or as extensive metropolitan highway and transit systems, but also as better housing, improved health, better nutrition, and augmented, enriched services. Over many of those years, improvements benefited city budgets, urban images, and many residents. City creativity worked along with national policy to diminish rather than increase inequalities and, haltingly, to reduce racial gaps.[14] Federal urban outlays increased phenomenally, from $3.3 billion in 1967 to $27.4 billion in 1979 (adjusted for inflation), from 2.1 percent of total federal outlays to 10.6 percent.[15] A redistributive example from the tail end of this period comes from Boston, when Ray Flynn was mayor, from 1984 to 1993. Faced with great demand for large projects, the city held off the issuance of permits, then announced in a public meeting with nearly a dozen large developers that they would be required to furnish "linkages." After a great deal of political objection, the developers (and the banks) yielded to the populist demands, creating substantial funds for the construction of affordable housing and other broadly beneficial investments.[16] From the New Deal until Jimmy Carter's presidential term, and on occasion, as in Boston, even later, federal policies often worked well in support of city agendas, reducing poverty and providing help for those who remained poor. Politics and policies worked along with economic expansion to reduce divisions of social class and to make cities better places.[17] Such improvements were generally seen as *urban* progress.

At the same time, the postwar consensus provided a slew of benefits to the growing middle class and working-class whites, as their suburbs took the greater share. Urban renewal destroyed much central-city housing, factory shutdowns took jobs out of cities, and the largest federal "urban" expenditures by far, for highways and homeowner mortgage tax credits, went to better-off suburban areas. When African American uprisings exploded in the late 1960s, they gave expression to frustration with these inequalities.

This complex and changing city situation gave geographic expression to broader national developments, whose economic and political patterns influence city fortunes still today. A lengthy political struggle over the direction of the economy and society preceded today's reliance on market-rule decisions. For decades, working people gained. From the 1930s to the 1970s, the government expanded protections for consumers and workers, instituted insurance for modest bank accounts, and regulated investment procedures. Public innovations of other sorts occurred at an astounding rate. Eleven federal regulatory agencies were established between 1933 and 1966, and a full dozen between 1970 and 1975.[18] Most of these activities can be seen as city-supportive in nature, and many of them helped cities' neediest residents.

Extensions of federal regulatory powers, together with the simultaneous expansion of redistributive taxation and spending over the same years, came about in good part because of "the extraordinary array of social movements that remade American society."[19] Organized labor, the civil rights movement, the New Left, the environmental movement, feminism, counterculture pressures, and sexual liberation all played a part. This sort of redistributive social growth is, as noted earlier, quintessentially urban in nature. Historically, workers have organized in the city crucible. As historian Joshua Freeman writes, in New York in 1945, only weeks after the end of World War II, more than "a million-and-a-half workers milled around the streets or stayed home" in a solidarity walkout. The economy lost an estimated $100 million, and federal tax revenues fell by tens of millions, as a strike in commercial buildings led "fifteen thousand elevator operators, doormen, porters, firemen, and maintenance workers" off the job. Governor Thomas Dewey intervened, and his appointed arbitrator settled in favor of the strikers. Months later President Truman intervened in a tugboat strike, which Mayor William O'Dwyer pushed to arbitration. Strikes continued in the city and took place across the country for more than a year. "The size, strategic importance, and demonstrated power of the working class allowed it to play a major role."[20]

Right-Wing Opposition   Opposition developed early on to this burst of redistributive, regulatory, progressive innovation, eventually morphing into the obsessive antitax movements that abound today and into pressures in favor of extreme market fundamentalism. Decades ago, when industrialists and investors anticipated increases in international competition and rising costs of broader social services, they acted. Foreshadowing electoral politics that would emerge by 1980, a small set of moneyed activists worked to set the redistributive clock back, to undo the New Deal, to prevent further leakage of increased productivity to the workers. The seeds of austerity were planted, to reduce the size and sweep of distributive programs.

As sociologist Isaac Martin has shown, organized efforts to redistribute income *upward* began earlier. In some senses, these ultraconservative efforts began more than one hundred years ago, in response to the Sixteenth Amendment in 1913, which authorized the Congress to assess income taxes.[21] From 1938 until 1958, business groups worked in a highly organized way for repeal.[22] Right-wing lobbying developed rapidly. The American Enterprise Association, founded in New York in 1938, became the American Enterprise Institute in 1943, when it moved to Washington, DC, and eventually took on an antiurban coloration.[23] The powerful National Association of Manufacturers also moved from New York, where it had been located to be near industry and finance, to Washington, to be located near increasingly influential policy makers. Only after many years did these efforts make headway in city-damaging ways.

It was in August 1971, still a decade before the election of conservatives Ronald Reagan in the United States, Margaret Thatcher in Britain, and Helmut Kohl in West Germany, before the term *neoliberalism*, before the "Age of Austerity." Lewis Powell, about to be appointed to the Supreme Court, wrote a memorandum to the U.S. Chamber of Commerce in support of a conservative political resurgence. Powell proposed that people of means "set up professorships, . . . institutes . . . where intellectuals would write books from a conservative business perspective, and . . . think tanks."[24]

Urban Liberalism Continues   After World War II and through the 1950s, the economy stayed strong, forcing opponents of gradual progressive change to fight uphill even when Republicans held power, against the stay-the-game temper of the times. Many economic leaders acted with moderation, believing that "they had an obligation to act as disinterested stewards of the national economy."[25] A letter that President Dwight Eisenhower sent to his brother in 1954 suggests the moderating power of such mainstream ideas. The president expressed skepticism about the reach of reactionary politics: "Should any political party attempt to abolish social security, unemployment insurance, and eliminate labor laws and farm programs, you would not hear of that party again in our political history. . . . Among [those who contemplate such things] are H. L. Hunt (you possibly know his background), a few other Texas oil millionaires, and an occasional politician or business man from other areas. Their number is negligible and they are stupid."[26] As least for that time, Eisenhower saw things clearly. The country continued along its gently positive redistributive trajectory, keeping ultraconservatives on the fringe.

Following the 1960 and 1964 elections, under exploding pressure from the civil rights movement, Democratic presidents John F. Kennedy and especially Lyndon B. Johnson moved the country in progressive directions, establishing and expanding opportunities for the poor, the disenfranchised, and African Americans with voting rights, health care provisions, housing subsidies, and other programs under the banners of the "New Frontier" and the "Great Society." As we have seen, this period saw tremendous increases in federal spending for urban areas. After the election of Republican Richard Nixon in 1968, cities continued to hold their own. The negative income tax facilitated efficient transfer of income to many low-income working adults, and the new Environmental Protection Agency responded to the environmental movement, promoting legislation to protect air and water.

Thus for four decades and through five administrations—FDR, Truman, JFK, LBJ, and initially Nixon—federal programs worked gradually to reduce inequality and to help cities, as the country developed with a rapidly growing economy based on consumer spending. As William Julius Wilson writes: "Lower-wage workers benefited from a wide range of protections, including steady increases in the minimum wage, and the government made full employment a high priority. There was also a still-prosperous manufacturing sector in or around cities with a strong union movement that ensured higher wages and more nonwage benefits for ordinary workers."[27]

Growth of the Right

Membership in the U.S. Chamber of Commerce doubled between 1974 and 1980, and its budget tripled. The Heritage Foundation and the American Legislative Exchange Council, ALEC, both were formed in 1973, the Cato Institute in 1977, and the Manhattan Institute in 1978. By one measure, corporate lobbying offices in Washington, DC, grew from one hundred in 1968 to more than five hundred in 1978 to nearly twenty-five hundred by 1982.[28]

Conservative think tanks, unlike mainstream institutions, often set clear political goals.[29] For instance, while the mainstream Brookings Institution, much like a university, stresses nonpartisan, independent, objective research, the Heritage Foundation openly proclaims its mission "to formulate and promote conservative public policies based on the principles of free enterprise, limited government, individual freedom, traditional American values, and a strong national defense." While the mainstream institution works to tamp down the influence of any single line of thought, the conservative institution works at focused promotion of one ideology.[30]

Meanwhile, two political currents flowed in favor of suburbs and against cities. The Nixon administration was almost pathologically anxious about liberals, and the Republican Party designed an electoral strategy to break the Democratic Party's hold on southern white voters. When these currents combined, a river of federal money flowed away from cities and toward suburbs. Reductions in federal budgets for cities mainly harmed minority populations, as the White House preferred to use resources in growing suburbs, where white voting majorities both North and South were accustomed to federal subsidies that had begun in the post–World War II boom. This all gathered into a political realignment linking "racism, antigovernment populism, and economic conservatism,"[31] easily directed against cities. Thus, *New York: Drop Dead!*

In the 1970s negative ideas toward cities and mounting city troubles had already reinforced one another, with manufacturing collapse and lost jobs, ghetto rebellions, aging infrastructure, and budgetary crises. Cities turned into bull's-eyes for fiscal and programmatic retrenchment, and their opponents subjected them to rhetorical abuse. As I document in the next chapter, cities became "real-world laboratories for . . . experimentation," thus becoming the focus of a long-term assault that hammered poor families, minority families, immigrants, and the cities themselves.[32] To add insult to injury, right-wing ideologues used cities as symbols to illustrate what was wrong with the nation. The pejorative meaning of *urban* was abetted by media-induced fears that gripped an increasingly suburbanized and ever more insulated majority population.

Hostile Rhetoric and Legislation

Cities thus came to serve as political targets to provide justification for the very austerity policies that damaged them. While fiscal stringency and reduced services have broader effects, in suburbs, towns, and rural areas, much of the fiscal retrenchment itself has been aimed at cities. The ideological use of cities diverts attention, promoting broad false consciousness as people vote against their own material interests. For the cities themselves, the demonization punishes directly.

City Words

Herbert Gans once warned planners and scholars against their use of the popular term *underclass*.[33] Today's terms would be *the disadvantaged*, *the underprivileged*, or, on Fox News, *parasites*.[34] *Underclass*, a euphemistic "buzzword for the urban poor," originally referred to men and women chronically without decent work, stuck in a hopeless labor market. Later the term shifts blame onto the underemployed themselves. "The issue," writes Gans, "always boils down to whether the fault for being poor and the responsibility for change should be assigned more to poor people or more to the economy and the state."[35]

Words like these work as code to blame African Americans and Latinos, easily stretched to include others, such as immigrants. A labeled person, Gans points out, may get unwarranted attention from the police and courts, potential employers, welfare offices, and schools. Such labels merge problems with schools, housing, addiction, and street crime, even though they require separate and distinct responses. The term *underclass* eventually morphed into a description of any *neighborhood* ripe for intervention, helping to justify destruction of city housing and neighborhoods, as similar terms still do.

People use the city itself as a stand-in to speak or write tactfully about uncomfortable subjects. Building up from the term *neighborhood*, or just *'hood*, a bevy of euphemisms get their start. City-words are used to support racial bias against dark-skinned people.[36] *Urban music* means music by African Americans. *Urban attire* is clothing made stylish by its black wearers. *Urban schools* are troubled, minority schools. The *inner city* and the *central city* are seen as places where African Americans, Latinos, and immigrants live. *City Year* is the internship program that places college students as teachers' aides in schools with high dropout rates. The word *urbanicity* refers to the percentage of black students in the school population. Students in my classes have written about "urban cities"! As city planner Tom Angotti notes,

> Since the early twentieth century "urban" problems were equated with new immigrants and African Americans. Suburbia, though clearly an integral part of the modern metropolis, has been defined not as part of "the city" but as the legitimate place for the single-family "American Dream" house. Conservatives in Congress have long demonized cities; for example, they opposed investment in public housing by arguing that it only encourages migration to cities. In the 1950s, before central city neighborhoods exploded in rage against institutional racism, conservatives . . . declared that central cities with large black populations were "cancers." The prescription was surgical removal via "urban renewal," or they would be allowed to self-destruct if government only ignored them (this was the policy of "benign neglect" invented by Richard Nixon's advisor, Daniel Patrick Moynihan).[37]

Recent research confirms "that Americans associate big cities with African Americans" and that cities themselves are "a 'racialized' concept." "A commitment to helping central cities can be viewed as a commitment, however indirect, to helping African Americans." The data show that "even Americans who do not hold prejudiced views associate urban problems with African Americans, suggesting that social policy . . . will always need to contend with racial attitudes."[38]

From the Manhattan Institute to the Janitorial Staff

In one of the more striking efforts to establish a beachhead to challenge established progressive changes, a group of activists and intellectuals with seed money from British millionaire Antony Fisher in 1978 started the Manhattan Institute. This research and publicity operation, initially focusing on city affairs, by 2008 had an annual budget over $10 million, its own quarterly journal, a sizable staff, more than four dozen affiliated scholars, and a host of highly prominent political, media, and academic supporters.[39] The institute was the think tank for New York City mayor Rudy Giuliani in the 1990s and has served as a patron of notable New York–based supply-side economists, welfare critics, and others pushing for "limited government, free markets, individual self-reliance, lower taxes, [and] cultural reform."[40] Novelist Tom Wolfe wrote enthusiastically about "revolutionaries" at the institute, who dynamited "the conventional wisdom" of liberal mainstream elites.[41]

The Manhattan Institute's development paralleled that of other institutions better known in the growing national conservative movement, as they campaigned for "tax reductions on business, deregulation in transportation and finances, labor law 'reform' designed to weaken unions, and austere fiscal policies."[42] The Manhattan Institute is notable for growing in a city that had been long accustomed to fragments of European-style social democracy and public intervention.[43] The institute used the "urban crisis" of the 1960s and 1970s as a symbol of the defects of the Great Society, and it continues to undertake a general attack on liberalism, blaming the city's problems on public employee unions, bloated bureaucracies, social engineering, and tolerance for disorder. The city-focused institute brings together Wall Street people and other financiers, ultraconservative intellectuals, and cultural leaders. Its city-based work eventually helped shift the terms of the *national* political debate far to the right.[44] In late 2012, when a senior fellow at the institute was invited to respond to the statement that "the IMF and others say that income inequality represses economic growth," she argued that "increasing inequality isn't an obstacle to economic growth," but rather that inequality is growth's natural result, which itself promotes growth.[45]

A more nuanced reading suggests that rising inequality constrains growth. For example, it constrains the ability of families to invest in their children. It is a reasonable assumption that all parents and child-care givers would choose schools where their children are more likely to learn, yet many cannot do so. Residential segregation imposed by income and race combined isolates the rich from the poor, increases disenfranchisement, and leads better-off people into ignorance. While knowledge leads to compassion, ignorance leads to condescension and contempt.[46]

Deep national biases have emerged against redistributive policy, expressed for example by the outraged South Carolina citizen who told his congressman in 2009 to "keep your government hands off my Medicare." Such ideas fit the neoconservative urban program. They were evident, for example, when the Manhattan Institute used its physical presence to bring the urban crisis "literally to the doorsteps of white middle- and working-class New Yorkers," stimulating "long-simmering racial resentments."[47] This city groundwork later influenced national attitudes, helping to make anticity political statements more acceptable, even when they are nonsensical. Some publicists and politicians suggest without evidence, for example, that city neighborhoods by their very existence are breeding grounds for indolence, crime, and antisocial behavior. Running in the 2012 Iowa Republican presidential primary caucuses, the former Speaker of the House of Representatives, Newt Gingrich, a master at the use of incendiary language, pushed on these buttons of resentment to tie together emotions about poverty, neighborhood, race, and crime. With startling inaccuracy and evident cynicism, Gingrich said "children in really poor neighborhoods have no habits of working . . . no habit of showing up on Monday . . . unless it's illegal. . . . What if they cleaned out the bathrooms, what if they mopped the floors? . . . and they didn't have to become a pimp or a prostitute or a drug dealer."[48] Congressman Paul Ryan, the 2012 vice presidential candidate, says, "We have got this tailspin of culture, in our inner cities in particular, of men not working and just generations of men not even thinking about working."[49]

Reactionary Media Rhetoric

In debates on austerity policies, proponents and opponents use a series of key words to describe themselves and other parties. As the celebrated scholar Albert Hirschman points out in his book *The Rhetoric of Reaction*, critics of reform react in three unreasonable ways. They argue, against the facts, that proposed reforms will have *perverse* effects and will exacerbate the very ills the reformers hope to reduce. They argue that reform attempts are *futile* and will result in little or no change; and they argue that the reforms, should they be instituted, will *jeopardize* earlier, valuable accomplishments. They make their deceptive reactionary arguments (as Justice Powell urged) in order to win power and resources.

By the 1990s, institutes and think tanks serving as incubators for right-wing ideas "were poised to capitalize on emerging—and unregulated—media sectors such as cable television, talk radio, and Internet commentary."[50] By 2003, Americans were listening to fifteen hundred hosts on conservative radio talk shows.[51] Conservatives campaigned to dominate the airwaves. Their attack on the mainstream media has had considerable effect, not least because in good part it reinforced anticity bias that had already grown rampant.

As Steve Macek has shown, in research focused earlier, on the 1990s, even mainstream print media paints an unjustifiably ugly picture of the nation's cities. The news then depicted cities as "violent and out of control, populated by murderers, muggers, drug addicts, and lowlifes, places where the rules of normal, decent behavior no longer apply." Two *Time* magazine cover headlines made the point: September 17, 1990, "The Rotting of the Big Apple," and April 19, 1993, "Los Angeles: Is the City of Angels Going to Hell?" These biased mainstream representations of cities employed ideas and images from conservative interpretations of the urban crisis, amplifying the fears of white middle-class suburbanites. The bias arises in part from pressure brought by advertisers, which prompts even leading newspapers to be "fairly brazen" in attempts to "drive away inner-city readers." According to Joseph Lelyveld, then executive editor of the *New York Times*, "The advertisers we cater to are not thrilled when you sign up a bunch of readers in some poverty area for home delivery."[52]

On television, the bias in coverage is similar, or worse. When Dan Rather opened the *CBS Evening News* on September 22, 1995, the visual frame for his lead-in depicted a "city skyline with the word 'CRIME' in the foreground," underscoring "the association between the city and criminality suggested by Rather's words." As moviegoers now know from *Central Park Five*, by filmmaker Ken Burns, the news stories of the April 1989 rape and near murder of a jogging white investment banker in Central Park were wrong. Police persuaded five young black men from Harlem to give false confessions, and the media framed them as "wilding" in the park. These innocent men arguably became key elements in "the specter of a rising 'youth crime wave,'" helpful for those who wanted expanded police forces and more investment in prison construction, but devastating for urban affairs by creating a false comprehensive view of the city. Rather's introduction gives the viewer plenty to be scared about—joggers murdered, little girls gunned down, the worst still yet to come—suggesting, with its mentions of Central Park and Los Angeles, that the primary object of fear is the inner city itself.[53]

State Legislation Affecting Cities

Manifestations of ideological antiurban bias have multiplied, with powerful harm to city fortunes. Because cities are legal creatures of the fifty federated states of the union, entirely subject to state rules, *existing* legally only by virtue of state-granted charters, then state-level legislation can be crucial. Conservative gains in state legislatures and governorships have imposed new burdens on cities. The Detroit bankruptcy case may be the most extreme example, but it is instructive. Robert Kleine, the director of Michigan's Office of Revenue and Tax Analysis and later the state treasurer, explains how the state's "hostility" over three decades drove the city into bankruptcy. The state could have chosen not to reduce revenue sharing, so as to have reimbursed losses from Detroit's income tax cut. It could have set up regional districts for fire and police protection, seized mass transit opportunities with federal funding, maintained residency requirements for city workers, arranged for either tax-base sharing or regional government, and even—within sight of bankruptcy filing—allowed emergency managers more time. Each of these strategies has been employed elsewhere, but instead, in this case, state politicians chose to "blame Detroit's problems on corruption, unions and overly generous pension benefits," none of which, according to the former state tax director, "were the primary causes of bankruptcy."[54]

One influential body promoting anticity action across the country has been the American Legislative Exchange Council. ALEC encourages states "to advance the Jeffersonian principles of free markets, limited government, federalism, and individual liberty," in ways of considerable import to cities. ALEC promotes legislation that is business-friendly and tax-hostile. With more than two thousand members, ALEC, founded in 1973, claims to be "the nation's largest, non-partisan . . . association of state legislators." ALEC staffers draft proposals for state legislators, generating "hundreds of model bills, resolutions, and policy statements," supported with funding from the nation's largest corporations and immensely wealthy individuals. Exempt from lobbying restrictions and requirements, ALEC managed for thirty-nine years to avoid identification with state legislation, even though its models end up reproduced *verbatim* in actual bills, until its activities became more widely known in 2012.[55]

Many of ALEC's activities have a built-in antiurban, austerity bias. For example, as we shall see below, ALEC affected the small city of Woonsocket, Rhode Island, when the state legislature reversed itself to rule against local officeholders and city voters who had decided to tax themselves to rescue their schools and balance their municipal budget. ALEC has promoted city-threatening legislation not only on schools and municipal budgets, but also on census counts, voter qualification. safe neighborhoods and immigration, and gun ownership and sales.

In New Jersey a series of ALEC-inspired bills to institute austerity reforms would cause damages to "urban" schools. The proposed Urban Hope Act would allow "nonprofit companies to run public schools in the state's most beleaguered cities," privatizing the profit while socializing the losses. Titles of other New Jersey bills were "Innovation Schools and School Districts," "Great Teachers and Leaders," "Next Generation Charter Schools," "Parent Empowerment and Choice," and "Parent Trigger." Among other effects, these bills would lower standards by loosening "training requirements for charter-school teachers," and they would leave charter school administrators and teachers "exempt from all state laws, rules and regulations of any school board of education." Still other ALEC-inspired New Jersey bills with potentially damaging urban effects were the New Jersey Right to Work Act, filed in 2012. which would weaken unions, and the Pollution Control or Abatement Flexibility Act, drafted in 2010, which would weaken environmental protection.[56]

ALEC has taken on broader anticity issues, too. Because highly reliable estimates indicate that the 1990 census undercounted the U.S. population by about eight million people, missing predominantly city people of color, the census proposed statistical sampling as a measurement technique to reduce errors. Because the census is the basis for decennial congressional redistricting and also for the allocation of some federal funds, undercounting tends to reduce city power, influence, and federal transfers. Statisticians and census officials, as well as census authorities in other countries, agree that sampling techniques produce more accurate results than enumeration. Sampling is also cheaper. Nevertheless, and in line with insistence from Republicans in Congress, ALEC's Public Safety and Elections section opposed the use of statistical sampling in its model legislation in 1998. This unscientific opposition continues, and the Census Bureau has pulled back from sampling plans.[57]

To increase voter registration and add time and flexibility for casting ballots, progressive activists liberalized voting procedures in many states. One goal is to enroll larger numbers of poor and minority city voters and get them to the polls. Many of these potential voters are residents of inner-city neighborhoods. ALEC fought against this push to increase city voting with its 2009 model, the Taxpayer and Citizen Protection Act, intended to limit voting times and especially to restrict voting booth access through various photo ID requirements. Provisions in the model Protection Act—and in subsequent laws passed in many states—would make voting more difficult for poor people. "Researchers have long warned that voter ID laws disproportionately affect—and potentially disenfranchise—minorities, the poor, young people and the elderly (groups, as many have noted, that tend to lean Democratic)."[58] Low automobile ownership among African Americans in cities denies them the most commonly accepted ID, the driver's license. Memphis, for example, has 41,000 households with no vehicle, Houston, 129,000, and Madison, 19,000. Tennessee, Texas, and Wisconsin all passed voter ID laws.[59] In March 2012, the Pennsylvania governor signed a strict voter ID law that requires voters to present a photo ID for every visit to the polls. In Philadelphia, 18 percent of registered voters do not have ID cards, double the statewide percentage. Barack Obama's win four years earlier had depended heavily on Philadelphia, where he received 83 percent of the vote. Obama did carry Pennsylvania again in 2012, but the bias introduced by the photo ID exclusion surely made the results closer. Other restrictions have been imposed as well. In Wisconsin's voter ID law of 2011, for example, an ID must show the voter's current address. Since poor people, especially city renters, tend to move more often, this requirement lowers voting probabilities, with permission uncertain even if a voter could show proof of voting-district residence by presenting utility bills.[60] This political struggle has continued.

Black Lives Matter

Rhetorical hostility to things "urban" and practical punishment of cities and city residents reinforce one another. They work like two hands clapping.

The noise became louder when news stories and then private YouTube videos began to document police or quasi-police killings of unarmed black men and women.

Early on New Year's Day 2009, a transit officer shot and killed Oscar Grant at BART's Fruitvale Station in Oakland, California. Oakland suffered forty-five police shootings from 2004 through 2008. Thirty-seven victims were black, and none was white, according to the NAACP. In February 2012, a neighborhood watch coordinator shot and killed Trayvon Martin in a Miami suburb. In July 2014, police on Staten Island put Eric Garner in a chokehold, and he later died. Also in July 2014, a policeman shot and killed Michael Brown in Ferguson, Missouri. That August, a police officer shot and killed John Crawford III while he held a toy gun in a Walmart store near Dayton, Ohio. In November, a policeman shot and killed Akai Gurley, who was walking in his Brooklyn apartment's stairwell. Also in November 2014, police shot and killed twelve-year-old Tamir Rice in a playground in Cleveland. In March 2015, a policeman shot and killed nineteen-year-old Tony Robinson in Madison, Wisconsin. Also in March, a policeman shot and killed Anthony Hill, who was wandering naked in an apartment complex in DeKalb County, Georgia, outside Atlanta.[61] In a third March event, a policeman shot and killed Naeschylus Vinzant in Aurora, outside Denver. In July Sandra Bland was found hanging in her jail cell on the edge of the Houston metropolitan area, three days after being arrested by a Texas state trooper for changing traffic lanes without signaling. She was on her way to a job at her alma mater, Prairie View A&M University. Also in July 2015 a Cincinnati University policeman shot Samuel DuBose for driving away after a traffic stop. Grant, Martin, Garner, Brown, Crawford, Gurley, Rice, Robinson, Hill, Vinzant, Bland, and DuBose, all African Americans, were all unarmed, and at least nine of the twelve appear to have posed *no* threat to police or anyone else. *USA Today* reports that each year on average from 2006 through 2012, ninety-six black persons, nearly two each week, were killed by a white police officer.[62]

In response to this almost unbearable sequence of tragic events and aided by the immediacy of communication, the collective pleas of "Hands up, don't shoot," "I can't breathe," and "Black lives matter" have become widely recognized symbols of the need for justice, a requirement for peace. Too rarely noted, however, is the background to the biased police violence, the long-term, steady practice of police-on-black (and on-Hispanic) repression as the principal element of the long-running "war on drugs" and the closely related explosions of the prison, parole, and ex-convict populations. Michelle Alexander calls it "the New Jim Crow," and she is right.[63]

As it turns out, gun laws and related public "safety" regulations have served as a favorite target of ALEC, and again, ALEC targets cities. New York mayor Michael Bloomberg tried for years to build a coalition of big-city mayors and others to restrict gun ownership and trafficking. His principal opponent was the National Rifle Association. In 2011, the NRA was the corporate cochair of ALEC's Public Safety and Elections section, whose model legislation has promoted pro-gun legislation across the country. The most notorious case may be Florida's 2005 "stand your ground" provision, exposed during the Trayvon Martin killing.[64] When cities can be vilified with words, set aside and isolated by municipal boundaries, and when the word *urban* has come to mean *poor and dark skinned*, then perhaps it should be no surprise that a black young man can be challenged and then shot to death for walking in a place that thinks of itself as *not urban*.

Cities as Budget-Cutting Targets

Cities themselves and their poorer neighborhoods serve as magnets attracting increasingly severe federal cutbacks. While it is true that the cutbacks weigh heavily also beyond city boundaries and that a few city centers escape the downward drag, austerity since the Great Recession weighs most heavily on cities.

From the 1930s to the 1970s, as we have seen, federal spending for cities grew tremendously. Writers often mark these few city-helpful decades as special, calling them "the American Century," referring to "the Great Compression," and noting the 1950s and 1960s as a uniquely positive time.[1] During these decades politics worked with economic expansion to reduce social class divisions and to make cities better places. Admittedly, these city improvements occurred unevenly, were marred by the destruction of "urban renewal," and were outpaced as suburbs took most of the prizes.

Since the mid-1970s, policies have tended wholesale in the negative direction, to increase class divisions across the nation and within each metropolitan area. The pressures of globalization and technical change as well as poor national economic management have stimulated austerity, but, in the main, political decisions have mattered most. The nation took a purposeful "great U-turn," so that by 2014 even "Wall Street analysts" and observers "within top consulting firms" acknowledged the erosion of the middle class "with a frankness more often associated with left-wing academics than business experts."[2]

For an extreme example, figure 2.1 shows the dramatic increase in the share of income going to the top 1 percent in New York City from 1980, when they took about 12 percent, to 2008, by when they took about 44 percent. After a Great Recession dip, their share rose back up to 39 percent by 2012. Over the longer term, such increases indicate an extraordinary shift in the distribution of income. Wall Street is the center of global capitalism, so its earnings do produce spectacular inequalities for both city and state, but the pattern occurs nationally even if in a less exaggerated manner, as depicted in the figure's bottom plot. The share of income to the nation's top 1 percent rose dramatically, from 10 percent to 23 percent.

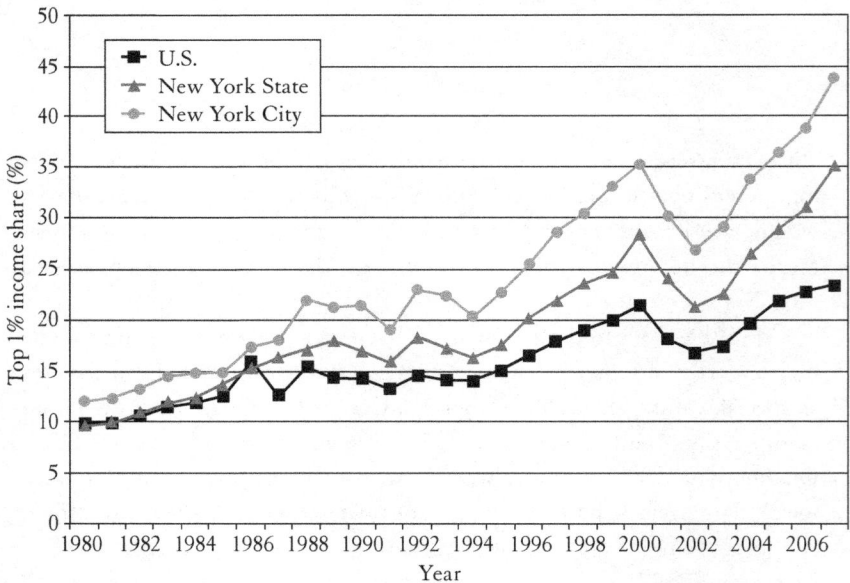

Figure 2.1. Changing 1 percent share of total income, 1980–2012: United States, New York State, and New York City. Parrott et al. 2012, figure 2, for NYS and NYC: FPI analysis of NYS Department of Taxation and Finance data. Piketty and Saez 2015, table A3, updated, income inequality for the United States.

As I showed in the previous chapter, the shift toward inequality did not happen on its own. Inequality is not a natural result of autonomous and uncontrollable market forces, whether local, national, or global, nor is it a result of changing technology and globalization. As Thomas Piketty and Emmanuel Saez, the global gurus on income statistics, point out, while the economists' favorite villain causing inequality is "skill-biased technical change," or SBTC, that cannot be right. SBTC and globalization have affected France and Germany just as they have the United States over the past century, but the two European nations have had drastically less change in their income distributions. (See the French-U.S. difference after 1975 in figure 2.2, showing that the share of income to the very wealthy increases by roughly half in France, while in the United States it rises eight times as much, roughly fourfold. Matching common perceptions of the range of regulatory restraint, the United Kingdom takes intermediate paths.) Peter Edelman, Georgetown law professor and former high official in the Clinton administration, points more directly to abandonment of antipoverty policy. Jacob Hacker and Paul Pierson, political scientists at Berkeley and

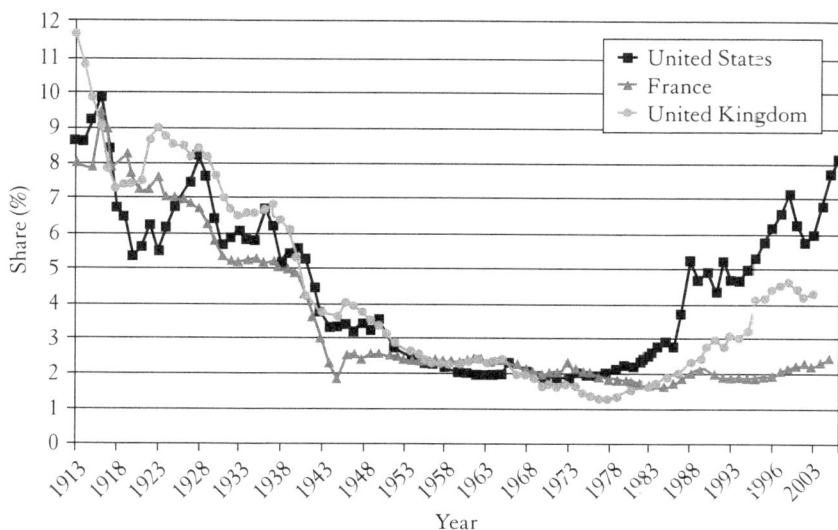

Figure 2.2. Top 0.1 percent income shares in the United States, France, and the United Kingdom, 1913–2014. Data from Alvaredo et al. 2013; World Top Incomes Database, http://topincomes.parisschoolofeconomics.eu/; updated in Piketty and Saez 2015, table A3, income inequality.

Yale, show how powerful people made decisions that changed the structure of the economy as they weakened public policy.[3] Piketty, using data
spanning three hundred years for seven countries, notes the "violent political conflict" inherent in capitalism's "deep structure of inequality," a structure that requires collective action and substantial redistribution outside
the operation of markets.[4]

Presidents and governors, legislators, and top administrative officials,
when pushed steadily by organized business executives to increase austerity over the past forty years, enacted changes. They loosened market
regulations, weakened social protections, and wrote laws and cut budgets in many areas, from patent protection to immigration labor regulations to urban transit. Whether intentionally or inadvertently, with their
actions—most of them insistently austere—these officials put the nation
on a downward slide. "Our political system has shaped our economy in
ways that have led to this high level of inequality," points out the Nobel
Prize–winning economist Joseph Stiglitz.[5]

Federal Withdrawal

The politics of *urban* austerity developed in the conservative think tanks,
and when a key proponent gained public power, policy shifted. William Simon, serving as secretary of the treasury from 1974 to 1977 in
the Nixon-Ford administrations, regarded cities as enemies, bastions of
resistance to free markets, rife with regulations restricting free enterprise, redistributive programs, and a culture of dependency. They needed
to be brought to heel. In response to the fiscal crisis, Simon pushed New
York to minimize intervention and let the market do its work. He called
bluntly for spending cuts, to enlist public action in service of the market.
He channeled narrowly, as have austerians over the subsequent forty
years, ignoring opportunities to cut the largest federal domestic subsidies,
for suburban housing and highways, military contractors, and giant farms
and ranches. But regarding New York City, according to journalist Sam
Roberts, Simon made "politically suicidal demands to city officials—raise
transit fares, abolish rent control, scrap free tuition at the City University."
These demands "prompted Victor Gotbaum, the municipal labor leader,
to complain that Mr. Simon barely believed in government at all, except

for police and fire protection, 'and he's not sure about fire.'"[6] By 2010, many conservative spokespersons were calling proudly for shrinking the government almost to the vanishing point.

State governments and sometimes cities themselves promoted austere city budgets. Crucial local needs depend upon local finances. School districts with help from state governments pay roughly 90 percent of the cost of elementary and secondary schooling. States, municipalities, and authorities spend in excess of $200 billion each year for health care. States and localities fund almost three-quarters of the nation's public infrastructure, and they employ six workers for every one employed by the federal government.[7] As federal funding declined, local pressures rose, but often budgets fell.

New York's liberal Democratic governor Hugh Carey set up the Municipal Assistance Corporation (MAC) for New York City, giving its directors, nine private citizens, authority to borrow nearly $10 billion (about $43 billion in 2014 terms), assuring timely repayment of outstanding debt to municipal bondholders.[8] Against the needs of city residents, MAC took aim, along with the treasury secretary, at three targets, proposing to cut services and raise fees for transit, housing, and higher education, rather than taking the alternative route of raising taxes. Similar pressures were felt in many cities. Thus, twenty years after President Eisenhower expressed skepticism about the influence of "stupid" politicians and businessmen, precisely these people had moved into the mainstream, empowered to overrule an elected mayor and city council.

Austerity policies—though rarely then called that—grew into a broad national assault on budgets for public services, with spending cuts and privatizations in health care, public schools, public spaces, housing, transit, the arts, and various other municipal functions. To a great extent, these policies focused on cities. As city populations declined, tax collections dropped and budgets were further cut. The Nixon-Ford administrations eliminated the mandate to spend on the inner city and introduced block grants allowing local officials to ignore needy populations.[9]

Democratic president Jimmy Carter, elected in 1976 with the key support of white suburbanites, only briefly slowed the Nixon-Ford drawdown of city support.[10] Initially, Carter's advisers wrote of "a commitment to urban America and America's cities." His treasury secretary focused on "the question of cities," his HUD secretary said "the White House is now in the hands of a friend of the cities," and urban aid budgets were scheduled to *increase* between 11 percent and 45 percent, according to *A New Partnership to Conserve America's Communities*, released in 1978. This would be the last time the government would even speak of a supportive "urban" policy, and the Congress ignored the report.[11] *Urban* had become synonymous with *minority poverty*. Just two years later, Carter's "National Agenda for the Eighties" served as an urban-policy burial oration.[12] Charles Orlebecke, who worked for HUD secretary George Romney, reports that despite the "impressive rhetorical commitment to address the economic and fiscal problems of older central cities," Carter was ambivalent and the final budget proposals minimal, as California's antitax "Proposition 13 sentiment moved east to the Potomac."[13]

In Cleveland, bankers opted to drive the city into bankruptcy. Brock Wier, the president of Cleveland Trust, Ohio's largest bank, decided to punish the city and its mayor, Dennis Kucinich, for their defense of a public electricity distribution system.[14] The bank refused to play its annual game, the refinancing of city bonds, and on December 15, 1978, it forced the city to declare bankruptcy. While the theatrical events in Cleveland and New York made for press coverage, similar fiscal problems confronted cities nationwide.

The election of Ronald Reagan as president came five years after the New York fiscal debacle, two years after Cleveland's bankruptcy. The Reagan election symbolized and solidified a national move to the right in political style as well as content. Austerity became a key part of national social and economic policy toward cities.[15] From 1978 to 1983 federal fund sharing fell by a third.[16] In 1983 Reagan proposed and the Congress approved $14 billion in cuts to welfare, food stamps, and child nutrition. In 1987 the government canceled revenue sharing, which had disbursed $85 billion to cities over fourteen years.[17] From its peak in 1978 to 2012, the biggest city-aid program, Community Development Block Grants, fell from $12.7 billion to $3 billion, a cut of five-sixths per capita.[18] The bad news for cities was worse still for the large numbers of African Americans, Latinos, and immigrants forced by circumstances to live in impoverished city neighborhoods.[19]

Over five presidential terms, Republican administrations under Ronald Reagan and then father and son George H. W. Bush and George W. Bush acted with indifference to cities, at times with zealous hostility. The decline in city support came steadily, reinforcing political pressures that then demanded further decline. "Direct aid to cities fell by almost one-third" between 1978, its peak, during Carter's term, and 1988, after Reagan's two terms. As a proportion of all federal aid, aid to cities declined from 28 percent to 17 percent. At the same time, "general aid . . . to States and noncity localities, such as counties, suburbs, and rural districts, increased almost 100 percent . . . from $69 billion to over $114 billion.[20] "The Reagan/Bush team also owed substantial ideological debts to their supporters, who were mostly suburban or rural and, in the main, conservatives and self-made New Federalists. They believed that the best government was the one that governed least. The antiurban attitude of the Reagan era lasted throughout the Bush Presidency. Ronald Reagan danced with the mainly nonurban constituents who brought him to the Presidency. George Bush, Reagan's Vice President for two terms and his successor, inherited and continued to fill out Reagan's dance card."[21]

Once the Republican Party had launched its ideological revolution openly promoting budgetary austerity, Democrats under Jimmy Carter and Bill Clinton yielded to conservative demands, adopting much of the austerity rhetoric, continuing many city-starving policies, and cutting adrift a raft of programs that helped people in need. Clinton ended welfare entitlements, instituting block grants to states, leading to disastrous cuts in benefits. In the 1980s and early 1990s about four of five entitled poor families received AFDC benefits, but by 2005, only about two in five did—so that only 2.1 million rather than 4.2 million families received welfare (now known as Temporary Assistance for Needy Families, TANF).[22] Other public guarantees, such as the minimum wage, eroded drastically, as did many private supports. As Edward Goetz writes, the nation undertook "an intentional rollback of social welfare policy in service to neoliberal policy initiatives to reduce government, privatize, and facilitate investment growth in cities," a "race-based strategy for reclaiming central city space."[23]

Cities and the Great Recession

When the economic crisis post-2007 hit the cities, they responded by drawing down rainy-day surpluses and shrinking public activities. Forced to lay off personnel and to delay or cancel bridge and road repair and other projects, they deferred maintenance, leading to potholes in streets and then collapse of the undersurface foundation, and near-failures and bridge closings. Cities have held off maintenance of water and sewage treatment plants and other public works, and they have cut services and hours in libraries, parks, and other major recreation facilities. The accumulated municipal infrastructure deficit is huge.[24] As the executive director of the National Association of State Budget Officers reports, when state revenue surpluses return after years of emptying coffers, "the money is not going to be enough to satisfy everyone's expectations."[25]

School districts have let teachers go and increased class sizes, and they have deferred maintenance, saving money in the short run but adding costs over time. Austerity cuts of today cause social costs for tomorrow, in lost productivity and costly social work, policing, and prisons. A stitch in time would have saved nine.

Municipal austerity means shorter hours and more layoffs—unemployment. Between peak employment in August 2008 and the beginning of 2012, state and local governments lost 668,000 jobs nationwide. In earlier recessions from 1973 to 1990, jobs losses were followed by dramatic recovery. This time, however, even more so than after the recession of 2001 and despite the resumption of hiring by the private sector, state and local hiring did not pick up, a large cause of persistently high unemployment rates.[26]

In a 2011 survey by the National League of Cities, more than 80 percent of finance directors reported increased costs for health insurance, pensions, and infrastructure, and nearly two-thirds reported increased costs for public safety. At the same time, 44 percent of the surveyed cities reported decreases in federal aid; 53 percent had shrinking local tax bases, and 60 percent were hit with reduced state aid.[27]

As of late 2012, at least thirty-one states had reduced municipal aid, "from straight reductions in aid to localities to funding cuts for specific programs, such as K–12 education, road maintenance and property-tax relief." Thirty-seven states imposed across-the-board percentage cuts, thirty-seven forced use of rainy-day funds, and forty-three cut specific, targeted programs. To downsize workforces, thirty-three states used layoffs, while others used furloughs, salary reductions, cuts to benefits, and early retirements. Thirty-one states reduced aid to localities, twenty-three imposed fees for parks and other uses, and nineteen added fees for colleges, court proceedings, and transportation. Fifteen states imposed business-related fees.[28] Without the Federal Recovery Act of 2009, known as the "stimulus package," which "injected $134–140 billion into the coffers of state and local governments," many municipalities would likely have collapsed fiscally.[29] Some did.

Municipalities responded in widely varied ways. Nevertheless, with few exceptions, cities have encountered serious difficulties. San Jose, the nation's tenth-largest city and the largest settlement in fabulously wealthy Silicon Valley, just south of slightly less populous San Francisco, suffered massive cuts to municipal staff, from 7,418 a decade earlier, to 5,400 in 2012. Four hundred ninety firefighters and sixty-six police officers lost their jobs, shrinking the police force by about a fifth. City tax collections in 2012 were expected to be lower than they were five years earlier, when the city had a smaller population. As the police chief says, "It's no longer 'Do more with less,'" . . . "It's doing less with less."[30] "'We're Silicon Valley, we're not Detroit,' said Xavier Campos, a Democratic city councilman representing San Jose's poor East Side. 'It shouldn't be happening here. We're not the Rust Belt.'"[31]

In cities less favorably situated, conditions have been worse. Stockton, California, less than eighty miles from San Jose, had to initiate Chapter 9 bankruptcy proceedings in June 2012, after its tax base collapsed. The city instituted layoffs of a quarter of the police, a third of the firefighters, and 40 percent of other city employees, and it reduced health care and pension benefits for most remaining employees. Despite spending cuts of $90 billion, the city faced a budget gap (2012–2013) of $26 million, so when Moody's rating agency severely downgraded the city's borrowing ability to a very low "Caa3," Stockton filed for bankruptcy.[32]

As David Harvey has argued, when shifts occur at the end of a coherent phase of economic development, urban policy and urban affairs usually play central roles. During the upward shift authorities undertake urban reform: they fund highway and other infrastructure projects, assist commercial building, build public monuments, and subsidize (market-rate) housing developments. These public investments proceed as key elements of economic expansion. When the expansion has played itself out and the boom collapses, then cities must shift down, absorbing much of the decline.[33] The up-and-down process of capitalist boom and bust involves both city building and city destruction. In the process, inequalities increase dramatically. Each metropolitan area, with variation not only from one jurisdiction to another, but from one household to another, has to respond to the collapse.

For reasons noted earlier, formal public bankruptcies like Stockton's are extremely rare, a troublesome option that governments fiercely resist and that many states prohibit.[34] Nonetheless, about fifty municipalities and other local entities, such as school districts and utility authorities, filed for bankruptcy between 2010 and April 2013.[35] In addition to Detroit, now under the control of its state-appointed monitor whose authority trumps the mayor or city council, other Michigan cities, including Detroit's nearby cities of Highland Park and Pontiac, collapsed fiscally.

In a growing number of cases, state governments add to city problems, with their indifference, or worse. Woonsocket, Rhode Island, mentioned in the previous chapter, sits about fifteen miles north of Providence, with a population of just over forty thousand. The city had a $10 million deficit in 2012. Its school department, surprised by a shortfall in 2011, eliminated nearly twenty teachers and support staff in its budget for fiscal year 2013.[36] The superintendent told the community that the "school department is like an accident patient in an emergency room."[37] As economic affairs columnist Joe Nocera reported, "Woonsocket's problems stem from the decision of Rhode Island's previous governor . . . to balance the state's budget by cutting state aid to the cities." When Woonsocket tried to solve its problems, the state senate voted to allow the city to increase its own property tax by 13.8 percent—strong medicine, but self-administered. The Rhode Island House of Representatives, however, killed the bill. Two right-wing Woonsocket representatives pushed for the city to go into receivership, following the lead of ALEC, which abhors taxes and prefers to shrink public budgets. A state budget commission now oversees and overrules the both the city government and the school district.

Woonsocket shares severe fiscal problems with neighboring municipalities. When Rhode Island cut state aid to cities, Providence, the state capital, renegotiated to reduce benefits for its municipal workers. Another Rhode Island city, Central Falls, went into receivership, after which the state-appointed receiver cut retiree benefits by 55 percent, closed the library and a community center, and laid off workers. One of the two conservative representatives who killed the relief bill for Woonsocket, himself a member of ALEC's national board, likes these austerity moves: "You never move faster than when you have a piano hanging over your head," he said. "The receiver is that piano."[38]

The geographies of city reality and imagery are complex. As a result of the mortgage meltdowns at the core of the recession, even the suburban advantage began to slip away for many home buyers. Yet despite their shared economic difficulties (even if less severe), people outside cities seem deaf to pleas for increased relief, displaying disdain for redistributive justice. They blame victims and seek retribution. In this political climate, the idea of *urban* usually retains its pejorative sense, now applied also to a good number of poorer suburban enclaves. For astute observers, these enclaves are themselves "cities," with all their problems. At the same time, in some places the idea of *city* has become a symbol of youthful wealth and sophistication, in safety zones created for a super-privileged urban elite—Center City Philadelphia, much of Manhattan, nearly all of San Francisco, and other places, too.

Even in those energized places, however, the situation can be complex. On June 20, 2013, the city council of Portland, Oregon, one of those celebrated, vibrant cities, unanimously approved a pared-down budget, but only after a long struggle with grassroots opposition to austerity. Early in the year, the newly elected mayor, Charlie Hayes, told each city department to cut its budget by 10 percent, to fill an announced $25 million general fund deficit, requiring further program reductions and personnel layoffs, despite several previous years of cuts. On April 11 more than four hundred protesters arrived at a council meeting, including "members of the Metropolitan Youth Commission, Laborers International Local 483, Portland Community College, Friends of Trees, Portland Safety Net, SUN Schools, Eastside Action Plan, Elders in Action, AFSCME Local 189 . . . Jobs with Justice, the People's Budget Project, and Solidarity Against Austerity." They were later joined by city firefighters and housing advocates.

The protest groups proposed raising revenues rather than increasing unemployment and cutting services. Reportedly breaking with years of unanimous budget voting, Commissioner Amanda Fritz, noting that she was the only woman on the council, voted no on May 29, arguing that the social safety net and environmental programs were "just as vital as roads and utilities and cops." After several specially scheduled council budget meetings, some surprising financial revelations, and considerable adjustment, a budget was approved, including many of the austerity cuts, although the announced deficit was reduced by several million dollars. As two Oregon economics professors wrote, "Our elected officials are in a tough spot, and federal and state decisions have dramatically reduced their room to maneuver. Our Congress and president prioritize deficit reduction over fiscal stimulus. Our Oregon Constitution is interpreted as barring the government from running deficits and [it] requires the state to rebate 'excess' tax collections, and property tax limitations."[39]

Negative congressional action limited extension of welfare benefits. The Obama stimulus package in 2009 did contain an Emergency Contingency Fund (ECF) that expanded TANF to put "more than 260,000 low-income parents and youth in paid jobs," but after Representative Eric Cantor called for abolishing the ECF, it expired at the end of September 2010, dropping one hundred thousand families from TANF benefits.[40] In 2012, with election-year deadlock, indifference to urban needs showed up again in congressional debate, not only by the absence of city-aid items but also by key negative actions. As historical novelist Kevin Baker opines, the Republican Party has become, "more than ever before in its history, an anti-urban party, its support gleaned overwhelmingly from suburban and rural districts—especially in presidential elections."[41] In late January 2014, after negotiating with the Senate, the House passed the farm bill, more than two years overdue, cutting food stamp allocations for about 850,000 families by some ninety dollars a month, despite persistently high underemployment and poverty.

Another measure of the lost political status of cities and the poor is that during the twelve hours of the four presidential and vice presidential debates of 2012, none of the four major-party candidates—not Barack Obama, Mitt Romney, Joe Biden, or Paul Ryan—mentioned either cities or the poor. Nor did they mention disenfranchisement. Nor, except when they could not avoid it—in response to questions about immigration—did they mention people of color.[42]

When the Obama administration inherited the Great Recession, pressures from the Senate and the House limited its options, so it focused on stabilizing the economy through the rescue of Wall Street investment houses, big banks, giant insurance companies, and the auto industry. Not only the Congress but also the administration neglected, and not infrequently blamed, just the people and places most likely to be victimized by decline in cities. The neglect and blame are a consequence of the strength of the austerity ideology, for these victims are part of the Democratic Party's traditional constituency.

Budgets and Ballast

As reflected in the seventy years of debates reviewed in the previous chapter, combined with the budget cuts I note in this chapter, cities have met dual needs of their congressional enemies. On the one hand, federal conservatives gain materially when their austerity policies starve city budgets and reduce benefits to city residents. On the other hand, they gain ideologically when heavy city problems resulting from reduced budgets provide ballast that keeps the ship of conservative politics from keeling over. In the Great Recession and its aftermath, "urbanized" suburbs have joined cities—in underemployment, idle or antiquated capacity, and human misery, and as symbols of failure. There should be little surprise here, as our metropolitan geography has long been arranged according to exclusionary principles following which poor people and minorities are segregated into less desirable and poorly served zones. Especially in times of stress, struggling cities and their poor residents are blamed for their own bleak situations. The political and economic decline of cities has thus worked in a self-reinforcing circle.

Although the economic crisis post 2008 severely aggravated urban problems, neither the policies nor the damaged cities were new. Since the late 1970s, the fortunes of cities and their minority populations have moved on a trajectory of decline, pushed by the reactionary policies of austerity.

Urban planning theorist Peter Marcuse points out that the language of the Occupy movement had it right: austerity is something the 1 percent *do to* the 99 percent.[43] As Jamie Peck says: "It is something that Washington does to the states, the states do to cities and cities do to low-income neighborhoods."[44] Most central cities and now many suburban enclaves are double victims. They are victims of the neglect resulting from a conservative rejection of long-standing liberal reforms, and they have become victims of "free market" mania enforcing austerity at both national and local levels.

Reversal of austerity politics and austerity economics at the national level will deliver profoundly beneficial local effects, improving conditions for residents and local governments alike in cities and newly poor suburban areas. The prospects for federal change have seemed particularly dim with Republican control of the Congress and conservative control of the Supreme Court. At the municipal level, in contrast, as we have seen, a good number of encouraging elections took place in 2014 and 2015, and the movement to increase wages has gathered steam. In statehouses, flickers of resistance to austerity can be seen here and there, with school funding, wage-increasing legislation, and even progressive taxation. California under Governor Jerry Brown's leadership has begun what may be large increases in state spending for schools. A few Republican governors have resisted conservative legislative pressures and signed on to Obamacare, to expand their Medicaid rolls. Two neighboring states "with similar populations and economies" provide "something close to a laboratory experiment," by pursuing "radically different strategies." Minnesota's governor opted for "good government, progressive taxation, and high-wage policies," while Wisconsin's chose "shrunken government, fiscal austerity, and a war on labor." The upshot—progressive Minnesota outperformed reactionary Wisconsin "in population growth, jobs, pay, and quality of life," all key ingredients of more progressive urban policy.[45]

3

Troubled City Schools

City schools in the United States are failing. As we shall see, they are separated by social class, race, and territorial markers. They trail behind their counterparts in the suburbs. They rank well below schools nationwide in Western Europe, Japan, Canada, Australia, Singapore, and South Korea. Urban school failings drag down the national economy, undermine social relations, and tear at an already strained political fabric. They also cheat the very students who most need good schools and deny cities their full potential.

Evidently, school policy ought to be of central concern for those concerned with cities, since not only do nearly all children attend schools close to home (perhaps not in their neighborhoods but nearly always in their municipality), but in addition the schools are for the most part governed and funded locally. My arguments of this and the next chapter will go further, pointing out that unless city schools are repaired, other aspects of city life will continue to slide downhill. Yes, in a few special places, city centers have revived, but probably no central city has thriving public schools.

This city-school problem, a crucial piece of urban affairs, will *not* be solved with city resources and city politics alone. The national government and the states need to do better budgeting, improve regulations, and provide open-minded support.

While a near consensus holds that U.S. city schools fail their constituents and their country, political debates obscure the root causes of the failure. Solid evidence rejects the notion that low school rankings originate from ineffective teachers or their unions. Nor are failures the result of weak school principals or bureaucratically inept administrators. The problem cannot be linked simply back to the home environment, to shift blame onto the supposed uninterest of parents or weakness in community culture. Rather, as I will show in this chapter, the pattern of failed city schools is a symptom of four underlying flaws: profound and growing inequalities rooted in the national economy; built-in municipal fragmentation that isolates cities and impoverished suburbs from their surroundings; austerity politics, including an unreasoned penchant for the privatization of public services; and continuing bias against people of color. As long as these flaws remain central features of the society, the problems they cause will remain, and city school improvements will occur only in limited cases.

Nearly 50 million children attend public schools in the United States, kindergarten through high school, and almost 5.5 million more attend other schools.[1] Counting all, including the 10 percent who attend parochial or private schools or are home schooled, roughly one-quarter go on to college and graduate with a bachelor's degree. In this chapter I am mainly concerned with the others, the *least* schooled, those who will not get any college degree. As figure 3.1 shows, of all adults twenty-five years old or older, 63 percent stop school short of a two-year associate's degree, and 71 percent stop short of a bachelor's degree.

It used to be that as children moved into adulthood and took their place in the economy, formal educational certification didn't matter so much. Some children learned skills like reading and basic mathematics outside school, and others easily joined the workforce without these skills. In 1950, most jobs (60 percent) did not require a high school diploma, and as late as 1973, still a third of jobs were available to those without a high school diploma.

That world is gone. By 2007, only 10 percent of U.S. jobs were available to someone without a high school diploma.[2] In today's world, even factories and trucking firms demand literate and numerate workers. Offices,

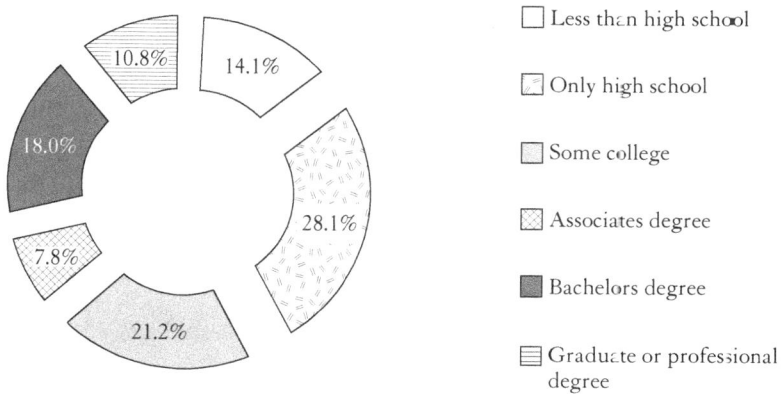

Figure 3.1. Adult educational attainment, 2013. U.S. Census Bureau, 2013. American Community Survey, five-year estimates, 2009–2013.

stores, public agencies, nonprofits, community organizations, and most other employers want job applicants to arrive with formal school credentials and good skills. Yet in spite of these stiffening requirements, many young people don't finish high school on time or at all, and even among the students who stay to graduate, large numbers score unacceptably low in math, science, and reading. When eighth-grade students took the National Assessment of Educational Progress in 2009, for example, many could not deal with the most rudimentary questions, and 37 percent of them apparently were unable to "understand" science.

At the bottom of this ranking, each student who does not graduate from high school loses about $260,000 in lifetime earnings and pays about $60,000 less in taxes. These school leavers have much worse health—a forty-five-year-old dropout has the health of a sixty-five-year-old high school graduate, and dropouts can expect to die nine years earlier. People who rank low in schooling are stigmatized and more likely to confront problems of physical and mental health. Workers with only a high school diploma earn barely half what college degree holders earn.[3]

Segregated and Unequal

Schools in cities (as defined by the U.S. Census) enroll just under one-third of all public school students, with suburban enrollment accounting for another third. At last count some seventeen hundred high schools, one in ten, were "dropout factories," defined as schools in which about a third of the students or more drop out before becoming seniors.[4] Nearly all these problematic schools are in big cities, and nearly all their students are African American, Latino, or immigrants. In other school districts, the deprived include growing numbers of white children from poor households. "The imbalance between rich and poor children in college completion—the single most important predictor of success in the work force—has grown by about 50 percent since the late 1980s."[5]

When districts are ranked by the portion of their students who do not graduate high school *on time*, the city of Indianapolis tops the list, with fewer than one in three ninth graders going on to a timely graduation. In other cities, including Detroit and Cleveland, fewer than 40 percent graduate on time. In thirteen more big-city districts the on-time graduation rates are higher, but still under 50 percent: Milwaukee, Baltimore, Atlanta, Los Angeles, Las Vegas, Columbus, Nashville, Minneapolis, Oklahoma City, San Antonio, Tulsa, Albuquerque, and Omaha. Counting children who drop out *before* ninth grade, the true graduation rates are lower.[6]

Many of the children who *do* graduate don't learn as much as they should. In the Charlotte, San Diego, and Boston school districts, for example, half or more of the students lack basic science concepts. This proportion grows even larger in New York, Houston, Chicago, Cleveland, Los Angeles, and Atlanta.[7] In New York City only 21 percent of the cohort that started high school in 2006 left prepared to go to college. In Rochester, New York, that success rate was only 6 percent.[8] New York City's rates are better than Rochester's because some New York City students can attend specialized and magnet high-performing schools, while in Rochester nearly all students must attend troubled schools. The total population of the twenty-three school-troubled cities listed in these two paragraphs exceeds thirty million.[9] Figure 3.2 provides a very rough division of enrollments in cities, suburbs, towns, and rural areas.

The relatively few city-schooled children who go on to college have a more difficult time than their classmates. They take less-demanding college majors, get worse grades, take longer to graduate, and drop out more often. They encounter difficulties mainly because when they leave their high schools, they are less well prepared for collegiate success, they lack confidence, and they feel like fish out of water. All in all, young people

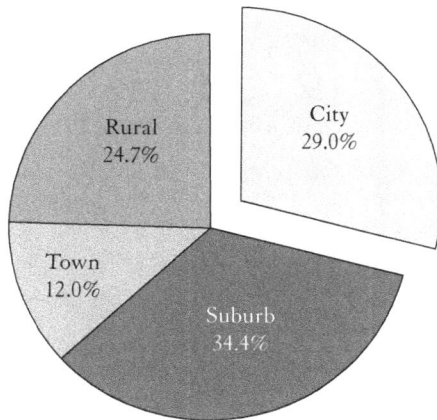

Figure 3.2. U.S. public school K–12 enrollment in cities, suburbs, towns, and rural areas, 2010–2011. Data from U.S. Department of Education, National Center for Education Statistics 2012.

from standard city high schools—teacher Vicki Madden appropriately calls them "urban students"—enter the world less able to contribute to the economy and the society, and less satisfied with their places in the world.[10]

Sometimes city schools themselves, along with problems in the neighborhood, present almost insurmountable obstacles, despite students' and families' own high hopes. To write the book *Our Schools Suck*, four researchers got to know black and Latino youth in South Central Los Angeles, Harlem, and the Bronx, the sorts of young people often blamed for their own failures. These young people do not suffer from any "culture of failure." They want to learn and often go to great lengths to do so, but they run into barriers with dilapidated school buildings, poor instruction when inexperienced or unsupported teachers have too many unprepared students in the classroom, and heavy demands outside school. In *Savage Inequalities*, Jonathan Kozol wrote about the extraordinary misery in inner-city East Saint Louis schools, which flooded with sewage when it rained. Such physical and environmental obstacles to learning, he found—like those created by unsafe sidewalks, dilapidated school buildings, or the dangers of the streets—deeply injure inner-city children. Kozol found similar problems more than twenty years later, this time when he revisited schools in the Bronx.[11] A middle-school girl from San

Francisco wrote of her relief at having left the violent streets of Hunters Point, but her relief was short-lived, because the violence repeated itself after her move across the bay to East Oakland, where street shootings again provided the soundtrack for a night's loss of sleep. Her large middle school was not up to her needs, despite the efforts of an eager, competent, and forceful principal. There were too many obstacles: some teachers were burned out, and *every* child came from a household with a low income, where caregivers had too many other pressures on their time and energy to assist their children. The school couldn't provide the extra instruction the children needed.[12]

These deplorable situations repeat themselves in city after city across the country, and the shortcomings are almost self-reinforcing. Yet it makes no sense. Why does a country that once displayed its public schools with pride now leave a large portion of them in such miserable shape, especially when reform proposals abound? Ideas for school reform include programs for inclusion, graduation by exhibition, high-stakes testing, whole-school improvement plans, cottage campuses, academies, high expectations, standard uniforms, and the federal government's forceful intervention, begun under President George W. Bush and modified under President Barack Obama, as No Child Left Behind (NCLB), then Race to the Top.[13] So many good ideas, but nothing works near well enough: what is the problem?

Those who are most directly involved with individual city students—their teachers, administrators, and families—typically face the brunt of the blame for school failure. The prominent education scholar and adviser Diane Ravitch, for example, long laid the blame on problems such as poor curricula, as well as selfish unions, teachers, and administrators who pursued their own interests.[14] Political scientists looking at "civic capacity" scale up their thinking a degree further, to an institutional level. They predict that more effective involvement of elites in city politics will enhance a school district's capacity for reform. But even these highly respected theorists take a circumscribed view, seeing each set of failing schools in isolation, rather than seeking a national pattern.

One can explain much more about school failures by employing a structural theory of inequality. From this extended perspective, commonplace school reforms operate merely at the surface. Below the surface level, schools and students are held back by the extraordinary chasm of educational apartheid: the isolation of children from poor households in minority school districts in nearly all inner cities and some poor suburbs, unable to access the benefits afforded children from the middle class in predominantly white and almost exclusively suburban districts.[15] While integration has been occurring in predominantly white schools, mainly in the suburbs (where the average percentage of white students has dropped from about 82 percent to about 75 percent), in predominantly black and Latino schools the "integration" of whites has for years been *declining*. Gary Orfield and his associates report that nationally, after "major gains in integration . . . from the mid-1960s through the mid-1970s" and some progress in the 1980s, "the share of white classmates for black and Latino students has been continuously declining for three decades."[16]

For the cities, this exclusionary system, based not only on race but also on social class distinctions, is not airtight. Communities have devised various schemes to overcome it. In some places, special schools bring privilege into cities. In other places, special programs send city minority students to find relief in the white suburbs. Even when reforms breach the walls of privilege, however, they do not knock them down, so these reforms, being exceptions, prove the apartheid rule. Key aspects of exclusion include inadequate funding for city schools and the exclusionary nature of suburban middle-class or upper-class schools.

Don't Blame Families, Teachers, or Administrators

Pedro Noguera and Randi Weingarten are correct when they write that "without a shred of evidence to back their claims, a new batch of so-called reformers and their allies in the media have asserted that charter schools are superior to public schools . . . that mayoral control is an inherently better form of governance than locally elected school boards and that ending tenure for teachers and evaluating them based on student test scores are the most powerful instruments that could be used to improve instruction and hold teachers accountable."[17] Many critics who worry about failing city schools incorrectly find salvation in charter schools, mayoral control, an end to teachers' tenure, and promotion tied to test scores.[18] They place the blame for school failures on problems of administration, curriculum, and organization, and on the selfishness of unions and weakness of teachers. Even in excellent suburban districts, it is true that administrative, curricular, and organizational problems occur, that unions can act self-ishly, and that teachers can be weak.[19] Such problems are to be expected in any complex organization with contradictory goals. But good school districts rather easily manage these common problems. Why, then, do the problems overwhelm central city schools?

Critics also incorrectly blame the bad attitudes of students. And they blame caregivers, including parents, grandparents, and others, for not paying sufficient attention to their children's school needs. These caregivers, it is said, do not talk up the importance of attendance, study, and good behavior, do not participate in school events and governance, and do not help with homework and other assignments. These criticisms contain important half-truths, but we need to know why students do not behave as critics prefer and why their caregivers do not provide sufficient support.

The key problems of central city schools do not result from lack of interest by caregivers, from students' bad attitudes, from spiteful administrators or weak teachers, or from the fact that the schools are public and part of a district rather than private or separately chartered. Instead, the problems of the schools arise from deep social and economic gaps in the underlying structure of the society. These gaps take economic form in exaggerated disparities of household income. They take social form in disrespect, dis-crimination, and stigma that mark the poor and ethnic groups. They take physical form in a metropolitan geography arranged to isolate rich from poor and people of color from whites. They are exacerbated by austerity policies and unjustifiable support for privatization. City schools that fail the children of poor African American, Latino, and immigrant families are located in neighborhoods with underperforming labor markets and dilapidated housing. In those neighborhoods, food deserts limit nutrition, city departments limit services, and conditions on streets, playgrounds, and other public spaces limit safety. Social stigma marks these places, their inhabitants, and the schools.

Yet many education critics persistently ignore these problems and over-simplify, to put the blame on families, teachers, and administrators. In a provocative book called *No Excuses*, Abigail Thernstrom and Stephan Thernstrom level exactly these kinds of blame. First, they examine race and ethnicity. They acknowledge that black and Latino children, who make up one-third of all students nationally, fail massively everywhere in (primarily urban) public schools, with lower scores, fewer AP classes, and higher dropout rates. The Thernstroms correctly see education as the central civil rights issue of the time, because the nation's failure to provide first-class education leaves children without good options in an economy that demands math and reading skills even for ordinary jobs. They assert (probably incorrectly) that NCLB was intended mainly to close the racial/ethnic achievement gap. And they observe, correctly, that some special schools in big cities are terrific, with great leaders and teachers, high academic and behavioral standards, and even nonstop schedules with longer school days, weeks, and years. Why, they ask, don't most schools improve? What is wrong?

Rejecting the most odious of past false claims, the assertion that black and Latino students are genetically inferior, with lower IQs, the Thernstroms turn to two main arguments: First, that teachers and administrators are damaged by a "traditional educational culture," which makes them unimaginative, without ambition, and resistant to innovation. Teachers and administrators "operate in a straightjacket . . . [and the] enormous power of teachers' unions stops almost all real change in its tracks."[20] This standard popular argument is logically flawed, since many, many *successful* school districts operate throughout the nation, mainly in the suburbs, employing administrators with the same certification and teachers who join the same unions that are said to be strangling the cities. Yet no straightjackets tie down suburban school districts. So why do the unions, the teachers, and the administrators cause problems in city schools?

The frequency of arguments blaming administrators and especially teachers and unions has increased. In 2009 and 2010, critics feared that Obama administration "radicals" intended to undermine NCLB, and they proposed sensational reforms to solve the problem quickly—just weed out all the terrible teachers and destroy the monstrous unions, then the children will learn.[21] Such proposals, in mutual reinforcement with the NCLB emphasis on testing and teacher assessment, became a steady diet on radio, television, and the press, captured on the big screen in two well-attended movies, *Waiting for Superman* and *The Cartel*. Funding from the Gates Foundation added still more pressure, to push for a quick-fix business model originally aimed to eliminate tenure and later to base teachers' pay not on seniority but on achievement.[22]

The Thernstroms' second argument is about the "cultures" of families or groups, applied to neighborhoods or even school districts. "Some cultures are academically advantageous," they write, but others are not. Here, "culture" means "values, attitudes, and skills that are shaped . . . by environment." Some minority cultures do not encourage their children to take school seriously, they claim. "The Hispanics who are flooding into American schools today," for example, seem to them to resemble the Italian peasant immigrants at the beginning of the twentieth century, who told their children to quit school and get jobs. Asian students today, on the other hand, have the right culture, as they "are typically more deeply engaged in academic work . . . cut classes less often, and enroll in AP courses at triple the white rate. . . . The explanation: family expectations. . . . The group . . . has most intensely embraced the traditional American work ethic."[23] Others quite commonly claim—also using pseudo-psychological rather than solid sociological explanations—that Asian American students are fulfilling the expectations of an Asian culture, rather than the "traditional American" one.

Black and Latino parents do not demand that their children do well in school, the Thernstroms claim. The children don't "speak politely to the principal, teachers, and strangers; they [don't] learn to dress neatly, to arrive at school on time, to pay attention in class, finish homework, and [to] never waste time."[24] The solution is to change the "culture" of the lagging groups. Television comedian Bill Cosby's statements and writings popularized broad assertions of this sort, however imprecise and superficial they were.[25] In many ways, these arguments turn the blame onto victims of oppressive economic conditions, troubled neighborhoods, and collapsing schools.[26] The closing scenes of the documentary movie *Waiting for Superman* vividly contradict this victim-blaming stance. In the film, we see whole families of "inner-city" parents, siblings, and relatives sitting painfully together with hundreds of other hopefuls through cruel lotteries in hopes that *their* student will be one of the lucky few who gets chosen for the well-funded charter school, thus escaping the underfunded and low-performance neighborhood school. The vast majority of these students and their caregivers—all of them hoping fervently for a chance at a truly good education—will be disappointed. The film thus unintentionally puts the lie to the assertion that children and their families don't value education.

Despite their imprecision and superficiality, and their evident appeal to racism, however, these arguments about culture cannot be completely ignored. Peer pressure, for example, works as an influential part of the adolescent experience for all children, serving as one special mechanism to enable a neighborhood to support or neglect its children at school. For children of color—African American, Latino, Asian, and American Indian—peer-group influence can be especially negative or positive, and it can be extremely powerful.[27] Minority children who are poor and sense that their ethnic group is despised can suffer severe social difficulties when challenged by their peers. If they do well at school, African American girls and boys are sometimes accused by their peers of acting "white." Researchers report strongly negative pressure of the sort illustrated in the *Boondocks* cartoon student who complains to his teacher about his C-minus grade. How can he move on, he asks, if she insists on giving him such a grade? His street companions, after all, expect their friends to get Ds if not Fs. Gang influence among children in large Latino neighborhoods can be similarly negative about doing well in school. Sometimes, when minority children "cross over," either residing in racial isolation in white neighborhoods or commuting from the ghetto or barrio daily to attend enriched and racially integrated schools, they must struggle with the paramount issues of identity and self-regard, often in an environment with staff untrained to mentor minority children or even to understand their needs.[28]

Schools are racially segregated, the Thernstroms acknowledge, and they observe that residential segregation causes school segregation. They observe, also, that schools "cannot . . . magically become racially balanced given existing residential patterns." Ostensibly in the interests of practicality, they therefore reject the logical options, which are to break down the "existing residential" segregation or to change the underlying conditions that produce the segregation. They fail to mention the Supreme Court's July 1974 decision in the crucial *Milliken v. Bradley* case, which disallowed the imposition of busing beyond the boundaries of a single school district. Nor do they speculate on what might have happened had the majority then supported Justice Thurgood Marshall's dissent, which argued in favor of allowing the plan for integration *across* district boundaries to stand. That plan, devised for a group of city and suburban school districts, would have integrated the mostly black Detroit pupils together with the mostly white suburban pupils in fifty-three districts.

As Justice Marshall wrote, despite "widespread and pervasive racial segregation" in Michigan and Detroit schools, "the decision . . . guarantee[s] that Negro children in Detroit will receive the same separate and inherently unequal education in the future as they have been unconstitutionally afforded in the past." As Justice William O. Douglas wrote in his separate dissent: "If this were a sewage problem or a water problem, or an energy problem, there can be no doubt that Michigan would stay well within federal constitutional bounds if it sought a metropolitan remedy."

Forty years later, segregation has remained so entrenched that it is easy to claim that only politically infeasible solutions (magic, as the Thernstroms say) can work to correct the school-performance defects of highly segregated neighborhoods. David Kirp, a professor of public policy at the University of California at Berkeley, is sorry to agree: "In theory it's possible to achieve a fair amount of integration by crossing city and suburban boundaries or opening magnet schools attractive to both minority and white students. But the hostile majority on the Supreme Court and the absence of a vocal pro-integration constituency make integration's revival a near impossibility."[29]

In *More Than Just Race*, sociologist William J. Wilson deals helpfully with the tangle of causation involving structure and culture. He is concerned with concentrated poverty, the condition that prevails in neighborhoods where schools fail most wretchedly. In a nod to the cultural critics, Wilson reports that some ghetto residents do engage in counterproductive behavior, but he finds that the obstacles enforcing inequality exert much greater negative power.[30] These obstacles are built into the structure of things, which includes underlying politics, punitive legislation and regulation, insufficient public budgets, as well as the political boundaries and land-use regulations that produce racial and economic segregation. Other obstacles that form part of the underlying structure include changes in workplace technologies that have led to the exclusion of unprepared minority workers, weak inner-city labor markets that cut off the flow of employment information, and poor transportation networks that block access to jobs.[31]

The contrast between city schools and suburban schools brusquely reveals the underlying inequality. Nearly every U.S. metropolis has two distinctly different sets of schools, successful in the suburbs, failing in cities and broken-down inner suburbs or minority districts. Going from the city to the suburbs is like moving from one nation to another. Judge and author James Ryan calls it "A World Apart."[32] Most suburban public schools have high on-time graduation rates—75 percent or higher, often 90 percent or more. These are the successful districts that surround America's largest cities.[33] Suburban children have much higher rates of college attendance and graduation, so that jobs requiring college degrees are open to them. In Kozol's terms, these suburb/city disparities reveal "savage inequalities."

Ryan argues correctly that politicians don't dare to assert that segregated schools are a good thing; but they come close to asserting that segregated *neighborhoods* are. Indeed, it was on this nuanced distinction that Nixon's suburban electoral strategy worked, confirmed in *Milliken v. Bradley*: if schools happen to be segregated, then we must provide adequate funding to make separate be equal, but we will not challenge the neighborhood separations! We have not provided the funding, it is true, so while the neighborhood question remains beyond reach, concern has only increased about failing city schools.

The Blame Game

Mainstream commentators and political "realists" often reject such blunt assessments of suburb/city disparities. To sidestep the impracticalities of overcoming these disparities and to avoid the discomfort of discussing the implications about race and class, scholars and popular-opinion leaders have turned their attention to city-to-city variations in three areas: community support, municipal leadership and programs, and civic solidarity. Cities with strong and persistent support from an organized community, they argue, will have prosperous school districts. We know from successful suburban school districts that activism and pressure can make a big difference in guiding municipal and school district leadership. But few cities enjoy such organized support.

When cities lack strong bottom-up strategies, the blame for failures logically transfers to poor top-down strategies, with calls for greater leadership at the mayoral or superintendent level. This approach is popular in the media, with sound-bite simplicity and superstar reformers. The daily news is salted with hopeful stories about inner-city school reforms, in some cases to be performed by highly compensated, newly placed superintendents portrayed as potential heroes. Incoming mayors often select these leaders, wrapping promising education reform ideas into their campaign strategies. Sadly, few of the stories have happy endings.

Oakland on the West Coast, for example, and Yonkers on the East Coast installed new superintendents with great fanfare, but there are no reports of stunning achievements. Heralded reform efforts in Detroit, from 2009 to 2011, also failed. Michelle Rhee won great praise for the vigorous changes introduced during her tenure as Washington, DC, school superintendent, but her radical experiment ended in bitterness, including electoral defeat for the mayor who had supported her, test scores manipulated to falsely claim improvement, and little if any evidence of better education for the children. Cases from Chicago, Los Angeles, and New York provide poignant examples from across the nation. Unfortunately, none of these cases delivers the dazzling success that was promised.

Two strong Chicago mayors made school improvement a top priority. After earlier administrations had established magnet schools, Chicago's first black mayor, Harold Washington (1983–1987), responsive to the needs of the African American neighborhoods that backed him, made school improvement a primary goal for his second term. But the city did not gain jurisdiction over its schools until Mayor Richard M. Daley's tenure (1989–2011). Daley was among the first nationally to announce a school strategy of tough love by mandating strict grade-promotion requirements and instituting required summer school for failing students. In 2001, Daley appointed Arne Duncan as CEO of the Chicago Public Schools, starting a campaign focused on increasing test scores, closing failing schools, and supporting new charter schools. As in other cities, in Chicago the changes from the top somehow missed support from below, despite activism from inner-city families. On many occasions mothers (black and poor) protested in front of City Hall and met with their aldermen to protest school closings.[34]

In his Renaissance 2010 speech, delivered in 2004, Mayor Daley promised more than one hundred new charter schools in underserved neighborhoods over the next six years.[35] Chicago charter schools have since tripled enrollments, with the opening of over seventy new Renaissance 2010 schools, but serious doubts persist. Test scores and graduation rates showed improvement, according to the city's reports, but critics lacked confidence in the results. On May 22, 2013, the Chicago school board followed Mayor Rahm Emanuel's push by voting to shut down forty-nine elementary schools and one high school. The administration, plagued with underperforming schools, cites "an exodus from the city . . . of middle-class

African American families." Of the district's more than four hundred thousand students, 87 percent come from low-income families, and more than 91 percent are minority children.[36] At best, reform measures showed improvement in elementary and middle schools as test score gaps decreased moderately, but high schools did not show improvement even after several years.[37] Michelle Rhee's positive reports for Washington, DC, schools also proved inaccurate.

In Los Angeles, Mayor Antonio Villaraigosa tied his political campaign to school reform during the 2005 election and made high-profile visits to schools known to be particularly violent. The Los Angeles Unified School District has eleven hundred schools that enroll more than six hundred thousand children. Many come from families struggling with deep poverty, and two-fifths of the elementary school children speak English as a second language, so school reform is on nearly everyone's agenda. Only two years after his election, however, Mayor Villaraigosa decided *not* to tackle the school problem. The weakness of his office was no match for the magnitude of the issues—including gang warfare at the most troubled schools and the difficulty of reaching agreement with big-money political donors, key state legislators, and various influential city figures. The mayor of Los Angeles doesn't really have control over the school district, which overlaps twenty-seven mainly "inner city" municipalities.[38] His attempts to gain control failed. Through his Partnership for Los Angeles Schools, he really controlled only ten campuses.

In New York City, Mayor Michael Bloomberg won strong authority over the school board and appointed former federal assistant attorney general and corporate CEO Joel Klein, who ran the schools like a business firm, slashing jobs in the central bureaucracy with broad political support, and hiring managers rather than educators to raise funds, streamline affairs, and seize control at the top. From Klein's perspective: "In the end it is my responsibility to say, this is the right policy. . . . The mayor holds me accountable, and the city holds the mayor accountable. We should not have 'shared decision-making.' That's what marks all unsuccessful school reforms." Unfortunately, for the students, the top-down model didn't help.[39] From 2002 to 2004, Caroline Kennedy served as director of the city's Office of Strategic Partnerships for the Department of Education. In this role, she raised millions for the schools while working for a dollar a year. In 2003, retired General Electric CEO Jack Welch, famous for his corporate restructuring, slashing jobs, and improving GE's value by 400 percent, led the advisory board of an academy that trains public school principals. That same year, the Gates Foundation donated millions of dollars, mostly focused on closing failing large high schools and turning them into small schools. Despite these efforts and more, the testing and graduation rate gains are "respectable, not historic."[40] After Klein left, in 2010 Bloomberg appointed publishing CEO Cathie Black, formerly of the Hearst Corporation. From the mayor's top-down view, Black would thrive despite her lack of experience with public schools, teaching, higher education, or the business of education. Black failed, lasting only three months on the job.

Despite the support of education-focused mayors, reform-minded administrations, and acclaimed new superintendents, many city schools continue to lose their best teachers. When lower-middle-class families can escape to put their children in suburban schools, they do. And the city schools still have high dropout rates, low scores, poor behavior, and little learning.

To more accurately pinpoint responsibility for failures in "urban" schools, as well as to identify ingredients for success, one extremely thorough research project concluded that success results from effective city-wide politics and administration.[41] In the Civic Capacity and Urban Education project, noted political scientist Clarence Stone and his team conducted more than five hundred interviews in eleven large central cities, each of which had attempted reform in the late twentieth century. Rather than simply asking whether tough top leadership would turn the trick, the researchers sought much greater detail. They grouped the cities by level of solidarity that connects business elites, city hall, and the community. Atlanta, Denver, Saint Louis, and San Francisco were the least mobilized politically, with the lowest levels of solidarity. Pittsburgh, Boston, and Los Angeles were the most highly mobilized for sustained reforms; and Baltimore, Houston, Washington, DC, and Detroit were in the middle. In a related study the same researchers asked whether minority ethnic control over city hall and the school district matters. They expected benefits for black neighborhoods and families in cities where a black mayor and black influential figures had taken political control and a black superintendent was heading up the school district, so researchers contrasted the four black-led cities—Atlanta, Baltimore, Detroit, and Washington, DC—with the other seven cities, all white-led.

The team checked whether nonschool characteristics mattered. Political machines dominate some of the eleven sample cities, while others have more open politics. Some base their economies on manufacturing, others on corporate headquarters, public administration, or finance. Some of the cities are in economically growing regions, others are in declining regions. Surprisingly, none of these factors correlates with the success or failure of school reform. Nor do the specifics or the quality of the reform proposals matter much, at least not when comparing these eleven cities one with another. Good proposals were made nearly everywhere for improving teaching style, boosting administrative efficiency, and streamlining system-wide organization. At the broad city level, not even the election of a black mayor and the appointment of a black superintendent made any real difference in the quality of schooling.

Stone's Civic Capacity researchers argue convincingly that the degree of political solidarity in the city is the most important factor for school success. For a reform to succeed, for schools to really excel, they explain, reform efforts must persist over a number of years, and persistence requires solidarity. The cooperation that first unites business CEOs can then lead politicians, teachers, school administrators, and voters in favor of sustained, long-term improvements in the schools.[42] In the cities with the lowest levels of political mobilization (Atlanta, Denver, Saint Louis, and San Francisco), the reforms could not mature. In the cities where highly mobilized leaders did work together (Pittsburgh, Boston, and Los Angeles), some modestly successful change occurred. In the middle cities (Baltimore, Houston, Washington, DC, and Detroit) the results were in between.

Unfortunately, even according to the researchers, *none* of the eleven cities really succeeded at improving its schools in a substantial way. Pittsburgh, sitting in the top spot for elite solidarity, did integrate its schools modestly by relying on long-standing, high-level cooperation among corporate officers, city officials, and the school board. Against any reasonable measure of achievement, however, Pittsburgh fails, despite being the city with the highest level of mobilization and the most momentum for school reform. School improvements were small even there, limited because neighborhoods remain racially segregated, and most black students continue to attend predominantly black schools, where performance standards are lower. In Boston, the next most mobilized city and next best at school reform, improvements were even more limited because business leaders kept out of the action. They didn't operate even behind the scenes, evidently uninterested in solving school problems.[43] Although Los Angeles earned relatively high ranking, subsequent evidence, as we have seen, shows little success at school reform beyond raising the issue among the electorate. The mayor campaigned hard to fix the troubled schools but could not arrange even modest agreement among key parties, which include the independent school board, state officials, and teachers' unions. In Los Angeles's East Side District Five, fifty-nine of ninety-one schools in 2007 were judged to be "chronic failures."[44] At the bottom end of the solidarity scale, in Saint Louis, where segregation is historically most severe among the eleven sample cities and where business-city-school interest and cooperation by leaders was less even than in Boston, no progress was made at all.

Even in the central cities with successful civic mobilization, the Civic Capacity researchers found that school districts had no purposeful, carefully managed school coalitions. These cities fail to bring together parents, teachers, administrators, and especially leading politicians and business executives. The missing piece, kept off the game board by the restrictive research design, finishes the puzzle: the *suburbs* surrounding each central city have precisely these qualities and capacities in great supply. They display great political solidarity, especially in matters of schooling. In most suburbs the powerful players (usually acting as householders and home-property owners, rather than leading politicians and business executives) support and reinforce their school systems, superintendents, administrators, principals, and teachers, who then relatively easily manage to provide good schooling to the children. Indeed, the most profound finding from this extensive research effort sneaks in from outside the researchers' box: although the nature of a school district's political regime *does* matter for effective reform, particularly the degree of involvement by community leaders, the big political-regime variation occurs not from one city to another, but between each city and most of its suburbs.

These powerful results lead us to new directions. The optimistic question is, what makes school reform work in cities? We can now answer that nothing works, as long as the focus stays narrowly on the cities' schools. As thoughtful school reformers attempt to remedy the failing situation, most of them focus quite understandably on tangible, school-based programs to improve preparation of teachers, supervise them more firmly while allowing them professional autonomy, modernize the curriculum, evaluate courses more carefully, and administer schools and districts more effectively and efficiently. But, as we have seen, narrow changes do not work. The Civic Capacity researchers themselves on occasion exhibit frustration with their inability to extend beyond these issues to broaden the scope, evidently wanting to introduce factors beyond the failing schools and outside the cities. They complain in footnotes or brief comments about their self-limiting sampling procedures, which in turn fenced in their data collection and analysis. This self-imposed restriction, which kept the researchers focused entirely *inside* each city's boundaries, denied them the chance to examine the profound school differences that separate each central area from its suburbs beyond. At some points, the research teams despair of identifying the things that really matter, like the much inferior economic situation of city residents compared to suburbanites, or the greater catch-up needs of city children with nutritional shortages or second-language difficulties. The researchers quietly acknowledge that suburban leaders sustain school reforms just the ways they theorize that city leaders ought to. The researchers excuse these limitations on their research by explaining that they must be pragmatists who accept urban-suburban disparities, so as to ask how the cities themselves can improve their schools under the status quo. By taking the situation as given, these researchers consciously deny the possibility of sufficient change.

To change the reality of city/suburb school inequality, one must somehow overcome the negative effect of municipal boundary lines. Advocates of metropolitan regional government, or even simple service coordination, have long struggled against the difficulties caused by a multiplicity of authority. Gerald Frug, the Harvard Law professor who writes on these issues and worries about schools in particular, proposes a broad form of cooperative metropolitan politics. To those who complain that his proposals are utopian, he responds with the suggestion that his radical proposal may in the end be more practical than the problematic status quo. I agree, and I think that to break with things as they are, to pursue any radical approach for city schools, without which they are unlikely to improve in any significant way, we must look directly at a series of structural issues that frame the city-school problem.

Fragmentation, Suburban Exclusivity, and Racial Exclusion

An excessive market-driven inequality, extensive municipal fragmentation, the almost complete exclusivity of suburban public schools, and racial segregation combine to leave city public schools and their millions of students abandoned and ignored.

Social Inequality and Unequal Schools Reinforce One Another

To account for the effects of social class distinctions, the starkest theory of educational inequality argues that a society with great inequality *needs* workers who willingly take undesirable jobs for low pay. To create or sustain such a class of workers, the society's major institutions, schools above all, must operate with bias. They need to prepare groups and individuals who will be "naturally" inclined toward one pole or another, either up to success in skilled and well-paying jobs, or down to a class of underemployed workers.

Political economists Samuel Bowles and Herbert Gintis long ago proposed a theory of polarization to explain educational inequality. Their theory helps explain the persistent gap between successful and unsuccessful schools, assigning them roles as built-in parts of the society's structure. In this scheme, the particular function of schools is to produce two distinct sets of people—leaders (winners) who expect success and wealth, and followers (losers) who expect to be kept in their place, with meager rewards. The argument is not that anyone *plans* school systems to produce inequality, but that the society structures itself to operate this way. Following this theory, schools create and maintain the divisions that underlie status quo social relations. Comparable social relations govern not only the mainstream economy, but also government agencies, the military, and other major institutions, such as the media and organized religion, as well as schools. The Bowles-Gintis set of arguments cleanly rejects the myth that public schools offer—or even that they mean to offer—paths to success for nearly all.[45]

A construct of this sort can be particularly useful as a heuristic device, to free one up for new ideas. The theory treats expectations—it does not predict that everyone who attends a leading school will succeed, nor does it deny that some who attend a school for followers will themselves succeed.

Thus, as in the larger society, cross-class mobility is not impossible, but it is limited. Nor does the theory require that anyone *intend* these unequal outcomes. The biases do not result from conspiracy. Instead, social forces will lead the society's major institutions, including the schooling system, to behave typically in dualistic ways, since the normal operation of the society requires that some people be prepared to fill jobs that require high skills, others, low skills. Some people should have high expectations for pay and respect, and others, low expectations. Nor, of course, is the situation simple duality; rather, success and failure in the real world lie on a gradient of gradual differences.[46]

As people and institutions act in their own selfish interests, the system that produces the inequalities is reinforced. To justify the inequalities, an ideology develops to assert that people are paid what they are worth. That ideology, put forth by neoclassical economic theory, contends that a worker's status (and pay) reflects his or her productive contribution to society. While the discipline of the labor market may be cruel, the theory goes, it makes for an efficient economy, of benefit to all. In 2010, after the market crash, a successful but repentant Wall Street banker wondered whether such an ideology makes sense. Pointing out how bankers and bond traders make "self-aggrandizing claim[s] to . . . socioeconomic util-ity," he asks: "You mean to tell me [their] work . . . is worth more to society than a firefighter? An elementary school teacher? A combat infantryman in Afghanistan? A priest? Good luck with that."[47]

Direct evidence to support such a stark dualistic schooling theory should be difficult if not impossible to produce, yet circumstantial find-ings abound. Many critics contend, for example, that when the George W. Bush administration introduced NCLB they aimed not so much at improving education in troubled schools and districts, as at handicapping what would be too-costly efforts at true reform. Again, the theory asserts not that the administration planned for unequal schools, but that its other objectives would stand in the way of policies to reduce school inequality. Thus, whether consciously or not, even if they expressed a desire to reduce inequality, they would fail. Meghan Behrent, a public school teacher in Brooklyn, writes: "By setting unrealistic standards that don't take immi-grant and learning-disabled students into consideration and then pun-ishing schools with children who fail to meet those standards," NCLB engages "in propaganda to drum up support for school vouchers," thus weakening city public schools. Behrent says, "Bush turned schools into test prep factories, setting them up to fail and then punishing them when they did."[48]

Linda Darling-Hammond, who holds a chair in education at Stanford University, gives credit to NCLB for shining "a spotlight on longstanding inequalities" and for insisting that all students get qualified teachers, but she finds these merits far outweighed by "unfunded costs and dysfunctional side effects." Her analysis suggests that NCLB might have been intended to reinforce public school operations that divide rather than unite, by focusing on testing rather than investing, de-emphasizing teacher preparation and development, discouraging the use of curricula that encourage critical thinking, not supporting high-quality preschool and health care for poor children, and labeling needy students as failures and punishing them and their schools. The alternative: "For an annual cost of $3 billion, or less than one week in Iraq, the nation could underwrite the high-quality preparation of 40,000 teachers annually, enough to fill all the vacancies . . . seed 100 top-quality urban-teacher-education programs . . . insure mentors for every new teacher . . . and provide incentives to bring expert teachers into high-need schools, by improving salaries and working conditions."[49]

City critics have responded with similar skepticism to the Obama administration's extension and modification of NCLB into a program called Race to the Top. They worry about its focus on intensely competitive assessment and formal measures of achievement and about its disregard for troubled schools and their teachers.[50] At the same time, the very inequality itself stimulates certain forms of resistance from teachers. Teaching in troubled inner-city schools can be especially hard work. But standard rules across the work world give seniority preferences for choice of work location or hours, especially where unions are strong. Experienced teachers are likely to flee troubled schools and also to resist the substitution of extra pay for tough assignments in place of seniority pay.[51]

Colleges and universities reinforce the public school divisions, just as they reinforce the society's overall status divisions. Admission to competitive colleges is not based on native ability, but almost entirely on school achievement, which is tightly tied to social class membership. Students from the top 25 percent of the socioeconomic ranking "are 25 times more likely to attend a 'top tier' college than students from the bottom quartile." According to former Princeton president and economist William

Bowen, disadvantaged students "get essentially no break in the admissions process." But they need breaks so as to compete with children tutored by expensive consultants from toddler age, taught in small classrooms by the most skilled teachers in their elementary and secondary schools, and encouraged by the most school-oriented parents. "Only a vigorous policy of class-based affirmative action that accounts for the huge class differences in educational opportunity has a chance of altering this pattern."[52] Without such action, schooling reinforces existing class divisions, pushing students up or down, to be winners or losers.

With rising requirements for job qualification and intensifying competition from distant places in the globalizing economy, the inequalities that have long differentiated schools in the separate municipalities of each metropolitan area take on added significance. Poorly educated graduates and dropouts from the city schools find themselves more abandoned today than were their poorly schooled parents and grandparents in the past, because today the traditional industrial alternatives have shut down, no longer providing unskilled jobs that offer passable incomes.

Municipal Fragmentation Protects School Inequality

Municipal fragmentation is the principal means through which schools are so easily segmented into those for winners and those for losers. Although small-area governments can provide capacity to bring democracy close to home, and can offer a local sense of security by erecting gates, the resulting fragmentation reinforces ordering by social class, race, and ethnicity. Residential segregation is a hallmark of the U.S. metropolis. Books by sociologists, political scientists, and city planners proclaim its prominence, carrying titles like *American Apartheid*, *Two Nations*, and *Separate Societies*. Even as minority populations have suburbanized with the movement of blacks, Hispanics, Asians, and immigrants from cities outward to occupy an older, inner ring of suburban municipalities, residential areas themselves and especially school populations have tended to repeat the long-standing racially separated patterns.

Schools are not the only municipal institution showing the effects of fragmentation. In times of national economic crisis, as described in earlier chapters, city budgets sink while suburban budgets stay afloat. City streets, bridges, water systems, and parks tend to be aging and much in need of expensive repair, while suburban infrastructure is newer and enjoys a better tax base to fund maintenance. Except for grocery stores, and sometimes only small corner stores, retail commerce has drastically shrunk in all but a few inner cities, while commerce succeeds in the suburbs.

Topping all these differences, disparities among schools may be the crucial ingredient, the most significant dividing line that separates central cities from their suburbs. The school effect shows up not only in pervasive inequality of opportunity for students, but also in other ways. For example, in a growing number of cities, the residential population is considerably whiter than the school population, because people without children need not worry about the poor quality of the public schools. In the city of Seattle, for example, the residential population is 30 percent minority, but the school population is 58 percent minority. In Cincinnati, the authorities have fought long and hard to drive out poor and minority populations, and they have recently succeeded. They have captured neighborhoods like Over the Rhine to encourage real estate investment by white middle-class residents without children, either empty nesters or young professionals. As Anna Brawley points out for Columbus, Ohio, in various cities middle-class white families with children, wanting city life, manage to find good elementary schools, but then move to the suburbs when their children reach secondary-school age.[53] An influential few may stay in the city and send their children to the small but expanding number of expensive private schools.

Municipal fragmentation reinforces the effects of inequality, since school budgets rely heavily on local taxation. As cities decline and suburbs prosper, their relative abilities to fund all municipal services, including schools, diverge. Given other inequalities, the two self-reinforcing spirals spin on.

Suburban Public Schools Are Effectively Privatized

School disparities are pushed by a third underlying element, the exclusivity of suburban schools. As formulated by Harvard law professor Gerald Frug, suburban public schools function essentially as *private* schools. Their barriers to entry come about not *de jure*, not by means of legislation, regulation, or case law, but simply through the restriction of attendance to those who can afford the real estate. Frug argues that suburbs as municipal entities construct private ownership *de facto* by privileged residents, who reserve for themselves (and their children) what are generally considered to be public goods. In the limiting case, when this sort of jurisdictional exclusion takes place one property at a time, as happened when a firefighting crew watched a house burn down because its owners had not paid their fire fee, the problem makes dramatic headlines (if only briefly).[54] When residents of suburban districts treat their schools like collective private property, conveyed to them by seemingly innocent municipal boundaries, there is no dramatic event to notice.

In this view, suburbs are like clubs with high entry fees. Clubs exclude those unable to pay and provide members with the privilege of good services.[55] Supportive evidence comes from many others. Connecticut law professor Terry Tondro, an authority on land-use regulation, found that city planners manipulated affairs in order to protect multiple groups of suburbanites who benefited from his state's checkerboard pattern of restrictions on land use and housing, which are set by each small township.[56] Probably the most highly prized benefit of this manipulated pattern of district boundaries is the locally financed and controlled public school, each open only to residents of its own small district.

Such facts are stark. The logic of a system with two kinds of schools— one set to produce winners and one set to produce losers—needs a way to hide its undemocratic nature.[57] People need to see the division as reasonable, fair, and natural despite its inequality-producing effects. Such a mechanism exists for blamelessly segmenting schools into the two groups: the *private* nature of the suburban *public* school offers this obfuscating mechanism, especially when multiple districts serve fragmented municipalities. The variety among these many districts submerges the essentially dual structure of social relations. Thus the city-suburb division in schooling serves to maintain the society's divided and divisive reproduction requirements, while making it all appear as a matter of individual choice.

Suburban public schools work like private schools, and that's how they deliver middle-class privilege. When suburban kids score, they think they've hit home runs, forgetting they were born on third base. As Luke Delvin, a 2009 Bronxville alumnus, wrote, when a college sophomore: "The lure of Bronxville is the unbelievable education that the school provides, and the teachers are the reason Bronxville is able to maintain this reputation. I attended Bronxville schools from kindergarten through 12th grade. Any academic success I have had in my life is a result of the fantastic teachers who inspired me to learn and to achieve my potential. Bronxville sends many of its graduates to top colleges. Clearly the schools are doing something right."[58]

On average, each Bronxville homeowner pays nearly $36,000 in school taxes each year. As one homeowner says, it's cheaper to pay these hefty school taxes than putting two or three children in private schools in New York City. Since Bronxville, in Westchester County just north of New York, is one of the wealthiest residential enclaves in the United States, anyone with property there can likely afford the school tax payments.

Racial Exclusion Remains the American School Dilemma

Historically, American children of different races studied in separate schools, and they still do.[59] As Jonathan Kozol writes in *The Shame of the Nation*, "Apartheid education . . . is alive and well and rapidly increasing. Hyper-segregated inner-city schools . . . are the norm, not the exception, in most northern urban areas." Although numerous white children fail at school, their failure *rates* are much lower than minority failure rates. Nationwide, 6 percent of white students drop out before completing high school, 10.4 percent of black students, and 22.4 percent of Hispanic students.[60] Since failure rates correlate highly with poverty as well as with race and ethnicity, and since poor white children usually mix with not-poor children in schools, white *schools* have lower dropout rates as well. Bias is all too evident, revealed even by data on *pre-K suspensions*! According to a study by the U.S. Department of Education released in 2014, black children receive nearly three times their share of pre-K suspensions.[61]

In a comprehensive study of city schools versus suburban schools, the Desegregation Project at the Harvard School of Education examined racial segregation. In their report, project director Gary Orfield emphasizes three points: school districts suffer pervasive racial segregation, suburbs exclude minority residents, and segregation has not diminished, but has grown since the 1980s. Today, most Americans live in highly segregated districts, districts in which large majorities of schoolchildren are in classrooms and schools with groups of similar children.[62] Even fiercely conservative Supreme Court justice Clarence Thomas, who rejects most proposals for reform, laments the urban results of this racial segregation: "Today many of our inner-city public schools deny emancipation to . . . minority students. . . . Failing urban public schools disproportionately affect minority children most in need of educational opportunity. . . . The promise of public school education has failed poor inner-city blacks."[53] The most serious school segregation lies not within individual school districts, but between them.[64] Justice Thomas again: "While in theory providing education to everyone, the quality of public schools varies significantly *across* districts."[65] Shifting demographic patterns exacerbate the variation the justice notes. In 1970 eight of every ten public school students were white. Now, they make up just over half. Latino students rose from one in twenty to nearly a quarter.[66]

Despite discussions of a "post-racial" society, one that can elect an African American to the presidency, levels of residential segregation remain startlingly high. Three examples provide stark evidence. In the Los Angeles metropolis, Hispanic, black, Asian, and white census tracts are sharply segregated.[67] To even out the proportions, more than two-thirds of the nearly thirteen million people in the area would have to move to another tract.[68] In the very different Buffalo area, nearly every census tract in 2010 was more than 85 percent white, or black, or American Indian. More than 73 percent of the 1.1 million people would have to move to even things out. In Milwaukee, the nation's metropolitan area with the highest segregation (as measured by dissimilar tracts), 82 percent of the 1.6 million people would have to move. Many of Milwaukee's central tracts are more than 85 percent black or 85 percent Hispanic, and many others are more than 50 percent minority, while in the suburban ring virtually every tract is more than 85 percent white. In other metropolitan areas segregation may not be quite so severe in the statistics, but nearly everywhere most minority residents live either in their "own" central tracts or in "suburban" minority concentrations.

Yet the Supreme Court rejects consideration of district-to-district differential in quality. Decades earlier, in his powerful dissent to the *Milliken* ruling on Detroit, Justice Marshall argued despairingly in favor of integration across district lines: "Our nation, I fear, will be ill-served by the Court's refusal to remedy separate and unequal education, for unless our children begin to learn together there is little hope that our people will ever learn to live together."

The Court acted then, in 1974, to disregard the city-suburb divide in schooling, and its position against cross-district remedies has only hardened since. Although school segregation for black children and poor children had declined for some years until late in the 1980s, it has been on the increase since, and the segregation of Latino students has risen to very high levels. As Justice Marshall knew, if the society is to function well, our children must go to school together.

Updating forty years and shifting attention to a much less noticed case, in Seattle, where the overall proportion of minority students is small, neighborhoods are still highly segregated by race, as are schools. Nevertheless, the sharpest racial line separates Seattle city schools from their suburban counterparts. And, as a study of the nation's ninety-one thousand public schools for the 2011–2012 school year shows, black and Latino children compared to whites are less likely to attend preschool but much more likely to be suspended, four times as likely to have less-experienced and lower-paid teachers, and less likely to have access to rigorous classes in math and science.[69]

Inside school district boundaries, segregation takes different forms. In New York City, for example, whose population is greater than thirty-nine entire states and whose public schools enroll more than a million students, some segregation is achieved via elite specialized high schools. The school population is 68 percent black and Hispanic, yet three of the very top schools—Stuyvesant, Bronx Science, and Brooklyn Tech—have very low black and Hispanic enrollments, which have recently decreased. The proportion of black students in these celebrated schools dropped from 11.8 percent in 1995 to 4.8 percent in 2006, and Hispanic enrollments also dropped.[70] In Omaha, the only black representative in the Nebraska legislature sponsored a bill to try to fit the law to the reality, envisioning three subdistricts for city schools, one white, one black, and one Hispanic.[71]

Resegregation has taken place in a context in which many Americans seem comfortable to ignore the facts.[72] Although desegregation has often worked well, many people erroneously believe that white flight makes desegregation impossible. Despite surveys showing that all racial groups broadly support the idea of integrated schools, many people believe that both white and black residents are hostile to integrated schools, preferring that public funds be used for compensatory education. And although private school attendance rates have held steady for decades at 10 to 11 percent of all children, many people believe that enrollments have shifted massively to private schools.[73]

One cannot be sure of the reasons for a misinformed public, but ideology and politics play a part. William Rehnquist, in the 1950s a fresh Stanford law graduate serving as a clerk in the Warren Court, wrote approvingly of the 1890s' rule of racial oppression known as "separate but equal." While acknowledging in his own words that his illiberal position was "unpopular and unhumanitarian," Rehnquist wrote: "I think *Plessy v. Ferguson* was right and should be reaffirmed."[74] In 1979, then Justice Rehnquist wrote his own minority opinion against desegregation, vehemently criticizing advocates of racial mixing, chiding the majority for their favoring of "integration *über alles*."[75] The southern strategy of the Republican Party pushed these kinds of ideas for votes, as the party pumped up white fears that originate in prejudice. The Nixon administration intentionally undermined successful school integration, as one act in a long conservative play whose audience is presumed to prefer racially segregated over integrated schools.

Finally in 2007 the conservative majority on the Supreme Court managed to deliver the public school affirmative-action coup de grâce. Seattle made the news along with Louisville, as Americans learned that the Court had decided five-to-four to reverse the 1954 mandate for in-district desegregation in *Brown v. Board of Education*.[76] Both cities had struggled with desegregation, Seattle with little progress, Louisville (under court order) with considerable success. Both city districts proposed to assign very small numbers of students to schools outside their own neighborhoods in order to diminish extreme segregation. In Seattle, the city was trying to overcome high racial imbalances in its schools, countering residential shifts that had, for example, turned its Franklin High from 21 percent white to only 9 percent white. An extremely modest policy would have applied each year to about three hundred students of forty-six thousand in the district. In Louisville, following three decades of court-ordered desegregation, a 2001 survey "found that 85 percent of . . . high school seniors reported that because they'd attended integrated schools, they were better equipped to live in a diverse society."[77] Yet despite the timid approaches and the positive results, the Supreme Court found even these most modest desegregation policies unconstitutional. As Berkeley public policy professor David Kirk puts it: "Chief Justice John Roberts wrapped himself in the mantle of *Brown*. 'The way to stop discrimination on the basis of race is to stop discriminating on the basis of race. When it comes to using race to assign children to schools, history will be heard.' But Roberts must have flunked American history, since to pretend that there is no difference between Little Rock circa 1957 and Louisville circa 2007 upends history."[78]

The statistical findings of the Resegregation Project, with data from 239 school districts in the year 2000, help focus attention on the steady failure of *each* city school system to deliver good educations, when compared with its own suburbs. As noted earlier, the study found increasing segregation nearly everywhere for black and Latino students. It found resegregation in the South, "after two and a half decades in which civil rights law broke the tradition of apartheid" to make southern schools the most integrated in the country. (Little Rock was released from its court-ordered integration after fifty years, in February 2007.) With major increases in Latino school enrollments, studies find rising Latino segregation, even more severe than black segregation.[79] Black and Latino students enroll in suburban schools that are themselves segregated. And although it found a growing number of multiracial schools, those schools mix minority groups, most often without whites.[80]

4

OPTIONS FOR CITY SCHOOLS

What ties it all together is this: public school disparities mirror neighborhood disparities, showing race and ethnicity tied closely to income levels, with homogeneous groups segmented by municipal boundaries. School differences correlate closely with class differences. Middle-class children and wealthy children get decent schools. Poor children do not, especially poor children who live together in poor neighborhoods. The public school crisis will continue unless the nation moves dramatically to reduce racial segregation of residential areas and to enact policies to reduce class distinctions. Equity in public schooling—a fair chance for every child—requires these changes.

Special Schools and Select Children

In the absence of actions to reduce the society's disabling racial and class differences, an overall national program of school reform is called for, one that uses federal funding for economic stimulus. Such a reform would also radically rethink the nation's overall approach to public schools. Fortunately, a model exists, though in a much smaller and less diverse nation—Finland. We will turn later to Finland's remarkable success in turning around its once failing schools. As we dream of such reforms, small successful American experiments suggest possibilities. André Gorz, speaking of social change more generally, urges "non-reformist reforms," social innovations that empower those who benefit from the improvements, enabling them to push further reforms. Such positive feedback cycles create their own energy for change.

Two examples stand out: special schools as parts of larger city school systems, and programs that help city children to attend suburban schools. Both work, but only on a small scale. With massive funding, select city schools build laboratories and playgrounds, employ better-trained teachers supported by administrators, and create safe environments.

A Few Special City Schools Can Work Well

School districts, city officials, principals, and teachers as well as children and their parents often introduce privilege into a small selection of schools. As Deborah Meier, the founder of Central Park East schools in New York, writes, "A more equitable society would go a long way toward making schools more effective, but . . . in the meantime, there's a lot schools can do all on their own."[1] Experiments with public or quasi-public schools and small successful schools prod others into competition. Among excellent select and privileged schools one finds individual magnet schools, members of the Coalition of Essential Schools, special alternative schools that emphasize self-governance and graduation by exhibition, high-achievement schools in elite neighborhoods, and a few excellent charter schools. Exceptional individual classrooms exist *inside* schools—in the 1988 movie *Stand and Deliver*, Jaime Escalante breaks stereotypes as he teaches calculus to otherwise turned-off Latino students at Garfield High in East Los Angeles. Quasi-public, nonprofit, one-off ventures operate in cities across the country, some succeeding admirably, like Central Park East, which Deborah Meier founded as an alternative New York City public school in the 1970s.[2]

Many propose charter schools as solutions to city school difficulties. Some operate as nonprofits. The SEED boarding school in Washington,

DC, enrolls more than three hundred children, grades six through twelve, who get room and board along with their academic support, all for free.[3] Among many new nonprofits, a company named Rocketship runs nine schools in Silicon Valley, two in Washington, DC, and schools in Milwaukee and Nashville. They use computers more, and teachers less, many of them inexperienced "Teach for America" interns. Rocketship's leaders include owners of for-profit companies that sell it DreamBox learning lab software and rent it facilities, prompting questions about conflicting interests. In California, school privatizers spend lavishly on school board election campaigns.[4]

The Harlem Children's Zone, an area of ninety-seven blocks and ten thousand children, includes two elementary-through-high-school "Promise Academies," and it offers community services as well as schooling.[5] Overworked and underpaid teachers and administrators at Cesar Chavez Public Policy charter schools in Washington, DC, keep underprivileged children for long days and work insistently with parents to counteract neighborhood pressures of poverty and resentment. Led by CEO Irasena Salcido, honorary board chair Alma Powell (the wife of the former U.S. secretary of state), and enthusiastic partners, this group of schools has proposed to "replicate the Harlem Children's Zone" to provide a broad selection of social services in the surrounding neighborhood. They had hoped to be supported by a Promise Neighborhood grant from the Department of Education.

To provide support, Education Secretary Arne Duncan proposed in the first Obama administration a giant national experiment funding Promise Neighborhoods in twenty cities, budgeting a few *billion* dollars per year. The actual budget—post economic collapse, and against opposition in a recalcitrant Congress—was funded at one five-hundredth, or $10–20 *million* per year. Such special schools improve the schooling of city students, but each school finds itself greatly restricted in scope, as illustrated by the heartrending lottery scenes in the documentary film *Waiting for Superman*. Among the 455 applicants entering the lotteries for the Harlem Success Academy, the Washington SEED School, and KIPP Prep in Los Angeles, there was room for only 85 students, so 81 percent of the applicants lost their chance.[6] "As Rocketship cofounder John Danner explains, critics shouldn't worry about charter schools skimming the best students, because eventually 'we're going to educate all of the students, so there's nothing left to skim.' "[7] Perhaps, but the Milwaukee Rocketship school pales by comparison with Wisconsin's top ten (public) elementary schools, which "have twice as many licensed teachers per students; offer music, art, libraries, foreign languages and guidance counselors; and provide classes that are taught in person by experienced educators."[8]

On a larger and more sustained scale, many large cities operate special public schools. Some selective magnet schools are top ranked academically, such as New York's Bronx Science and Stuyvesant High Schools, Boston Latin, San Francisco's Lowell High, and Philadelphia's High School for Creative and Performing Arts. Such special schools admit students from throughout a district only by examination or to pursue a specialized curriculum, overriding neighborhood school zone boundaries. They deliver high success rates—graduation from high school, high likelihood of a college degree, and a good professional career—so that as in well-financed charter schools, competition for admission is often fierce, and most applicants are turned down. Other special school experiments are more prosaic, such as New York City's splitting of large underperforming high schools into smaller schools, each with a specific orientation. Examples are the High School for International Business and Finance in Manhattan, one of four small schools that replaced George Washington High School, a "factory of failure" in its predominantly Dominican neighborhood, and the School without Walls in Rochester, New York.

City residents whose children manage to get in applaud these selective magnets. Equivalent to top suburban schools, for some families they provide the only hope, and for others, an alternative to an expensive private school. Applauded by municipal leaders who seek upper-middle-class support for public schools, they also serve poor residents. The Dayton Early College Academy, for example, an experimental public high school in Cincinnati that put poor children into accelerated classrooms, sent all thirty-two of its first graduating class to college. Other city residents, however, criticized arrangements that provide more experienced and qualified teachers, smaller classes, more Advanced Placement courses, better-equipped laboratories, and superior supplies, because they served only lucky applicants and the most qualified of the city's students. Other district schools suffered fiscally and also from the loss of students with successful classroom skills. As the most involved and active parents focus energy on their children's magnet schools, other schools suffer from lessened demand for improvements. Thus, in New York City, nearly half the city's students attend overcrowded schools.[9] In the Cincinnati case, the district faced $30 million in budget cuts and had to close two schools and lay off two hundred employees, so it chose to drop the Dayton Academy in 2007. The district shifted the school to charter status under sponsorship by the University of Dayton. Even with private foundation start-up funding and before the national fiscal meltdown, the costs for this good school were too high for the district to bear.[10]

In the 1970s, a sort of "domestic colonialism" argument was used to explain the U.S. city school situation. Does this notion apply again, given the conditions of underdevelopment that now prevail in so many cities? Privileged minorities attend good schools either privately or via public charters, magnets, and alternative schools, while the majorities suffer as the public school system operates in a collapsed form. This situation, which pits the lucky and the few standout performers against the many, occurs commonly in countries where large majorities of the children are poor. In most Latin American nations, for example, while the best universities are public, free of tuition, and endowed with scholarships that pay living costs, preparation for the demanding entry examinations typically involves many years of study at costly private elementary and secondary schools, sometimes topped by a year of post–high school individual tutoring for the entry exam. The public purse thus provides top-quality, free college to the small minority sufficiently privileged to have attended good private schools, but it excludes the majority, who attend or drop out of ill-equipped and overcrowded public schools with overworked and undersupported teachers. The defense of the excellent public university is easy—an exceptional teaching and research corps helps the country develop and prepares leaders for government and industry. The system provides opportunity for at least a few exceptional students from the lower classes to elevate themselves, as good examples, above the masses of impoverished citizens. But the vast majority of children stand no chance. Political realists in these countries contend that the national situation rules out sufficient taxation and investment, so the poor majority cannot hope for the teacher preparation, school construction, and payrolls to bring public primary and secondary schools up to satisfactory levels.[11]

Most recently in the United States, political conservatives have begun to advocate privatization of schools supported by vouchers. Even some groups of politically liberal minority residents support school vouchers, which try to bring the putative benefits of markets to school choice. These residents hope either that their own children may benefit directly, or that the experiments may induce system-wide spreading of some of the achievements of the exceptional individual schools. The attraction of the school business to private firms begins with the profit potential from the $550 billion annual public expenditure on primary and secondary education.[12]

On the face of it, nearly all these experiments show the potential for good "urban" education. Good schools *do* manage to operate in big cities, in districts dominated by weak schools with large numbers of students who drop out, and they run highly successful programs. The involved parents and children give them high marks. Why not, then, replicate the experiments so that all students can join in? The answer is unsurprising: funding for such privileged programs is limited and will likely continue to be grossly insufficient. If public funding through vouchers or otherwise were ample enough to pay full fees for private schools, or to pay for the city equivalent of good suburban schools, then in theory the extra money would go far toward solving the urban school problem.[13] Considerable funding is needed to compensate for the smaller classes or special instruction required for students who need to learn English as a new language, to overcome setbacks from disadvantaged childhood, and to offset other school-related disabilities.[14] Funding in poor neighborhoods needs to overcome family-income deficiencies to increase the likelihood of active parental support. Various experiments demonstrate that this sort of support works well. Unfortunately, almost insurmountable fiscal obstacles diminish the political reality of extending these experimental programs to citywide student bodies.

One of the most developed "voucher school" programs began in Milwaukee. Looking at Milwaukee's Parental Choice Program (MPCP), John Witte, a political scientist at the University of Minnesota, published perhaps the first authoritative study of vouchers. This initiative was then the country's largest voucher program, enrolling eight thousand students by 2000, about 8 percent of the city's school-age population. Witte's well-balanced book, *The Market Approach to Education*, published in 2000, examines MPCP from its inception in 1990 until 1995, when it served just over a thousand children. Each student had the benefit of an annual subsidy worth between $2,500 and $4,600, more on average than the per-student expenditure in the public schools. Although a few vouchered Milwaukee children enrolled in a dozen private schools in those first five years, nearly all attended only four formerly Catholic parochial schools. The outcomes are uncertain, at best. Parents of the vouchered students were indeed happy with their ability to choose, but test results show the educational differences to be nil when comparing these "choice" schools to the "non-choice" public schools, even despite the private schools' advantage of selectivity (in theory all applying children had to be admitted, but in fact the more problematic students were excluded). Even though the voucher schools in Milwaukee were somewhat more expensive per student than the public schools, the voucher teachers on average worked for less pay. Witte's major conclusion offers profound skepticism about the positive effect of vouchers for system-wide reform.[15] He writes:

> My foremost conclusion is to challenge the proclamation that the MPCP could be the vehicle for reducing the gap between white and minority students by a very large amount. (p. 150)

> What happened in Milwaukee was that private schools, many under considerable financial stress, received money, and that money improved their schools. In several cases, that allowed the schools to survive as options for families—some of whom would not have been able to take advantage of that option without vouchers. Those are not trivial results in the micro world of this program. But it is very difficult to see how those results predict what would happen to the full system of schools in a universal voucher system. (115)

Subsequent studies of Milwaukee and various studies of charter schools in other cities result in counterclaims and much confusion. Our interest is whether charter schools make much of a dent in the colossal failure rates of city schools. The evidence, unfortunately, is negative. Even despite great publicity and sometimes huge per-student special funding supplied by wealthy donors from high finance (Wall Street financiers support the Harlem Children's Zone), success rates are limited. Researchers have thus extended the questions, to ask whether compared to public schools generally, charter, private, and religious schools do well.

A thorough analysis published in 2006 by Teachers College at Columbia University should have settled many of the controversies. Using a 2004 report by the U.S. Department of Education, with data on an enormous set of test scores, for 190,000 fourth graders and 153,000 eighth graders, the Teachers College analysis concludes that charters, voucher schools, and other private schools provide *no advantages* at least for the teaching and testing of mathematics.[16] Contrary to the "common wisdom [which holds] that private schools achieve better academic results," "this analysis of U.S. mathematics achievement finds that, after accounting for the fact that private schools serve more advantaged populations, public schools perform remarkably well, often outscoring private and charter schools."

The analysis finds that "public schools significantly out-scored Catholic schools" and that among private schools, "Lutheran schools performed the best" but still not better than public schools. Conservative Christian schools, with a little over 1.5 percent of all students nationally, were the fastest growing but "the lowest performing," way behind the public schools in their test scores. Compared to regular public schools, charter schools score worse in fourth grade and trivially higher (with no statistical significance for the difference) in eighth grade.[17]

These comparisons of test scores account for the level of advantage of the student populations. At one far edge of the set are private, "independent" schools (many in big central cities), which *Forbes* magazine still calls prep schools. More than eleven hundred independent/prep schools enroll approximately 1 percent of the nation's student population. These schools tend to be extremely expensive, with tuition rates similar to those at elite private colleges. Student-to-faculty ratios are very low, often only six students per teacher, so class sizes are small, allowing close critical attention to student work. It is no surprise that students at such elite schools do well on entrance competitions for college. Many "1 percent" families live in exclusive suburbs and send their children to excellent suburban public schools (which as we have seen, perform like private schools), but others send their children to these expensive independent schools.

At the other extreme, where working-class or poor households are concerned, the *funding* of voucher schools presents severe difficulties. *No one* with the public's ear has proposed that the government provide *enough* money in vouchers to actually allow large numbers of children in poor families to get access to the very best schools. Even the outlandishly extravagant voucher program proposed for California by the libertarian Silicon Valley billionaire Timothy Draper would have spent only $4,000 per student, about 70 percent of California's average per-student expenditure at the time of the proposal and about 60 percent of the national average.[18] Facebook founder Mark Zuckerberg's multimillion-dollar donation to Newark's schools (not for vouchers, but for other CEO-favored reforms), when spread over five years, was to supplement the district's $940 million annual budget by only about 4 percent.[19] The costs of vouchers in most cities would increase if they included the compensatory funding typically required for students with special needs, to help with adjustments to the English language, or to provide for disabilities. Any system that "creams" off some students leaves others with limited funding. Thus some children will rise to the top to take the advantage, just as cream separates in an old-fashioned milk bottle. The majority of the children will be abandoned to still weaker and less-well-funded public schools. In practical terms voucher programs—like magnet schools, alternative schools, and other progressive options—promise to benefit very few.

A Few City Children Can Get to Good Suburban Schools

After a jury found her "guilty of . . . tampering with records," Kelly Williams-Bolar "was given two concurrent 5-year sentences" by the Ohio court. She had claimed her daughters lived in the Copley-Fairlawn suburban school district with their grandfather rather than in her Akron housing project, so they could attend a better school.[20] After Williams-Bolar had spent nine days in jail, the governor reduced the convictions to misdemeanors. Between 2005 and late 2011, the district resolved similar issues with at least forty-seven other families.[21] In another case, Tanya McDowell was charged with larceny and conspiracy for sending her son to a suburban school even though he lived in Bridgeport, a Connecticut city.

Some programs offer city children the opportunity to commute to suburban schools, and others offer city families the opportunity to live in suburbs that have good schools. Shedding light on the second option, findings from a much studied Chicago housing experiment suggest that lower-income black families benefit from the opportunity to live in higher-income white neighborhoods. In the late 1960s Dorothy Gautreaux filed suit against the Chicago Housing Authority on the well-supported grounds that the authority had persistently segregated blacks from whites in its subsidized housing. The court eventually agreed that the CHA needed a geographically inclusive, metropolis-wide remedy and allowed housing advocates to examine the results of its mandate: families applying for CHA housing were asked to select housing either in predominantly white suburbs or in predominantly black and much poorer Chicago neighborhoods. Except for their different locations, the two groups of families were similar by race (nearly all are African American), income level, family size, and other attributes. Researchers were able therefore to ascribe differences in outcomes to the difference in housing location. The results met expectations: the children who moved to the suburbs did better in school, graduated high school at higher rates, and got in trouble with the police less often than the children who stayed in Chicago. Similar findings in 2012 came from a study of HUD's Moving to Opportunity program, showing that children did better in school when their low-income families were helped to move "from severely distressed, high-poverty housing projects" in Baltimore, Boston, Chicago, Los Angeles, and New York to "high-opportunity" neighborhoods with low poverty, nearby jobs, more college graduates, and higher proportions of white residents.[22]

It is important to emphasize that although such school integration programs appear to be based on race, in fact the barriers derive also from differences in income. The urban/suburban distinction is key, as location, family income, and race all play roles. Most poor white students do not live in the city, and so they attend schools with middle-class majorities, but large numbers of black and Latino students live in cities or inner suburbs, and so attend schools with very large majorities of students from households that are poor. The point may be clear from the inverse situation, in the very few racially integrated suburbs at the higher end of the income scale, in which African American students attend public schools in upper-middle-class districts. In those cases, they enjoy relatively high degrees of success. In affluent suburbs like Hastings-on-Hudson in Westchester County, outside New York City, and Shaker Heights, outside Cleveland, all residents, of any race, are upper middle class, and graduation rates are high.[23] But these situations are atypical.

In Boston, the nongovernmental Metropolitan Council for Educational Opportunities supports school desegregation not by relocation of housing, but by busing from the city to the suburbs. The METCO program, which black parents and educators established in 1963 "to offer students an opportunity to attend suburban schools," enrolls more than three thousand students each year from Boston into a program with (declining) financial support from the state. Participating children come from poor city families (the typical family income was $25,000 in 1997), are minorities (77 percent black, 16 percent Hispanic, 4 percent Asian in 2006), and attend schools in the suburbs in which typically at least 90 percent of students are white. Evaluations from the students, their parents, and suburban school officials are overwhelmingly positive. This experiment has been running for more than four decades, with evolving and improving practices and with strong support from participants and potential enrollees and their families. The waiting list has as many children as the number enrolled.[24] Were the program to be expanded, it is expected that enrollments would grow rapidly, but limits on state funding preclude growth. Were the program to cease, three-quarters of parents say they would *not* enroll their children in their Boston neighborhood school.[25]

Severe limitations restrict opportunities for programs that place poor city children in privileged suburban schools. Given historical experience and practical considerations, such opportunities are limited by scarcity of funding, limits on organizational energy, and resistance against innovation or, worse, disruption. Without transformative changes, such as the sort of integration proposed for Detroit and its fifty-three surrounding suburban districts in the 1970s, the effects of small experiments will be minor, and the numbers of disappointed applicants very large. Participants and even applicants aside, much larger majorities of poor city students will remain in their failing schools.

Confronting Barriers of Class, Race, and Place

People use relative measures to define poverty and privilege, but among people living in the same society, absolute conditions, or thresholds, provide markers, too.[26] Below certain thresholds, communities, schools, and children tend to give up when the situation seems impossible. But above the threshold, something magical happens. The tangible, material differences that signal entitlement also trigger optimism, a can-do attitude, and a *sense* of privilege that in many ways can be just as important as material privileges themselves.

Children in ordinary suburbs who attend good schools get their edge from tangible, measurable advantages. They benefit from small classes and well-prepared, experienced teachers, equipped laboratories and libraries, elaborate field trips, and safe play areas. They may benefit as well from homework assistance from parents, tutors, and peers. These good fortunes blend together with imagined ones, to offer students who attend good-enough schools or live in good-enough districts a crucial sense of privilege. As Garrison Keillor says about Lake Woebegone when introducing his weekly radio broadcast of *Prairie Home Companion*, "All the women are strong, the men are good looking, the children above average." That better-than-average normalcy indicates the sort of attitude that city scholars like Roberto Quercia and George Galster expect from stable, supportive neighborhoods or districts, where conditions rise above a threshold defined not relatively "but by the *absolute* conditions there."[27]

Such a threshold of entitlement applies similarly to families or individuals, marking a notion of adequacy. Less than adequate equals poverty. People define poverty with relative and absolute levels of well-being in mind, to figure unconsciously whether they themselves or others are getting along, to take into account the various elements that generate feelings of social belonging. The idea that better than average is normal (Isn't everyone like me? Doesn't everyone get what I get?) can extend still further, in the manner suggested by Peggy McIntosh in her widely noted article "White Privilege: Unpacking the Invisible Knapsack." Drawing from feminist studies showing that men take for granted a sense of privilege and power over women, which derives from their tangible, material advantages, McIntosh explains how "white privilege" combines material, social, and psychological elements. Whites build on a set of unacknowledged advantages, while remaining unconscious of their source, often even unconscious that the advantages exist.[28] The same sort of privilege comes from living in the right place. No sphere of American activity relies on these notions of spatial entitlement more than school attendance at one of the thousands of "normal but above average public schools."

For children to succeed in schools, of course, a *sense* of privilege will not be enough. The reality matters, too, with the reinforcing privileges of class, race, and place. Overwhelmingly, children who succeed in school tend to be in the middle class or higher, with class privilege. Vastly disproportionate numbers of successful children are white, enjoying racial privilege. Successful children tend to live in well-connected, safe, and well-served neighborhoods, which provide them with geographic privilege.

For children who are white, belong to the middle class, and live in suburbs—*no particular privilege is apparent*. To these students and their parents, their satisfactory situations appear as birthrights, taken for granted. Like the children from the immensely wealthy New York suburb of Bronxville, most white, middle-class, suburban children have no idea how much they lose from living in a society divided by inequality, let alone any sense of the losses of others.

Children holding *two* of the three privileges usually still enjoy sufficient margin for success in school. For some children, even *one* privilege is enough, but not for many and not often. At the other end of the spectrum, the boy or girl who faces *three* underprivileged counts—not white, not middle class, not suburban—finds his or her educational chances extremely limited. An exceptional child, perhaps also with an exceptional parent, can escape this prison of circumstance, but only by relying on special individual capabilities and aptitudes or the extraordinary intervention of others.

Notable books appear when poor city children of color beat the system. Claude Brown (*Manchild in the Promised Land*) moved from poverty, alcohol, heroin, and gangs in Harlem in the 1940s to Howard University and law schools at Stanford and Rutgers, going on to the lecture circuit and to his work with at-risk adolescents. Kai Ting (*China Boy*) survived tough streets in San Francisco, reflecting that he "was trying [at age seven] to become an accepted black male youth in the 1950s—a competitive, dangerous, and harshly won objective. This was all the more difficult because I was Chinese."[29] Cedric Jennings (*A Hope in the Unseen*) overcame the poverty of a single-parent household in a drug-infested, violent neighborhood in Washington, DC, in the 1990s. At Frank W. Ballou Senior High School he suffered the derision of his neighborhood classmates, and at Brown University, the condescension of middle-class black students. Brown, Ting, and Jennings offer inspiring personal stories, but each insists that his exceptional case breaks the odds, proving the rule, which is that the obstacles of poverty, racism, and neighborhood isolation bring defeat to most who dare to challenge them.[30]

As suggested indirectly by the Civic Capacity studies I discussed in the previous chapter, which examined elite solidarity in Pittsburgh, Boston, Atlanta, and eight other cities, children are most likely to succeed at school when helped by strong community support and superior school quality.

These requirements for success are virtually undisputed in the literature on schooling. In separate ways, families (or households) and schools depend on neighborhood quality and available money. Each child's experience at school depends on support from home and on the school's quality. When the school is weak, failure is the probable outcome, even despite home support. If on the other hand the household does not provide support but the child attends a supportive school, the result is indeterminate, depending on how closely the school monitors the child and involves the family. A supportive family plus a well-run school promise likely success.

Neighborhood quality is a very complex notion. Well-functioning job-search networks, positive role models, good sidewalk supervision, ample space for recreation, and good public services offer extremely important aids for children but are weak or absent in many inner-city neighborhoods. A household is better able to support its children at school when its income is adequate *and* when it and the children get help from the community. In brief, a household stands a modest chance of overcoming the problems of a bad neighborhood only if it has an adequate income. Poor *and* located in an unsupportive neighborhood, a family is unlikely to be able to provide adequate support.

A school has needs much like a household. The extraordinary cases—the magnet, alternative, and experimental schools in which gifted, dedicated principals operate special and successful programs with low budgets in poor neighborhoods—provide exceptions. Rarely in troubled neighborhoods will budgets be large enough to overcome the disadvantages.

In combination, the burdens of poverty, racial discrimination, and a disorderly neighborhood usually bear down on children who attend public schools. In the Mott Haven neighborhood of New York City, for example, despite reductions in crime, the opening of new charter schools, and an infiltration of residents with higher incomes, children who lack all three sets of privileges belong to remaining families that are poor, play in a neighborhood that is still disruptive, and attend a very weak school, where it happens that all children are black or Latino.[31] Many of the students receive poor grades and scores, few finish high school, and still fewer go to college.

From many inner neighborhoods in New York's region, including "suburban" enclaves with impoverished groups in New Jersey, Connecticut, and Long Island, almost no one graduates from college.[32] In contrast, in the surrounding truly suburban areas of Westchester County, Long Island, Connecticut, and New Jersey, where many children enjoy all three privileges, the schooling results are positive. Suburbs like these are central to American society, not peripheral; they are predominantly middle class, not poor; and they are predominantly white, not black, Latino, or immigrant. They are "above average," privileged, ranking above the key threshold levels. Nearly all the suburban children graduate from high school and attend college. A high proportion graduate from college.

In nearly every state of the union, given the reliance on local property taxes, individual school budgets are determined largely by the income of the neighbors (either in the immediate neighborhood itself or citywide, versus the suburbs). Many people of color have long lived isolated in underserved and dilapidated city neighborhoods, where household incomes are generally low. In recent decades the very poorest people of color have become increasingly concentrated in ever worse neighborhoods, whether in central cities themselves or in inner suburban enclaves. Against these neighborhood difficulties, school reforms can achieve little.[33]

A National Focus on Equality

Peter Schrag, author of *Final Test: The Battle for Adequacy in America's Schools*, writes that "the crucial gaps in the schools serving the nation's neediest kids . . . stem from the lack of good teachers, books, or materials, and often all three." Conservatives claim that teachers' unions fight to protect all teachers, rather than culling out the weakest. This may be true, but it is largely irrelevant. In every profession, skills and capabilities of individuals are arrayed across some sort of bell curve, with a few individuals way above average and a few way below. The problem occurs because districts assign weaker teachers to teach in schools with the neediest children. This problem is not of any union's making. Furthermore, teachers (whether average, poor, or top notch) in the most problematic schools are also more likely to find themselves and their students short of good books and other teaching materials and equipment.

Summing up, the argument is threefold. First, U.S. schools must improve so that nearly all students attend, learn, gain competence and confidence, and graduate with high school diplomas. But success will come only if education authorities improve the worst schools. Second, the society must reduce class differences that separate, isolate, denigrate, and underserve the poor. Finally, the nation must confront racial and ethnic disparities head-on. As long as large numbers of children of color attend inferior schools, whether because they are segregated residentially or for other reasons, the school problem will persist.

Other nations have made great progress in schooling at the same time that the United States has fallen behind. They have done it by improving schools and lessening inequalities. What are the chances that we in the United States can act to improve schools and also reduce social inequality? The first thing the evidence shows is that if we do not do both things, we cannot do either.

Lessons from Finland

In the not so distant past, Finnish schools were *not* particularly successful. Linda Darling-Hammond compares Finland's schools in the 1970s with schools then in the United States, and she concludes that Finland was the loser.[34] An achievement gap separated students in accordance with the incomes and social status of their households. School quality differed greatly by neighborhood. These differences existed despite overwhelming ethnic and racial homogeneity. Today, however, Finland wins. In education circles around the globe, Finland has become the model. The enthusiasm stems from the remarkable achievements registered by public school students on international comparisons. In 2003, Finnish fifteen-year-old students ranked first as the top scorers worldwide on assessments by the Program for International Student Assessment, or PISA. Finns scored at the top on all four examinations, in reading, mathematics, science, and problem solving.

One can think of Finnish school issues in the 1970s in terms of New York City today. In New York since 2008, the public school system has offered a small number of *kindergarten* places for "gifted and talented" children. As the Center for New York City Affairs of the New School reports, "In parts of the city where the overall quality of the neighborhoods schools is poor, gifted programs may offer a refuge."[35] Of the children in the fall of 2012 who took the two tests the city administers, one for "reasoning" and the other for "knowledge," almost five thousand qualified, marking them off from the thousands who either scored too low or, much more commonly, didn't take the tests at all. Even among the select few, there are rankings: the five *most* selective schools have room for four hundred students, those who score in the top 3 percent of test takers, followed by a lottery. To up the chances, parents send their toddlers to prekindergarten schools, and they pay big money to run them through test-preparation programs. It is hard to know who loses more—the five-year-olds pressured to "learn" and take tests, or the vast majority relegated to inferior kindergartens.[36]

To compare schools across the globe, PISA examinations began in 2000; they are conducted every three years. In 2003, more than 250,000 students from forty-one countries took the examinations.[37] In mathematical literacy, while the United States ranked number twenty-eight or twenty-nine of forty-one (tied with Latvia in 2003), Finland was number one. Next to the top, and close in their scores, were Hong Kong, South Korea, the Netherlands, Lichtenstein, Japan, and Canada. Only 10 percent of U.S. students scored in the top two math categories, compared to 24 percent of Finnish students (even more, 31 percent, in Hong Kong, and between 24 and 26 percent in South Korea, the Netherlands, Japan, and Belgium). The results for reading were similar, with the United States at number eighteen and Finland number one. In science, the United States ranked twenty-second, and once again Finland ranked first. On the problem-solving test, the United States ranked number twenty-nine, Finland number two or three (just below South Korea, tied with Hong Kong).

The truly remarkable result, however, is not that Finnish students on average did so well or that so many Finns scored in the top categories. Instead, the relative equality among Finnish students is most remarkable. At the bottom, whereas more than a quarter of U.S. student test takers (26 percent) scored in the lowest two mathematics categories (worse than twenty-four OECD countries, above only Portugal, Italy, Greece, Turkey, and Mexico), only 6 percent of Finnish students scored so poorly. On every test, *large* percentages of Finnish students scored in the top categories, *and* a markedly small percentage of Finnish students scored in the bottom categories. *Unusually large percentages of Finnish students earned test scores near to their national average.* This national average was very high, the highest among nations.[38] In the bargain, many near-average-scoring Finns did better than many of the higher percentile students from other countries.[39]

Statisticians use the coefficient of variation to summarize how scores are spread out. It measures dispersion of values, to indicate whether values are clumped tightly together or spread out widely.[40] When test scores are tightly clumped, with relatively little spread from the low scores to the high scores, then students are learning relatively equally. Sometimes equality can be a problem—perhaps the strong students are not very strong, so that all scores are low. Maybe not—perhaps all or most students do quite well, so that the great majority of scores are relatively high. That high-end equality is what Finland's schools produced. On each of the four tests, Finland's students yield small coefficients of variation, the smallest of any nation, yet their average scores are high. *Nearly all* Finnish students have high scores, which drives up the national average, while also allowing a large portion of students to earn the very highest test scores. The Finns are having their cake and eating it too.

To repeat: In the early 1970s, Finland's school system was weak, lagging behind the United States. Now it ranks much higher. The achievement is reflected in the high average PISA scores, but there is more: "More than 99 percent of students now successfully complete compulsory basic education, and about 90 percent complete upper secondary school. Two-thirds of these graduates enroll in universities or professionally oriented polytechnic schools. And over 50 percent of the Finnish adult population participates in adult-education programs. Ninety-eight percent of the costs of education at all levels are covered by government."[41]

What accounts for this remarkable achievement? How does a nation create and operate a school system that prepares top school achievers in math, reading, science, and problem solving while educating nearly everyone at a very high level? How does the nation pay for such success? Can a school system produce only winners?

Education as a Human Right

In the United States, proponents of more equal public school funding and performance have struggled in courts and state legislatures across the country. In at least nineteen states, courts have ordered reductions in interdistrict funding disparities. Justices lace their court opinions with outrage at states' failures to provide adequate funding. Sometimes the justices write with fury at legislatures, state bureaucracies, or political systems incapable of even minimal functioning, despite constitutional requirements. In California, numerous studies document the geography and demography of school successes and failures. Suburbs stand out from cities, as do well-off city neighborhoods from poor ones. Other states provide parallel evidence of funding disparities: huge in-city disparities have been documented in Washington State, Ohio, and Texas. Landmark court cases have challenged school inequality in New Jersey. The Supreme Court of Washington State unanimously held the legislature in contempt in September 2014 for failing to obey the court's order to provide funding for public education consistent with the state's constitution.[42] Bowles and Gintis argued the right theory: the way school systems are set up, at least in the United States, is to produce winners *and* losers.

A happy exception that may have proved the rule, an exception that was once seen as a pointer for the future, is a successful program that crosses municipal boundaries in the Wake County School District, or WCSD, centered in Raleigh, North Carolina. In 2000 this district shifted from its court-ordered and by now historic agenda of racial integration to *economic* integration. The shift occurred partly as the school board anticipated constitutional objections at the Supreme Court to race-based decision making, but mainly because of research findings that confirm the educational benefits of income mixing. As one former Raleigh school board member and education researcher says, disadvantaged students "do much better and advantaged students are not hurt if you . . . avoid concentrating low-achievement students."[43] The goal in Raleigh is to have no school with more than 40 percent of its student body poor; as a result of the program, most of the schools either meet the goal or come close. The WCSD incorporates Raleigh with its sprawling suburbs to form the twenty-first-largest school district in the nation, and the district is still growing rapidly, adding to its 130,000 students in more than 140 schools, 46 of them operating year-round. More than 97 percent of the children attend either a "neighborhood" school within five miles of home or a magnet or some other school by choice. About three thousand children, mainly poor children bused from the city to the suburbs, take involuntary placements to schools outside their neighborhoods, in pursuit of the district's economic-integration goal. Most of the district's poor children are African American and Hispanic. In 1995, only 40 percent of black students met state requirements in grades three through eight; but after the program had integrated schools economically, by 2005, 91 percent met requirements, and results are similar for Latinos. Measured over the short term, the results please administrators and parents. Four "unusual circumstances . . . make the politically delicate task of economic integration possible" in Raleigh: a countywide school district includes city and suburbs, busing for racial integration has a thirty-year history, the local economy was booming, and business leaders, including newspaper editors, provided solid support.[44]

This good news from Wake County excited school reform advocates, but it displeased others. In 2010, Tea Party Republicans gained a majority on the county school board and pushed what critics term "an ideological agenda aimed at nothing less than sounding the official death knell of government-sponsored integration in one of the last places to promote it." The new school board chairman, responding to critics who point out that poor children will again be concentrated in high-poverty schools, justified the board's decision to allow de facto segregation by income (and by race) with this comment: "If we had a school that was, like, 80 percent high-poverty, the public would see the challenges, the need to make it successful. . . . Right now, we have diluted the problem, so we can ignore it."[45]

In Finland, when the school reform movement began, the goal was not school excellence, but equality. The world can't stop talking about the high levels of achievement of Finland's schools, but Pasi Sahlberg points to the high level of equality, fulfilling the idea that *all* children in Finland should attend equally good schools under equally favorable conditions. It is true that Finland's small population is much less diverse than America's, with only a small proportion of immigrants. Nevertheless, since 1990, immigrant groups have entered from "Afghanistan, Bosnia, India, Iran, Iraq, Serbia, Somalia, Thailand, Turkey and Vietnam; new immigrants speak more than sixty languages. Yet, achievement has been climbing . . . and growing more equitable, even as it has been declining in some other OECD nations."[46] As Sahlberg writes: "Education sector development has been grounded on equal opportunities for all, equitable distribution of resources rather than competition, intensive early interventions for prevention, and building gradual trust among education practitioners, especially teachers."[47]

An American journalist summarizes the approach: "Decades ago, when the Finnish school system was badly in need of reform, the goal of the program that Finland instituted, resulting in so much success today, was never excellence. It was equity."[48] Finnish researchers, and their counterparts looking from the outside, find that as the Finns pursued equality of schooling, they found excellence.

One important element in equality is budgets. Budgets affect class size, and class size matters, whether in Finland or the United States. For many city schools in the United States, the evidence is not promising. The city of San Diego made a special effort using state and federal stimulus funds to aid its thirty poorest schools by driving down class size, to seventeen children on average, for kindergarten through second grade. As anticipated, the smaller classes yielded improved test scores. But after the district used up its federal stimulus money and was subject to budgetary restrictions, in 2012 average classroom numbers bounced back to thirty students or more for most schools. Only in special schools and in a few well-off neighborhoods where parents and support associations provide ample supplementary funding did class sizes remain small. The neighboring Coronado district, with thirty-two hundred students, raised donations from parents and others to the tune of $1,500 per student in 2010, compared to less than $20 in much less wealthy San Diego.[49] This private funding pattern beyond taxes occurs in wealthy neighborhoods across the nation.

Authorities have chosen larger class sizes as a means to deal with fiscal difficulties, a standard invocation of austerity principles. School reform leaders including Microsoft's Bill Gates, Education Secretary Arne Duncan, New York City mayor Michael Bloomberg, and New York's former schools chief Joel Klein advocated larger class sizes as one method to resolve budget shortfalls. Each of these particular leaders, by the way, like President Obama himself, attended elite private schools, where class sizes tend to be very small.

In Finland, one element of the pursuit of equality has been to keep class sizes small, in *every* school. They have also kept *schools* small—enrollments run from three hundred to nine hundred students. The intended result is close attention to every student. Finnish education leaders now worry greatly about those few students who remain unequal—the roughly 6 percent of students, for example, who get failing scores on the PISA examinations. And they worry that boys read much less than girls, so they are working on programs to interest boys in reading for enjoyment. Their overall idea is to find out for whom the system is not working, and then find solutions. The result, so far at least, has been that by pushing for equality among schools and providing strong support for students everywhere, they achieve excellence. Can fairness and equality come first in U.S. schools? Would excellence among all students then follow as it has in Finland?

It is worth adding that in Finland, there are no privately funded schools and very few independent schools at all. There are no schools run for profit. Nearly everyone attends public schools, from pre-K through university, without fees. All schools provide free lunch. Speaking at Columbia University, Sahlberg said, "Here in America, parents can choose to take their kids to private schools. It's the same idea of a marketplace that applies to, say, shops. Schools are a shop and parents can buy whatever they want. In Finland parents can also choose. But the options are all the same."[50] In the United States, a sensible place to begin is universal pre-K, well known to improve performance for low-income students. Vetoed as "communal child-rearing" in 1971 by President Nixon, it is now high on the agenda of increasing numbers of school reformers and political leaders.[51]

Teacher Training, School Autonomy, and Responsibilities

In nearly all U.S. states, public school teachers must hold four-year university degrees and a master's degree that includes courses in pedagogy and in specialized subject matter. They also need a practice teaching internship. That preparation puts them on an educational par with other professionals—social workers and counselors, accountants, engineers, lawyers, dentists. In helping to prepare the next generation of citizens and producers, teachers perform one of the society's most essential roles. Yet in the United States teachers are under attack. The adjectives used to describe teachers indiscriminately include *uncaring*, *irresponsible*, *weak*, and *unprepared*. Many teachers, especially in city schools, are necessarily inexperienced, and some, including those highly motivated college graduates who win coveted places with Teach for America, are sent into problem schools with only a four-year degree and very little preparation to teach. Teachers in city schools often find themselves unsupported by administrators, unable to take advantage of professional development programs, and paid too little in comparison with other highly trained professionals who hold comparable responsibilities, not to mention their suburban colleagues. Nearly all teachers are forced to teach "to the test," and many burn out from overwork and disregard. Many feel undermined by opponents who vehemently object to tenure, seniority pay, unions, and various prerogatives other professionals take for granted.

The comparison with the situation in Finland is revealing. There, teachers and school administrators as well take on a great deal of responsibility, and they are rewarded with high prestige as well as decent pay. Competition to become a teacher is intense. "Teacher training programs are among the most selective professional schools in the country."[52] Of those college graduates who apply for graduate school in teaching, only 15 percent are admitted, and they are paid while in graduate school. Once on the job, teachers get ample time during the workday ("at least one afternoon each week") for joint work on curriculum development, and more time for professional development and for work with caregivers.[53] In-service training is rarely compulsory; it is seen as a right. Teachers, together with administrators, design their curriculum, select texts, and govern their small schools. "If a teacher is bad, it is the principal's responsibility to notice and deal with it."[54]

Forty years ago, Finland's schools were centralized, national standards were rigid, and national testing was all-important. Today the many small schools are managed locally, with teachers designing curricula to follow minimal national standards. As Sahlberg points out, Finland chose *not* to copy reforms undertaken elsewhere. The Finnish school authorities do not have standardized school curricula, and they encourage music, art, exploration of new subjects, and problem solving, in addition to basic mathematics and science. They administer very few tests (nearly all students take only one examination, optional, upon high school graduation). The Ministry of Education encourages alternative methods of teaching, with no stress on rewards or sanctions for either students or teachers.[55] "Compared with the stereotype of the East Asian model—long hours of exhaustive cramming and rote memorization—Finland's success is especially intriguing because Finnish schools assign less homework and engage children in more creative play. All this has led to a continuous stream of foreign delegations making the pilgrimage to Finland to visit schools and talk with the nation's education experts, and constant coverage in the worldwide media marveling at the Finnish miracle."[56]

Well-Being of Children

Schoolchildren in Finland know they are favored. One can imagine they enjoy the same sense of privilege that prevails at Lake Woebegone, where *everyone* is superior. Long anticipating more recent reforms elsewhere, schools in Finland have served free lunch for all students for decades. Two postings by elementary school students, evidently written in English, give us some of the flavor of lunch:

> Our school lunch is served every day at 11am . . . quite normal Fin[n]ish food . . . doesn't cost anything. . . . We always can take as much as we like, and we also have to taste everything even we don't like it. Today . . . was one of our favorite dishes: spaghetti bolognese and salad. . . . The spaghetti was integral [whole wheat] pasta which is of course healthier. . . . There is also a very small amount of fat and salt in the sauce.
>
> Today . . . the fish was ok but everyone didn't like the pesto. . . . In Finland it's quite common that potatoes . . . we have to peel it before we eat it. Everyone don't like to do it because you may burn your fingers, but cooking potatoes with skin keeps more vitamins inside it. . . . Most of [us] liked today's salad especially the watermelon.[57]

As in most public schools in the United States, books and supplies are free, as is transportation. Other key provisions make a difference: Finland has universal, close-to-free health care, including occupational health and dentistry. A European Commission report issued in 2000 notes that 88 percent of Finns were satisfied with the hospital system, more than double the satisfaction rate in the rest of the European Union.[58] Universal child care and pre-K options, from the age of six months, help children to be successful.

Reducing Unequal Funding of Schools

When measured against the educational needs of the children they serve, city schools in the United States do not get adequate budgets. Although variations from school to school *within* city districts can create zones of privilege amid general neglect, the broader disparities divide needy cities from well-funded suburbs. The most visible distinctions segregate black and Latino children in the cities from white children in the suburbs. Here we return, unavoidably, to arguments about city versus suburb first encountered earlier, in the discussion of austerity.

It is not as though the problem of highly unequal schools lies unrecognized. Evaluation research shows conclusively that when more money is spent sensibly on public schools, it helps. Some of the most expensive items, such as preschool education and small classes in early grades, help the most.[59] Knowing the importance of adequate funding (and leaving race aside), *state* courts have often found that neighborhood-to-neighborhood and district-to-district spending inequalities violate state constitutional requirements that require provision of good schooling to all children.

In a series of California cases, bracketed by the 1971 and 1976 *Serrano* decisions, the state supreme court ruled that children in poor districts suffer unconstitutionally, because districts with higher property values have "a substantial advantage in obtaining higher quality staff, program expansion and variety, beneficial teacher-pupil ratios and class sizes, modern equipment and materials, and high-quality buildings."[60] In response, the California legislature centralized control over the bulk of school financing, so that some 80 percent of California budgeted school funding is allocated according to state and federal rules. With Proposition 13 in place, however, which passed in 1978 to impose drastic limits on local property tax increases, funding didn't go up in city schools, and went down in the suburbs. Prop 13 caused California to fall from its top rankings for public schools, crashing near the bottom among the fifty states.[61] A summary of twenty-two university studies costing $3 million released in March 2007 notes that the "problems are so deep-seated . . . that more funding and small, incremental interventions are unlikely to make a difference unless matched with a commitment to wholesale reform."[62] In the 1980s and 1990s, even facing its responsibility to meet special needs of the quarter of its students who do not speak English as their first language, "California [was] well below average in the nation in its per-pupil spending and dead last among the major industrial states. . . . Its academic achievement in math and reading . . . was near the bottom among the states, even in interstate comparisons of the same ethnic groups . . . largely attributable to California's larger classes, lower preschool and kindergarten participation, higher teacher turnover, and inferior classroom materials and other resources for teaching."[63]

In spite of statewide efforts to equalize financing, given the lowered standing of California schools *on average*, it is hardly surprising that, in the bland words of the most comprehensive study, the public schools "manifest inequality of opportunity."[64] Researchers use the euphemism *demographic* to soften the effect of their observation that problems in schools correlate with skin color and poverty. Because the schools face unreliable and inadequate financing, California's problem schools have difficulties meeting the tougher accountability requirements of No Child Left Behind, the Race to the Top, and parallel state edicts.

Many California suburban schools are okay. Despite lower student achievement scores statewide, many schools still work well for their students. The averages obscure great gaps separating the test scores of students who are middle class or affluent, placing them far above the students whose test scores reflect their "economic disadvantages." For all the problems of California's meager public school budgets, many suburban schools still perform well, as local per-student budgets are more robust, and parents and "friends of the school" groups pay large sums to supplement supplies and to fund sports, music, travel, and even Advanced Placement classes. At the other end of the spectrum, school problems abound in the big urban districts: Los Angeles, with its six hundred thousand students, and the contiguous Orange County and Long Beach districts, San Francisco, San Diego, Fresno, Oakland, and others.[65]

The contrast with Finnish schools could hardly be greater.

District and Neighborhood Boundaries

When the Supreme Court outlawed school segregation in *Brown v. Board of Education* in 1954, suburban schools with mostly white students already outclassed many city schools. Nevertheless, the huge gaps that would increasingly separate suburban from city districts lay hidden below the surface of the legal arguments. The Court firmly rejected *Plessy v. Ferguson*'s separate-but-equal doctrine, which for more than fifty years had permitted racially segregated schools, and the Court condemned the evil of segregation as practiced within individual school districts. When in 1957 the openly racist governor of Arkansas defended the segregation that the Court found so patently odious, President Dwight Eisenhower, the former supreme commander of Allied Forces in World War II, enforced the law. He sent one thousand helmeted federal paratroopers to Little Rock, to escort black students into Central High School.[66] Unfortunately, as case after case later affirmed, the Court applied its findings only to racial segregation *within* school districts. It never ruled against classroom segregation *across* school district boundaries. This narrow scope restricting the Supreme Court's application of the Fourteenth Amendment's equal protection clause has powerfully affected metropolitan politics, real estate practices, and land development ever since.[67]

Boston offers a good illustration. As Harvard psychologist Robert Coles famously pointed out, although the Court found a pattern of school segregation *within* Boston and therefore mandated busing in 1974, by so doing it pitted low-income whites from South Boston against low-income blacks from Roxbury. This arrangement left the suburbs undisturbed, safely protected with their higher incomes, tax-paying capacity, and institutional stability, so they could continue to shield their privileged, highly segregated schools.[68] In the areas surrounding cities across the country, better-off families, predominantly white, continued to insulate themselves in the suburbs, sending their children to extremely segregated schools, with no objection from any court. So, even though *Brown v. Board* did attack racial inequality in schooling in a formalistic way, it did *not* propose to overcome the deepest inequality of all, the profound fiscal and managerial difference that distinguishes minority school districts from white ones. The Boston situation was repeated across the country. In 2002, the richest quarter of the nation's fourteen thousand school districts (those with the lowest percentages of poverty) received $1,350 *more* in state and local funding per student per year on average than did the quarter of districts with the highest poverty rates. Similar gaps separate high-minority districts from mostly white districts.[69] New York State had the largest income-based gap, with more than $2,600 per student separating impoverished city neighborhood classrooms from well-off suburban ones, which can translate into more than $65,000 per year for a single classroom, about a million dollars for a typical elementary school with four hundred children. The gap in Illinois came in almost as high.[70]

In 1970, Detroit was the prototype metropolis, a black center in a white doughnut with about a million city people, nearly all black, surrounded by about three million suburbanites, nearly all white. Suburbanites earned about three times what city householders did, and the vast majority of suburban public school students were white, in contrast to overwhelming majorities of black students in the city.[71] Yet, as we have seen, when in 1974 local officials devised an arrangement for cross-district application of *Brown v. Board* that would bus students between city and suburbs, the Supreme Court rejected the concept wholesale. Reifying municipal boundaries as if they were not temporal lines drawn by Michigan state law, and holding to the false pretense that suburbs do not belong to the same social and economic universe as their central city, the Court stated explicitly that between-district segregation was *not* unconstitutional. To the Court, the Detroit suburbs bore no responsibility for the de facto segregation that separated their superior white schools from the city's inferior black schools. Justice Marshall dissented prophetically that the nation would pay a high price for decades to come.[72]

To no one's surprise, fiscally burdened city districts, along with some troubled suburbs, enroll the majority of impoverished children, as well as the majority of children of color in the United States. As leaders have served new portions of austerity, the bad taste has become worse. In California, school funding inequalities have isolated cities and subordinated them to suburbs. Statewide declines in the fortunes of public schools resulted from the limits imposed by Proposition 13 and various radical right-wing shifts in governance that have occurred since Ronald Reagan was governor. These statewide inequalities match quite closely the class and race distinctions that isolate cities from suburbs, which were revealed inadvertently by the Civic Capacity study. As we observed earlier, each school district in the eleven cities in that study, including Pittsburgh, Boston, and Atlanta, as well as San Francisco and Los Angeles, suffers markedly compared to its suburbs, which enjoy superior fiscal conditions.

In big-city school systems, the disparities appear neighborhood by neighborhood as well, from one school to another, and especially when comparing special magnet schools with ordinary schools. Researchers have compiled evidence from districts in California, Washington, Ohio, and Texas. In San Francisco's Mission District, Balboa High School has about twelve hundred students, a quarter of them black, a quarter Latino, a quarter Filipino, a fifth Chinese and Samoan, one-twenty-fifth white. As Peter Schrag has shown, Balboa ranks right near the bottom on the state's performance index, with circumstances that prevent many of the children from learning. Balboa rotates in and out its many substitute teachers, who are even less experienced than the poorly qualified regular teachers, does not supply enough textbooks, leaves its bathrooms filthy, and expects little from its students.[73] Just across town *in the same school district*, other high schools with different "demographics" employ permanent, experienced teachers with advanced degrees, supply a surfeit of teaching materials, and demand excellent work from their students.

This pattern of in-city inequality is repeated endlessly. In one-quarter of U.S. districts with two high schools or more, a pay gap of at least $5,000 per year separates teachers in schools with the most from those with the fewest black and Latino students.[74] Although each district *claims* roughly equal per-student funding from state and local sources, closer examination shows wide variation. According to a 2011 report by the U.S. Department of Education that analyzed data from nearly ninety thousand schools, many schools that enroll low-income students are underfunded when compared to schools with better-off students. Forty-six percent of Title I elementary schools (those enrolling larger numbers of poor children) received less funding per student than their districts' non–Title I schools.[75]

Researchers at the Center on Reinventing Public Education at the University of Washington, probing with case studies before the release of the federal data, found strong spending biases in Seattle, Cincinnati, and Houston. In Seattle, for example, contrary to formal district reports that claim higher spending on poor children, close examination reveals that the schoolchildren at privileged Wedgwood School on average cost the district 37 percent more, $4,019 per child per year, compared to only $2,928 for the children at the underprivileged Martin Luther King School.[76] In a single classroom of twenty-five students, that advantage adds up to more than $27,000 each year, not counting the very substantial voluntary contributions that middle-class parents donate to buy sports uniforms, hire coaches and musical instructors, buy art supplies, and—most expensive of all—fund trips to out-of-town destinations, even including flights to Europe. How can a single district maintain such contrasting school-funding situations, given state and federal mandates for equal funding? Are districts aware? Do districts hide the discrepancies? The answers for Seattle were pretty straightforward: the district cooks the books.

> The district charges schools a fixed false rate for all teachers, principals and other administrative staff, regardless of what these staff are actually paid by the district. The district then pays out the real salaries [which] vary substantially with experience and other qualifications.
>
> Schools such as Wedgwood, which can attract the best teachers (typically the most expensive teachers) can really benefit from this scheme. . . . The district's budget reports don't even reflect that Wedgwood teachers are some of the most expensive in the district.[77]

If such flimsy falsifications of funding are allowed to stand *inside* single school districts, despite legislation mandating roughly equal expenditures, then why should anyone expect to find spending equalization *between* school districts? In fact, legislators rarely vote for serious equalization. In spite of the legal requirement that funding by the state in California equalize schooling opportunity, for example, it did not do so. Mark Rosenbaum is a Los Angeles ACLU attorney who joined other civil rights litigants in *Williams v. California* in May 2000 on the anniversary of *Brown v. Board*. He refers to "the Mississippification of California schools, a separate but unequal system that would make [*Brown v. Board* litigant] Linda Brown shudder."[78] But the problem crops up all over: "In 1993, the Cleveland suburb of Cuyahoga Heights, with a 22-mill (2.2 percent) property tax levy, could spend nearly $12,000 per pupil; East Cleveland, taxing itself at triple that rate, could spend just over $5,500."[79]

The bright statewide exception may have been New Jersey. Over a quarter century, in a series of decisions, the New Jersey Supreme Court ordered a thorough reorganization of the state's public schools, building on the 1973 *Robinson* opinion, which built on California's *Serrano*. The thrust was for equalized funding—in 1976 the court, in frustration with the legislature, actually closed New Jersey schools for eight days, which caused the state to institute an income tax. In 1981 the court found in *Abbott v. Burke* that the state had still failed to remedy spending disparities, and in 1990 the court ordered the state to fund every student at the level "of the more affluent suburban districts" and to add something for special disadvantages.[80] Finally, in 1997 the court ordered the creation of twenty-eight "Abbott districts" in the poorest jurisdictions. The now thirty-one Abbott districts serve nearly three hundred thousand students, more than a fifth of the state's public school students, and they receive a little over half the money the state supplies to its 616 school districts.

Three major difficulties burden the Abbott system: Residents of better-off (non-Abbott) districts complain of their obligation to tax themselves more heavily to support their good schools, and they complain about spending Abbott funds on some relatively successful districts, especially those that have recently increased their numbers of middle-class residents. Some non-Abbott districts do not receive adequate state aid to help their poor children. And some districts use the state funding corruptly, with little benefit to the children. Overall, however, the program still earns high praise. Students in Abbott districts raised their fourth-grade language proficiency from 29.5 percent in 1999 to 66 percent in 2005, still below the state average of 88.5 percent, but a big improvement. As the director of the National Institute for Early Education Research reports, the evidence is clear that "this is good use of state taxpayer money."[81] But even in New Jersey with these powerful court directives, vast discrepancies have remained. Without stubborn inequalities, why would Mark Zuckerberg of Facebook have felt the need for his $100 million to match Mayor Cory Booker's fund-raising for rehabilitating Newark's schools?[82] If Governor Chris Christie has his way, the focus will not be on educational inequalities, but on attacking teachers' unions by switching to merit-based firing, pensions, and pay, increasing funding for higher education, and expanding programs for charter schools.[83]

Across the country, school funding disparities have become material for lawsuits, and, very often, state courts have found violations of state constitutions. Individual justices have shown outrage. Strong judicial majorities have ruled fiercely against governors, legislatures, and school authorities. Adjustments have been halting, slow, and subject to reversals. Racial desegregation in schools reached its peak decades ago, and the separation of racial and ethnic groups in schools has been on the increase since the late 1980s. Funding disparities continue, and across the country urban school districts fail to serve millions of poor and minority children. Outside the cities, in the suburbs, schools tend to be successful.

The nation needs to base remedies for broken schools on fairness. The system in tiny Finland, which to produce school excellence focuses first on the need for equality, points the way. It is evident what sort of choices we need to make in order to fix the schools, but it is not clear how to pursue these choices. In the following chapters, on city issues related to food and drugs, the stories I present have different subjects, but the issues all stem from inequality, our ever-growing problem.

Glimmers of Hope

In July 2013 the governor of California signed into law the Local Control Funding Formula, the LCFF, simultaneously giving K–12 school districts more authority and (especially in needy cases) much larger state allocations of money.[84] This new school-funding program will not restore California public schools to their highest-in-the-nation standards of a half-century ago (and even then substantial quality differences distinguished district from district and neighborhood from neighborhood)—far from it. But it will begin to redistribute resources to districts, schools, and classrooms that need them.[85] Districts will be relieved of many state mandates, free to allocate all but the supplementary needs-based funds on their own. Community groups fought successfully, so will be involved in monitoring. Totally bucking the trend, state authorities will not punish troubled districts, but help them. Shades of Finland?

To be implemented over eight years, the new California formula shifts state aid to high-needs students—those with low incomes, needing help with English, and living in foster homes—favoring additionally districts with high concentrations of such students. The law specifies state funding at least 20 percent (plus inflation) above the district basic per-pupil grant for each needy student, with an additional "concentration grant" of up to 22.5 percent for each needy student in excess of 55 percent of total enrollment. Although well-off school districts will still provide funds from local sources, to allow smaller classes and special classes and activities, state funding for poor districts will increase substantially.[86] Funding has already recovered from the Great Recession, but class sizes are still too large. The new formula will help, but it is not clear how much.[87]

Any state that very substantially boosts school funding will lessen the burden on districts and schools in poor cities or neighborhoods. A boost in federal funding will have similar effects. If school improvements can be seen as elements of urban policy, then if enacted along with lessened austerity restrictions, better nutrition, and an end to the violence of the drug war, these improvements will make poorer city neighborhoods and poor suburban districts themselves less unequal, and cities will be better off.

5

THE PARADOX OF PLENTY

Short of money, without automobiles, and with poor transit options, many city residents shop in small local markets, where they find few fresh fruits or vegetables and pay high prices.[1] Surrounded by fast-food restaurants, they use them. They lack farmers' markets and cannot arrange efficient transit to good supermarkets. They share these problems with poor residents of inner suburbs. Robert Lustig, a pediatric endocrinologist at the University of California medical school in San Francisco, reports that 80 percent of the six hundred thousand food items sold in this country and nearly all foods provided to the poor "are laced with added sugar."[2] The results are devastating. In New York City, 40 percent of adults "are overweight or obese. Obesity . . . kills 5,800 New York City residents per year . . . [striking] particularly . . . black, Latino, and low-income communities."[3]

Schools have districts and superintendents, buildings and principals, classrooms and teachers, families with children, contractors and suppliers. City food systems have no bureaucracies, no defined clienteles. Education is heavily freighted with ideological content, but food is merely something to eat. Schooling is a public responsibility, but stores and restaurants supply food privately. Students, guardians, and others can identify and influence schools, but almost no one can challenge food corporations or their lobbyists.

To add food and nutrition as elements of urban policy breaks a supposedly natural boundary. Food and nutrition policy have long been thought to be subjects not for cities, but for departments of agriculture, health authorities, and regulators of large corporations. Federal agencies and states regulate food production, marketing, and sales. Antitrust enforcements break up grocery chains. The government heavily subsidizes farming and purchases food for the military. States purchase food to supply prisons.[4] Federal programs provide food in many poor neighborhoods through food banks, food stamps, school meals, and other programs.

Yet it is highly appropriate to add food and nutrition as elements of urban policy. City health departments play big roles in guaranteeing food safety. School districts cook and serve enormous numbers of meals. Cities, worried about problems like obesity, prohibit some food ingredients and restrict the use of others. The *geography* of nutrition across the city and metropolitan checkerboard plays out unevenly, so some neighborhoods have plenty of nutrition, while others do not.

Food and nutrition come into the picture as one of the "external" or "upstream" urban policies in need of improvement, demanding attention to the ways nutritional deficits vary from neighborhood to neighborhood. The problem of food insecurity (the technical term that has replaced *hunger*) troubles the poorest neighborhoods. Styles of intervention and cognition vary, as we will see when as we find the sources of nutritional difficulties to originate in deep elements of the political economy.

Neighborhood Nutritional Deficits

Health levels in cities depend on many things—hazardous industry or other sources of toxins, pollution from trucks and other traffic, structures with poisonous lead paint, and indoor air pollutants. Health levels depend on the social environment. Is the community well organized or disorganized, isolated in psychological and social senses? Can residents depend on neighbors?[5] Is health care available and affordable? Finally, health levels depend on food quantity and quality—the subjects of this chapter—varying with purchasing capacity, quality of information, access to supermarkets or other fresh-food providers, distance from fast-food restaurants, and public provisioning. Conditions vary from suburbs to cities and from neighborhood to neighborhood.

Robert Lustig, the San Francisco medical researcher, points out that "even when all foods are available at low cost," poor people are pushed to rely on junk food, "fast food or pizza," by lack of refrigerators, no space for cooking, or pressure on time as a result of multiple jobs.[6] Households in the poorest city neighborhoods consume unhealthy foods, sometimes go hungry, and often worry and stress about hunger.[7] Residents suffer complications from obesity, diabetes, heart disease, and injuries, all exacerbated by improper or inadequate treatment. "Food insecurity (from worry to hunger) may cause diabetes as the body adapts to cycles of bingeing and fasting . . . and diabetes can lead to food insecurity when the cost of medications and treatment sap family resources."[8]

Chicago's Neighborhood Differences

From 2002 to 2008, medical researchers surveyed ten large Chicago neighborhoods, most with populations the size of a small city, ranging from forty thousand to ninety thousand inhabitants. Residents surveyed in two of the neighborhoods are all (100 percent) white; in another, all Asian; in two, 98 percent and 94 percent black; and in another, 77 percent of Mexican origin. Household income differences correspond with race and schooling levels. In the neighborhoods of color, from half to more than four-fifths of households report very low annual incomes, $30,000 or less. In the two white neighborhoods, nearly half report high incomes, *above* $70,000.[9] The differences correlate highly with health and nutrition.

Six neighborhoods of color and poverty report diabetes rates nearly double the city average, more than triple the rate of the two white neighborhoods.[10] Compared to either the white survey neighborhoods or Chicago overall, the neighborhoods of color have higher blood pressure and more pediatric obesity and asthma.[11] In five of the neighborhoods that are predominantly poor and either African American or Latino, more than one-third of the population is obese. In North Lawndale and Roseland, nearly all black, about 40 percent of the adults are obese, nearly double the percentage in the white neighborhoods of Norwood Park or West

Ridge, or in Chicago overall. The researchers find these high rates to be serious matters: "Obesity is a risk factor for adult-onset diabetes, coronary heart disease, and several other serious medical conditions that can lead to poor health and premature death."[12] In the impoverished neighborhoods of color, high proportions of the adults (up to 40 percent) find nutritious foods too costly, but in the two well-off white neighborhoods, only 10 percent and 13 percent of respondents reported similar cost problems.[13] Community residents on the survey design committee argue the need for improved access to "cheaper healthy food options in the community."

Food Deserts

In many inner-city neighborhoods and in a growing number of poor suburbs, supermarkets are scarce, while distant ones are hard to get to, putting relatively inexpensive food out of reach. Bayview–Hunters Point in San Francisco confronts these problematic conditions. Following decades of urban renewal and dislocation elsewhere in the city, the neighborhood is home for San Francisco's largest African American population (a third of the neighborhood), and it has the city's lowest incomes.[14] It lies adjacent to former Candlestick Park and a highly toxic decommissioned naval shipyard, a Superfund site. Even with pollution, unemployment, and poverty, however, one of the residents' top two complaints in 1999 was unreliable bus service to get to satisfactory grocery stores. Corner food markets in the neighborhood sold high-priced, poor-quality foods, devoting an unusually small portion (only 2 percent) of their shelf space to fresh food. The stores also served as locations for dangerous drug-sales activity.[15]

Such conditions prevail in many city neighborhoods, with too few supermarkets and too many fast-food outlets. When supermarkets *are* present, diets sometimes improve. One study concluded that with each additional supermarket, a neighborhood's intake of fruits and vegetables went up 32 percent for African American and 11 percent for white residents.[16] Other studies suggest that more is required.[17] Local options (usually convenience stores) tend to be more expensive, offer less choice, and sell food that is less healthy and less fresh.[18] To get to better stores, householders without automobiles get rides from others when they can, walk, take transit, borrow a car, pay for a taxi, and pool purchases with neighbors who drive.[19] With the inconvenience and their dependence on payment dates for Social Security and food stamps, they shop infrequently.[20]

Sales of fresh foods increase when shelf space increases. Despite income constraints, if healthy fresh foods are offered, people buy them.[21] Limits to access and high prices are particularly damaging for children, the elderly, and those with health problems. In the most troubled big-city neighborhoods, residents also sometimes restrict their own visits to food stores because they fear violence on the street.

Finally, as studies show in Chicago and New York City by researchers who advocate improved labor protections and higher local wages, when local markets do make fresh food available in poor neighborhoods, a burden falls on super-exploited workers.[22] Employers may deny safety equipment, penalize workers who take scheduled breaks, and degrade work in other ways. Poor neighborhoods tend to have non-chain, locally owned stores, often owned by immigrants, with nonunion workers. Many choose not to pay full wages. They can even undercut prices, on meat for example, by avoiding unionized butchers.[23]

Neighborhood health-service "deserts" spread, too. "Urban and suburban areas have lost a quarter of their hospital emergency departments over the last 20 years. . . . In 1990, there were 2,446 hospitals with emergency departments in non-rural areas. That number dropped to 1,779 in 2009, even as the total number of emergency room visits nationwide increased by roughly 35 percent."[24]

New York City's Nutritional Worries

In December 2006 New York City's Board of Health required the posting of calories on menus and menu boards for fast-food restaurants and other places that sell uniformly sized foods and already provide nutritional information. The new regulations also bar trans fats from *all* restaurants. According to Mayor Michael Bloomberg and his health commissioner, New York took these extraordinary regulatory steps because of the city's "exceptionally high rates of obesity and heart disease," which were getting worse, and they wanted to reverse the direction of change.[25]

Forty years earlier, in 1965, McDonald's restaurants served soda in a seven-ounce Styrofoam cup. Now they serve soda in a forty-two-ounce paper cup, having increased the size sixfold. This enormous quantity has become the fast-drink standard for restaurant chains, and diners may supplement the first supersize serving with free and easy refills. When a researcher ordered a medium iced tea at a McDonald's in a remote Missouri town, she was offered the large, since it was cheaper![26]

In New York in 2012, the mayor tried to prohibit restaurant soda servings larger than sixteen ounces. Earlier that year, the city Obesity Task Force had issued a report called *Reversing the Epidemic*. Despite the good news that obesity rates had dropped 5.5 percent over five years for children in kindergarten through the eighth grade, the bad news dominates the report, as the following summary statements suggest:

> Obesity is not a cosmetic problem. Epidemic obesity has led to massive increases in prevalence of Type II diabetes, which can result in blindness, hypertension, and amputations. One in three adult New Yorkers now either has diabetes or a condition known as pre-diabetes. Obesity also increases cancer, heart disease, arthritis, depression, asthma and a host of other problems. Severe obesity leads many to immobility and depression. In New York City as of 2007, there were 2,600 hospitalizations for amputations related to diabetes and 1,400 people who ended up on dialysis due to diabetes.[27] In addition, applying national estimates to the New York City population, over 100,000 adults have diabetic retinopathy (eye disease) which if untreated, can lead to blindness.[28]

These are neighborhood problems, poverty problems, and race problems, "striking New Yorkers unequally." Residents of the poor minority areas of East New York or Bedford Stuyvesant "are four times more likely than a resident of the [mostly white, well-off] Upper East Side to die of diabetes. Black New Yorkers are almost three times more likely, and Hispanics twice as likely as whites to die from diabetes."[29]

Food Insecurity

With the Great Recession, city health agencies, school districts, and federal researchers recognized that food insecurity worsened. The number of food stamp participants increased more than 2.7-fold between 2000 and 2012.[30]

The Department of Agriculture, USDA, refers to hunger and worry about hunger as "food insecurity." In the argot of USDA, *marginal* households worry but make do, anxious but rarely changing eating habits. *Low food security* households get enough to eat, with "little or no indication of reduced food intake," but they reduce the "quality, variety, or desirability of diet." *Very low food security* households report "multiple indications of disrupted eating patterns and reduced food intake."[31] In plain English, someone doesn't get dinner. Children from low food security and marginally secure households receive about a quarter of their daily caloric intake from school lunch programs.[32] Surprisingly large numbers of people are either hungry or fear that they will be. Nationally, despite parents' efforts, and SNAP (food stamps), WIC (Women, Infants, and Children, a nutritional subsidy program for pregnant women and young children), and school lunch and breakfast programs, and *after* the recession ended, more than four hundred thousand children and probably more adults went hungry at various times through 2011. Figure 5.1 shows rising levels of food insecurity—the top line shows, for example, that in 2011 nearly 15 percent of households were at some point short of food; this statistic was still at 14 percent in 2014. There were 48.1 million people in these households. The bottom line shows that since 2008, between 5.5 and 6 percent of households were at some point severely short of food. In 2014, there were 12.4 million adults and 914,000 children in these truly hungry households.

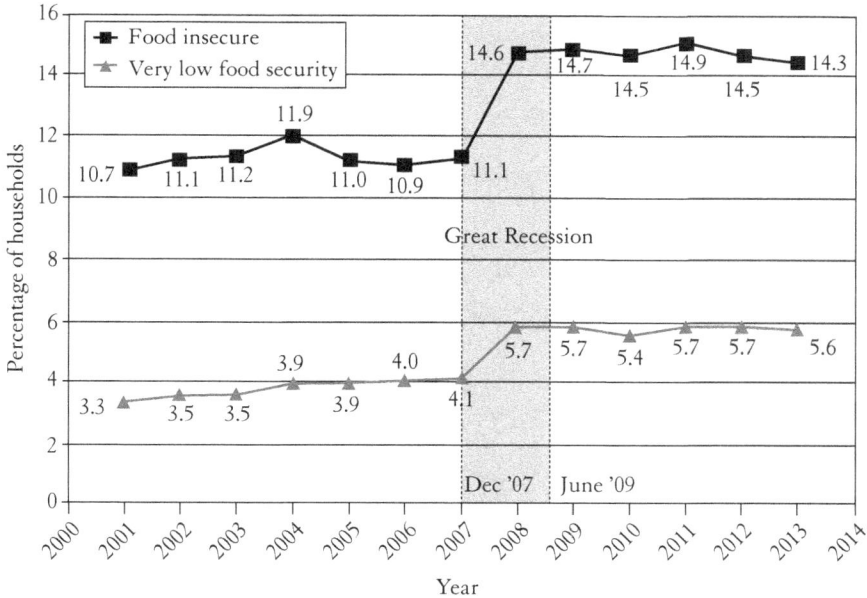

Figure 5.1. Timelines of food insecurity, 2001–2013. Income growth before taxes, adjusted for inflation. The prevalence of food insecurity increased in 2008 and has remained near that level. **Food insecure households**: Households that were unable, at some time during the year, to provide adequate food for one or more household members because of lack of resources. **Very low food secure households**: Normal eating patterns of some household members were disrupted at times during the year and their food intake reduced below levels they considered appropriate. Source: United States Department of Agriculture, Economic Research Service, 2014, "Food Security in the United States," http://www.ers.usda.gov/data-products/food-security-in-the-united-states/interactive-chart-food-security-trends.aspx.

In comprehensive studies for Chicago and Los Angeles, researchers have connected low-quality food and low nutritional intake with high rates of infant mortality, high rates of cancer and heart disease, and other health problems.[33] Many children are either hungry or close to it—observers see longer lines at school cafeterias on Mondays, along with eager eating by children still in the lunch line (despite the rules). On Fridays children express concern in anticipation of weekends or winter vacation when families are more likely to be out of food stamps and children will not have school breakfasts and lunches.[34]

Before the recession, well over a quarter of the households made the insecure list on a Washington, DC, neighborhood survey: more than 21 percent of them food insecure, topped by an additional nearly 7 percent actually hungry. Using estimates derived from interviews with Latino and Asian immigrants who visited big-city clinics and community centers, researchers estimated food insecurity rates in poor neighborhoods to be about 40 percent in California, Texas, and Illinois.[35]

To measure household food shortage, the USDA asks a series of survey questions. People worry about food running out, meals being made smaller or sometimes skipped altogether, or missing of meals for a whole day. Hunger and worry about hunger affect a higher proportion of households in principal cities (33 percent more) than in other parts of metropolitan areas, and as table 5.1 shows, these difficulties are prevalent in households with children headed by a single woman (or a single man—rare), black

TABLE 5.1. Food insecurity by household characteristics, 2014

Household characteristic	Food insecurity (%)
All households with children	19.2
Households with children under age 6	19.9
Households with children headed by a single woman	35.3
Households with children headed by a single man	21.7
Black, non-Hispanic households	26.1
Hispanic households	22.4
Low-income households[a]	33.7

Source: United States Department of Agriculture, Economic Research Service, 2014, "Food Security in the United States," http://www.ers.usda.gov/data-products/food-security-in-the-united-states/interactive-chart-food-security-trends.aspx.
[a] Households with incomes below 185% of the federal poverty threshold, which was $24,008 for a family of four.

and Latino households, and poor households. These categories, of course, overlap. For example, of all households with children headed by women, 35.3 percent were food insecure in December 2014. Many of these households are black or Hispanic, and poor; food-insecure portions are shown separately in the table.

City Planning, Personal Change, and Structure

At the turn into the twentieth century, when cities were extremely unhealthy places, planners had to pay attention to health issues, but they did not bother with food. A public health historian tells us that New York City in the post–Civil War period suffered "the depths of disorder and disease." In 1912 the health department "picked up over 20,000 dead horses, mules, donkeys, and cattle from the city's streets," to say nothing of more than five million pounds of spoiled meat and "1,946 cubic yards of night soil." Tons of horse manure and other waste littered the streets.[36] People avoided living in cities if they could.

A Century of Limited City Food Planning

Public health practitioners and urban planners worked together to modernize the city. Civil engineers piped in safe water and piped out sewage, crews removed manure and other waste from the streets, and housing authorities reduced crowding and introduced light and air in tenements. Companies constructed streetcar lines and subways, and authorities reduced density by encouraging peripheral residential construction, thus stemming rampant TB infections.[37] The emergent social science branch of planning took concern with the health of vulnerable populations, including the poor, immigrants, and the homeless. City food was hardly on the agenda.

City planners did attempt to improve food distribution, advocating efficiency and sanitation. As part of the City Beautiful movement, boosted by the World's Columbian Exposition of 1893 in Chicago, planners reorganized messy agglomerations of food businesses into more rationally planned wholesale food markets and modern distribution facilities, usually central "terminal" markets located by rail lines.[38] These wholesale "halls" survived until 1970 or later, when peripheral distribution facilities opened, as city land-use patterns around the world adjusted to the transportation dominance of highways and trucking. Otherwise, analysis of food and nutrition rarely took settlement patterns into account, and analysis of cities and things urban rarely took food and nutrition into account.[39]

Over the centuries, city food supply has on occasion raised official concern. Ancient Rome conquered colonies to find land and workers who would ship grain and other foods on Roman-built roads to the capital. Whether or not Marie Antoinette actually said "Let them eat cake," city hunger was at stake. In Chicago, concern about rising food prices during World War I led neighborhoods to lobby for farmers' markets, and then in the 1930s, Chicago pushed to modernize its markets to keep food prices down for consumers.[40] Long into the twentieth century, Third World city masses died in famines for lack of money to buy bread or rice.[41] But the idea that food was a basic need in U.S. cities and should be distributed more fairly would wait for another day.

Ann Spirn's 1984 book *The Granite Garden* reminded students in landscape architecture, urban studies, and city planning in the late twentieth century that they needed to pay attention to nature. As Spirn wrote, the health and welfare of city residents still "depends on the efficient provision of sufficient energy, water, food, and other resources."[42] When students read the book in my freshman course on the American city, it occurred neither to me nor to the students to discuss food. Spirn's rich and detailed examples hardly raised food as an issue.

With the turn to the twenty-first century, food appeared on the national agenda, and city advocates took note, with intense discussion in classrooms and the public sphere. Eric Schlosser's book *Fast Food Nation* came out in 2001; Michael Pollan's *The Omnivore's Dilemma: A Natural History of Four Meals*, and Michele Simon's *Appetite for Profit: How the Food Industry Undermines Our Health and How to Fight Back*, in 2006. Barbara Kingsolver's *Animal, Vegetable, Miracle: A Year of Food Life*, and Raj Patel's *Stuffed and Starved: The Hidden Battle for the World Food System*, came out in 2007; Christopher Leonard's *The Meat Racket: The Secret Takeover of America's Food Business*, in 2014. Independently produced movies on food were released and viewed widely: among them, *Super Size Me* in 2004, *Fast Food Nation* in 2006, *King Corn* and *Food Inc.* in 2008, *Ingredients* in 2009, *Forks over Knives* in 2011, and *Feeding Frenzy* in 2014.

Meanwhile, scholars in public health, medicine, and urban studies shipped out a boatload of studies on nutrition, the food industry and its economics and politics, public regulation, and efforts at reform. Advocates now work to reduce diet-related illnesses, to oppose corporate control of the food industry, to question genetically modified organisms (GMOs), and to aid people at risk of hunger. They also worry about loss of farmland to suburban or exurban building booms, such as the loss of potato fields on Long Island that occurred long ago as the New York metropolis developed its close-in, modest suburbs and occurred again later, as second-home estates occupied more remote sites.[43]

Health advocates and city planners have recently seized on the food movement. As late as the year 2000, interviews revealed that most city planners were *not* involved because they thought food was a "rural issue," to be dealt with by agriculture interests and regulators or by agencies such as public health departments. Planners now work to assist food distribution efforts or to conduct assessments of food insecurity.[44] A series of mainstream professional and scholarly journals on cities and planning have put out special issues on food and the city.[45]

How much will cities be able to change their food and nutritional practices? Will improvements arise through changes in individual behavior? Will social groups influence people's diets and purchases? Will cities, states, and the federal government change policies? Will the structure of the corporate-dominated food economy shift?

Personal or Social Change

Will children eat vegetables? Yes, if they are involved in producing them. Will cities support better food policies? Yes, if they are shown the way and provided the resources to attract supermarkets, help corner stores to stock healthier foods, support farmers' markets, establish or protect community gardens, and even protect farmland from development. Do city administrations and school boards worry about hunger, nutrition, and obesity? More and more they do, especially if they see the potential benefit from job creation, tax revenue, and reduced health care costs. But these concerns and attitudes alone will not produce the needed changes. The "food problem," much like the "school problem," has deep roots.

If the obstacles to change lie buried deeply in the structure of the society, and if limits are imposed by an uneven distribution of resources and power, where can change begin? Advocates for food and nutrition reforms answer by operating in two areas, in the realm of personal or individual change, and in the realm of social or collective change.[46]

In disputes over nutrition (as in disputes about schools, and drugs), one finds mentions of deep structure and change. Michele Simon speaks darkly of the "powerful forces that control our modern food system." An upheaval that challenges the increasingly unfettered operation of corporate economic and political power may indeed be required before sufficient improvements can be made in the food system. But nearly all of the food and nutrition game is played within a more limited set of boundaries, so that even theorists who advocate (or anticipate) major structural shifts try meanwhile to work actively for more modest reform, while others limit their hopes to changes in individual behavior.

Many influential Americans display an ideological preference for personal rather than social or collective change. When Tommy Thompson, the former governor of Wisconsin and George W. Bush's secretary of health and human services, spoke on obesity, he focused on individuals, saying that first of all, "we have to continue to work hard to spread the gospel of personal responsibility."[47] This focus on individual responsibility is hardly unusual.

Many churches encourage parishioners to take personal health responsibility. T. D. Jakes, a popular televangelist pastor who broadcasts from the Potters House in Dallas, "has been at the forefront of the health crusade in the black church." Jakes himself lost forty-five pounds and continued working toward another thirty-pound reduction, saying, "We have to continue to create an atmosphere where people can talk openly about their issues and have healthy solutions." Rev. Grainger Browning, pastor of the Ebenezer AME (mega) Church in Fort Washington, MD, just outside Washington, DC, with more than ten thousand parishioners, says: "As our memberships get older, we are pastoring out of necessity because we see people who are literally digging their graves with their teeth. . . . I was at a men's meeting and 75 percent of the men at the meeting were on medications." James Tate, a former high school football lineman in his mid-thirties, lost two hundred pounds by joining the weight loss program at the First Baptist (mega) Church of Glenarden, in Prince George's County, Maryland, on the edge of Washington, DC. Tate used to have to sit in one of the wider seats in the handicapped section. The church operates an active health ministry to prompt change in individual behavior.[48] In Oklahoma City, health worker Michael Bailey goes door to door visiting neighborhood barbershops and convenience stores. "Look at the kids, overweight, huffing and wheezing. Their lives will be miserable if this doesn't change." Bailey thinks food is slowly killing his community, but he focuses on individual change.[49]

Renette Dallas, a physician who is also a member of the Mount Pleasant Baptist Church in Washington, DC, sees health activism as a fad and is not optimistic about individuals taking responsibility for their own nutrition. Commenting on the health and fitness programs that Dallas herself conducts for her church, she says, "People are giving out free cotton candy and hamburgers. . . . We do things because everybody else is doing it. . . . The president is talking about fitness, the first lady is talking about fitness and big business is talking about fitness, and churches are big business. It is a trend but it doesn't mean anything."[50]

Social or Structural Change

As Robert Lustig writes in *Fat Chance*, "The concept of personal responsibility . . . doesn't always make sense."[51] The documentary movie *Feeding Frenzy* shows how food marketing overwhelms personal responsibility. To allow people to take responsibility, influential New York University nutritionist and sociologist Marion Nestle argues, schools should promote "eat less, move more," involve teachers, ban commercials for foods without much nutritional value, end sales of the worst of them, make meals fit the USDA Dietary Guidelines, and provide physical education and sports. Packaging should display nutritional information including sugar, salt, and fats on soft drinks and snacks, and on fast-food wrappers. Television ads should be restricted, and equal time should be demanded for constructive messages. Food ads should disclose calories (in a manner that is easily assimilated by consumers) and not contain misleading health claims. Taxes should be imposed on soft drinks and other junk foods, the money used to fund "eat less, move more" campaigns. Fruits and vegetables should be subsidized.[52] Farm subsidies for the production of corn and sugar should be abolished.

Recent city actions on food and health demonstrate remarkably different municipal approaches to tackling such issues through the setting of health goals. New York City and San Francisco both put out plans in 2004. Take Care New York recommends clinical preventive medicine for individuals: see the same doctor or other health care provider regularly, don't smoke, keep your heart healthy, know your HIV status, get help if you are depressed, avoid drug addiction or alcoholism, get cancer checkups and immunizations, set up home to stay safe and healthy, have a healthy baby.[53] Each recommendation is a good one, but the question arises, under what circumstances do these good individual options become feasible?

San Francisco's Prevention Strategic Plan implicitly asks exactly that question, then aims to alter the circumstances. Looking beyond individuals, to examine the society and to promote alterations in social and political structures, the plan recommends advocacy for livable wages, programs to move to full employment, including job training and placement, and an affordable supply of high-quality child care. The plan also recommends improved quality and quantity of housing, strong social safety nets, improved public transportation, increased public participation in political and social organizations, improved availability of respite services, and equal, fair education policies.[54] Unfortunately, since San Francisco's population comprises only about 10 percent of its metropolis, with powers that derive entirely from the State of California, itself only one-fiftieth part of its larger political union, these recommendations may fall on too few ears. New York City, comprising nearly 40 percent of its three-state metropolitan population, stands a better chance, were it to attempt such collective or "structural" reforms.

Such things as reductions in unemployment, provision of child care, reductions in housing costs, and of course reductions in poverty, wherever their political support, are essential ingredients for full solutions to problems of food and nutrition. Yet for key improvements in city living, simpler and more direct changes in food and nutrition can be made, even as more basic problems persist. Food First is an activist organization with a strong record of radical research and advocacy. In its mission statement it takes on major structural problems, calling for ending "the injustices that cause hunger, poverty and environmental degradation throughout the world." Its supporters "believe a world free of hunger is possible if farmers and communities take back control of the food systems presently dominated by transnational agri-foods industries." Food First thus calls implicitly for challenging powerful global corporations, consistent with its history of calls for liberation of nations long subject to colonial rule and foreign corporate domination.

At the same time, in its 2009 report on Food Policy Councils, Food First moderates its goals, suggesting small reforms within structural limits, to bring "the weight of local, county or state government behind grassroots initiatives." Food policy councils across the country have been advocates for modest change. In an apparent bow to the power of the food industry, the politics of city "growth machines," and the importance of regional boosterism, Food First presents studies showing how local councils have helped stimulate their city's or broader areas' economies. "To many, those 'food dollars' represent an opportunity to capture more wealth in the community."[55] Other groups that normally focus on redistribution have also stressed how much "local" food production can help the general economy. A study of northwest Wisconsin shows food economy potential for growth of $1.13 billion a year, and a study of the Chesapeake Bay region shows "that a 15% increase in local food purchases would bring in three times more dollars to farming communities than federal subsidies currently bring to the region."[56] A study of the greater Seattle area estimates that if the area "were to source just 20% of its food locally, it would inject an extra billion dollars per year into the city's economy."[57]

Mark Winne, the director of the Community Food Security Coalition, recommends caution more directly, warning against trying to defeat "the big boys: factory farming, GMOs, etc." Winne says that food policy councils have not been able to take on the big issues. "FPCs that have tried to take on factory farming, industrial agriculture, or the industrial food chain have found themselves on the short end of the stick. For the time being I think it is prudent to avoid those big fights. Taking on the oligopolistic forces of multinational agribusiness is not yet within the scope of Food Policy Council work."[58]

The contrast between Food First's radical mission statement and its reformist activities produces a tension present in many situations, inducing reformers to work at two levels simultaneously, dovetailing short-term changes into longer-term goals. Possibly, in a feedback loop from individual behavior to structural reform, modest food reforms in public schools can lead to long-term changes. If children learn to shop and eat with more discrimination, grow their own vegetables, and cook nutritious food, then their adult demands in the marketplace can bring changes in regulation and corporate behavior. Innovations over the last decade or so have occurred in many places. Individually, each is a small effort. Collectively viewed, they are promising. Grassroots grow into healthy lawns.

Eating Outside the Market

The private food system is gigantic, with total retail sales around $600 billion per year, roughly $40 per capita per week, some 13 percent of all retail sales.[59] Yet, as we have seen, many find the market out of reach of their pocketbooks. Various programs extend food access for city residents. Food "subsidies" come via *nonfood* public spending that provides families or individuals with welfare payments, medical care, housing, and retirement income. Aside from Social Security, which offers extremely important food support for the elderly, the principal *indirect* programs are the negative income tax, welfare (TANF), and assistance for housing. The main *direct* food programs are school meals and SNAP (food stamps). Two smaller programs are WIC (food for pregnant women, infants, and children) and food banks. For recipients with two or more children, three programs—the negative income tax (Earned Income Tax Credits, EITC), SNAP, and TANF—transfer on average more than $2,500 per family each year.[60]

School Food Programs

School programs serve lunches to income-eligible children, and they also serve breakfasts, summer-vacation food, and child-care meals. These programs have provided food and nutrition to children from poor families since the 1930s, lessening inequality and relieving hunger. Financed by the USDA, school food programs deliver in excess of seven billion meals each year, and they cost more than $50 billion. The lunches are not haute cuisine; indeed, they fall far below the quality of school lunches in a number of other countries, but they do meet federal dietary standards.[61]

The National School Lunch Program operates in nearly all public schools and some private ones, providing some subsidy to more than twenty-one million children on an average day in 2011. The School Breakfast Program, started in 1966, operated in fiscal year 2012 in more than eighty-nine thousand schools, serving more than 12.9 million children every day.[62] In many city schools *all* the children receive subsidized lunches. School cafeterias also serve what they call "competitive foods," which any students can buy à la carte; these foods need *not* meet federal standards. Students also buy food from snack shops or vending machines, which offer junk in 98 percent of high schools, 97 percent of middle schools, and 27 percent of elementary schools.[63] In 2010, the leading text on school lunches observed that "the lunch lady serving a government-approved hot lunch is but a dusty icon. The most popular school lunch in California [was] a small pepperoni pizza, nachos, a peanut butter cookie and a diet soda . . . a dietary bomb containing 1,116 calories and 51 grams of fat."[64]

Following pressure from public health and nutrition advocates, much publicity by Michelle Obama, two studies for the Congress by the prestigious Institute of Medicine, and the 2010 Healthy, Hunger-Free Children Act, the USDA released new food and nutrition standards in January 2012. The improved standards reduce saturated fat, sodium, and calories, and they increase quantities of whole grains, fruits, and vegetables.[65]

SNAP (Food Stamps)

The number of SNAP participants peaked at nearly forty-eight million in September 2012, later declining moderately. As a report from the Urban Institute notes, "SNAP does more than combat hunger—it is an antipoverty program, a work support, a promoter of health and nutrition, and an automatic stabilizer in recessions."[66]

Researchers found that over decades SNAP became more important in the safety net. "During the recession, it filled in where . . . other programs fell short," assisting anyone who is poor, including those just above the poverty line, and "not limited to families with children or to the elderly, as many safety net programs are." Nearly all eligible persons (96 percent) who were enrolled for welfare payments also used food stamps in 2008–2009, as did nine-tenths of those who were officially poor. Benefits reached more than forty-seven million income-eligible persons in fiscal year 2013, at a cost of $82.5 billion.

Among the working poor, eligible persons with recorded earnings, 60 percent used food stamps. Since 2008, as a result of rising unemployment *and* removal of time-limits as part of ARRA (the recovery act passed under the Obama administration), the number of able-bodied adults without dependents in the program increased by 60 percent (in fiscal 2009) and by another 23 percent (in fiscal 2010) to total 3.9 million persons.[67]

After much debate in the Congress in 2014, SNAP was cut by 1 percent, resulting in household cuts of about $90 per month atop a November 2013 cut of $36, leaving benefits averaging about $1.40 per person per meal.[68]

Women, Infants, and Children (WIC)

The Women, Infants, and Children program served almost nine million pregnant women and their children monthly in fiscal 2013, operating through more than eighteen hundred local agencies. Budgeted at $6.5 billion, WIC provides cereals for infants and adults, fortified with iron, fruit and vegetable juices rich in vitamin C, and "eggs, milk, cheese, peanut butter, dried and canned beans/peas, and canned fish." Recently added foods include beverages and tofu made from soybeans, fresh fruits and fresh vegetables, "baby foods, whole wheat bread, and other whole-grain options." The Farmers' Market Nutrition Program, which WIC started in 1992, provided free "fresh, nutritious, unprepared, locally grown fruits, vegetables, and herbs" to 1.5 million participants in 2013. WIC also spent nearly $2 billion for nutritional services delivered at more than nine thousand clinics.[69]

Food Banks

One national nongovernmental organization, Feeding America, funds and regulates more than two hundred food banks and emergency food rescue organizations across the country.[70] It supports some fifty thousand local charities that run more than ninety thousand food distribution operations, from pantries to soup kitchens, and it supplies food during emergencies, food after school, and a program called Kids Cafe.[71] With funds from charities and federal grants, Feeding America helps thirty-seven million people.

The Political Economy of Food

Leading food authority Marion Nestle says Americans have a "paradox of plenty." On the one hand, overabundant food is produced and sold, and many people eat too much. On the other hand, surprising numbers of people are short on nutrition. Too much and too little.

Food corporations promote overeating, interfering with human needs for nutrition, just as tobacco firms once interfered with health. They claimed "that smoking is a matter of individual choice and that it is wrong for government to interfere." They confused the public by presenting phony science. "They set the standard in use of PR, advertising, philanthropy, experts, political funding, alliances, lobbying, intimidation, and lawsuits to protect their sales." And they pushed smoking "to children and adolescents; to minorities, women, and the poor," as well as overseas. Food corporations do similar things to sell food. Nestle suggests we should not be surprised, since *"cigarette companies sometimes owned food companies."*[72]

Yet criticism is muted. "Badmouthing the food industry or the Farm Bill is the 'third rail' of American politics. Because it's all about Iowa. Iowa is the first presidential contest for both parties. And that means no one wants to diss corn, or any corn-based product."[73] In Rochester, New York, the interests of food corporations may conflict directly with the nutritional needs of poor city residents. The board of directors of Rochester's Food Link includes representatives from such food giants as ConAgra, Kroger, Mars Food, Walmart, and Procter & Gamble.[74] Feeding America's Leadership Partners include General Mills, Kellogg's, PepsiCo, Cargill, ConAgra, Kraft, Kroger, Target, Walmart, and Sam's Club. In food banks, much of the food is prepackaged, salty, high calorie junk, which studies suggest do more harm than good.[75]

Michele Simon, in *Appetite for Profit*, argues that "we must confront the powerful forces that control our modern food system head-on."[76] Food corporations do not openly advocate an unhealthy lifestyle, but they promote one by using science to discover and add addictive ingredients, advertising with hype and half-truths, and employing lobbyists. They tailor marketing campaigns to children, ethnic and racial groups, and the urban poor. They focus on factory food rather than fresh food, profiting from longer shelf life and cheaper production methods.

For millennia human beings struggled to get enough food. They learned to sample things nature provided, to seek foods high in nutrients. But these foods are also relatively high in salt, sugar, and fat, and since storing up extra fat on the bones meant survival through scarce times, humans evolved over hundreds of thousands of years into eating machines pleased with the tastes of sugar, salt, and fat. Then, suddenly, food production and provision went through a revolution as large parts of the world moved suddenly (in evolutionary terms) from scarcity to stability to abundance furnished by increased agricultural productivity combined with improved manufacturing, storage, and shipping.[77] Rising farm productivity and more efficient food corporations did solve the scarcity problem for most Americans, but they created new problems.

Selling Food

Food firms produce or buy harvested commodities, transform, package, and deliver them, attract customers, and sell, all the while taking care to obey laws and regulations and maintain safe standards. Facing stiff competition, they must constantly innovate. The affair is complicated, since firms in aggregate produce hundreds of thousands of distinct items brought to consumers by myriad farmers, ranchers, traders, processors, and retailers, hyped by an enormous number of ads on television, in cyberspace, in newspapers and magazines, and with direct mailings and discount coupons. The dilemma: when sales promotion comes into conflict with good eating practices, promotion often wins.[78]

To sell more, food corporations create tastes, tweak recommendations of nutritionists and public health specialists, increase shelf life through additives, advertise, and manipulate the regulators. A Snickers candy bar, it turns out, is an impressive piece of design that keeps buyers coming back. "As we chew it, the sugar dissolves, the fat melts and the caramel traps the peanuts so the entire combination of flavors is blissfully experienced in the mouth at the same time."[79] Fast-food restaurants design other foods aiming for the "bliss point," with just the right combination of sugar, salt, and fat.[80] Eateries make locational choices to find the most customers, and the problem for city neighborhoods develops.

Food companies find themselves squeezed, pushed on one side by advocates for good food and on the other by shareholders,[81] so they adopt "voluntary self-regulation as the primary strategy."[82] They lobby, attack critics, promote healthy physical activity, and push state legislators to protect them from legal liability. A lawsuit against McDonald's for making someone obese is preposterous, yet the idea has sufficient traction so that twenty-three states had passed business protection laws by 2006.[83]

Marion Nestle writes that it is "difficult to know about the industry's behind-the-scenes efforts in Congress, federal agencies, courts, universities, and professional organizations to make diets seem a matter of personal choice rather than of deliberate manipulation."[84] Even the Academy of Nutrition and Dietetics (AND) has taken funds from food corporations and their lobbying fronts, such as the National Dairy Council. AND represents seventy-four thousand dietitians, generally among the strongest proponents of dietary improvements. Nevertheless, to one informed, critical observer, the annual AND conference worked like a "junk food Expo," with prominent displays offered by food, beverage, and restaurant firms, corporate booths, food giveaways, and other forms of persuasive publicity. A good number of AND's members accept food-corporation funding for their research, but keep it quiet. Nearly a quarter of the three hundred speakers at its 2012 meeting "had undisclosed financial ties to the food industry," having consulted with Sara Lee, Monsanto, McDonald's, Ocean Spray, Nestlé, Coca-Cola, Hershey's, Burger King, and others.[85] At least twenty-six speakers at that meeting were employees of food or pharmaceutical firms, and some sessions were sponsored by firms. A registered dietitian attending the meeting complained that one "session on children and beverages titled 'Kids are Drinking What?' was essentially an hour-long advertisement for milk."[86] Information on corporate connections was obscure, not provided in the program, except in notes at the back.

The corporate connections are sometimes not so subtle. The staff director of the Senate Agriculture Committee, appointed in early 2015, moved directly from being a senior lobbyist for PepsiCo, which produces the soft drink and also Cheetos and Lay's potato chips. PepsiCo lobbied furiously "to beat back local soda taxes and ensure that junk food remained available in schools." They even "requested the redefinition of a 'school day' so the company could continue to sell its sugary sports drinks at 'early morning sports practices.'"[87]

According to the Centers for Disease Control, "children are uniquely vulnerable to the effects of advertising."[88] Accordingly, to manipulate children to develop food habits (which they likely will carry over as they become adults), companies develop cartoon images like SpongeBob, sponsor TV shows, decorate cereal boxes, and invent entertainment characters like Ronald McDonald. Food corporations "spent approximately $870 million on marketing to children under the age of 11 and over $1 billion on marketing to adolescents" in 2006. Two-thirds of the spending promoted "carbonated beverages, breakfast cereals, and fast food restaurants," and the other third promoted "non-carbonated beverages, snack foods, and candy."[89] By contrast, the public-interest "5 a Day" campaign promoting fruits, vegetables, and grains operates on an annual budget of under $7 million, according to Yale University's Rudd Center for Food Policy and Obesity.[90] Many of the worst effects occur in poor neighborhoods and among minority populations.

As Simon shows, food firms push junk through regulatory loopholes to hit children with nonsense advertising, claiming "health benefits of even the most nutritionally bankrupt of foods." The food industry's own Children's Advertising Review Unit gives its blessing to absurd claims, "[overstating] the benefits of their self-serving, loophole-ridden marketing policies." Coca-Cola, for example, claims it doesn't market to children under age twelve; the company's own model guidelines recommend no sales in elementary schools; and Coke brags that it doesn't advertise on children's TV programs. But it *does* advertise on "mixed" shows (for children and adults), inserts thousands of product placements with its logo, puts its brand on toys, and, despite its own guidelines, permits sales in schools. In Kentucky, where 44 percent of *elementary* schools had vending machines, Coke "lobbied for four years running against state legislation designed to fix [the] problem."[91]

Food ties in with schools and with austerity, but in complicated ways. Whether Coke aimed its Kentucky lobbying effort at long-term brand allegiance or short-term sales revenues, or both, it found backing from school administrators, who find the income helpful to their budgets. Casting a broader net, we find that national sales of snack foods and beverages in schools are estimated to total $2.3 billion annually, and school districts themselves are estimated to earn $750 million from vending-machine sales alone.[92] These sorts of infiltrations, twisting the eating preferences and patterns of children, often target poor city populations.

School Food

Atop the revenues from school meals, the industry assigns high priority to long-term influence over taste buds, projecting future sales to older teenagers, young adults, and on. Although food firms subtly manipulate marketing, evade standards, avoid regulations, and sow confusion about requirements for good nutrition, they have cooperated powerfully with nutritionists to defend school programs.

So while ideological and budgetary hawks have attacked school-food programs for a long time, they have had limited success, losing repeatedly to alliances uniting such disparate groups as public health scientists and nutrition advocates, school administrators, factory farm operators and ranchers, small organic producers connected to local farmers' markets, and giant food and beverage corporations. President Ford wanted to cut the budget by converting the school lunch program to block grants, but without success. The Reagan administration cut "a whole host of programs serving poor and working-class families," but it proposed to cut lunch subsidies only "in the full price category—thus converting schools meals into just the sort of welfare program it was elsewhere attacking."[93]

More than a decade later, when conservatives won the Congress in the midterm elections of 1994, Newt Gingrich as House Speaker proposed his "Contract with America," with a provision to radically limit (or eliminate) school lunch subsidies, and conservatives repeated calls for block grants, to end "entitlement to breakfast, lunch, summer food, and child care meals." Nutrition advocates and others feared loss of the automatic expansions in times of economic downturn. They feared increased state-to-state inequalities. And they feared that local autonomy would shortchange hungry children. A giant coalition, including farmers who had been sparring with USDA on separate issues, once again saved the lunch program.[94]

Another decade along, the George W. Bush administration in 2004 pushed for "extensive income verification procedures that would almost certainly have denied free and reduced price meals to millions of eligible children," entire school populations in many big-city districts. Again, a diverse coalition won big enough to regard the 2004 Child Nutrition Reauthorization Act "as a great victory." The chief lobbyist for the Food Research and Action Center reports that this was the "only unanimous legislation" that congressional term approved by the House, the Senate, and ultimately the White House to provide "new federal funding to any of the human needs programs."[95] Despite these victories, from 1980 on, the fiscal squeeze has been "the constant preoccupation of most [school] food service directors."[96]

Public responses to the 2012 improvements in school food programs are curious. Protests against the improved dietary standards were organized to celebrate teenage cravings via school theater productions, on Facebook and Twitter mailings, and in various places, including suburbs outside Pittsburgh and Milwaukee, in western Kansas, and in Parsippany, New Jersey. A reporter for the *New York Times* put it this way: "Because the lunches must now include fruits and vegetables, those who clamor for more cheese-laden nachos may find string beans and a peach cup instead. Because of limits on fat and sodium, some of those who crave French fries get baked sweet-potato wedges. Because of calorie restrictions, meat and carbohydrate portions are smaller. Gone is 2-percent chocolate milk, replaced by skim." The improvements will have their greatest effect in schools with high proportions of poor students, but the commentary has been widespread. As a high school senior in Brooklyn said: "Before there was no taste and no flavor. Now, there's no taste, no flavor, and it's healthy, which makes it taste even worse."[97] Not so, says David L. Katz, the director of the Yale University Prevention Research Center and editor in chief of the journal *Childhood Obesity*:

> Taste buds are adaptable, and when children can't be with the foods they love, they can learn to love the new foods they are with, in as little as a couple of weeks. Time, then, is needed to know if there is genuine resistance to new school nutrition standards, or merely the inevitable and temporary resistance to change. . . . Either way, school nutrition would change more readily for the better if this were not only about cafeterias but also about culture. The job of changing the food demand—of making our children care about nutrition and health—resides not with our schools but with ourselves.[98]

One letter to the editor following the front-page stories said: "I'm having a hard time processing the complaints. Aside from the price of the meals, sympathizing with students is shortsighted and a breach of educational and parental duty. I don't *really* want to go to work, pay the rent, save for retirement or go to bed early, but my 4-year old *will* eat his broccoli." Another letter remembered an earlier era: "When I prepared dinner for my children, I would let them help me cut the peppers, mushrooms and broccoli and would tell them that they could have a taste as long as they didn't tell their brother or sister that I let them. That's all it took for those items to be special in our house."

In October 2012, when a Republican candidate for Congress in the small upstate New York city of Watertown ate a school lunch, the portions were too small. He said, "My campaign manager and I had to get a snack after lunch. I was only allowed two ketchup packets. Swear to God."[99] Kansas representative Tim Huelskamp (also a Republican), ignoring the fact that the USDA has been setting school lunch nutritional standards for decades, said, "I think decisions about the lunchrooms should be made . . . with the parents and the school district, not some bureaucrat in Washington."[100]

Hopeful Reforms

In cities across the nation, advocacy groups and city agencies are working with people in poor and minority neighborhoods to attract a grocery store or supermarket, build a farmers' market, encourage corner stores to stock better-quality fresh food, identify healthy fast-food retailers, change zoning and other land-use regulations to permit community and even rooftop gardens, and persuade transit agencies to establish good routes and schedules to out-of-neighborhood supermarkets and farmers' markets.[101] As of 2014, the website of the Association of Collegiate Schools of Planning provides access to twenty-seven college course syllabi dealing with these sorts of topics.[102] The examples of local changes that follow show a wide variety of city innovations in food and nutrition. These innovations are highly time-sensitive, as conditions in cities change year by year, and as the social learning curve moves from place to place.

Food Policy Councils, Community Gardens, and More

Alfonso Morales, professor of urban planning at the University of Wisconsin, documents advances in community food research, street vending, and good-food markets, as he promotes food systems for communities and regions.[103] Jason Corburn, professor of city planning at the University of California at Berkeley, in *Toward the Healthy City*, points to the founding of the San Francisco Food System of the Department of Public Health, or SFFS, which encourages community gardens and works to focus social service programs on food adequacy. Since food and nutrition problems concentrate in minority communities, one charge to the SFFS was to cope with racism. Food advocates at SFFS focus on "job training, business skill development, urban greening, farmland preservation and community revitalization and redevelopment," even extending to land ownership and control outside the city. They won improvements in transit, the early introduction of electronic food stamps, or EBTs, at the Alemany Farmers Market (electronic benefit transfers have since been adopted widely), a 15 percent increase in fresh produce at corner stores, and community involvement employing teenagers as survey interviewers.[104]

New York City has experimented with tax incentives and rezoning to attract grocery stores and to encourage existing stores to carry more fresh produce. Minneapolis passed a Food Code in 2012 to require every grocery store to offer at least five varieties of vegetables or fruits and at least two varieties of meat, poultry, fish, or vegetable proteins, two of bread or cereal, and two of dairy or substitutes. The idea is to prevent a grocery that does *not* provide these good foods from "occupying an area and preventing new businesses" from coming in.[105]

Food Justice movements try to reframe issues for farmers and for consumers. Food advocacy becomes political. As researchers in Buffalo write, "Pressure is increasing from nongovernmental actors to incorporate food . . . into municipal policies and plans."[106] Even when focused on "from below" (composting, community gardens, etc.), organizing can help shift power so as to provide help for vulnerable, food insecure populations, to encourage food advocacy.[107] For its report on food policy councils in 2009, discussed above, Food First found councils in sixty-five cities and counties or regions (typically centered on cities), supplemented by seventeen state councils.[108] The Harvard Food Law and Policy Clinic reports that there were 111 food policy councils by 2010 and 193 councils by 2012.[109] One of the first was in Knoxville, Tennessee, starting in 1982. Soon after, partly in response to a 1984–1985 effort of the U.S. Conference of Mayors, local food policy councils were established in the mid- to late-1980s in various cities, including Saint Paul, Syracuse, Philadelphia, Kansas City, and Charleston, SC.[110] By 2013 they seemed to be almost everywhere.

Philadelphia has been known as a city with high poverty, streets too unsafe for exercising, and high rates of obesity. Its Food Trust, founded in 1992, works to ensure "that everyone has access to affordable, nutritious food." It "works to improve the health of children and adults, promote good nutrition, increase access to nutritious foods, and advocate for better public policy." The Food Trust operates more than twenty-five farmers' markets across the metropolitan area, in the city and in suburban towns in both Pennsylvania and New Jersey, marketing food harvested on farms mostly within a sixty-mile radius of market. The markets accept WIC coupons for locally grown fruits and vegetables, and they accept EBTs, with a two-dollar "Philly Food Bucks" bonus coupon offered for every five dollars of food stamps spent. Philabudance, the region's largest food bank, opened the nonprofit Fair and Square supermarket in Chester, a poor, black community thirteen miles to the south.[111]

In growing numbers of cities, farmers and consumers of food have come together to form CSAs, community-supported agriculture ventures, in which community members become partners with farmers, arranging, sometimes collectively, for weekly delivery of fruits, vegetables, and often also meat, bakery goods, eggs, and other farm products. The advantage, especially to small producers, is a guaranteed income, earned even if bad weather destroys crops (drought or flood, for example). The advantages to households are regular delivery of farm-fresh, usually unadulterated food, possibly at a good discount, and various payment plans that usually accept food stamps. People's Grocery, in the East Bay (Oakland and other cities across from San Francisco), opened the Grub Box in 2009 to deliver fresh produce, eventually shifting operations to another group, Dig Deep Farms & Produce, a project of the Alameda County Deputy Sheriffs' Activities League. Dig Deep is a highly developed CSA that produces on a set of five farms, three on city parcels and two on nearby rural hillsides. Dig Deep packs and delivers throughout the area. Consumers can sign up for the entire season or year, but they can also make weekly decisions for produce boxes to feed from one to five persons for a week, ranging from ten dollars to twenty-five dollars (in early 2013).[112] Since 1995, Just Food has operated in New York City. It has helped develop more than one hundred CSA sites across the city, provides services to community gardens and farmers' markets, runs food education programs and workshops, works with the state's Hunger Prevention and Nutrition Assistance Program to support food pantries, and operates a two-year adult educational program at its Farm School, which offers individual courses and awards an Urban Agriculture Certificate.[113]

In Chicago, the mayor, concerned with the "crisis of the 'food deserts,'" met with the "leaders of six major grocery-store chains in 2011." Quicker change may come, instead, from nongovernmental and noncorporate organizations. One such group, called Food Desert Action, delivered fresh produce to some of Chicago's neediest neighborhoods using a mobile grocery store. Their operation, called "Fresh Moves," used a large bus donated by the transit authority and beautifully redesigned by Architecture for Humanity. Fresh Moves began working as a mobile grocery store in May 2011, originally making three stops, two days a week, with some of their produce furnished at a discount by Goodness Greeness, a supplier of organic foods, some purchased in more standard ways. In principle, food left over on the bus was donated to homeless shelters, but most everything sells, and only three months after the operation opened, high demand had already pushed the group to expand its operations.[114] (With the end of a one-off federal subsidy, the bus operation ceased late in 2013.) Also in Chicago, an organization called Growing Home "offers life and job skills training on three organic farms across the city to formerly incarcerated, homeless, and low-income individuals." Two-thirds of the participants in the program have moved on to full-time employment.[115]

In 2008 Michael Pollan called on the president-elect to appoint a farmer in chief.[116] Local action is more likely. When the City of Baltimore began to think seriously about its many food deserts, different city agencies and groups had been working toward different objectives: the Planning Department to improve grocery stores and accessibility, the Health Department to reduce obesity and cardiovascular disease and to improve nutrition, and elected officials to improve their constituents' quality of life. For each group, the "solution turned out to be exactly the same thing: access to healthy food."[117] In 2010 the city appointed a food policy director, funded by the philanthropic Baltimore Community Foundation.[118] The director is charged with improving access to fresh food by developing overall policies, promoting healthier shelves in grocery stores, establishing vegetable gardens in the city, and improving school foods. Baltimore cooperates with the Center for a Livable Future at Johns Hopkins University and receives funds from Kaiser Permanente, the Annie Casey Foundation, and others.[119]

In March 2010 Baltimore set up two experimental online grocery stores where shoppers can submit their orders from the public library, paying with cash, credit, or food stamps. "I pay with my charge card. They swipe it right here. I come back to the library tomorrow and they'll have it all bagged up and ready to go," said one shopper. Another shopper, "a single mother of three who works as a custodian," gets books from the library, and she says: "Fruit is fresh. The vegetables are fresh. I get the butchered meat and all. It's really good." The libraries are across town from one another, each in a food desert with some of the city's highest rates of death from diet-related health problems: "one neighborhood is mostly African-American and working-class, the other racially and economically mixed."[120] In another project, started in 2012, Baltimore connected city farms with corner markets to provide fresh vegetables. One of the farms "was once the neighborhood's retail hub, home to fish markets, cobblers and tailors. . . . But, as residents fled to the suburbs, the stores emptied out and became havens for drug dealers. The city razed the buildings about two decades ago, and a community garden and farm sprouted in their place."[121] The Baltimore food policy director hopes that a new zoning code will not only allow but also encourage more urban farming, to increase the supply of produce in the city.

Toronto has been a beehive of city food activity. Its Food Policy Council, now a subcommittee of the Board of Health, operates probably the premier city food program in North America, which emphasizes communications, capacity building, and public education.[122] In 1991 the Toronto Food Policy Council wrote its Declaration on Food and Nutrition, responding to more than a year's work done by the Food and Hunger Action Committee, or FHAC. Later the city council approved a program of grants for Food Access that allocated $2.4 million "for kitchen purchases in 180 schools and social agencies." In 2000, the FHAC published *Planting the Seeds*, providing "an inventory of food and hunger-related initiatives in which the City of Toronto is involved," as well as information from interviews with consultants and a set of recommendations. In 2001 the FHAC published *A Growing Season*, offering an "action plan" for food and hunger in Toronto. The focus in Toronto is on "equitable food access, urban agriculture, regional food self-reliance, 'fair trade,' 'buy local' and 'eco-label' products." The City of Toronto even established an executive position in its administration for a full-time director of the Food Policy Council, a line in the city budget.

School Food Improvements

In many school kitchens "real cooking" equipment is worn out, discarded, or mothballed. Staff members don't know how to use tools like slicers, and they don't have "basic knife skills." Skilled cooks have been "replaced by less-skilled food service assistants, many of whom, like their young customers, are full-fledged citizens of the fast food nation." They are used to microwaved meals and drive-thru windows. "They don't know how to cook; they don't know how to operate the machinery. We're hiring them because they are breathing."[123] And, of course, they can be paid less.

But the time may be right for a turnaround. Despite the continuous pressure from giant food businesses, there are signs of a spreading resistance. Some advocates express optimism. Anxious about the health risks of obesity, parents and school personnel have begun to work with nutritionists and food activists "in demanding better, healthier meals. And we know how to provide them; exemplary programs abound. . . . Our choice is between doing a better job now or paying much more later for medical care."[124] Across the country, schools and districts have been experimenting with lunch programs and beyond.[125] Administrators, cafeteria staff, parents, teachers, and the children take part. Some schools make arrangements with nearby small farmers; others grow their own food. Some sell school-produced food in the community. Many make curricular changes to accompany new approaches to food and nutrition.

In the Troy Howard Middle School in the small city of Belfast, Maine, population sixty-seven hundred, the teachers talked the authorities into converting a gravel bed slated to become a bus garage into a garden, making topsoil from seaweed, local farm manure, yard waste collected by city crews, and lunchroom table scraps. The first year, 2001, students harvested "80 varieties of vegetables, including onions, Savoy cabbage, peppers, and multiple varieties of tomatoes," nearly all from Maine-purchased seeds. They planted in spring and harvested in fall. They received a grant to build a greenhouse, but worried about the cost of fuel for nighttime heating, so later they built three hoop houses that don't need heating. Half the school's 150 seventh graders work in the garden as the core of their academic program, along with a few from other grades. The food/garden core accounts for about 90 percent of seventh-grade social studies, 30 percent of art, and 20 percent of math, language arts, and science. Each student is an "employee" in the Compost, the Seed, or the Garden Stand group. The program now supplies fresh food for all Belfast's schools, donates to the local soup kitchen, sells produce and seed at its own farm stand, and runs a "restaurant" that sells pizza made almost entirely from locally grown ingredients. The children get their business plan checked by the investment officer of a local bank, and they break even, except for the salary of one teacher. They take pains not to compete with local farmers, who provide help in various ways. A key teacher in the project says, "One hundred percent of the kids eat vegetables without prompting."[126]

Eight of the top ten obesity states are in the South, where school-food alternatives are particularly important, as poverty goes together with fried chicken, biscuits, and gravy. To combat obesity and to expand their incomes, a group of African American farmers outside Tallahassee started a collaborative that now involves between sixty and a hundred farmers for farm-to-school programs that combine healthy food with nutrition education. Their group, the New North Florida Cooperative, provides income to farmers and delivers fresh produce to over a million students in more than seventy school districts in Florida, Georgia, Alabama, Mississippi, and Arkansas. Needs for change meshed: farmers wanted timely payments and a system to deliver their crops in good condition; schools needed dependable delivery of high-quality crops like collards, cabbage, peas, butterbeans, and sweet potatoes, the right amount, on time, and not too costly. Co-op members cut, chop, bag, and refrigerate their produce, guaranteeing high quality, saving the school districts money, and improving diets. Students visit farms on programs run by the farmers. Nationwide, farm-to-school programs have caught on. By 2009, there were more than nine thousand schools, in all fifty states, that participated in one form or another.[127]

Riverside County, an outer suburb of giant Los Angeles, has a population 46 percent Latino, 7 percent African American, and 7 percent Asian.[128] More than half (53 percent) of the forty-three thousand students come from at-risk homes. Two-thirds buy lunch at school, and much of what they buy is at the salad bar. The idea came along with a food director, Rodney Taylor, when he shifted his job from the affluent Santa Monica–Malibu district, where an active parent had prodded him to try a farm-fresh salad bar in a two-week summer child care class. Taylor was sure it would not work, but now says, "When I walked in the first day and saw the youngsters grabbing food off the salad bar, I was changed forever. I didn't even need to go back the next day." In Riverside, Taylor's new program received start-up grants, talked farmers into discounting sales for a pilot project, and encouraged PTAs at the district's better-off schools to contribute funds for the first two years. Parents volunteered to work, cutting up the fruit and vegetables into small pieces for small children. The salad bars now compete with pizza and sloppy joes served at the school cafeterias and just about break even, selling not only to the schoolchildren, but also to teachers, Meals on Wheels, small private schools, nonprofits, and business firms.[129]

School-food changes even involve class schedules and lunch times. A study by Western Washington University found that elementary students who ate lunch *after* recess, rather than before, ate more fruit, vegetables, and milk, wasted 30 percent less food (by weight), and consumed 14 percent more iron, 35 percent more calcium, and 13 percent more vitamin A. In Berkeley, California, the well-off inner suburb across the bay from San Francisco, adjacent to Oakland, the John Muir Elementary School involves in its garden children attending kindergarten through fifth grade, and it teaches classes in a cooking room. The school rescheduled lunch to come after recess and extended the lunch period by ten minutes. The teachers were highly skeptical and resisted both innovations, but in the end they were enthusiastic about "integrating the curriculum around food, health culture, and the environment," to the point of volunteering on their own time for the planning team.[130]

Resistance

"Good nutritional advice is notoriously complicated and hard to follow, isn't it?" an interviewer once asked Marion Nestle. Nestle replied, "No, it's not complicated. It's simple; eat more fruit and vegetables, and don't eat too much. And be active and don't smoke."[131]

Locally initiated improvement in food policy, to promote fruit and vegetables and slow down fast foods in neighborhoods and schools, is cause for optimism, but better policies will have most effect if eventually they cause changes in national pricing, taxing, and subsidy structures. It should be cause for optimism that some 350 food co-ops operate today as viable alternatives to corporate food, as Anne Meis Knupfer argues in her enthusiastic history, yet she warns that the recession harmed "financially fragile fledgling cooperatives," forcing some to close.[132] Hundreds of communities now have food policy councils. City governments have moved to promote better nutrition, to nudge restaurants into offering healthier options, and to improve access and encourage markets to sell fresher food and more fruits and vegetables. Municipal and consumer support has grown for markets that sell produce from local and smaller farms. Administrators, school-teachers, and parents have become more active on food issues, teaching children about better nutritional options, involving children in growing crops and preparing meals, and organizing to purchase locally not only to provide fresh foods but also to support area farms. Nevertheless, consider-able evidence suggests that very high obstacles may stand in the way of further local change.

One obstacle arises with racial and class boundaries. A food activist wrote about the tension in her work in Rochester, New York, where "most of the good-food movement people are white and upper-middle class." Helping to run a 99 percent white volunteer-led program in 80 per-cent black communities, she says, "It's troubling."[133] Co-ops selling nutritious food, even when offering discounts keyed to income, have problems attracting poor or minority customers, although Malik Yakini, director of the Detroit Black Community Food Security Network, reports success based on "good will from its previous projects."[134]

The *Good Laws, Good Food* handbook put out by the Harvard Law School displays the sort of optimism that many of our examples have illustrated. The handbook can indeed be used in practice, as its authors propose, as a legislative, regulatory "toolkit" to assist food activists, food councils, and local policy makers. At the same time, the handbook can be interpreted pessimistically, even in the absence of concerns about race, as it provides evidence of structural limitations. Federal and especially state prerogatives normally delimit local legislation and regulatory options. "Local governments do not have any power except that given to them by the state. . . . States almost always have ultimate authority over local governments . . . [and] state laws play a significant role in local areas."[135]

Judge John Dillon of the Iowa Supreme Court early in the nineteenth century recognized that the Constitution provides no powers to local governments. Thus, the so-called Dillon's Rule, "still relevant today, holds that local governments have only those powers that are expressly given to them by the state." "*Home Rule*, on the other hand, is a broad grant of power from the state that allows municipalities to independently handle local matters without the need for special legislation by the state, as long as the municipal laws do not conflict with state laws."[136] State by state, the tension between these two principles is worked out in legal and political practice. The general rule is that local governments are persistently subordinated to the wishes of state executives and legislatures. That local subordination is expressed either by state constitutions, broad legislative pronouncements, or particular state laws.

State preemption of local laws poses significant restraint on food reform, and federal powers pose additional restraint. As the Harvard handbook points out, different levels of government play special roles in a number of food areas. On food safety, the federal FDA recommends but does not impose safety provisions for restaurants and stores, it regulates the processing of meat and poultry, and it exercises some authority over food recalls. State governments implement food safety laws, mainly on the model of the FDA food code. Although some local governments have their own food safety ordinances, they mostly enforce *state* laws. *Land-use and zoning* regulations, which can, for example, affect the location of grocery stores, are usually delegated by states to localities, but federal court decisions have set powerful guidelines. Rules governing *geographic preference in food procurement*, such as giving an advantage to local or regional farms in their bidding for school-lunch provision, must follow federal guidelines when federal funds are used, and otherwise generally must follow state law. Rules for *food labeling* vary. Federal rules apply to ingredient and nutrition labeling for packaged foods shipped across state lines as well as for chain restaurants and vending machines. States may set labeling rules for non-chain restaurants, and they may require other labeling information (for example, Alaska requires that farm-raised salmon products be labeled). Local governments may require labeling in restaurants, but their authority has been contested. *Food assistance benefits*, as we have seen, are provided almost exclusively by the federal government, or by private charities.

Different local interest groups navigate this hodgepodge of rules and regulations differently—via nongovernmental organizations, changes in local laws, even the appointment of a food policy director, perhaps creating a relatively autonomous and powerful city food agency.

On the other side of the equation, business resistance to change continues. Restaurant associations resist local laws and regulations by promoting "legislation at the state level. States like Florida, Alabama and Utah have statutes that reserve for the state the authority to set rules that individual restaurants have to live by." Sometimes, the ground shifts. After the City of Cleveland banned the use of trans fats by restaurants, in April 2011, as part of its "Healthy Cleveland" program, the Ohio Senate reacted They amended the state budget to *prohibit municipal regulation* of ingredients used by fast-food restaurants. Such state legislative action is well within normal bounds. But then lawyers for the City of Cleveland discovered that the amendment had been written by the lobbyist for the Ohio Restaurant Association and sent by e-mail to the state's department of agriculture. The lobbyist had written that this sort of local regulation "is exactly what we want to pre-empt with the attached amendment." The offending e-mail was exactly what food advocates needed. Cleveland foodies had their day, as another state court reversed the decision, finding the preemption unconstitutional.[137]

In other states, food-related decisions have gone differently. The pattern of outcomes will be known only after more years pass. While New York City, San Francisco, and Chicago have instituted rather strict reforms, imposing requirements for posting salt and sugar content, the Arizona legislature prohibited local governments from limiting the use of fast-food consumer incentives like giveaway toys.[138]

Nearly all parties who take an objective, informed overview—medical researchers, nutrition specialists, the Centers for Disease Control, children's advocates, and the many scholars cited above—raise concerns about deep structural issues. As long as powerful food business firms, in pursuit of their own understandable objectives, exert disproportionate influence over federal tax, spending, and regulatory policies, then small producers, local producers, and—most of all—fresh food producers face a steep uphill journey. Under those conditions, even the best and strongest local food achievements will encounter continuing obstacles.[139]

As an illustration of the broad reach of such conflicts, consider the proposed settlement of the Greek financial crisis. Greece has long required that milk stay on grocery shelves no more than five days—so Greeks enjoy tasty, fresh milk. Western European milk suppliers seizing the moment demanded that Greece loosen its regulations, to allow their cheaper and less tasty but longer-lasting milk to compete on those shelves.[140]

Three central obstacles stand opposed to the progressive changes that would be particularly helpful to people in poor city neighborhoods, Nestle points out. The big food companies lobby powerfully, carrying their influence into Congress and to state legislators and regulators. Research universities operate with bias, accepting heavy funding by big agriculture, food corporations, and government agencies under the same influence. And powerful advertising influences us all, much of it especially aimed at children, minorities, and poor people. The food industry contributes positively to our lives in important ways and makes it inexpensive and convenient to meet biological food needs. Taken all together, it is true that industry activities have come close to eliminating (in the United States) the problem of hunger, but they have led to the problem of getting either too much food or too many bad foods, or both. Because food companies must get people to buy more of their products but not their competitors' products, the companies pay huge advertising and political lobbying fees just to keep going. These activities are supported by public policies. Thus at its base, sound nutrition policy, which should be "eat less," would contradict the food industry's whole system.

To create the conditions in which we can solve city problems, Americans will have to tackle food and nutrition, along with austerity, school inequality, and drugs. To be sure, nutritional maladies in cities originate far "upstream" and involve high-level federal, corporate, and research establishment power. They also arise from down-home, long-enjoyed personal and cultural preferences. As such, they come to be deeply imbedded and often well hidden in our ways of life. Food and nutrition issues are key elements of many aspects of urban life, so their solutions must come in good measure as parts of a revived, reconsidered urban policy. The daily news is salted and peppered with examples of progress—as I write we learn that the consumption of added sugar is down, mainly because people, especially children, chug down fewer soft drinks. Tentative results are good: reduced obesity, reduced illness. The pressure for change has come mainly from cities. The good results will be gradual, and they may be self-reinforcing.

6

DRUGS, PRISONS, AND NEIGHBORHOODS

In earlier chapters I described how cities suffer from budgetary austerity, lack of support for schools, and conflicts with corporate goals about food. Flawed policies lack fairness in each area, causing expansion of inequality and holding cities back from their potentials. Weak cities then damage their metropolitan areas, harming the economy and spreading social discord. Often, however, the sources of these inequality, schooling, and food problems remain obscure. Even at the city level, the damages can be diffuse, and the connections indirect, making it difficult to connect the dots. The combined effects of poverty, racial animus, and municipal fragmentation obscure the problematic policies that block needed reforms.[1] Yet each of these issues, we have seen, should constitute a key part of urban policy.

The drug war is different, with dramatic, evident effects. Those who enforce drug laws attack inner-city neighborhoods directly, drastically disrupting the lives of poor black and Latino residents. Cities at their best are highly productive and just, but the drug war powerfully undercuts that potential. It discourages diversity, fairness, and democracy. It reduces social, technological, and economic innovation. Solid arguments demand the inclusion of drug issues as part of urban policy.

As I will show in the next chapter, the drug war is different in another way. As public policy, it contradicts the broad conservative push for urban austerity, while at the same time exacerbating the need for public expenditure. For decades, public spending on the drug war and closely associated prison operations has constituted a major growth industry. And yet, much like defense spending, drug-war spending is supported most strongly by those who otherwise favor austerity. Growing segments of the public have come to question the drug war and the prison-industrial complex, and modest changes have begun, but there remains a very long way to go.

Why Have a Drug War?

Drug war and prison issues overlap unavoidably, but instructively. Since the surge in drug arrests and imprisonment that began almost simultaneously in the 1980s, prison issues have taken on a life of their own. Even as evidence mounts about wrongful convictions, political leaders are only beginning to notice the most horrific of prison conditions. Solitary confinement is commonplace, standard practice in so-called supermax prisons. In Pelican Bay State Prison in California, prisoners are kept twenty-three hours or more each day in a cell measuring 7.7 feet by 11.6 feet without windows, the only view out through 2,220 perforations in a steel door, to a blank wall. Ernesto Lira spent *eight years* in such a cell. He had been stopped in his car ostensibly for a hairline crack in the windshield and then charged with transporting three grams of methamphetamine wrapped in foil. Sentenced to eleven years (he had been in jail before), he was incorrectly categorized as a gang member by prison authorities. A federal court later ruled that he was wrongfully convicted on unreliable evidence, but his life had already been destroyed. More than three thousand California prisoners are kept in solitary confinement, often for many years.[2]

Our focus begins before prison, mainly on poor neighborhoods in relatively large cities, but it will necessarily shift from neighborhoods to prisons, and back, just as so many prisoners do. Even when prisons are located far from the neighborhoods, in distant rural areas, they function in many ways as integral parts of neighborhoods, their economies, and their social lives.

The drug war helps fill prisons mainly with black and Hispanic men arrested in and removed from city neighborhoods.[3] Governments imprison people for many reasons other than drug violations, but starting about 1980 the intensive, selective enforcement of drug laws pushed like a mainspring to expand what has become a gargantuan U.S. population of prisoners, former prisoners, and their kin.[4] It is odd to think of the so-called "correctional institutions" that now speckle the American rural landscape as extensions of city neighborhoods, but in many ways, that is what they are.

The overall system of federal, state, and local prisons and jails exerts a militarized political influence not only inside the lockups but also far outside the walls. Jutting out from the prison tree, thick branches cast shadows over many city neighborhoods. Prisons and these neighborhoods have become part of the complex military-industrial-congressional arrangement that President Eisenhower wanted to warn about in his 1961 farewell address.[5]

U.S. prisons and jails constitute the largest penal system in the world, holding more than 2.3 million men, women, and children in hundreds of institutions. Another five million persons exist on probation or parole. After many decades with rates low and steady, the numbers rose drastically from the early 1970s until about 2006. Figure 6.1 counts prisoners,

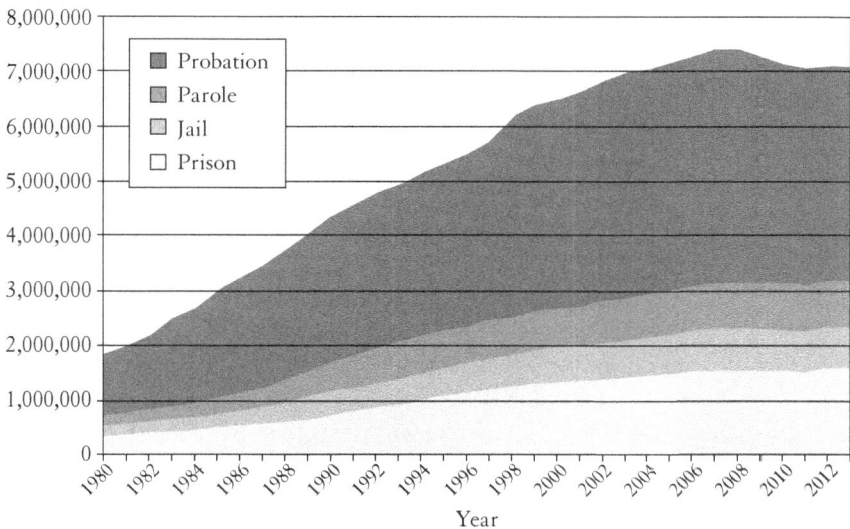

Figure 6.1. Rising incarceration rates, 1980–2013. Data from *Sourcebook of Criminal Justice Statistics* (1980–2011) published by the Hindelang Criminal Justice Research Center, University at Albany, SUNY; Glaze and Kaeble 2014.

parolees, and those on probation from 1980 to 2013.[6] Many released prisoners live in the same inner-city neighborhoods in which they were arrested, where the families of most prisoners and parolees live. Prisoners move in a dreary cycle from neighborhood to prison and back again. Millions of people who do *not* reside in impoverished neighborhoods and are not confined by the prison system are nevertheless part of it. They work either as public employees or for private local businesses, national firms, or global corporations tied economically to prisons. Together, these many millions of people form an entangled community of sorts, with its majority trapped in cities, subjugated whether intentionally or not by others who seek moral satisfaction, profits, job security, or local economic development. They form part of a system that relies on physical repression, poverty, racial bias, and severe limits on opportunity.[7]

The drug war has been a key element in the growth of this neighborhood-prison "community," "a major factor in the construction of the carceral state."[8] To understand the connection, one must consider a key distinction between the drug trade and the drug war. In depressed neighborhoods, the drug *trade* serves as a key business, albeit highly risky. The drug *war*, including the illicit drug trade, introduces violence. The *trade* creates local jobs and income, but at the same time it brings danger and stress. On the highly dubious positive side, drug dealers provide jobs for youth, spend money on local business, and support some community activities. But of course the negatives overwhelm these small positives. The violence and disruption associated with the illicit drug trade destroy communities. Gangs can constitute informal governments and rule through violence. When police enter to enforce drug laws, they undergird the violence and also function as the main conduit from neighborhood to prison. The coexistence of a sometimes-thriving drug economy with neighborhood violence brings bad news not only for the suffering residents and the damaged local economy but also for people in the broader society and economy. The difficulties spread out not only to surrounding city neighborhoods but also to the metropolitan areas and the nation. The worst effects result not from drug use nor even from drug marketing, but in the ruin of neighborhoods attacked by drug prohibition itself.

By comparison with other city-damaging policies, the drug war stands out. Damages to cities and city residents from poor schools, insufficient nutrition, or, say, mismanagement of immigration, appear over time and indirectly. Those who ought to legislate and administer better policies can shift the blame. In the case of the drug war, however, given the evident and pronounced nature of the harms caused, officials and war hawks find it difficult to evade responsibility, so they need to offer strong justification, which they do by way of asserting that the war works, claiming such dramatic reduction of drug use that the benefits outweigh the costs.

Crime fighters find it self-evident that when they put a stop to selling and street use, they either reduce drug use or at least stem its growth. Politicians and pundits call meaninglessly for a "drug free society," ignoring not only tobacco and alcohol, but also abusive and theoretically illegal drugging by prescription.[9] Assertions that the benefits of the drug war outweigh the costs are highly questionable: these claims generally overestimate the extent to which drug use would expand in the absence of the drug war and underestimate or ignore the extremely high costs of the war.

Scholarly studies of drug use are more cautious, even though conclusions vary widely. At one end of the spectrum, in an excellent popular summary, published in 2011, of studies of the drug war and drug use, three experts, professors of public policy—Mark Kleiman, codirector of the Rand Corporation's Drug Policy Research Center, Jonathan Caulkins, and Angela Hawken—assert that more permissive legislation would lead to dangerously increased drug use. They point out correctly that because no country permits *fully* "free legal commerce in cannabis, cocaine, heroin, or methamphetamine," we cannot know whether or by how much drug use would increase if legal commerce were to be permitted. Their 2011 book *Drugs and Drug Policy* offers no quantitative estimate of the likely increase in the use of drugs were the war to cease. Yet they pose the question in a greatly exaggerated way. What, they ask, would happen "if the level of abuse . . . were to quadruple or quintuple—results that cannot be ruled out based on any knowledge currently available"?[10] Kleiman and his colleagues are correct to warn that we do not know how much change legalization will bring, but their warning sounds tendentious.

To scientifically estimate potential effects, one must compare today's situation, in which prohibition is the law, with the alternative, in which drug use would be permitted. Such a "social experiment" would be difficult to undertake. An adequate comparison would require large changes, introducing not only drug legalization in some form, but also new regulatory controls. In roughly comparable situations, however, some localities and even countries *have* greatly liberalized drug use under restricted conditions, with evidence extending over a number of years. By mid-2015, in twenty-three states medical marijuana is legal; Washington, Colorado, Oregon, Alaska, Maryland, and Delaware have authorized or decriminalized recreational marijuana; and discussion proceeds in other states. During Prohibition (which made production, trade, and sale of alcohol illegal in the United States), consumption levels changed, allowing (in theory) comparison of before with after. Regulations have changed for dangerous substances other than illicit drugs and alcohol, namely tobacco and prescription medications, also offering contrasting experiences. Analysis of all these cases, each of which can be seen as a highly constrained social experiment, allows the uncertainty to be narrowed.

In contrast to the views expressed in *Drugs and Drug Policy*, most drug-war scholars doubt that making drugs illegal causes much reduction in use, if any at all. Most scholars venture that liberalization would not open the gates to floods of drugs. The Global Commission on Drug Policy, in its report *War on Drugs*, concludes from evidence on liberal policies in several European cities that "decriminalization initiatives do *not* result in significant increases in drug use"[11] Because changes in policy are limited in scope, evidence one way or the other is necessarily incomplete and inconclusive.

Whatever the future of drug *use*, the current drug *war* has strong downsides—this conclusion is not seriously disputed. Multibillion-dollar costs burden public budgets. The war destroys communities. The nation faces a pervasive incarceration regime, fueled in good part by the drug war. Pronounced racial bias permeates prison administrations and the neighborhoods of released prisoners. Many people have suffered "civil death," living imprisoned beyond prisons, suffering from probation restrictions, barriers to employment, and other limits on citizenship.[12] The domestic society has become notably more militarized, and international relations suffer. Given these negatives, advocates and supporters would be able to make a case *for* the war only by showing that it achieves at least its principal objective, the reduction of drug use. This they cannot do. Weighing the certain damages against doubtful achievements, most social scientists, economists, legal experts, historians, and independent observers are firm. They judge the drug war to be a failure.

In the face of these almost overwhelmingly negative judgments, why does such a strategy persist? Two plausible answers are available. The first answer is familiar from earlier chapters: the direct and visible damages of the drug war mainly burden cities. They burden the poor. They burden African Americans most, Latinos next, and poor immigrants. They burden, especially, city neighborhoods and inner suburbs where darker-skinned and poorer people live. Elected authorities, and the voters who elect them, have been largely exempt, experiencing no fallout in *their* neighborhoods. Few influential groups need consider the heavy damages to troubled neighborhoods.

The second answer to the question—Why does such a failed strategy persist?—is that various groups make use of the war to satisfy their own institutional, financial, and ideological interests. People in these groups are not poor, for the most part they are not dark skinned, and they are not residents of poor city neighborhoods. Local firms provide jail supplies. Major corporations manufacture and sell goods, from prison food to paramilitary equipment. Guards and their unions, specialized federal agencies, construction companies, operators of private prisons, arms manufacturers and dealers, and money-laundering banks benefit from the drug war. Voters in many rural communities are sustained by prison construction and operation. Voters in other depressed communities hope for such sustenance. Each of these parties stands to lose influence and income with fewer prisoners.

Politicians at all levels—with notable exceptions—support the war in recognition of the power of the myths that surround the evils of drug addiction and drug marketing—addicts and dealers are bad people, who deserve punishment, who should be removed from society. The war isolates "them," delivers retribution, and signifies moral outrage focused on cities. The war stigmatizes a segment of society, a social element that people see as an enemy. Only an unusually brave or well-situated active politician speaks the full truth about the drug war. At its root, the war on drugs works as the ultimate antiurban policy, an attack on poor residents of color in inner-city neighborhoods.[13]

Drugs and Booze

Prohibition offers many parallels. Drugs and alcohol support substantial economic sectors, where manufacture and distribution generate sizable profits. Where politicians once could reap rewards by taking a moral or community-safety stance in opposition to drinking, now they can oppose drugs. Prohibition created battle-zone damages, but it was never so vigorously prosecuted, and finally it was repealed. The drug war creates worse damages, is vigorously prosecuted, and persists.

The alternatives to the drug war are similar to the alternatives that replaced Prohibition: expansion of medical treatment and social support for addicts, substantial rehabilitation programs for addicts and their families and communities, and decriminalization of drug use accompanied by licensing and restrictions. Many critics move one major step further, to legalization accompanied by strict regulation and deterrence. That step would make the situation for drugs parallel to the current situation with alcohol, legal but tempered by high taxation and warnings akin to the antitobacco warnings, greatly reducing violence and neighborhood destruction.

The Alcohol Business versus the Drug Business

Alcoholism and drug addiction—via alcoholics and addicts—impose heavy burdens on families, communities, health care systems, and public budgets. About this parity there is little dispute. The drug war, however, imposes two additional, and heavy, burdens. The first is the vast increase in the imprisoned population, which we have noted and will return to below. The second burden arises because the *business* end of the drug industry is markedly different from the business end of today's alcoholic beverage industry.

For a start, the drug business offers a considerable local economic benefit, however contradictory that benefit may be. In cities of any substantial size, the liquor trade mostly sends neighborhood money out, to liquor store owners who live in the suburbs or out of the area, and to distributors, manufacturers, and tax authorities. The drug trade also sends money out, to suppliers, shippers, and manufacturers. In contrast, however, the drug trade brings outside money into the neighborhood, some of which goes to residents, for payrolls and local profits. Furthermore, whereas neighborhood liquor stores sell almost exclusively to walk-in local customers, drug merchants sell mainly to drive-in outsiders. In this sense the drug business, for the poor neighborhood, performs as a successful city export industry, providing jobs for unskilled workers, in theory just the sort of enterprise many advocates of neighborhood economic development favor.

Although in other ways the street-corner drug trade looks economically much like the trade of liquor stores, officials regulate the two activities differently as aspects of land use. When planners and neighborhood activists consider neighborhood alcohol issues, they aim to break up concentrations of liquor stores, which not only reflect the troubled lives of residents but also feed the troubles. Thus zoning codes may prohibit issuance of a permit for the location of a liquor store near one that exists, or in a school zone. However, when *drug* sales concentrate in vicinity, the regulatory responsibility and authority fall not on city planners, but on the police. In the alcohol case, the policy is to disperse sales points or prohibit sales in school zones. In the drug case, the policy is to arrest the merchants. Although even when located far from others a liquor store may have negative influence, as it takes money out of the area and injects fuel for irresponsibility and misconduct, still the individual store is not taken as a problem for public policy to solve. If public officials concern themselves with liquor stores at all, they spend little time worrying about problems of drinking, and city councils do not discuss the litter of beer bottles. Yet officials do worry about street-market drug "stores," they worry about problems of "using," and they discuss evidence like the litter of discarded needles.

In a second way, the drug business differs from today's alcoholic beverage business. While outsiders typically own liquor stores, city residents typically own neighborhood retail drug businesses. Most often, African Americans have what some call an "ethnic lock." In some neighborhoods, Latinos exercise local dominance. The pattern is normal. Earlier ethnic locks and related "identity politics" (some persisting today) involved Irish cops in Boston, Jewish schoolteachers in New York City, local restaurateurs in ethnic neighborhoods, or midwestern WASP men as bankers, business owners, and U.S. senators. In the case of drugs, this sort of monopoly of the neighborhood trade in black and Latino enterprises takes on great significance for the economy and for politics.[14]

Minority dominance of the neighborhood retail business, however, does not translate into minority preponderance in *purchasing* or *use*. Minority users exercise no monopoly on drug use. Contrary to what appears in highly visible street selling, and in newspapers, newsmagazines, television, and movies, however, African Americans do not depend upon, use, or abuse drugs at higher levels than whites. Getting accurate information on consumption of an illegal substance is tricky, but surveys tend to give consistent results, showing very little racial or ethnic difference in rates. "There's a perception among many individuals that African Americans as a group—regardless of socioeconomic status—tend to abuse or use drugs at higher rate," says Duke University researcher Dan Blazer, but his national samples, when controlled for socioeconomic status, show that blacks have lower drug-use rates, 5 percent, compared to 9 percent for whites and 7.7 percent for Hispanics.[15] Another national study, published in the *Archives of General Psychiatry*, revealed that despite having more opportunities to use drugs, African American adolescents have lower rates of use than white adolescents.[16] Figure 6.2 presents data from the standard national survey on drug use. The survey includes adults and adolescents and does *not* control for income, education, or any other relevant

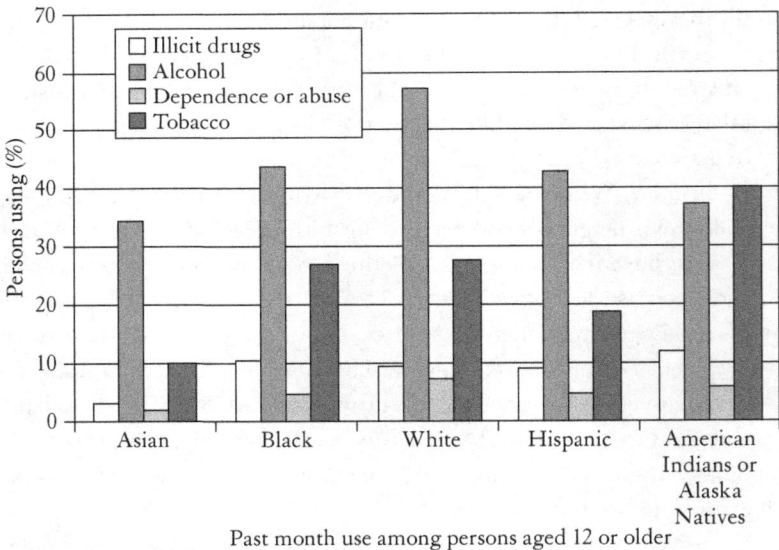

Past month use among persons aged 12 or older

Figure 6.2. Substance use or abuse of by race/ethnicity, 2013. The terms "dependence" and "abuse" indicate high levels of drug abusing or drinking, i.e., likely addiction or alcoholism. For illicit drugs, alcohol, and tobacco, data from Substance Abuse and Mental Health Services Administration 2014. For heavy alcohol use, data from Substance Abuse and Mental Health Services Administration 2008.

difference.[17] Drug-use rates are low for Asian Americans, high for Native Americans and Alaska Natives, and grouped at about 9 to 10 percent for black, Hispanic, and white Americans. For comparison, the table also shows widely varying rates of tobacco use. For drug *addiction*, together with *alcoholism*, the third column shows highest rates for whites.[18] Applying these rates to the varied population sizes, we see that the vast majority of U.S. drug users (and abusers), just over 70 percent, are white.

Illegality

This difference between drugs and alcohol is key: alcohol is regulated, but drugs are prohibited. The enforcement mechanism is the drug war, prosecuted with bias. Three men elected president, twice each—Bill Clinton, George W. Bush, and Barack Obama—admitted they had smoked marijuana, breaking the law. In middle-class suburbs, central business districts, and high-end restaurants, authorities tend to ignore even flagrant evidence. Police and prosecutors, who decide whom to arrest, what charges to levy, and what sentences to request, focus instead on targeted wholesalers, a certain class of retailers, and users in select neighborhoods.

Authorities thus fight the drug war in run-down minority neighborhoods, inflicting massive "collateral" damages. The authorities take down drug lawbreakers by real war, not like the federal War on Poverty, where authorities use words and budgets, and not like local zoning wars, where planners use public meetings and zoning regulations to thin out liquor stores. The war on drugs is fought with troops in uniforms. They carry weapons, ride in attack vehicles, engage in battle, and send people to prison. The warriors who fight against drug traffic in poor neighborhoods are not rogues. They operate with popular support. The war generates its own internal growth dynamic, enriches profiteers, and demonizes an enemy. One tactic is to stop and then search pedestrians, who when told to empty their pockets sometimes reveal traces of drugs. In New York City in 2011 the police conducted more than 685,000 such "stop-and-frisk" operations, 87 percent involving blacks or Latinos. In the end hardly any of the persons stopped were prosecuted and convicted.[19]

By stretching, one can imagine a strict alcohol Prohibition in effect today with legislation declaring the liquor business as well as liquor itself to be illegal—thus prohibiting the manufacture, shipping, wholesaling, retailing, purchasing *and possession* of wine, beer, and hard liquor. Jack Daniels and Anheuser-Busch would go underground or ship from overseas. Bars would shut their (front) doors, spend a percentage to entertain top officials, judges, and local cops, raise their prices to cover the extra expenses, and serve stronger drinks (which provide a higher profit margin) to recoup costs. With no recourse to the courts to enforce contracts, bar owners would hire hoodlums rather than lawyers. Restaurant owners would undertake similar initiatives, paying off authorities, raising prices, stiffening alcohol content, and hiring goons to threaten violence. Microbreweries would stop helping with neighborhood social and economic revivals; pubs or bars would no longer serve as friendly gathering places after the factory whistle or the Wall Street closing. To drink at home, people would be forced to patronize criminal dealers, pay premiums, risk low-quality or adulterated drinks, lower their window shades, and do without favorite brands. Worst of all, neighborhood residents, particularly those living near entertainment zones or clandestine liquor distributions points, would have to protect themselves on the streets against the dangers that surround bootleggers. They would also have to insulate their homes against random shooting in drive-by attacks and also to avoid the authorities, if not actively fear them. Police departments would seize personal assets for forfeiture, including cash, electronic equipment, automobiles, and real estate, by conducting legal raids on selected households where people who own valuable property might be caught with alcohol.[20]

This fantasy of alcoholic beverage control enforcement even tougher than Prohibition mimics the drug war. The drug war costs tens of billions of dollars annually. It makes already poor and underserved neighborhoods worse off. The war does not diminish drug traffic to any notable degree; it just shifts it around. Among its other bad effects, the war inhibits local economic development. Because legitimate firms cannot make, ship, sell, or possess drugs legally, illegal business firms take over at all levels, from agricultural production, processing, and manufacture, to overseas and domestic shipping, to wholesale and retail marketing. In afflicted neighborhoods, where sellers meet consumers in evident concentration, street gangs often dominate. In the most depressed areas, gangs may be among the larger employers in the area, their jobs going to high school dropouts and others with few good options. The jobs come, however, with life-threatening danger and no security. Job choices shrink still further because the illegal trafficking truncates social life, cuts off normal access to other neighborhoods, inhibits effective community policing, and stunts politics.

Nearly all the most troublesome effects in the neighborhoods come not from drug sales or use, but from their illegality. Battles occur occasionally with the police and more often among rival distribution "firms." In afflicted neighborhoods the drugs, just like alcohol, feed irresponsibility, but with drugs the illegality adds another dimension, stimulating rampant violence. For local leaders and outside volunteers, those who hope to improve neighborhoods and assist residents with jobs, housing, schools, and social services, the violence poses insurmountable barriers. The much milder side effects of Prohibition led to repeal.

The Drug Economy

The value of the global drug trade has been estimated to be between $260 billion and $300 billion annually in production, transportation, smuggling, and distribution.[21] Rand Corporation researchers, under contract to the U.S. Office of Drug Control Policy, report that U.S. drug users alone spent roughly $100 billion in 2010 for four illicit drugs—cocaine (including crack), heroin, marijuana, and methamphetamine.[22]

In 2010, 22.6 million people used illicit drugs in the United States, 8.9 percent of the population twelve years old and older, with about 90 percent of the users at least eighteen years old. More than three-quarters of these people used marijuana. The total cost to society for dealing with this illicit drug use is gigantic. For everything, including law enforcement and prison administration, property damage, medical costs, and—most of all—lost productivity, the estimate for 2007 is $193 billion.[23]

As direct expenditure, the federal government budgeted $25.2 billion in fiscal year 2012 on drug-related matters, including $10.5 million for treatment and prevention, and $15.1 billion (nearly three-fifths) for domestic law enforcement, border interdiction, and overseas interventions. Drug-war funds are allocated mainly to the Departments of Justice, Defense, State, and Homeland Security. When local and state agencies are included, total direct public spending in response to illegal drugs amounts to well over $50 billion annually.[24] Total prison and jail expenditures exceeded $80 billion in 2010.[25]

A better estimate of the fiscal costs of the drug war adds in the potential tax receipts. Even ignoring potential reductions in overseas drug-fighting ventures, nearly $3 billion per year, economists Jeffrey Miron and Katherine Waldock calculate the net annual fiscal gain from legalization of all drugs to be $88 billion, half derived from spending cuts at local, state, and federal levels, and half from new tax revenues to states and the federal government, assuming rates comparable to those on alcohol and tobacco. The researchers stress that these are "ballpark" figures, and they calculate smaller savings and tax receipts for decriminalization rather than full legalization, because only the latter eliminates arrests for trafficking and cuts the subsequent legal and incarceration costs.

Neighborhoods and Prisons

The modern-era drug war began officially June 17, 1971, when President Nixon declared "all-out, global war on the drug menace." Earlier, in 1968, responding to increased use of heroin and marijuana, President Johnson had reorganized federal agencies to form the Bureau of Narcotics and Dangerous Drugs. When the Nixon White House created the Drug Enforcement Administration, the DEA, in 1973, it employed 1,470 special agents and spent less than $75 million annually.[26] The war was to focus on treatment for addiction rather than law enforcement, and to help those in need, including troubled neighborhoods and cities. But soon after, strategies aimed differently: to seal borders against imports, to arrest and imprison targeted dealers and users, and to disrupt drug production overseas. Border controls and drug-war collaboration with violent overseas regimes became staples of foreign policy, and at home the war has focused on arrests of minority men in city neighborhoods. Law-and-order surges with intensified arrests and prison growth occurred repeatedly, most often in states with Republican administrations, but also following harsh penal policies introduced by Governors Nelson Rockefeller and Mario Cuomo in New York and Ann Richards in Texas, and Presidents Ronald Reagan and Bill Clinton.[27] The drug war formed part of the response to "powerful institutional, cultural, political, economic, and racial forces" of the post–World War II period. "Unlike many other Western countries, the United States responded to escalating crime rates by enacting highly punitive policies and laws and turning away from rehabilitation and reintegration."[28]

The Domestic Drug War

In the climate of a moral imperative to conduct the drug war, drug convictions fueled growth of the prison population. Law enforcement became broadly more punitive. Judicial discretion in sentencing was curtailed, and mandatory minimum sentences for jail terms were introduced. Three-strike laws, which legislatures enacted in twenty-four states, led to long-term imprisonment, including life sentences for nonviolent crimes. Juveniles increasingly faced trial as adults.[29] In 2009 there were "just over 100 people in the world serving sentences of life without the possibility of parole for crimes they committed as juveniles in which no one was killed. All [were] in the United States."[30] The great bulk of illicit drug law enforcement takes place in black and Latino neighborhoods, including "zero tolerance" policies, like New York's stop-and-frisk arrests.[31]

The federal government and states joined as allies with inventive and punitive crime-fighting legislation, mushrooming arrests, stiffer sentencing, prison construction, and incarceration. In 1970, 415,000 people were arrested nationwide on drug charges. Drug arrests grew slowly at first, then rapidly, to 581,000 in 1980, more than a million in 1990, and nearly two million in 2006, as shown in figure 6.3. Roughly 13 percent of all arrests in the United States are for drug violations, and about 20 percent of all prisoners have been convicted of breaking drug laws. Of the drug arrests, more than 80 percent are for possession, rather than sale or manufacturing, and a good portion of the possession arrests (estimates run from 33 percent to 85 percent) are for "stand-alone" possession, meaning the arrest was not for any other violations, which range from speeding to armed robbery.[32]

Along with the explosion in arrests, prison populations swelled as new laws led to more convictions and longer sentences.[33] From about forty thousand prisoners held in federal, state, and local prisons for drug violations in 1980, the count has grown to about a half million. That twelvefold increase over three decades not only extended poor neighborhoods of color into distant prisons, but extended prison emotions, styles, and routines back into the neighborhoods. The increase in drug prisoners played a key role in making the United States the most prison-intensive society on earth. Counting *all* who are locked up in federal, state, and local institutions, as a proportion of the population, America imprisons five times as many as Spain or Britain, six times as many as Canada, seven to nine times as many as France or Germany, and fourteen times as many as Japan. The

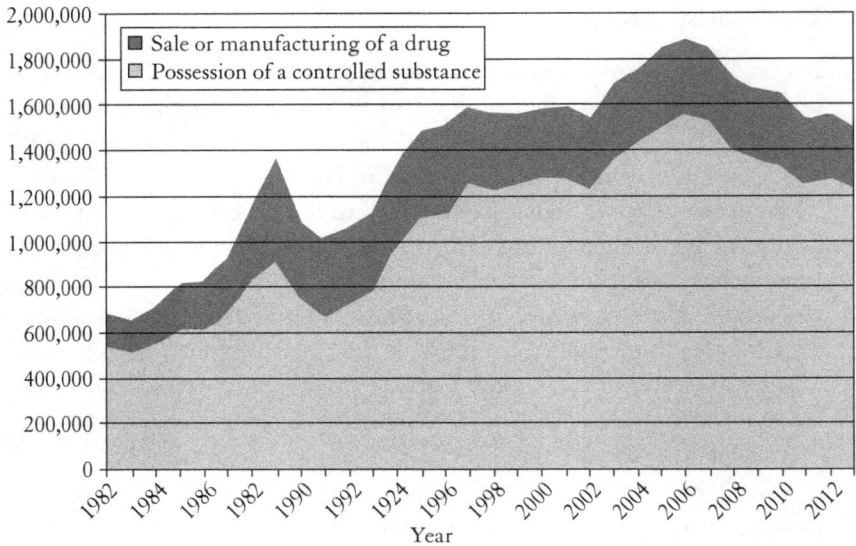

Figure 6.3. Number of drug-related arrests, 1982–2013. Data from Bureau of Justice Statistics, estimated number of arrests, by type of drug-law violation, 1982–2007, http://www.bjs.gov/content/dcf/tables/salespos.cfm; Federal Bureau of Investigation, Uniform Crime Reports (1995–2013), https://www.fbi.gov/about-us/cjis/ucr/crime-in-the-u.s.

thirty-year rise has leveled off, though the number of prisoners continued to rise slightly from 2012 to 2013. For the long historical series of the *rate* of incarceration, inmates per one hundred thousand population, we see in figure 6.4 that for forty to fifty years there was no increase, and then beginning in 1974 the rate exploded. As figure 6.1 shows, after 1980 the massive numbers of persons out of prison but still under supervision in the justice system, which trebles the total. In 2013 roughly seven million persons were under supervision.

The drug war expanded in part because the Congress and state legislatures issued ever-tougher penalties. Two years after the federal declaration of war, New York State, under Governor Nelson Rockefeller in 1973, passed draconian penalties: fifteen-year sentences for possession of four ounces or the sale of two ounces of illegal drugs.[34] In 1978, the Carter administration began a program of asset forfeiture, encouraging police to seize and keep money or other valuables. Federal "truth-in-sentencing" laws reward states financially if they keep prisoners for at least 85 percent

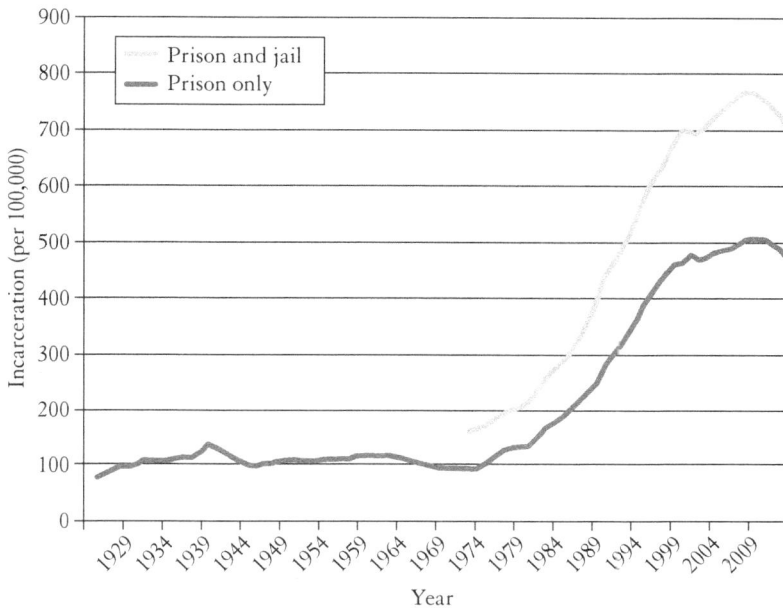

Figure 6.4. Long-term incarceration rates, 1925–2013. Data from Hindelang Criminal Justice Research Center, University at Albany, SUNY, 2013, tables 6.1.2011 and 6.28.2012; Glaze and Kaeble 2014.

of their sentences. Federal law in 1986, during the Reagan administration, created lengthy mandatory minimum prison terms for heroin, cocaine, and crack cocaine.

The residential location patterns of the overall prisoner and parolee populations, which are disproportionately poor and dark skinned, reflect bias against those convicted for drug violations as well as those convicted of other crimes. Total arrests (for drug violations and all other crimes) exceedingly target poor city neighborhoods of color, and arrestees are disproportionately poor, minority young men. For example, in most areas of Onondaga County, which includes Syracuse, in upstate New York, fewer than eight of every ten thousand residents (mostly white) are sent to prison each year. In a few rural zones of the county, the rate goes as high as twenty-seven per ten thousand. But in inner neighborhoods of color in the city of Syracuse, at the county's center, the rate shoots up 2,600 percent to as many as seven hundred of every ten thousand residents. Similarly skewed results appear in city after city across the nation, connecting race, class, and space with prison populations, illustrated by the *Justice Atlas of Sentencing and Corrections.*[35] Everywhere, neighborhood rates of prison admission correspond closely to the percentages of residents who are nonwhite.

In larger and denser Brooklyn, where arrest rates and racial concentrations also tally, on numerous city blocks of color public expenditures for keeping residents in prison exceed $1 million annually. In a few Brooklyn blocks, expenditures exceed $5 million a year. The larger the black population on the block, the higher the prison spending.[36] These extraordinary expenditures, focused so intensely on a very few neighborhoods in cities across the country, result from steady growth of the drug war and associated crime fighting. In the first Bush and the Clinton administrations, the war continued to expand, along with the growth of the Colombian cartels and the importation of cocaine. DEA budgets rose rapidly, overseas operations expanded, and arrests and prisoner counts grew.

George W. Bush shifted rhetoric but not strategic focus after taking office in 2001, announcing "aggressive goals to reduce drug use in the United States." He focused on the "morality" of drug use but kept the emphasis on crime fighting, yet with an ironic acknowledgment of the failures of drug wars past: "Thousands of children still live in homes torn apart by drugs. Thousands more are still considering whether to try drugs for the first time. . . . It's up to all Americans to be involved in this important struggle against drug addiction. It's up to all of us to urge our fellow citizens to make the right choice—and to help those who make the wrong choice understand the consequences and that there is a more hopeful future."[37]

Although President George W. Bush did sign the Second Chance Act aimed at helping ex-convicts reintegrate into communities and thus reduce recidivism, federal drug policy more generally adopted the president's tough stance, involving the Office of Homeland Security and using the PATRIOT Act. According to the White House National Drug Control Strategy of 2006, the war was "producing results," a public statement that ignored scientific findings of failure. The administration also refused to "end the unique government monopoly over the supply of marijuana available for Food and Drug Administration (FDA)–approved research." The American Civil Liberties Union, the ACLU, called this decision, which prevented privately funded research, "a parting shot to legitimate science."[38] Even while pressing hard against use of marijuana and cocaine, however, the government ignored local concerns with methamphetamine and border states' difficulties with drug smuggling from Mexico.[39]

Long before his first election, then senator Barack Obama described the drug war as an "utter failure," and four years later, in Oregon, when asked about medical marijuana, he added, "There really is no difference between that and a doctor prescribing morphine or anything else " He also promised not to use "Justice Department resources to try to circumvent state laws on this issue."[40] In the first Obama administration, Attorney General Eric Holder announced more liberal policies and promised restraint in situations when federal and state or local laws clashed. However, in 2009 Gil Kerlikowske, director of the Office of National Drug Control Policy, announced that the Obama administration would continue existing enforcement policy but would no longer call it a war. And in 2012, when Vice President Joe Biden met with President Felipe Calderón of Mexico, he rejected the idea of legalization despite Latin American wishes, saying: "On examination you realize there are more problems with legalization than with nonlegalization." President Obama, at the Summit of the Americas in April 2012, acknowledged that drug laws may do harm, but said "legalization is not the answer."[41] The Justice Department continued to make drug arrests and shut down businesses even in states and cities that permit them, either for medical purposes or otherwise. The administration pushed against proposals to liberalize state laws. "A Southern California man was sentenced [January 7, 2013] to ten years in federal prison for operating medical marijuana dispensaries, even though they are legal in the state."[42] California cities were at the forefront of the conflict, and when Washington and Colorado voters legalized marijuana for recreational use in November 2012, they put their states in more intense conflict with federal law.

International Mayhem

Through eight presidential administrations, from Richard Nixon to Barack Obama, the government has tried to reduce drug movement across borders. Early on, the drug war "stepped up diplomatic pressure against Turkey, a major opium source for the notorious 'French Connection' heroin traffickers, and it provided narcotics-control assistance to Mexico and Turkey." Later, in the 1970s, the government added "programs of crop eradication, substitution, and overseas law-enforcement."[43] Through the 1980s, the effort continued to reduce the frequency of border crossings.

In January 1990, President George H. W. Bush proposed a 50 percent increase in drug-war military spending. The 1991 budget was $2 billion for interdiction, spent mainly by the Department of Defense. Under Presidents Bush and Clinton, the international strategy shifted from border interdiction to vastly expanded efforts *inside* other countries to wipe out crops and destroy manufacturing facilities. That shift in strategy anticipated an interagency review by the National Security Council, which found that interdiction had failed to slow the trafficking of cocaine. "The NSC . . . argued that stopping drugs close to their source of production might prove a more effective strategy." Funding for foreign drug intervention, which had been cut in half between 1992 and 1994, down to about $330 million, was pushed back up.[44] By 1995, "anti-drug programs in Latin America . . . represent[ed] almost 20 percent of total American foreign assistance to the region, compared with only 3 percent" a decade earlier.[45] The overseas intervention had limited effect on shipments, however, repeating the failures of interdiction.

As a consequence of drug conflicts, international violence skyrocketed.[46] In Colombia in the late 1970s and 1980s, as the cartels consolidated operations and shipped unprecedented amounts of cocaine, armed conflict made much of the country ungovernable. For years, the ebb and flow of poppy production in Afghanistan has made a mockery of control efforts. U.S. officials evidently recognize the impossibility of eradication, but nevertheless continue with programs. In Brazilian cities, as became widely known with preparations for the World Cup soccer championships and the summer Olympics, neighborhoods are almost wholly controlled by drug lords, with heavy infiltration into police forces. In Mexico, during the *sexenio* (six-year term) of President Calderón, many thousands were killed in the border metropolitan areas of Tijuana (San Diego), Juárez (El Paso), and Matamoros (Brownsville), as well as smaller border cities and numerous places farther south, and the mayhem has continued. Overall in Mexico, catastrophic numbers of people have been murdered; sixty thousand is generally taken as an accurate minimum estimate of the carnage, and many cities and much of the countryside are ungovernable, ceded to warring drug cartels. Mexican officials including the judiciary, police, and army have been made virtually powerless. Residents have evacuated whole neighborhoods of border cities. Readers with courage can browse the forty-four photos of the horror posted by the *Atlantic* online.[47] No one anticipates a quick return to peace, short of a cessation of the U.S. drug war.

Race and Class

Many people have an acquaintance, perhaps a cousin or uncle, or even a mother or father or sibling or child, who is an alcoholic. Adult children of alcoholics, ACOAs, are well known to family counselors. Most people don't talk about it much, but it is there. When Carrie Nation chopped up taverns with her hatchet, to be arrested about three dozen times a century ago, she knew well the character of her targets, as her first husband had died of drink.[48] Threatened by deviant behavior (alcoholism) among familiar people, she and other radicals in the temperance movement focused their fanaticism on members of their own community. They didn't target strangers. Still today, people mainly view alcoholics as problematic family members, whose behavior does not merit the attention of public authorities.

The drug war is different. It targets strangers, who do merit the attention of public authorities. People rarely think, at least they do not think openly, that family members, friends, or others in their social circle abuse drugs. Instead, people imagine that strangers abuse drugs, deal drugs, and commit drug-related crimes. These strangers, "others," are part of *an other* community. This difference myth has for at least a century served as the basis for public drug policy. As reported by Mathea Falco, former assistant secretary of state for international drug strategies, "When the first drug laws were adopted early in [the twentieth] century, drugs were associated with immigrant groups and minorities: opium with Chinese laborers in the West; cocaine with blacks; and marijuana with Mexican immigrants in the Southwest. These drugs were seen as foreign threats to America's social fabric, undermining traditional moral values and political stability."[49]

When the current drug war began, President Nixon had already made clear his moral revulsion at the excesses of white, pot-smoking hippies. Apparently he felt threatened by their libertine behavior. Nevertheless, he trained the big guns not on these misbehaving whites, but on African Americans and Latinos, not seen as libertines but as criminals. The war built upon nativist, racist feelings about substance use, and the war has since targeted, arrested, convicted, and sentenced blacks and Latinos with vastly disproportionate frequency and severity. Outside minority neighborhoods, authorities tolerate flagrant use of cocaine by white, middle-class professionals. According to Dr. Herbert Kleber, director of the Division on Substance Abuse at the New York State Psychiatric Institute, drug come-ons are common. Notices appear, for example, on the Casual Encounters section of Craigslist. Powder cocaine use remains socially acceptable, and Kleber says that "people don't feel nearly as much the need to hide it . . . they feel that they can use it in a more open fashion."[50] Although national statistics show stable use of cocaine from 2002 to 2005, they also show a 20 percent increase from 2004 to 2005 among eighteen-to-twenty-five-year-olds. A companion study in London shows use among young adults tripling since the late 1990s. Yet in New York as in other U.S. cities, this almost flaunted use of illegal substances rarely incurs the wrath of the state.

White stockbrokers can sniff powdered cocaine at top-drawer restaurants without much worry, but in the 'hood, when black inner-city residents use crack cocaine, they need fear arrest, conviction, and prison. The penalties vary hugely, even though crack and powdered cocaine are chemically identical. When cheap crack flooded the streets in 1982, authorities from municipal law agencies to the U.S. attorney general asserted (incorrectly, it turns out) that crack was distinct from powdered cocaine and much more dangerous than other drugs. Crack is a black offense, while powdered cocaine, like drunk driving, is a white offense. In an atmosphere polluted by racist rhetoric about dangerous cities,[51] Congress mandated ten years in prison for someone caught with 1.75 ounces of crack (50 grams). Someone caught with 11 *pounds* of powdered cocaine (5 kilograms, or 5,000 grams) faced the same ten years. Thus the Congress codified the racial bias, treating a black user the same as it would a white user carrying one hundred times as much of virtually the same drug. It took thirty years, with the Fair Sentencing Act of 2010, for Congress to reduce—but hardly eliminate—the racial disparity. Under the reformed law, someone can still possess eighteen times as much powdered cocaine as crack and be treated the same.[52] This sort of racial bias has been standard operating procedure for a long time. Thirty years ago, First Lady Nancy Reagan provided a symbol for the permissive stance on white lawbreaking with her "Just Say No" campaign, directed at

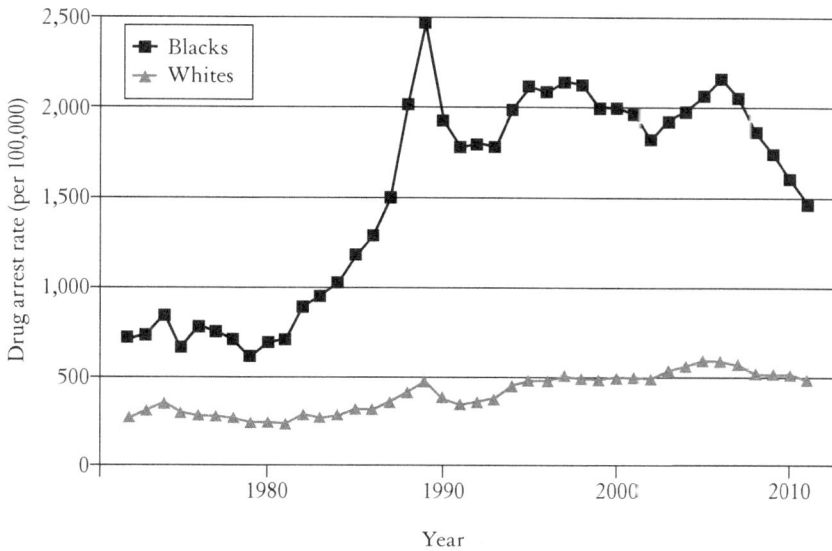

Figure 6.5. Drug arrest rates for blacks and whites per one hundred thousand population, 1972–2011. From National Research Council 2014, figure 2–13. Data from Federal Bureau of Investigation (1990): 1972–1979; Uniform Crime Reports race-specific arrest rates, 1980 to 2011, from Bureau of Justice Statistics, U.S. Department of Justice.

middle-class, white youth. Figure 6.5 shows the startling increase in black compared to white drug arrest rates beginning in 1980.

Jim Crow in Century Twenty-One

Prisons across the country now look like African American and Latino storage pens. They are constructed that way. As professor Marjorie Zatz writes: "Sentencing is the result of a long series of decisions . . . police decisions about where to focus their surveillance and when an arrest is warranted rather than a warning; the prosecutor's decision to accept or reject a case and which . . . criminal charges to file; the judge's decision about . . . bail . . . and other conditions of release; the prosecutor's and defense attorney's decisions regarding plea bargains . . . and the judge's or jury's decision about guilt."[53]

These judicial decisions filter out literally millions of white and middle-class defendants, while targeting those who are poor and dark skinned.[54] Roughly

20 million Americans use illicit drugs each year, but only about 1.5 million are arrested, the vast majority being people of color. As Zatz adds: "We find ourselves faced with a situation in which a sizable portion of our citizenry is politically disenfranchised, experiences long-term unemployment, has little reason to respect the criminal justice system, and views prison rather than college as the place where one becomes an adult."[55] This bias has nothing to do with patterns of use, or with patterns of sales. As Michelle Alexander writes in *The New Jim Crow*:

> The notion that most illegal drug use and sales happens in the ghetto is pure fiction. Drug trafficking occurs there, but it occurs everywhere else in America as well. Nevertheless, black men have been admitted to state prison on drug charges at a rate that is more than thirteen times higher than white men. The racial bias inherent in the drug war is a major reason that 1 in every 14 black men was behind bars in 2006, compared with 1 in 1065 white men. For young black men, the statistics are even worse. One in 9 black men between the ages of twenty and thirty-five was behind bars in 2006, and far more were under some form of penal control—such as probation or parole.[56]

The federal Bureau of Justice Statistics projects that if imprisonment rates hold steady, then of white males born in 2001, 5.9 percent will eventually serve a term in prison. Of Latinos, 17.2 percent will end up at one point in prison. Of black males, it is 32.2 percent, one in three, who can expect prison sometime in their lives.[57] Much worse—on average, every day in 2010, more than 35 percent of black male high school dropouts ages twenty to thirty-nine were actually in prison or jail.[58]

As we have seen, the United States has the world's highest incarceration rate—nearly 750 inmates for each 100,000 residents in 2007, or 1 of every 133 persons, counting men, women, and children.[59] Except for French Guiana and Russia, with rates almost as high, nearly every other country in the world imprisons at a much lower rate. The British have the highest rate in Europe, one-fifth the U.S. rate. A survey in 2011 concluded that close to one-third of twenty-three-year-olds in the United States, 30.2 percent, have been arrested![60] Racial disproportions in prisons sometimes reach fantastic levels. In the state of Illinois, black males were at one point fifty times more likely to be incarcerated than white males.[61]

Women are jailed at much lower rates than men—there are *only* about two hundred thousand women in prison and jail, compared to more than two million men—but their incarceration rates are similarly racialized.[62] For every 100,000 African American females, 142 were in prison or jail in 2009, compared to 74 Hispanic females and 50 white females. The racial differences for women apply to all age groups, but they are shrinking.[63] The rate for black women was six times as high as for white women in 2000, but by 2009 it had fallen to less than three times as high. Studies in particular states sometimes show rising arrest rates for white women as the cause of the shift, apparently due to methamphetamine epidemics, and sometimes they show declines in recent arrests of black women. A 9 percent decline in imprisoned women in a dozen states with comparable statistics shows the decrease as being almost *entirely* due to fewer or less drastic drug sentences.[64]

The disproportions also hold for young people. Black and Latino youth are about twice as likely as white youth to land in jail. More African American and Latino men in their twenties are in prison or jail, on probation, or on parole than in college.[65] For boys, detention facilities can be terrible places: the Texas system held young inmates in thirteen detention facilities in 2005, in an operation plagued by violence, sexual abuse, and mistreatment resulting in broken bones, unhealthy foods, filthy, unsanitary facilities, falsification of records, and breakdowns.[66]

The majority of prisoners, black, Latino, and white, are poor. Of prisoners with a source of income, 37 percent of women and 28 percent of men earned less than $600 in the month before their arrest. Sixty percent of women and 40 percent of men in state prisons were unemployed before their arrest. "Eighty percent of people accused of crimes are unable to afford a lawyer to defend them."[67]

Segregation extends inside prison walls. The State of California often segregates prison inmates into apartheid areas. "More than 25 years ago, California adopted the practice of placing inmates in double cells with cellmates of the same ethnic background for the first 60 days after their arrival at a prison." Authorities evaluate inmates for "propensity to violence, among other things," and then claim to assign them "permanent quarters on a non-racial basis." In 2003 the policy segregated "40,000 new prison inmates and several hundred thousand others who were transferred between prisons."[68] The lawyer for Garrison S. Johnson, a black inmate who successfully challenged the system, describes it "as nothing more than 'routine, blanket racial segregation' . . . based on a 'needless and dangerous' stereotype that assumed that all members of a racial or ethnic group acted and thought alike." *Nightline* television anchor Ted Koppel did a feature in which he concluded that "race guides every aspect of prison life" in Solano prison in Vacaville, with officials assigning cellmates by race, and fights almost always across race lines. He observed "as rigid a form of segregation as ever existed in this country."[69]

New Orleans has the highest rate of incarceration of any large U.S. city, just as Louisiana has the highest rate of prisoners in local jails. Flaws in due process keep arrestees locked up for months, sometimes as long as a year, waiting to be charged for nonviolent misdemeanors, when by law they should be released on their own recognizance. Family, friends, and neighbors can be powerless. According to Loyola University law professor Bill Quigley, "It's a vacuum, sucking poor people in and keeping them in. Being arrested now equals being sent to prison," where investigations reveal "dungeon-hole conditions" with no fresh air, overflowing toilets, and intense overcrowding. Prisoners in Louisiana serve on work teams for private firms—twenty-first-century chain gangs—and to facilitate such activity, the Louisiana state legislature granted immunity to prison authorities for any injuries to prisoners or damages to property resulting from the work program.[70] The drug war is far from the only mechanism for punishing poor dark-skinned people in New Orleans, but it has served to justify and excuse terrible excesses in the so-called justice system, and across the country it has been a major stimulus for growth of the prison system.

Why do people talk about the New Jim Crow? Berkeley sociologist Loïc Wacquant argues that today's arrangement of intensified ghettos tied to massive imprisonment works like a fourth phase of the "peculiar institution." Each phase, from slavery on, has offered two advantages to whites: the extraction of profits from cheap labor and the guarantee of social advantage. The second phase, after slavery, was Jim Crow laws of exclusion in the South. In the third phase (overlapping chronologically), whites extracted similar advantages from forced isolation of African Americans into the northern ghetto. Now, the system operates with intensified ghettos connected to prisons. In each case workers are disciplined to accept lower pay, and in each case social integration is impeded.[71]

The second phase, Jim Crow, started soon after the end of the Civil War and lasted a century, into the 1960s. White southerners constructed the infamous system of discriminatory restrictions, always with threat of violence. Voters, mayors, city councils, governors, state legislators, public prosecutors, judges, and juries, as well as the Congress, the White House, and the judiciary, imposed Jim Crow. Laws separated public facilities—so that from schools to bus-terminal waiting rooms to theater sections to parks and swimming pools to drinking fountains, "White only" was an expected sign. Jim Crow denied African Americans nearly all rights of citizenship, and it was legally undone only after a century of struggle and, finally, federal civil rights laws.

In northern cities, especially after the Great Migrations out of the South, blacks escaped Jim Crow to get employment in the expanded economies supporting World War I and World War II. But the black migrants found that whites constructed systematic restrictions in the North, too, that excluded them from labor unions, colleges, good jobs, and respect. They were denied innumerable other rights, and they were confined residentially to ghettos. These restrictions reaped advantages for whites, as business firms pushed down black wages and profited from inflated prices at local stores. White communities effectively prohibited school and interpersonal integration while reaping for themselves the benefits of government programs like the tax deduction for interest on home mortgages.

In the current arrangement, which is Wacquant's fourth phase, the drug war plays a key role. In this system of intensified, left-behind ghettos and their connected prisons, the drug war is not against drugs at all, but against poor people of color, exactly the people who live in deprived city neighborhoods.[72] How, Michelle Alexander asks, can such bias occur in a time when overt racism has all but disappeared? In three ways. First, police and prosecutors are given enormously wide latitude by the courts, a consequence of tremendous weakening of the protections of the Fourth Amendment to the Constitution, with eviscerated protection against warrantless stops and searches. As a consequence, and resulting from conscious and unconscious racial bias in the organization and activities of police and prosecutors, searches and arrests target poor people of color. Second, the courts have strongly blocked every avenue of appeal by those who demonstrate the biased results of police and prosecutorial acts.[73] Finally, drug convictions are now used as a way to limit access to many public benefits, from housing to job programs and, as we have seen, even the right to vote.

Biased Arrests

Just over 70 percent of drug users are white, about 14 percent black, and 13 percent Hispanic.[74] Police arrest many more African Americans and Hispanics than expected from their proportion in the population. Drug arrests take the lead. Drug users typically purchase from drug sellers of the same race.[75] Perhaps the police focus on impoverished minority neighborhoods to take advantage of more efficient arrest opportunities or to meet arrest quotas, easier to do in places with higher geographic concentrations of drug sales. Perhaps they share in the bias that led the Congress to their crack cocaine / powdered cocaine disparity. Perhaps police buy into the historical myth that drug use is a minority problem, so they "profile," "stop and frisk," and otherwise target people of color.[76]

A familiar case has to do not with drugs but with simple automobile stops, widely known as "profiling" or DWB—"driving while black" or "driving while brown." In a notorious case, boxing champion Hurricane Carter was presumably "profiled" when arrested in a New Jersey highway stop as part of a search for the murderer of three bar patrons in 1966, to be freed only twenty years later, in 1985, for lack of evidence. Top police officials and Governor Christine Todd Whitman finally acknowledged widespread New Jersey profiling. Less well known is the May 1999 case of the Detroit mayor's eldest son, stopped by police along with his date, herself a city prosecutor, on suspicion of auto theft, because they drove a Jeep through a well-heeled neighborhood where a look-alike automobile had just been stolen. Both subjects of the stop were black, while the police, who arrived in six cars, held him at shotgun point and handcuffed her, were white.[77] A 2002 national study by the Department of Justice concluded that Hispanic and black drivers or their cars, compared to whites, are searched about three times as frequently. As Brent Staples observed in June 2009, even though some speak of a "post-racial" era with the election of Barack Obama, racial bias in policing still victimizes people of color.[78]

Early in the drug war, in 1980, African Americans made up a quarter of arrestees, already twice their proportion in the population. Then, through the 1980s, as drug arrests nearly doubled, police nabbed record numbers of black people for drug violations and other crimes, too. By 1990, arrests of African Americans nationally had expanded until they accounted for more than two-fifths of all arrestees.

During the anti-crack frenzy "black women were ten times more likely than white women to be reported to child welfare agencies for prenatal drug use," despite narrower differences in black and white rates of illicit drug use during pregnancy.[79] Among fifty-two new mothers who prosecutors charged with "transporting" drugs to a fetus, only fourteen were white, while thirty-five were black, two were Latina, and one was Native American.[80] In April 2014 Tennessee began arresting women who used drugs while pregnant, "five black, four white, all poor."[81]

Authorities have used antigang statutes to reinforce the drug war in some cities, further penalizing African American and Latino residents and their neighborhoods. Years ago, in 1992, the Los Angeles County district attorney's office identified almost half of all African American men ages twenty-one to twenty-four as gang members. In Denver the police department put two-thirds of the African American boys and men ages twelve to twenty-four on its list of suspected gang members. Whites, who then made up 80 percent of Denver's population, accounted for fewer than 7 percent of the police's list of suspected gang members.[82] According to a 2005–2008 National Gang Center survey of law enforcement agencies in larger cities across the nation, 35.6 percent of gang members are black, 48.1 percent are Hispanic/Latino, 9.3 percent are white, and 6.9 percent are other.[83] These numbers serve best as indicators of alienation and exclusion, reasons for social and economic intervention (jobs, schooling, public assistance) rather than police action.

Changing drug habits have caused some adjustment in the racial contours of arrests. Arrests for crystal meth (the form of methamphetamine that is consumed illegally), used mainly by whites and initially in rural areas in the South and Midwest, have gone up. Usage spread and enforcement increased (Indiana state police found 1,260 labs in 2003, compared to just 6 in 1995), but in spite of a flurry of federal and state legislation regarding meth since 1989, penalties have not been increased to match the perceived danger.[84] Still, arrests shifted, so that between 1999 and 2005, the population of black drug offenders in state prisons fell by a fifth, while white offenders increased by two-fifths. Nevertheless, prison populations are still highly skewed racially: blacks, with Hispanics, constitute two-thirds of imprisoned drug offenders.[85]

Biased Convictions, Sentences, and Jail Terms

As noted above, courts tend to convict people of color with higher frequency compared to whites, thereby exacerbating the racial bias in arrests, and judges tend to give stiffer sentences, with longer prison terms. As in the case with arrests, the racial disproportion in prosecutions, convictions, and sentencing includes elements of social-class discrimination. Poor arrestees tend to be dark skinned, and vice versa. Poor defendants must rely on inexperienced and underpaid assigned counsel rather than privately retained attorneys, and they face the likelihood of social bias from prosecutors, judges, and juries.

Authorities can act without conscious discriminatory intent but still introduce racial and class bias.[86] When the Supreme Court nomination of Sonia Sotomayor was discussed, some prominent whites worried that her decisions on the Court might be biased because she was Latina (of Puerto Rican heritage) and had grown up poor. Turning the tables, it is hard to imagine white skin and middle-class status giving rise to similar worries among elites.

Federal, state, and local justice systems exhibit racial biases not only along the crack/powdered-cocaine divide, but also for other crimes, including drunk driving. Although groups like Mothers Against Drunk Driving (MADD) make their case with persistence, and even though teenage boys count among the most lethal drivers, district attorneys and judges nevertheless treat youthful drunk driving charges lightly. A severe penalty for possession of marijuana and cocaine (including crack) is seven times more likely than one for drunk driving. Arrested youthful drunk drivers tend to be white, and arrested drug offenders tend to be black. The bias is generalized: a national study in 173 communities found that local district attorneys prosecute minority youth much more severely. Prosecutorial choices and sentencing differentials display bias for students in eighth to twelfth grades, as reported by the district attorneys themselves. They punish black students with out-of-home placement, while for white students they seek lesser penalties, including suspension or dismissal of the case.[87] Courts themselves stereotype by race: in Iowa, court officials see delinquent young whites as merely misbehaving, boys will be boys; but the same officials see delinquent young African Americans as "undisciplined, as living in dysfunctional families that are primarily headed by young mothers, and as sexually promiscuous, dangerous, delinquent, and prone to drug offenses."[88]

These racial biases pervade the country, but they may be most evident where least disguised, in the South. A yearlong controversy (2006) over high school fighting in the small town of Jena, Louisiana, revealed familiar patterns. When white boys hung nooses and used lynching symbolism, the school superintendent and the district attorney both winked, but when black boys protested against the symbols, authorities imposed Jim Crow retribution. Following a nasty schoolyard fight, authorities did not charge white students, but they charged black students, originally with attempted murder. It is hardly an exaggeration in Louisiana to fear a murder charge as the first step to the death chamber.[89] In a less consequential incident, Solomon Moore, a reporter for the *New York Times*, found himself physically detained by police merely because he stood nearby in a neighborhood sweep. This was in Salisbury, North Carolina, and although drug sales had been taking place, no one was arrested. When Moore produced his journalism ID and objected that he had "a right to talk to anyone I like, wherever I like," one of the police officers trumped the reporter's naïveté—"Sir, this is the South. We have different laws down here." Moore is black.[90]

Sentencing bias, already noted, is widespread. Among persons convicted of drug felonies in state courts, only one-third of whites go to prison, but more than half of African Americans do.[91] In 1986, prior to mandatory minimums for crack offenses, "the average federal drug-offense sentence for blacks was already 11 percent higher than for whites. Four years later, following harsher drug sentencing laws, the federal drug-offense sentence averaged 49 percent higher for blacks."[92] Owing to unbending federal sentencing rules, the harsh Rockefeller drug laws in New York State, the unforgiving "three strikes, you're out" law in California, and similarly punishing legal codes in many other states, sentencing biases became so grotesque that "a disproportionate number of young Black and Hispanic men are likely to be *imprisoned for life* under scenarios in which they are guilty of little more than a history of untreated addiction and several prior drug-related offenses."[93]

Drug prosecutions constitute the single most common category of federal cases. Across the 1980s and 1990s, drug cases grew more prominent, rising from 21 percent of the federal caseload in 1982 to 36 percent in 1999. In 2011, drug cases represented 31 percent of federal criminal cases.[94] In state courts, persons arrested for drug trafficking more likely face felony convictions than do people arrested for robbery, aggravated assault, rape, burglary, car theft, or even murder.[95]

The ghetto-prison system operates with heavy bias against blacks, Hispanics, and the poor. Poor minority persons suffer disproportionate numbers of arrests, more zealous prosecution, higher rates of convictions, longer sentences, and discriminatory prison administrators and guards. A series of decisions by the Supreme Court virtually guarantees this bias.[96]

Neighborhood Collateral Damages

The place where race and class come together for the drug war is the neighborhood.[97] Outsiders, and sometimes insiders, do not refer to neighborhoods, but to black/African American ghettos or Hispanic/Latino barrios. Some of the residents in drug war neighborhoods sit at the bottom of the class scale, put there by their dark skins, their low incomes, and bad circumstances. Within these constrained places, occupied by designated "others," the war begins to make sense. As Alice Goffman shows in her book *On the Run*, about life on tough streets in Philadelphia, the tentacles of control and repression inflict their damages far beyond prison walls.[98]

With military action, what the Pentagon calls collateral damage occurs as unintentional killing and injuring of innocent civilians, disruption of commerce, and destruction of property by weapons aimed to kill enemy combatants. Whether or not such side-effect damages in real war zones are random and accidental, they are tragic. Drug-war damages to neighborhoods are similarly tragic. In war the soldiers are desensitized to the tragedy through training and by fear for their own safety, so the abuse to innocent bystanders can appear systematic and even deliberate. Police, put on the front lines by lawmakers and prosecutors, are not so desensitized, and abuses are much more limited in the drug war, but the neighborhood damages are nonetheless powerfully harmful, in good part because of warring among competing law violators.

Violence

Violence arises for many reasons in poor, underserved neighborhoods, making it impossible to disentangle the influences. Such neighborhoods suffer from a nexus of joblessness, poverty, poor schools, and low levels of public services. They lack recreation programs and facilities like parks and playgrounds. They are afflicted with racial and ethnic discrimination, and they are isolated. Single mothers and other caregivers sometimes do not have the wherewithal to provide support and supervision for their children.[99] Add the drug war, and an already problematic situation becomes impossible. The worst effects come as a result of police actions and especially gang violence related to drug marketing. The violence disrupts resident families, hampers local businesses, and endangers people at home and in public spaces.

In the most troubled neighborhoods, severe violence comes from the criminalized drug business, because drug-marketing networks operate much like occupation forces. As in real war zones, as much as residents loathe the occupiers, they come to rely on them for protection. Crazed drug users are not the chief sources of violence. Instead, the violence, including drug-related murder, usually relates to the *business* of drugs, including maintenance of market share through protection of turf.[100] No doubt turf violence will occur without the drug war, and other crime will occur, but both will be far less intense and less extensive.

The police respond in kind.[101] As Sudhir Venkatesh found in Chicago's Robert Taylor Homes public housing project, tenants grew "accustomed to police busts, sweeps, tactical units, mob action, mass search and seizures, fingerprinting, raids, and other paramilitary techniques."[102] Police departments have become increasingly militarized. In 2010, according to the Office of Management and Budget, thirty-two federal agencies spent more than $65 billion on "homeland-security related funding."[103] Much of this paramilitary activity supports the drug war.

Persistent neighborhood violence leads to adolescent alienation, constrains living spaces for all residents, promotes distrust of neighbors and of the social surroundings, restricts movement to only the safest zones, and shuts down much of the area for many hours of the day. As Harvard Business School economist Michael Porter points out, under such conditions legitimate business firms cannot survive.[104] The problems affect everyone in the area.

Children cannot play outside, adults cannot converse or play ball. All residents risk injury or death from stray bullets; that risk is sometimes so intense that mothers put their children to bed in bathtubs or on the floor, and children learn to identify which gun makes which sound. Middle-school students write essays about their lives of fear. Neighborhoods depopulate, leaving the remaining residents with still fewer resources. A stray bullet hit Patrick Daly, who was principal of an elementary school in Brooklyn, one morning in 1992 while he walked through the Red Hook projects to check in on a student to see why he wasn't in school that day.[105] Since the end of the crack epidemic, cities have been seen as much safer places, but in a comment on the small-town massacre at the Sandy Hook school in Connecticut in December 2012, an Oakland, California, high school journalism broadcaster expressed dismay and sympathy, but no surprise, as she lamented the persistent and pervasive gun violence in her neighborhood.[106]

More than a third of black and Latino parents surveyed nationwide, and a quarter of Asian parents, do not allow their children to play in the neighborhood, for fear of danger. Philadelphia mayor Michael Nutter focused his 2007 campaign on neighborhoods, with two controversial anticrime ideas: a tax credit up to $10,000 per year for three years for every released prisoner hired by a local business, and an aggressive stop-and-frisk procedure to stem burgeoning neighborhood crime. John Street, his predecessor, had a whole neighborhood transition initiative. Residents in tough Northeast neighborhoods of Washington, DC, struggle over whether policies to exclude the many ex-offenders living there would reduce the high murder rate.[107] These strategies may not work, but their popular appeal suggests the depth of dismay with the violence associated with the drug war.

Family Separation

The drug trade and the prison system produce other neighborhood effects. In low-income minority communities from which a disproportionate number of inmates are drawn, and to which parolees return, nearly everyone on the block knows several people caught up in the legal system. Fragile neighborhoods suffer heavily not only from the loss of income of those who have been removed to prison but also from the weakened social networks. "It seems likely that at least 20 to 25 percent of African American women" suffer from "being tied to an incarcerated man," thus lowering their status, interfering with family functioning, adding to stress levels and mental health problems, in addition to damaging community life. As a result of their connections with incarcerated men, these women also have increased incidence of obesity, diabetes, and hypertension.[108]

Women now go to jail in large numbers, though perhaps the increase has peaked. From 1974 to 2004, the number of females grew faster than any other imprisoned group.[109] In New York State, the rate of imprisoned women quintupled in thirty years.[110] The large numbers of women in federal prisons prompted Kathleen Hawk Sawyer, the director of the U.S. Bureau of Prisons in the George W. Bush administration, to question the entire system. When testifying before Congress, after pointing out that more than 70 percent of female prisoners are "low-level non-violent offenders," Hawk Sawyer said: "The fact that they have to come into prison is a question mark for me. I think it has been an unintended consequence of the sentencing guidelines and the mandatory minimums."[111] Female prisoners come almost entirely from inner-city neighborhoods.

Separation trauma is severe. Half the imprisoned parents do not see their children at all. Most prisoners are parents—three-quarters of the women, two-thirds of the men. Children have a hard time getting to a prison to visit; more than 60 percent of family visitors would have to travel more than one hundred miles from home, and many would have to go by bus, a time-consuming venture. Legislation makes it difficult for mothers to reunite with their children even on release from prison; the federal Adoption and Safe Families Act of 1997 requires courts to decide a child's placement within one year, effectively removing many children from mothers in prison and on parole.[112]

In the United States, 3.2 million children have either a mother or, much more often, a father in prison, on parole, or recently released; some have both parents incarcerated. Children of prisoners constitute 2 percent of all minor children and a whopping 7 percent of African American children. One-quarter of black children by age fourteen will have had a father or mother incarcerated. For children of poor African American young men, having a father in prison is commonplace.[113] Children of prisoners of any race miss the love of absent parents. They must adjust to the authority of grandparents, aunts, or uncles, move to foster-care homes, or deal with other adults, who are socially more distant. The children have to endure the stigma of having a mom or dad in jail. At the same time, in neighborhoods with many in prison, demoralized or cynical residents may take prison experience as a norm, so that the stigma of illegality may be reduced.[114] These and other abnormal conditions put stress not only on the children but also on those who deliver social services.[115] The incarceration of parents adds burdens atop poverty and other disabilities, to reduce children's school performance still further.[116]

Not only men and women, but also young people go to jail in large numbers. According to the Children's Defense Fund, about eighty-one thousand children are held on an average day in a juvenile lockup, and another ten thousand are held in adult jails and prisons. They are at risk of being sexually abused, worst of all in adult facilities.[117] Removed from families and neighborhoods, most of these young people are helpless, in spite of the enormous expenditures involved. Youth of color are sent disproportionately to the adult system.[118] "Youth who are transferred from the juvenile court system to the adult criminal system are approximately 34 percent more likely than youth retained in the juvenile court system to be re-arrested."[119]

Civil Death

Since the early 1970s, with the start of the drug war, more than thirty-seven million people have been arrested and jailed for offenses related to drugs.[120] Numbers of these people face insurmountable obstacles in finding jobs, registering to vote, or utilizing public programs for housing, college scholarships, and the like.

Residents of troubled inner-city neighborhoods, where the drug trade concentrates, spend much of their lives in uncomfortable association with the law enforcement system. Minor drug traffickers, often charged with possession "with intent to distribute," are arrested for transportation, storage, or selling. Prisons and neighborhoods connect so closely that stylish street dress came to be modeled on prison garb—including the low-hung, baggy pants that first moved out from prison to ghetto and barrio, but have now passed on to youth living everywhere. Parolees returning to their neighborhoods find that "support systems, like schools and public assistance programs, receive less money and attention than incarceration does."[121]

Especially when the economy is in the doldrums, inmates returning to their neighborhoods cannot find work. The habitual drug user may return from prison with no halfway house in the neighborhood, his child in the foster system, no legitimate business willing to hire him. Federal and state laws disqualify him from serving in the military or holding many government jobs. What does the released inmate do? He can't get welfare, he can't find work, and he can't feed his child. Exiled from legitimate work, he puts the community at risk. In prison he may have trained for a life of violence. In the drug business, he can put that training to work.

In recent history, in some inner-city precincts virtually no men have voted. Felony laws, holdovers from Jim Crow, disenfranchised an estimated 5.85 million people in 2012, about 9 percent higher than eight years earlier. These numbers include 7.7 percent of all African Americans, one in every thirteen. These numbers would be worse, but a number of states recently relaxed restrictions, so that between 2000 and 2010, "reforms in nearly two dozen states have led to 800,000 people getting their voting rights back."[122] For nonblacks, the disenfranchisement figure is 2 percent. State laws and procedures vary widely. In Maine and Vermont, prisoners can file absentee ballots. In a dozen states, however (including 2012 swing states Florida, Virginia, Nevada, and Iowa), convicts can lose the right to vote permanently. In other states, released prisoners may be able to vote after release, or after parole.[123] In sum, 13 percent of African American men, 1.4 million people *not in prison*, are denied the right to vote, making up a third of disenfranchised voters. Disqualified at a rate "seven times the national average," these men are greatly concentrated in poor city precincts.[124] With the aggressively pushed voter ID laws, still more citizens have lost the ability to vote.

Florida is the "felony disenfranchisement capital of the nation, with more than a million of its citizens struck from the rolls," including nearly a quarter of the state's African Americans.[125] Florida used to permanently bar ex-felons from voting. In 2007 the state facilitated registration of non-violent ex-felons, and more than 150,000 registered. Since the state took steps backward in 2011, almost no ex-felons have registered. To be *considered* for registration an ex-con must have had no new crime and wait five years from release for "non-serious" felonies and seven years for serious felonies. Registrations have practically ceased.

Some states prohibit felony drug offenders from getting food stamps or welfare, following the provisions of the federal Gramm amendment.[126] Public housing authorities evict tenants for drug-crime involvement, deny access to persons convicted of drug violations, and evict offenders' families. Substance users get cut off from federal disability payments.[127] Ex-convicts, even some long out of prison and entered into new lives, carry fear into every necessary involvement with the government, so even when they can, they often do not apply for driver's licenses or passports or jobs with public agencies or school districts. Although exclusion rules are unevenly enforced, they nonetheless threaten family stability, especially in poor neighborhoods and for minority families. One comprehensive study found that 41 percent of those deported for criminal convictions have drug felonies.[128] In nearly every metropolitan area, authorities for decades have concentrated poor people geographically by locating housing projects and assigning tenants in ways that increase segregation. The drug restrictions magnify the discriminatory effect.

The American Bar Association has identified thirty-eight thousand provisions in federal, state, and local laws that punish people who have been convicted of a crime, "pertaining to everything from public housing to welfare assistance to occupational licenses. More than two-thirds of the states allow hiring and professional-licensing decisions to be made on the basis of an arrest alone." Not a conviction, an arrest.[129]

Drug "Firms" and Neighborhood Labor Markets

Much of the drug economy flows through poor neighborhoods, outside the law. As Brendan O'Flaherty explains in his 2005 textbook *City Economics*: "Ordinary businesspeople selling a lawful product can rely on courts and lawyers to settle disputes; they can use checks and accept credit cards; and when they are robbed, they can go to the police. Businesspeople who sell drugs can do none of these things. Thus they must cultivate an image of toughness, hire hit men instead of lawyers, and handle large amounts of cash, which makes them attractive targets for robbers."

Following on the earlier discussion of Prohibition, if the Jack Daniels distillery and the Anheuser-Busch brewery were suddenly to be made not legal and pushed underground, they would not only change the way they operate. They would also receive premium payments because of the dangers involved. Their sales would stimulate the growth of an ancillary economy of laundered money, with clandestine and armed sites worldwide for production and shipping. As O'Flaherty reminds us, high profit rates are predicted by a fundamental financial principle: returns must be highest where the risks are highest. In the underground market, retail dealers use street corners, apartments, and runners. Producers use clandestine networks for shipment and distribution, instead of using legally sanctioned distributors with delivery trucks. Drug kings and dealers must expect high returns, because they face unpredictability and loss. Profit levels depend in large part on the illegality itself. A significant portion of the profits would vanish were the trade to be decriminalized, and many who now receive those profits either at the source or downstream would no longer have reason to participate.

The drug economy functions with great energy in many neighborhoods burdened with concentrated poverty, high unemployment, low wages, and meager public amenities. In such bleak environments, the drug economy provides entrepreneurial opportunities for some and an accessible although illegal means of earning income for others. At the street level of distribution, some of the market is organized by gangs, in which young people take jobs as low-rung lackeys, for low pay and an elevated likelihood of arrest, injury, or even death. Each retail drug distribution operation, like any McDonald's franchise, serves mainly to extract monies that flow in from sales and then out, to bigger dealers, shippers, and producers outside the neighborhood, beyond the city, beyond the national borders. Because the business is illegal, franchise fees in the drug business are steep, but each franchise's local economic function is the same: providing jobs and incomes.

Street gangs have been a feature of poor neighborhoods for many decades, but as drug sales have grown and the drug war has developed, they have escalated their violent tendencies. Historically, gangs served as organizations of social peers who felt isolated from the main society. Gangs sometimes engaged in turf struggles and frequently had trouble with the police, but normally they provided only minor irritants to the peaceful functioning of the city beyond their own neighborhoods, and only rarely did they have a deadly effect. Similarly, when traders of opium, marijuana, and heroin operated, violence was rarely extensive, and neighborhoods, though sometimes threatened, were not destroyed. The drug war changed the community rules, broke down the social controls that limited the violence, and canceled restrictions that held back the worst gang abuses.

Ever since the advent of crack in the early 1980s and the racially biased response by lawmakers, vigorous criminalization has altered the rules. In one of the most outrageous moves, federal drug czar William Bennett urged hospitals to routinely screen for cocaine in delivery rooms. Some mothers actually lost their babies on the spot, and, as noted earlier, some went to jail, "still bleeding from labor."[130] Update to 2014, a Columbia University neuroscientist reports that "in Brooklyn . . . you go to the family courtroom on any day, you can see parents losing their children for marijuana."[131] As a part of this climate of hostility and incomprehension, street gangs in many cities turned into business enterprises, operating as firms "systematically involved in the distribution of various narcotic substances."[132] These firms, in their normal business operations, engage in violence. If a firm (a gang) wishes to thrive and expand its market share, or even merely to resist going out of business, it must compete to defend its market: literally, its neighborhood turf. Under conditions of illegality, a gang defends or expands its turf by engaging in physical battle. As part of the business strategy, turf battles are frequent, and fighting is key.

The treasurer of one Chicago gang kept detailed accounts, which he provided to a sociology graduate student, who was closely involved with the gang. The treasurer was well educated and sophisticated in his accounting techniques, and his accounts provide a clear window into the clandestine business.[133] Interpreted as records of a normal business firm, the accounts include some surprises. To begin, drug dealing is not the high-end business one expects from reports in the popular press. Rather, the jobs for most employees look rather like so many entry-level, dead-end jobs in the service and retail sectors. The hours are not very good, and the jobs are "not particularly lucrative, yielding average wages only slightly above those of the legitimate sector. Hourly wages for those on the lowest rung of the gang hierarchy are no better than the minimum wage."[134] But the jobs are readily available.

Wages in the gang are highly skewed, and the very high rewards at the top attract unreasonably hopeful low-level employees. Given the lack of employment options in the neighborhood, entry-level workers behave as though they are in a tournament, gambling their lives or futures in hopes for a big win.[135] They risk jail and death more than do higher-up members of the trade, but even the latter—those on the management team—expose themselves to extremely high penalties for failure, risking beatings, long prison sentences, and death at the hands of either the police or rival firms.

Gang activities constitute whole underground sales networks, but large as they are, these activities show only one corner of the drug economy.

7

Drug-War Politics

Pressures for drug-law and prison-regime reforms have increased and spread since the turn of the twenty-first century. Numerous state referenda, legislative moves, and court rulings have liberalized marijuana restrictions, allowing medical prescriptions and in some cases recreational use. Legislatures have reduced penalties for use of many drugs and have lessened some of the racial bias. Arrests and jailings for African American men and women have diminished moderately in many cities. California spends more than $9 billion annually on its prison system and over the last three decades built twenty-two new prisons (but only one university).[1] As first steps for change, however, California voters decided with a huge majority in 2012 to reform the three-strikes law that had required life sentences even for minor crimes. More than one thousand lifers were released within a year. In 2014 Proposition 47 passed handily, to end felony sentences for nonviolent, low-level crimes, including possession for personal use of cocaine, heroin, and other drugs. A political science professor at the University of California, San Diego, says that Prop 47 "officially end[s] California's tough-on-crime era."[2] Along the same trajectory, the Obama administration announced in July 2015 an experiment with restoration of Pell Grants, canceled in 1994, to "allow potentially thousands of inmates across the U.S. to gain access to . . . the main form of federal aid for low-income college students."[3]

While many politicians have benefited from supporting the drug war, growing numbers of influential persons express opposition. While private firms may benefit handsomely from provisioning the war, state governments have become more cautious, sensitive to budgetary pressures. Among supporters for drug-law reform, nearly all endorse a policy known as harm reduction; many call for decriminalization, and growing numbers advocate legalization. Nevertheless, the drug war remains a major and damaging element of urban policy, with key supporters.

An Austerity Exception

Much of the money spent in the underground economy later enters the normal, legal economy. Most institutions involved with drugs operate either as legitimate private businesses or as public agencies, excepting the gangs and other retail dealers, drug producers, and distribution networks. Legally involved groups include the police, prisons, drug courts, rehabilitation centers, gangsta rap producers, courier services, construction firms, suppliers of all sorts, and banks. These institutions and their employees earn their livings connected to the drug trade, operating in the open. These private firms and public offices issue weekly paychecks, deal with unions and individual employees, pay taxes, and receive full support from the enforcement of contract law.

Institutional Sustenance and Good Jobs

Predatory practices that harm city people reach their zenith with seizures encouraged with federal incentives.[4] Police seize more than a billion dollars every year, much going into the Justice Department's Asset Forfeiture Fund.[5] Contravening traditional forfeiture laws in most states, which protect against unwarranted takings of property and stipulate broad public use of funds from seizures, Congress voted in 1984 to allow police departments to capture drug money and seize "drug-related" assets, sell them, and keep the money for themselves. Attorney General Richard Thornburgh later boasted: "It's now possible for a drug dealer to serve time in a forfeiture-financed prison after being arrested by agents driving a forfeiture-provided automobile while working in a forfeiture-funded sting operation."[6]

Such procedures carry the potential for abusing citizens' rights and contaminating police practices, compromising due process by tying police compensation, purchase of equipment, and other expenditures to the money seized in forfeitures. The rules allow police departments to get around state requirements "to share forfeited assets with school boards, libraries, drug education programs, or the general fund."[7] "Some small town police forces have enhanced their annual budget by a factor of five or more through such drug enforcement activities. . . . A 1993 report on drug task forces prepared for the Justice Department . . . noted that 'one "big bust" can provide a [drug] task force with the resources to become financially independent.' "[8]

Prison employment offers hope to small cities and rural areas, to prop up their economies.[9] Businesses that build and even operate prisons combine interests to form powerful electoral coalitions. Prison guards in California pressed for pay and benefits, to extract major concessions from the legislature.[10] Many once regarded this union as the most powerful lobby in California. Even though guards need only a high school education, they "had gained the most rapid pay increases of any state workers in recent years, with salaries . . . plus overtime . . . routinely . . . into six figures."[11] Most people who live in small prison communities are white, with big-city, predominantly minority prisoners.

Census population statistics reinforce the antiurban bias. Many federal agencies allocate expenditures in proportion to population. When authorities count prisoners as local residents, this inclusion displaces resources and political representation away from the prisoners' home neighborhoods in big cities.[12] Some two-thirds of New York State prisoners come from New York City and others from a few upstate cities with large minority populations, and 82 percent of the prison population is black or Latino, but virtually all prison cells (98 percent) are located in disproportionately white state senatorial districts.[13]

Day in, day out, many individuals benefit from drug-war expenditures by municipalities, states, and federal agencies. Like the institutional beneficiaries, these individuals are unlikely to take active interest in the health of the inner-city neighborhoods where so much of the war takes place. Police, prosecutors, judges and judicial personnel, jail and prison administrators, and guards constitute the public-sector part of this prison-industrial complex. Many other parties have allied interests. Counselors, psychologists, other medical personnel, and other specialists benefit by employment directly in the public sector or through contracts. They find work in the daily functioning of the drug war, earning their livings treating mandated clients, either inside prisons, taking post-prison referrals, or providing alternatives to the justice system. Taken together, these beneficiaries and their institutions weigh heavily in many local economies, and they exert influence in local and state governments.[14]

Making Money from the Drug War

Corporations and other private interests benefit, too. They sell to police departments and other enforcement agencies substantial quantities of arms, uniforms, specially equipped vehicles, advanced communications equipment, and a whole panoply of up-to-date paramilitary equipment. They provide services to prisons, including "security technology, vending machines, and products sold at elevated prices at the 'commissary,' where prisoners buy toiletries, food, and other necessities." Firms like Marriott hold large food-service contracts. Many of the advantages of cost-plus contracting known to be so inflationary in military procurement also prevail in prisons. When prisoners make telephone calls home, or people transfer funds in, or even when prisoners take their savings out on release, they often pay exorbitant fees to "inmate service companies."[15] These firms may share commissions, leaving authorities "no incentive to seek competitive bids."[16] One Alabama jail "collects 84 percent of the gross revenue from calls," while a Texas firm pays the county "at least $55 a month per inmate." In-state calls escape regulation, so that a fifteen-minute call in New Jersey can cost $8.50. To transfer funds into Clallam Bay prison in Washington, one pays $4.95; at the Tennessee Prison for Women in Nashville, the fee is $6.90. This is big business: in 2014 one firm, Global Tel-Link, a New York–based firm that earlier sold for $1 billion, had contracts with twenty-two hundred prisons and jails, with more than a million inmates.[17]

Funds flow to construction firms, general contractors and subcontractors, suppliers of materials and furnishings, and workers who build and maintain prisons. Prison construction became the basis of many a local growth coalition, in which civic boosters push their interests with support from labor. Money is made even with prisoner manufacturing. Unicor, which made $900 million in revenue in 2011, "is a government-run enterprise that employs over 13,000 inmates—at wages as low as 23 cents an hour—to make goods for the Pentagon and other federal agencies."[18] In this branch of the national economy, the prison-industrial complex, the larger the drug war, the more prisoners, the better.

Until about 1990 prisons were almost entirely public. Since then, private corporations have not only built and continued to supply prisons but now sometimes operate them. Nationwide in 2006, 154 private prisons in thirty-one states, the District of Columbia, and Puerto Rico held 120,092 prisoners. Texas then had forty-three private prisons, and California had twenty-two. By 2009 the number of people in private prisons reached 130,000, with an additional 16,000 civil immigrant detainees. Revenues for just two firms, Corrections Corporation of America and the GEO Group, reached almost $3 billion in 2010.[19] In addition to the private prisons, privately operated halfway centers, set up like prisons, hold many thousands more, sometimes in appallingly unsafe conditions, where "drugs, gangs and sexual abuse are rife."[20] Private prisons are less likely to help prisoners with programs for mental health, substance abuse counseling, high school and college courses, and job training. In California, Texas, and Arizona, the private sector holds significantly higher proportions of prisoners of color.[21] The incentives for sustaining the drug war and adding prisoners are straightforward, since more convictions and longer sentences translate into public spending. Business interests likely translate into lobbying at state capitals and in Washington, and they may furnish campaign contributions, all part of mainstream U.S. politics.

Other parties benefit from the drug trade. Banks and other financial institutions, despite theoretical requirements to register large depositors, manipulate procedures to move vast quantities of money across the globe. Banking records are notoriously secret, and public officials have imposed few strict controls even on well-known law benders such as offshore banks. Money transfer operations operate with near impunity outside banks as well: in Queens, in New York City, for example, launderers take large cash deposits and then split them into thousands of smaller amounts just below the legal radar (usually $1,000), paying token amounts to neighborhood residents who lend their names to facilitate the transfer of millions of dollars internationally.[22] Dictators, drug lords, and gunrunners all need bankers to turn a blind eye.[23]

Pharmaceutical companies are also eager to get their piece of the economic pie. According to a leading researcher in Scotland, "Big companies are starting to get interested in the field [of therapeutic marijuana]. 'We see them—Pfizer, GlaxoSmithKline, Novartis—all the time at the meetings of the [scholarly] society now.' "[24] The pharmaceutical industry is working its public relations machine to maintain laws prohibiting the growing of marijuana, presumably to secure profits upon the industry's development of substitute drugs,[25] meanwhile increasing profits from existing, legally available pharma-provided painkillers. At the other end of the production-to-market spectrum, testing for drug use has been a growth industry.[26] Much of the profit in these transactions depends not mainly on drug use but on its illegality.

Political Profits

The drug war has provided a target to help conservative politicians who seek justification for the cutting of expenditures for social services. Some aim for drastic reductions in spending and ultimately for comprehensive shrinking of the public sector. Others aim to hold down taxes while maintaining massive military and security programs. Both groups find they can lean on the drug war, which serves as a helpful political crutch. By demonizing an isolated group of people and warning that we must arm "ourselves" against "them," these partisan operators can extract campaign funding and help corporations that receive drug-war contracts, while simultaneously demanding lower taxes and budget cuts. It's an economy of fear.

Under these circumstances, political parties and candidates make easy use of anti-drug rhetoric. For a starter, it is easy to attribute the problems not to drug *prohibition* but to the *presence* of drugs, period. Even politicians who understand that the war works counterproductively may decide not to oppose it, to avoid being pronounced soft on drugs, soft on crime. Other proponents play on fear and prejudice, using their rhetoric to feed on ignorance and misrepresentation, maligning critics. For some, the strong racial bias of the drug war makes it politically convenient.

Generally, politicians have difficulty going against the trend and find it convenient to oversimplify, as did Charlie Rangel, Democratic congressman from Harlem, who said: "You can't get on a train, a plane, you can't do anything now that you aren't in fear that this epidemic is absorbing you. . . . Look at what drug abuse does to you and look at the heavy burden it is causing you, America. We've got to win the war."[27] Years later, Bob Riley, Republican governor of Alabama, said: "Drugs are the enemies of ambition—and when we fight against drugs, we are fighting for the future." It is a rare politician who breaks with standard practice, but sometimes retired politicians summon their courage to speak the blunt truth.

Various reasons lead politicians to ignore the evidence or sidestep rational discussion. Many voters oppose drug use and endorse punishment on religious or moral grounds—one thinks of the early struggle against drinking, with the temperance movement and Carrie Nation's call from God, which told her to enter taverns with her hatchet and chop up the bars. Stiff penalties like the Rockefeller laws in New York or three-strikes life sentences in California respond to public outrage not just against drugs but also against perceptions of waves of violent crime. For many, incarceration produces quick, solid, sure results, but treatment does not. Few voters or politicians feel the consequences of the drug war in their own neighborhoods, and they do not imagine how the war causes mayhem where others live. Legislators, prosecutors, judges, and juries do not connect their penalties (for fighting crime) with the budget-busting high costs of prison construction and added-up per-prisoner expenses.[28]

To sum up: For many politicians, the drug war offers extensive benefits. It disenfranchises large numbers of lower-class and minority voters who favor public expenditures for social programs. It adds census-count numbers to rural and small-town districts where the prisons are located, thus awarding them more federal funds and greater political representation. It creates convenient scapegoats for distracting attention from deeper and more serious social and economic problems. It satisfies those who oppose drug use on religious and moral grounds. It assists a key set of corporations, which can make campaign contributions. And it falsely shifts the blame for crime and disruption.

Rescuing Cities

Aside from narrow political gains, illicit jobs in poor neighborhoods, and direct and indirect financial benefits to public agencies and involved businesses, the drug war offers no benefits to the society at large, but many burdens. Critics search for better options. Four proposals stand out: demand reduction, harm reduction, decriminalization, or legalization. Legalization would create regulated and restricted markets like those for alcohol, tobacco, and prescription medications, accompanied by education and rehabilitation. Decriminalization would maintain criminal penalties for drug producers and dealers, but not for drug users. Harm reduction would focus on medical and social relief for addicts, and it would encompass demand reduction. Even a small part of the cost savings from reduced war spending would pay for the new policies.

Reformers take inspiration from the failure of Prohibition and lessons from innovative programs and policies in other countries. They have learned from experience with control of alcohol and tobacco, which have succeeded by regulating markets, limiting advertising, campaigning to persuade the public, and educating youth. In a dramatically successful U.S. example, cigarette smoking has declined sharply, thanks *not* to prohibition, but to higher prices, regulation of advertising, limits on smoking in public areas, public education, and consequent shifts in social habits.

Discussions of drug use and the drug war (two very different things) tend to be confused, uncomfortable, and unrealistic. For example, as I argued in the previous chapter, many people fear moderate drug users much more than they fear abusive alcoholics, even though recreational drug users cause fewer problems, of less severity. Critics of drug use tend to assume it is someone else's problem—and when those critics are middle-class, white, and in positions of authority, they readily attribute the problems to poor people of color. Thus discussion of drug use (and therefore the drug war) slides easily into discussion of "other" people and their bad behavior, even though, as we have seen, whites use drugs just as much as blacks and Latinos.

Social Scientists Oppose the Drug War

Nearly all scholars who have examined substance use and abuse and the drug war find the war counterproductive. Milton Friedman, the conservative icon who won the 1968 Nobel Prize in economics, strongly opposed the drug war, concluding that it leads to *increased* drug use and the marketing of *stronger* drugs, while destroying communities.[29] Friedman, together with two other Nobel laureates and more than five hundred other economists, signed a letter to President George W. Bush and other public officials calling for legalization of marijuana.

Orthodox economic theory offers helpful ideas about the possibilities for marginal change. Everyone agrees that *demand reduction* (in effect the same thing as reduced drug use) would shrink the drug war. People can be put into three categories: those averse to drug use under any circumstances, light and occasional users, and heavy users or addicts. Those at the two extremes, just like teetotalers or alcoholics, are unlikely to respond to regulation.[30] In the intermediate group, cautious, moderate users increase use with penalty reduction or decriminalization, but probably not much. The evidence (from the comparison case with alcohol—Prohibition—as well as from experiments in other countries) suggests that permissiveness would stimulate only small increases in demand. In the third group, addicts (like alcoholics and heavy smokers) will respond poorly to regulation. Overall, then, the demand for drugs is a poor candidate for *regulatory* control. The evidence from sharply declining tobacco sales suggests that demand (for drugs) will decline with price increases and changes in lifestyle, so legalization with sufficient taxation and social change can reduce use; but unless taxes are very high, short-run reductions in demand will probably be small.

Supply is another matter. The evidence, presented throughout the previous chapter, leads to the inescapable conclusion that even the most drastic controls will fail to reduce supply, except sometimes and in some places temporarily.[31] Powerful police and military forces from the United States and dependent countries have intervened to destroy crops and processing facilities, to capture and punish producers and traffickers, and to control shipments and especially importation into the United States. They have worked to arrest traffickers, destroy production facilities, and curtail shipments of marijuana and meth inside the United States. These interventions have failed. When the market demand for drugs is high, the suppliers continue their profitable work by shifting growing fields, moving production sites, altering shipment arrangements, and adjusting customer contact as necessary.

Theories of public order also offer bleak assessments. The Global Commission concludes that "punitive drug law enforcement fuels crime."[32] U.S. authorities have turned a medical/social issue into a criminal issue, at

once undermining city neighborhoods and creating a massive prison archi-
pelago. Under these arrangements, local authorities focus on maintenance
of public order and sometimes use the theory of the finger in the dike. At
the most local level, 7-Elevens and other stores broadcast classical music
in their parking lots, discouraging drug sellers from hanging out, plug-
ging that hole.[33] More generally and somewhat more formally, "broken
windows" theorists suggest that a strong and strict police control—an idea
that once found support from neighborhood groups—will stop misbehav-
ior at very low levels, thus discouraging higher-level crime.[34] The idea is to
insist on and enforce public order, making life intolerable for lawbreakers,
nipping problems in the bud. Aside from issues of civil liberties and civil
rights, the problem is that when the pressure is high, then as old holes in
the dike are plugged, new holes break through. Thus while police squads
can stop drug activity in focused zones, they are unable to reduce drug
trafficking overall in the larger area. Traffickers (and their customers)
merely move to other zones, and along with the traffic, the war moves,
too. In a similar adjustment, drug activity has recently shifted out of some
central-city neighborhoods only to increase in inner suburbs (the cause in
this case is not geographically focused police enforcement but changing
real estate prices and gentrification). This discussion pertains only to traffickers subject to high levels of police attention; others, such as Wall Street
traders wanting cocaine, buy in separate, segmented markets.

The problem can be stated more generally, in terms of regulation. In
theory, drugs are highly regulated—although, in reality, much of the drug
market itself is illegal, meaning that transactions, ownership, and use of
the commodity should not occur. But since in actuality this illegal market
exists and operates quite widely, and all its theoretically prohibited activities do occur, then the market is in practice unregulated. On the one hand,
drug production, shipment, and sales operate in a totally unregulated market; on the other hand, that market is disrupted by war. In one sense, then,
legalization would lead to the possibility of regulation.[35]

Theory from political economy and sociology focuses not on drug use
or drug users but on the drug war itself, probing its origins in history and
its function as a national institution. The United States has always used
the oppression of people of color, particularly African Americans but also
others, including immigrants, both for the extraction of value (through
low pay, long hours, and tough working conditions) and for segmenting

the population socially, which satisfies many whites. The drug war is thus deeply rooted in the American political economy, serving as a key element in the nation's most persistent social, political, and economic cleavage.

Given these pessimistic interpretations of the drug war, it is hard to recommend local actions other than to go along with the program and strive to create economic opportunities for workers and families, including transfer payments, improved schools, new and better social programs, and resistance to both police abuse and drug-gang mayhem. But on a larger scale, city planners and activists can push for national change—on issues of economic inequality, racial injustice, and, more directly, the absurdity of a drug war that not only creates damages and wastes money but yields no good. It is in the legislative realm of drug prohibition where changes will make a dramatic difference, since so many of the problems related to drugs stem not from use of the drugs themselves, nor even from the marketing, but from the prohibition on use and marketing. Economists can use their analysis of supply and demand to explain why the war will not stop drug use. Political scientists can show why focused repression (of drug trafficking) in particular neighborhoods will merely shift the problem around. But as the view from political economy suggests, larger improvements may depend on larger political and social changes, on integrating people of color and immigrants into the middle-class mainstream, the professions, and (much more) into politics, on empowering the poor, and on challenging austerity, thus reversing growth in inequalities in income and opportunity.

We can look beyond problems of individual addiction and its liabilities, to problems related to laws that make the entire economy of drugs illicit. For many, such a transfer of focus is difficult—from a focus on individual responsibility (drug use is evil, dangerous, and illegal) to a focus on a system-wide, abstract responsibility (drug laws are voted by legislatures and enforced by police and courts). For many, to leave off the attack on illegal individual drug behavior in order to take up an attack on the drug laws themselves is a big pill to swallow, because of the alien feelings that come from the disreputable nature of drug dealing, problems of sales to (and by) children, and reluctance to regard any laws as problematic.

Prohibition of alcohol failed miserably, and it promoted illegal rackets generally. Stiff regulation of tobacco has had dramatically good effect, without prohibition. The drug war—a new Prohibition—has not reduced drug use or drug production and shipment. No evidence suggests that even full legalization (with regulation) would lead to a substantial increase in drug use. Finally, tacitly legal drug use abounds in the United States. Middle-class, mostly white people, in restaurants and clubs, and in the suburbs, purchase and consume most drugs—the vast majority, if we add illegitimate prescription drugs—and they rarely suffer at the hands of the law. The drug war does not attack drugs, but it attacks the nation's most vulnerable neighborhoods and the people who live in them.

Public Leaders, Scholars, and Voters Oppose the Drug War

Although many skeptics will bet on the drug-war status quo—given continuing support from religious groups, involved corporations, small-town beneficiaries, and many politicians—optimists can bet on change. Prominent persons in various positions have risked retribution to speak in favor of alternatives. Officials have targeted the burden of prison spending itself, in response to tightened budgets. Courts have pressed prison systems from various angles. Community leaders fear loss of long-term community and social intervention capacity, as the costs of maintaining prisons have continued their growth. Voters have supported change.

It is difficult to tell whether the federal center can hold. Earlier, despite pre-election statements in 2008 that signaled openness to reconsideration of the drug war, the Department of Justice in the Obama administration has wavered uncertainly in its prosecutorial agenda, going from permissive to hostile, for example, on medical marijuana. Despite its liberal drug "czar" and claims about shifting toward nonwar prevention efforts, the Obama White House maintained a focus "on weapons [and] cash" to stem the importation of drugs.[36] Allocation of funding within the administration's drug budget shifted modestly *away* from rehabilitation and community support toward law enforcement and interdiction. A comparison of fiscal 2005 (final budget authority) and 2013 (enacted budget) shows that "demand reduction," which includes drug courts with other treatment and prevention expenditures, actually declined by nearly 3 percent (controlling for inflation) while "supply reduction" increased more than 12 percent.[37] Calls for change persisted in the second-term election, but for both parties, the 2012 campaign focused elsewhere. By early 2014, coping with conflicts between federal prohibition of marijuana and the many states with laws

allowing it, the Justice Department stopped prosecuting most "legal" dealers, and the Treasury Department issued rules to help banks do business
with these dealers.[38]

In earlier statements, high-level officials spoke out. Surgeon General Joc-
elyn Elders, federal district judge Harold Baer, and ambassadorial nominee
and former Massachusetts governor William Weld all opposed the war.[39]
Black mayors have spoken openly, despite pressure to blame the drug culture for their cities' problems. Cory Booker, when mayor of Newark: "The
drug war is causing crime. It's just chewing up young black men. And it's
killing Newark." Kurt Schmoke, when mayor of Baltimore: "Remove
the profit motive, and you put the dealers out of business." Schmoke proposed to "have government stores and buy marijuana cigarettes . . . nicely
wrapped . . . purity and potency guaranteed with a tax stamp."[40] Mike
Gravel, former senator from Alaska, in the 2007 Democratic Party presidential primary: "The scourge of our present society, particularly in the
African-American community, is the war on drugs. . . . If they really want
to do something about the inner cities . . . it's time to end this war. . . . All it
does is create criminals out of people who are not criminals."[41]

Many thousands of police officers and others in law enforcement belong
to the group Law Enforcement against Prohibition.[42] New York City
police commissioner Raymond W. Kelly, speaking in 2007 for scores of city
police chiefs, found the war's methods absurd, especially the irony of support by the gun lobby. More than 340 mayors and 200 police chiefs joined
Kelly to oppose extending Kansas representative Todd Tiahrt's amendment, which handicaps state and local governments, the Department of
Justice, and the Bureau of Alcohol, Tobacco, Firearms, and Explosives
(ATF) by prohibiting the sharing of "crucial information about guns used
in crimes."[43] Norm Stamper, the retired Seattle police chief, says, "I actually support the legalization of *all* drugs." The "more dangerous or sinister
or sensationally reported," the greater the advantage to legalization. Let
the government, rather than the cartels and the street gangs, do the regulating, which will put the cartels and the gangs out of business.[44]

Gara LaMarche, senior fellow at the Wagner School of Public Policy
at New York University and former CEO of the Atlantic Philanthropies,
went public, noting that right-wing politicians use crime and the drug
war as a "wedge issue to dislodge the pillars of the Great Society," inducing moral paranoia. "The hard-right foundations like Scaife, Bradley and

Olin" and the "bombastic media like Fox and Rush Limbaugh" make bogus use of race and crime, but they are rarely criticized in public. Despite this politics of mass incarceration, LaMarche hoped (in 2007) that politics was turning around, seeing "signs . . . everywhere that the prison-industrial complex is beginning to crack."[45]

Pat Robertson, the archconservative evangelical leader, onetime presidential candidate, and owner of the Christian Broadcasting Network, says, "This war on drugs just hasn't succeeded," and "I really believe we should treat marijuana the way we treat beverage alcohol."[46]

Confronted with recessionary tax pressures in the nation's post-2008 fiscal crisis, some state governments acknowledged the outsized magnitudes of their prison budgets, calling for drug-war and prison budget restrictions. Several states passed something like California's Proposition 36 (in 2000), which aims to shift emphasis from prisons to treatment. In some states, concern about restrictions on civil liberties has had some effect: Rhode Island, Iowa, and Florida restored some ex-prisoner voting rights. Prisoner numbers in many states exceed manageable capacity. In 2010, "nineteen state systems were operating above their highest capacity, with seven states at least 25% over their highest capacity."[47] Federal courts—without any comment on the drug war—found prison health conditions in California in violation of constitutional protections and ordered the release of forty thousand prisoners in 2009. With the state's "Golden Gulag" of prisons and its collapsed budgets, the order for prisoner release has facilitated the cutting of expenditures for purely fiscal reasons.[48] New York State dramatically reduced its population of drug prisoners, down 62 percent in the decade from 2000 to 2010.

Various states now pursue "justice reinvestment," a diversion of funds from prisons to social support. Numerous advocacy groups, including organizations of ex-prisoners, have entered public debate.[49] Many states have moved to decriminalize the growing, marketing, and use of medical marijuana. A former Washington, DC, federal prosecutor was surprised when juries of peers refused to send defendants to prison. He came to see their refusal as part of the struggle against the war on drugs, and as a law professor he now encourages juries to use their power to nullify.[50]

As draconian penalties have affected even some middle-class whites, the high social cost of drug prohibition has entered public conversation. In the mainstream, opposition to the drug war has grown—leading to increasing demands for drug courts in place of the traditional justice system, treatment options in place of prison, and decriminalization in place of prohibition. Filmmaker Eugene Jarecki found that wherever he went, "everyone involved—prisoners, cops, judges, jailers, wardens, medical experts, senators—all described to me a system out of control, a predatory monster that sustains itself on the mass incarceration of fellow human beings. Their crimes, most often the nonviolent use or sale of drugs in petty quantities, have become such a warping fixation for our prison-industrial complex that they are often punished more severely than violent crimes."[51]

Harm Reduction, Decriminalization, or Legalization?

In place of criminalizing the production, marketing, use, and possession of drugs, "harm reduction" deals with addiction as a health problem. This approach stresses the negative consequences of drug *use*—disease and death, family disintegration and other social problems, and lawbreaking. It emphasizes prevention of harm through education as well as treatment, and it takes into account both the useful characteristics of some drugs (medical marijuana, for example) and the varying addictive propensities and dangers to health and behavior. Advocates of harm reduction promote such interventions as heroin or methadone maintenance, the monitoring of drug purity, syringe exchanges, and safe injection sites. They also promote safe health practices for crack smokers, needle exchanges and other aids for intravenous users of cocaine and other substances, and safe practices for other drug users. They urge use of condoms, the disinfecting and disposal of needles, and the cleaning of utensils.[52] In Vancouver, British Columbia, public clinics allow heroin users to inject themselves with clean needles under supervision, and similar clinics are opening in Montreal and other Canadian cities.[53] An ample definition of harm reduction includes efforts to limit easy access to dangerous drugs, such as requiring a doctor's prescription for the purchase of methamphetamine, which has worked remarkably well in Oregon and Mississippi.[54]

Support Neighborhoods by Reducing Harm

Most thinking about rehabilitation focuses on the individual, especially the recommending of counseling for abstinence, following one or another of the models developed originally for alcoholism. Patients, often teenagers or young adults, enter various kinds of treatment programs, including weekly or daily meetings modeled after Alcoholics Anonymous, outpatient clinics for drugs or mental health, and residential substance-abuse rehabilitation programs with steady supervision and treatment from a few months to several years. Often participation is mandated by the court system.

Most harm reduction programs focus on individual or household/family problems. None has the capacity to deal effectively with the drug war's collateral damages to neighborhoods and their residents. This incapacity points to the need for community efforts that can rehabilitate and support not only drug users but also their neighbors and the drug dealers themselves, who need to unlock themselves from counterproductive activities and lifestyles.

Effective programs support neighborhood social rehabilitation and economic development, overlapping with improvements in schooling and expanded food and nutrition support. It takes a village to raise a child. Drug rehabilitation requires whole neighborhoods to receive assistance—household incomes must be increased through long-term efforts, from head-start schooling all the way to job training, public employment programs, and expanded income maintenance via EITC and unemployment insurance. Communities need entry-level jobs with promotion ladders. Communities need family services, child care, education programs, and housing assistance. They need police protection against ordinary crime and violence. They need more effective subsidies for housing and health care. Public services of all sorts need to be introduced and expanded, including especially safe streets, supervised after-school playgrounds, and day-care programs.

Any strategy for dealing with drug use, to be successful, requires individual and community rehabilitation as a central focus. A program of harm reduction will provide key support for both decriminalization and legalization.

Decriminalize Individual Behavior

Several countries have decriminalized drug possession. In 2001, Portugal, while maintaining criminal penalties for drug dealers, dropped criminal penalties for those found with small amounts (a ten-day supply) of drugs (marijuana, heroin, cocaine, LSD, and others). Instead of being arrested and jailed, apprehended users appear before a "dissuasion commission" of three people, including a lawyer or judge and a health or social services worker, who can release the user, recommend treatment, or recommend a small fine. The results appear to have been positive: warnings that Lisbon would become a drug users' haven have not been borne out, and dire consequences from drug overdoses, including death, have markedly diminished. Spain, Italy, and Mexico have also decriminalized drug use without dire results.[55] As of 2014, about three-quarters of the U.S. population lived in states where marijuana laws had been relaxed. Still, the lack of a nationwide decriminalization policy is problematic, as is the focus on marijuana alone. President Obama, on April 14, 2012, at the Summit of the Americas, acknowledging that drug laws may do harm, said, as noted earlier, that "legalization is not the answer."

A set of small steps will go a long way toward alleviating the neighborhood-destroying aspects of the drug war. Civil society groups have pushed for each of these steps. Walk them together, and the improvements will be dramatic. End mandatory sentencing. Fully eliminate the crack/cocaine disparity. Stop sending juveniles to adult courts and adult prisons. Rescind all the get-tough legislation, from the Rockefeller drug and three-strikes laws on to all their copycats that result in long prison terms for minor offenses. Stop putting in prison people convicted of minor, nonviolent crimes. Make use of drug courts, and copy or adapt the many intervention innovations pioneered in other countries. Eliminate the seizure incentive that can motivate police to make drug arrests. Adapt as drug-use restraints the many strategies that limit use of tobacco.

At least for marijuana, public support for legalization has grown dramatically. While more than 80 percent of Americans opposed legal pot as recently as the early 1990s, by 2014, 54 percent supported it.[56]

Rescue Neighborhoods: Start with Legalization?

The massive evidence of a wrongheaded drug war points many critics toward a more radical departure—a complete end to the war, decriminalization of drug use, and legalization of the drug trade, accompanied by steep regulatory barriers and harm reduction expanded to neighborhood rehabilitation and development. Stop the war and stop the violence, but rehabilitate neighborhoods.

Governing drugs the way we govern alcohol entails risks. In the case of food, business interests and the health of the public come into conflict. In the case of alcohol, the conflict is more focused, as corporations advertise and push sales, knowing that alcoholics make up their principal market. We should assume the same would be the case were now-illicit drugs to be sold legally. Legal corporations will do all they can to promote addiction, because it will increase their sales. Furthermore, we should expect that however high tax rates are set at the outset of drug legalization, they will tend to fall (as they have fallen with alcohol) because of the strength of the industry's lobbying. Finally, "doing drugs" will become more acceptable. These are serious risks, not to be minimized.

But the upsides make these risks worthwhile. Even in periods of general economic success, few harm-reduction programs can exist, much less prosper, in communities afflicted by drug commerce. Gangs control such commerce, and violence is their method. In periods of economic recession, the problems are worse, because community assistance programs are among the first and the hardest hit. Dissolve the drug war, and community rehabilitation begins with a fresh emphasis, offering opportunities and options that are taken for granted in stronger, better-off neighborhoods.

Decriminalize drug use, but limit it through education, regulation, intervention, and the provision of attractive alternatives. Legalize trade in drugs, but regulate, restrict, and license. The prospect of such changes frightens many. It looks like walking on a path to anarchy, and even the most optimistic of critics must fear political reaction. Yet, as many critics powerfully argue, abundant evidence calls for such changes.

Harm reduction, decriminalization, or legalization, combined with related reductions in prison, parole, and probation populations, will have positive short-term and long-term consequences for cities. Public spending on the justice system and incarceration can be reduced and transferred to neighborhood support. These are potentially very large sums of public funds, as illustrated by "million-dollar blocks"—city blocks where the state spends more than a million dollars on a single block's residents incarcerated each year.[57] The whole tenor of city life will improve when the drug war finally comes to an end. Safe streets, safe neighborhoods, families reunited, police focusing on serious crimes—these are all desirable things almost beyond imagination in city zones where the drug war has been contested.

Democracy, Inequality, Urban Policy

> We may have democracy, or we may have wealth concentrated in
> the hands of a few, but we cannot have both.
>
> Supreme Court Justice Louis D. Brandeis, 1941

American cities will not prosper unless the nation takes a new approach
to urban policy. Yes, federal agencies need to augment their contributions
for housing, and metropolitan areas need inter-municipal coordination.
Cities need enhanced environmental protection, accelerated economic
development, and protection against abrupt real estate booms and busts.
But for such improvements to occur more often and more robustly, the
nation must reject austerity and, together with the cities, improve policies
for schools, food, and drugs.

Recent history is not auspicious. Austerity policies continue to abet growing inequality and to intensify the fiscal difficulties of cities. Against President Obama's efforts—including his warnings in his first campaign and
again in the spring of 2014 against growing inequality, his arguments for a
higher federal minimum wage to be indexed by inflation, and his proposals for a host of progressive expenditures—the Congress resisted. At times
the president himself seemed persuaded by misleading anti-deficit rhetoric. Although the Congress did fund early and limited stimulus spending

proposed by Presidents Bush and Obama, it budgeted far too little for rapid recovery and decidedly did not aim at rescuing cities. Pundits and the media have placed school reform on everyone's agenda, but hostility to taxation and restraints on public spending nevertheless persist, leaving big-city schoolchildren in immense difficulty. Many and diverse parties support food reforms, but corporate resistance remains strong, and unhealthy obesity abounds. Liberal civil rights groups, conservative budget cutters, and billionaire financiers have joined forces pushing to reduce arrests, but drug-war advocates and prison profiteers persist, keeping the neighborhoods down.

In these conflicted circumstances, can politics shift so as to diminish city-damaging austerity, privatization, and inequality? Can the nation build on widespread concerns, to support city schools, improve neighborhood nutrition, and be done with the drug war? Much evidence on the national level is gloomy, anticipating further inequality and concentrated wealth. In his pessimistic dissent to the Supreme Court's 2010 *Citizens United* decision, which permits election expenditures by corporations, Justice Stevens wrote that "a democracy cannot function effectively when its constituent members believe laws are being bought and sold"—a sixty-year echo of Justice Brandeis.

In other ways, however, as we have seen throughout this book, better opportunities have arisen, especially on the urban scene. Even in the strongly anti-Obama 2014 midterm congressional elections, when advocates spent \$3.7 billion on the first post–*Citizens United* election and conservatives took charge of both houses, showing no interest in helping cities, progressive voting occurred. If the sun can keep shining through the heavy conservative clouds, perhaps it will energize reformers to aid city schools, improve city food, resist the drug war, and promote equality.

Fighting Austerity

Congressional conservatives like to cut city-aid budgets for the same reason Willie Sutton robbed banks—that's where the money is. Given the preponderance of the nation's metropolitan population, the vivid demarcations that separate rich and poor municipalities, and the political opportunity to cast blame on poor minority neighborhoods, pro-city spending programs offer the budgets from which the money can be extracted. Enact cuts to federal programs that aid cities, conservatives in Congress apparently believe, and everybody wins.

Austerity is not only a city problem, of course. Its bad effects show nationally in the collapse of highway infrastructure, in slowed industrial progress, and in a more unequal distribution of income and wealth. Many believe as I do, along with Justice Brandeis, that these unequalizing effects diminish democracy. Ian Ayres and Aaron Edlin, professors of law and economics at Berkeley and Harvard, invented the Brandeis ratio to put numbers to the concentration. Their simple quotient divides the average income of the top 1 percent by the median income. The higher the ratio, the more distant is democracy. In 1980 the ratio was 12.5, already higher than it had been, but a quarter century later, in 2006, it had tripled to 36. Ayres and Edlin remind us that "Brandeis lived at a time when enormous disparities between the rich and the poor led to violent labor unrest and ultimately to a reform movement." Today they believe the nation approaches another "Brandeis tipping point."[1] In cities, the drastic and cumulative spending cuts that have eroded services, especially schools, exacerbate the disparity, to make a turning point still more likely. Will it occur?

Not easily. We have seen how austerity is imposed on cities from federal and state levels. By now, an ideology of inequality has also taken deep root in city halls and among city influentials. In recent decades, while city leaders proudly doled out munificent grants for private development, they irritably objected to pushing up bottom-end wages. Under Mayor Bloomberg, New York City favored developers, awarding millions in subsidies to firms including Goldman Sachs, the Bank of America, and Ernst & Young for office skyscrapers. The city gave the Yankees hundreds of millions for their new stadium, even though baseball fans confront overpriced everything, from seats to hot dogs. But when New York labor organizers argued for the living wage, justly saying that "if you work full time, you shouldn't be poor," city leaders played the red card. Mayor Bloomberg "rumble[d] about threats to capitalism," just as Mayor Giuliani had earlier complained that advocates were "trying to rebuild the Berlin Wall."[2] These pro-inequality biases are repeated in cities across the nation, in favor of low taxation and shrinking services, but with subsidies for developers.

Conservative political theorists have long claimed that cities do best at collecting garbage and policing the streets, not at redistribution.

Progressive theorists have long bemoaned the difficulties of reform even in single *nations*, much less single cities. From both perspectives, whatever difficulties New York City may encounter at enacting progressive reforms, other cities across the nation will encounter them as well.

Furthermore, limits on every city's anti-austerity power come down from federal legislation. Four prominent *personal* income tax dodges allow well-off individuals and families to reduce their payments through loopholes that provide tax deductions for health insurance, mortgage interest, local tax payments, and retirement savings. These deductions award disproportionate benefits for the middle class and the wealthy, overwhelmingly favoring relatively well-off suburbanites, rather than residents of cities and poorer suburbs. Some $70 billion of federal tax expenditures annually provide deductions for payment of state and local taxes, including school district taxes. Further tax exclusions accrue on capital gains on home sales and other investments, as well as employer-paid health insurance. Forgone taxes for home mortgage interest deductions alone have totaled for many years well more than $100 billion annually. From such personal tax expenditures in 2011, totaling $592 billion, 72.5 percent of the gains went to the top one-fifth of taxpayers, favoring better-off suburban constituencies. For the bottom *three*-fifths of taxpayers, by comparison, refundable credits (EITC and related programs) total a paltry $96.5 billion.[3] Thus the average EITC recipient, likely a city resident, receives less than 5.6 percent of the average tax break awarded to those who are much better off.[4]

The national philosophy of taxpaying responsibility has shifted markedly in the austerity direction over the last half century. In the 1960s, the highest-earning taxpayers, those in the top 0.01 percent of the income distribution (that is, one of every ten thousand tax filers) actually *paid* on average 71.4 percent of their income in federal taxes (income, payroll, estate, and other taxes).[5] The highest 0.1 percent of taxpayers (including the 0.01 percenters) paid 60 percent, and the inclusive top 1 percent paid on average 44.4 percent. Such high tax payments are unheard of today. For the one percenters, average tax rates had crashed by 2004, to levels between 30.4 and 34.2 percent.[6] The next income groups—the vast middle class, three-fifths of the population—did not benefit from tax reductions, although rates for the bottom two quintiles did drop. (See figure 8.1.)

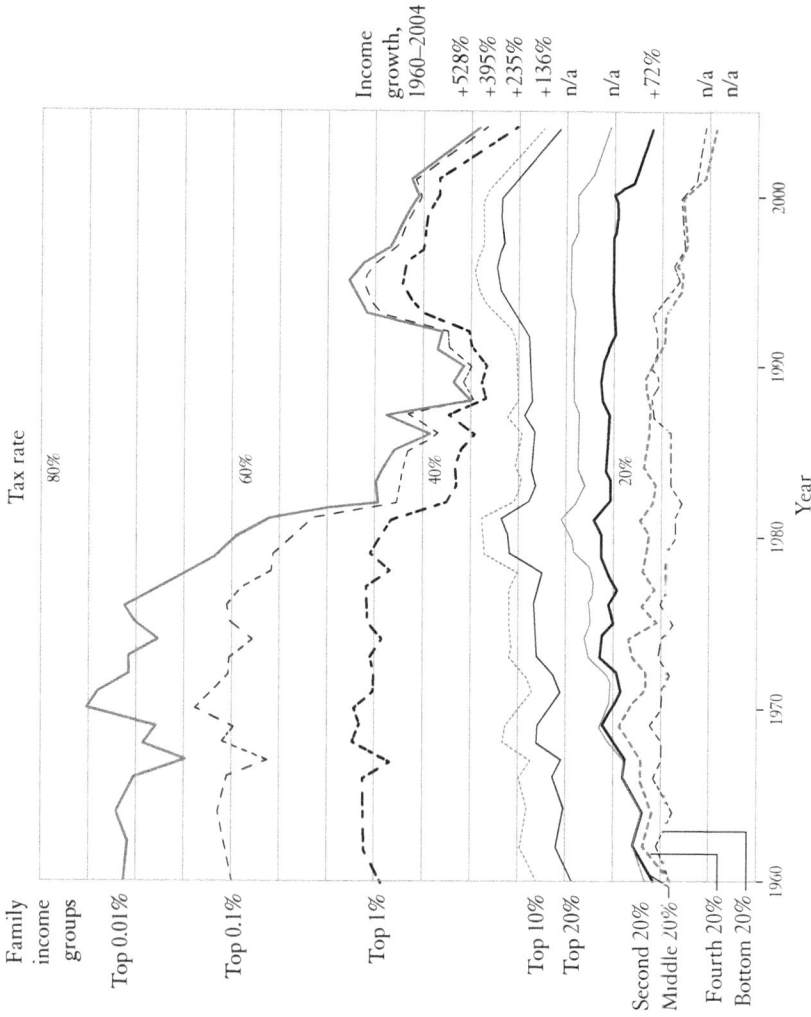

Figure 8.1. Average tax rates and changes in income, 1960–2004. Data from Emmanuel Saez, University of California, and Thomas Piketty, Paris School of Economics; Census Bureau (real median income growth from 1960 to 2004). Adapted from David Leonhardt, "Coming Soon: 'Taxmageddon,'" *New York Times*, April 13, 2012.

Tax reductions for the rich matched their runaway wealth accumulation. The pretax inflation-adjusted incomes of the top 0.01 percent grew by 528 percent over those forty-four years. Incomes also grew (on average) for the rest of the top 1 percent. But for everyone else, the 99 percent, incomes *declined*. If you are hungry, whatever your politics may be, from Tea Party to Socialist Party, you can find meat for your sandwich in those tax statistics.

The Fiscal Policy Institute explains the extraordinary income grab by New York City's 1 percent (displayed earlier, in figure 2.1). Three trends stand out to explain the widening disparities: wages have become less equal, favoring high-wage employees; wages have fallen compared to earnings on capital, favoring investors and owners; and particular public policies have aided the 1 percent. These policies include reductions of taxes on the wealthy, declining real value of the minimum wage, and difficulties put up by the National Labor Relations Board against workers who want to form unions and bargain collectively.[7]

Again, we should ask, are we approaching the tipping point? Rising inequality—resulting from markets that in all likelihood deliver unequal incomes, combined with parsimonious public policy—alarmed Justice Brandeis. Evidence today suggests people are alarmed again. Even in the Republican-led elections of 2014, anti-austerity forces gained ground as poorly paid workers organized, gained support, and caught the attention of voters. In Republican-dominated South Dakota, Nebraska, Arkansas, and Alaska, sizable majorities, ranging from 53 percent to 69 percent, voted to increase minimum wages. Illinois voters cast their ballots 2-to-1 urging the legislature to raise the minimum. Throughout 2014, a total of ten states raised the minimum, and since January 2015, the legal minimum wage exceeds the federal level in the District of Columbia and twenty-three states.[8] Pressure has been building in cities—with the highest minimums approved in Seattle and San Francisco, at fifteen dollars an hour. Referenda and initiatives to increase minimums appeared in Eureka, San Diego, and Richmond, California; Las Cruces, New Mexico; Washington, DC; and Philadelphia and Chicago. In New York State, city leaders pressed the governor, who agreed to push for a bill allowing cities to raise minimum wages locally, to exceed the state level. In July 2015 the governor of New York State ordered an increase in the *state* minimum wage to fifteen dollars an hour, and laws mandating paid sick leave have recently passed in eighteen cities, three states, and the District of Columbia.[9] And across the nation, living-wage laws now require city suppliers and contractors to pay more. More than 120 cities and counties have adopted these laws, often in the range of $12 to $15.[10]

Cities have also begun to help neighborhoods to resist gentrification. In some cities, long-term residents, typically those who have owned their homes at least ten years, receive relief from rising taxes and impossible-to-meet mortgage payments. Richmond, California, has used its power of eminent domain to rescue underwater mortgage holders. Boston, which the Cleveland Federal Reserve Bank found to have "the highest gentrifying pressure in the nation," aims to protect the one-quarter of its residents who live in gentrifying neighborhoods. The city council passed a bill to allow long-term homeowners to defer payment until the property is sold if they face property tax increases of at least 10 percent. Philadelphia passed two laws, the Homestead Exemption, which allows a $30,000 reduction of assessed value, and LOOP, the Longtime Owner Occupants Program, to freeze assessments for a decade if a household's income does not exceed about $110,000 and its assessment has tripled. Similar neighborhood pressures and plans have come up in Washington, DC, Pittsburgh, and San Francisco.[11]

Not only did the 2012 election of Bill de Blasio as mayor of New York City represent a notable reaction to increased inequality, but other New York officials pushing openly against austerity also won posts, to dominate the city legislature and occupy top political and administrative posts. They also persuaded the state to fund vastly expanded early public education, increasing enrollments for full-day preschool for more than seventy-three thousand four-year-olds by 2016. Already by fall 2014, enrollments in public schools and community centers exceeded fifty-three thousand.[12] The city proposed to increase taxation of the highest city earners, to cut back on subsidies to developers, and to demand cross-subsidies that will provide a larger stock of affordable housing—but these initiatives ran into state-level resistance.

Occupations of public space in hundreds of cities may have ended, but Occupy Wall Street generated a persistent shift of attention to inequality. Bill Peduto, the mayor of Pittsburgh, says his challenge is to find "good jobs for people with no PhDs but with a good work ethic and GEDs." As he asks how to make things better, he says, "All the mayors elected last year are asking this question." He believes that a demographic trans-formation, bringing "millions of Latino, Asian, and African immigrants and the millennials to the polls," is remaking the politics of many cities.[13] One index illustrates the new imbalance—Republicans control the Con-gress and many states in 2014, but only four of the thirty largest cities have Republicans as mayors.

Even the largest city in the nation, with a population exceeding eight million, however, cannot succeed alone at attacking austerity and eras-ing some of the worst stains of inequality. Arrayed against the progres-sive reformers in New York City are self-interested suburbs in three states and the New York State governor and legislature, responding to their own political ambitions as well as the voting preferences of many of the 57 percent of New York State's population who live outside the city. Most legislative and fiscal power lies with the state legislature, which responds traditionally with favors for the city's "growth coalition," includ-ing tax-shy wealthy households, real estate agents, developers, and other business interests. Similar or stronger obstacles remain to be overturned for other cities. On austerity, two steps forward, one step back.

Schools, Food, Drugs, and Prisons

From the political left to the political right, advocates see school reform as crucial—the nation's dilemma, the central civil rights issue of the time, even, according to the *Economist* magazine, an opportunity for the Repub-lican Party to win Latino votes by making up for their foot-dragging on immigration.[14] The agitation has produced some reforms—the number of eighteen-to-twenty-four-year-olds who have neither completed high school nor earned a GED fell steadily from 1998 to 2013. Hispanic drop-outs fell from 35 percent to 14 percent, and black dropouts fell from 16 per-cent to 5 percent.[15]

Pasi Sahlberg, the director of international programs in Finland's Min-istry of Education, has stated that "Americans cannot achieve equity with-out first implementing fundamental changes in their school system." Turn his sentence around, and he is still right: Americans cannot achieve funda-mental changes in their school system without first improving equity—not full equality, just more fairness. For Republican and Democratic office-holders, as well as residents of districts with good schools, this tight circle of causation and historical dependency often makes progressive change less attractive. Fairness depends on improving schools for *others*, but the improvements themselves require reductions in inequality. Pushed in the right direction, good policies can generate a self-reinforcing circle of improvement.

Food and the health problems associated with poor nutrition have also caught the nation's attention. In 2014, despite the $60 million or more that food corporations spent nationwide to defeat several municipal regulatory proposals by "nutrition nannies" (as *Forbes* calls them), two crucial voter initiatives passed. Berkeley voters approved a penny an ounce tax on soft drinks, the first in the nation. In San Francisco, a 55 percent majority voted for a two-penny tax.[16] Starting December 2014, a provision of Obamacare began to require prominent posting of calorie information at fast-food outlets, convenience stores, and even movie theaters. While the food industry objects, preliminary tests show positive results. Studies released mid-2015 suggest that consumption of sugary soft drinks has diminished and that childhood obesity is no longer on the rise.

With Republicans in control of the Senate, quick reform of drug laws and sentencing reforms may be unlikely, but with the momentum of marijuana reform and the growing recognition of the horrific international results of the drug war, including the mayhem in Mexico and El Salvador and the heavy emigration from Central America, eventual progress is highly likely. As Bill Keller, former editor of the *New York Times* and founding editor of the 2014 online Marshall Project, writes, "Criminal justice is one of the few areas of public policy where there is a significant patch of common ground between right and left."[17] The National Academy of Sciences research team reaches deep into history to conclude also in 2014 that fair, consistent, and transparent sentencing works better than severity and is in line with "fundamental and widely shared ideas about just punishment [in] the United States and other Western countries since the Enlightenment." Their report calls for initiatives that will shorten sentences, reduce racial bias, and curtail the war on drugs.[18]

On Democracy and Progress

The evidence throughout this book shows that the deprivation that afflicts cities, inner suburbs, and their poorest inhabitants is not only immoral, but also politically and economically unsustainable. It is economically illogical, and it may be, as even mainstream conservative politicians have begun to argue, politically suicidal. The Occupy movement and its one-percenter logic did much more than to upset decorum with disruptions in New York and hundreds of other cities. The forceful arguments also challenged the standard way of ignoring vast extensions of inequality and the multiple social and economic damages that result. Those who wish to protect the status quo of privilege with poverty have been forced to turn to more and more specious argumentation, turning, as Peter Marcuse says, "what should be wine into water."[19]

Regarding food inequality, Congressman Paul Ryan, the 2012 vice presidential candidate appointed chairman of the powerful Ways and Means Committee for 2015, and subsequently elected Speaker of the House, asserted when he chaired the Budget Committee that the nation cannot afford its SNAP (food stamp) bills and that federal and state governments should stop encouraging participation in the program (which both the Bush and Obama administrations and many governors encouraged). He also argued, contrary to the data, that SNAP is a work disincentive and that waste, fraud, and abuse are rampant. Ryan proposed turning SNAP from an entitlement into block grants to states, to reduce benefits further.[20] These selfish and (à la Brandeis) antidemocratic ideas leave those who are most vulnerable at the mercy of their poverty, their usually poor neighbors, and whatever charity they can find. These ideas are a throwback to less democratic times. They are being challenged in cities.

For centuries the ideas (and the practices) of citizenship and democracy, if they existed at all, were restricted to highly exclusive councils of land-owning elites. Starting in the eighteenth century, many cities and nations began to consider broader ideas of citizenship, from time to time responding to pressure to include larger portions of the population in the franchise. The U.S. Constitution, in practice, gave the vote to property-owning adult white males. The franchise later grew, at least on paper, to include such groups as non–property owners, persons freed from slavery, women, and younger adults. In some cities in several other countries today, most adult residents, including noncitizens, can register and vote in local elections. But formal democracy has strict limits in the United States. In the U.S. presidential election of 2012, Barack Obama received only 27 percent of the potential vote. Mitt Romney received 25 percent. Nearly half of voting-age citizens, 48 percent, cast no vote at all.[21] A cynic thinks that Congressman Ryan has carefully counted votes and is still gambling.

Fortunately, in the United States as elsewhere, ideas and practices of citizenship and informal democracy have spread beyond the act of voting to include a whole array of human and civil rights. Often these rights are instituted to protect individuals and groups, whether disadvantaged majorities such as women or nationally oppressed populations, or even smaller classes of people, such as those who are physically disabled. Rights may protect against the imposition of majority preferences or privileges as well.

Along another dimension, beyond voting and civil rights, and beyond human rights, ideas and practices of citizenship and democracy have spread into the realm of the economy. Democracy seen in this broader sense has developed to require that public bodies take on more responsibility to deliver goods and services. Over the long term, wage earners have won recognition as well as various rights versus the private firms for which they work and also versus the state. Today in the United States one can legitimately demand, for example, that laws be invoked to protect workers against retribution during organizing drives for unions, and that the state set and enforce health and safety standards in workplaces, though these matters are hardly settled. The eight-hour day is a legislative reality in all industrially advanced democracies, at least for most jobs in the formal sector, and often the workweek is set at fewer than forty hours, though this limit provides little help for those who must hold two or three jobs. Minimum wages are legislated nearly everywhere, even if their level is open to dispute and in the United States they do not yet guarantee a living wage.

During the years from the New Deal until the mid-1970s, these sorts of more inclusive ideas and practices dominated U.S. politics and powerfully influenced art, literature, and public discussion. People growing up in those generations came to consider it *normal* to expect and to win expanded rights of citizenship and ever more ample practices of democracy in politics, education, civil society, social life, and the economy. People did recognize the always-provisional nature of gains, and they knew that even long-standing achievements were contested and could be rolled back. They knew improvements had been won only through political organizing, labor strife, and social movements, and that there would perhaps always be a long ways to go. But optimism was the proven rule, and people mostly thought that despite hard-to-bypass blockades and painful setbacks, they, their children, and their fellow citizens, including immigrants, would win progress.

That optimistic period lasted about four decades, and for the generations then emerging, those were formative years. As urban populations swelled throughout the twentieth century, even political representation, which at first almost ignored cities, finally moved toward fairness. Although the Senate deprives metropolitan areas (and populous states) of equal representation, after the Warren Court's "one person, one vote" *Reynolds* rule in 1964, city (and suburban) voters had their say.

When the positive trajectory ended, sometime in the late 1970s, it took a while for the change to be clear. Was the new arrangement the real normal, a time when the odds stack up heavily against progress, a time when the rich get richer, when one percenters run things without so much trouble from the bottom 60 percent? Is the real normal a time when politics, social practices, and economics operate so as to maintain or exacerbate divisions by race, gender, and social background? Is it a time when presidential elections can be altered by five right-wing Supreme Court justices who themselves decide how the vote will be counted? Is it a time when the Republic suffers as the empire grows? As Paul Krugman has suggested, it has been a time when the *austerians* rule.

Market societies generate inequality, so reformers need always to anticipate a series of struggles, against the odds but never futile, for social transformation and persistent stepwise gains. Our best hopes, I think, may be for an endless repetition of two steps forward, and one step back. Most of the forward steps will be taken in cities. Taken most likely after external damages are reduced.

Historical Optimism

Historical precedents help us see into the future. On the balance of forces that may help or hinder cities, neighborhoods, and residents to deal with austerity budgeting, schools, food, and drugs, I am optimistic. Although the problems are not new, and in many ways they have become worse over the past thirty years, and especially over the past decade, still there are grounds for optimism. There is much evidence of positive response—from those who resist, who want to improve their status and that of their neighborhoods, and also from those who manage parts of the system but are either sensitive to the plight of others or worry about the corrosive effects of inequality and exclusion on the system overall.

Perhaps a fitting conclusion is to point to the long tradition in American politics of progressive reform, even of the influence of ideas from socialism and social democracy. In a political world in which right-wing ideological manipulators have turned American *liberalism* into an epithet, it is strange to suggest that ideas from socialism will be useful. But in fact many of the things Americans like best about their country operate in collective ways—good public schools, the National Parks, public water supplies, public libraries, municipal and state parks and recreation programs, even our streets and sidewalks. We collect taxes, and public authorities provide the services without fees or inexpensively. It works well, and, for the most part, we like it. These services, as well as socialized retirement benefits and socialized medicine for the elderly and the poor, were expanded quite dramatically through the twentieth century under presidential administrations that were (in limited ways) progressive—Teddy Roosevelt, Franklin Roosevelt, Dwight Eisenhower, John Kennedy, and Lyndon Johnson.[22]

In the first decade of the twenty-first century, even during years mostly under conservative Republican leadership, these democratic, redistributive programs have once again expanded, many of them because of entitlements still tied to rising needs as the economy turned sour. Federal transfer payments to individuals and families have grown tremendously, to the point where for the average family, transfers amount to almost one-fifth of income. Between 2000 and 2009, after adjusting for the effect of inflation, the per capita federal transfer payment had risen by 69 percent. The largest chunks are for Social Security, Medicare, and food stamps. These programs, as well as special transfer programs to support children, soften the blow of unemployment, and they help veterans. The programs were created to fight poverty, and to a considerable extent, they do. More and more, however, they have shifted from helping the poorest, to supporting people struggling to stay in the middle class.

A study by the Congressional Budget Office shows that the poorest fifth of households, those in the lowest quintile, received just over one-third (36 percent) of transfer payments in 2007, way down from the more than half (54 percent) they received almost thirty years earlier, in 1979.[23] A growing portion of benefits has been delivered to those who consider themselves as "self-sufficient members of the American middle class" and who oppose public spending, who may even belong to the Tea Party, but whose declining economic status makes them needy and also makes them eligible. One such recipient is the owner of an apparel shop in the small city of Lindstrom, Minnesota, whose annual income is about $39,000, who "wants you to know that he does not need any help from the federal government" and who says "too many Americans lean on taxpayers rather than living within their means." But for four years, and continuing, this middle-class shop owner himself received several thousand dollars of federal EITC payments, and he signed up his three younger children for free school breakfast and lunch programs, funded also by federal transfers. His mother, who is eighty-eight, twice relied on Medicare to pay for hip surgery.[24]

It is sometimes hard to believe today that these "collectivized" activities and various other elements of modern "social democracy" occur in the United States. Since the Reagan presidency, there has been almost deafening ideological noise from the austerian Right,[25] screaming that government per se is evil and that—as Margaret Thatcher asserted—society does not exist. Perhaps because of the political constraints in this ideological climate, up to the 2014 midterm election President Obama operated as though he believed—in John Nichols's words, "that everything public is inferior to everything private, that corporations are always good and unions always bad, that progressive taxation is inherently evil," and that the economy should be set up so the wealthy gain and the rest get only trickle-down.[26] After all, writes Nichols, the president who promised change later gave up on single-payer health care, saved the auto industry by funding GM and Chrysler but let them lay off thousands and relocate dozens of plants overseas, and left the Deep Horizon recovery in the Gulf of Mexico in the hands of "the corporation that had lied about the extent of the spill, had made decisions based on its bottom line rather than environmental and human needs, and had failed at even the most basic tasks."[27] There are better options, and they come from American history. Better options have been coming again recently from the nation's cities. It is high time to reexamine these options and to provide the conditions in which cities can thrive.

We can start by making the improvements suggested in this book. They can be the first steps in a larger effort to bring about another era when cities and their inhabitants can once more prosper.

Notes

Looking Upstream

1. Mier 1975, 1–2.
2. P. Williams 2014.
3. The Success Academy charter schools in New York have exceedingly high suspension rates. Taylor 2015.
4. See Dahl 1961 on pluralism, Miliband 1969 on elitism, Polantzas 1976 on capitalist structure. Also Katznelson 1994 and especially Piven 1994.
5. Tucker 2011. See Rumberger and Rotermund 2009 and the California Dropout Research Project 2014.
6. O'Brien 2012.
7. San Francisco and Marin Food Banks 2011.
8. Food Runners San Francisco 2015.
9. Open Hand 2012.
10. Alameda County Community Food Bank 2012.
11. Gafni 2010. *YoRaps* 2012.
12. Stephens-Davidowitz 2014.
13. See Castells 1977, 1983, and Goldsmith 1994.
14. Harvey 2012, 35ff. See Young 2013.
15. Storper 2011, 1079.
16. Glaeser 2011, quoted at 247.
17. Also see Clavel 1986.

18. *Democracy Now!* 2015.
19. Goldsmith and Blakely 2010.
20. Harris 2011.
21. On false "integration" see August 2014 and Ruiz-Tagle 2014.
22. "Anglo" would be more accurate than "white"—since Latino/Hispanic is an "ethnic" category orthogonal to "race."
23. Lemann 2011.
24. Shane 2012.
25. Bischoff and Reardon (2013) show steadily rising income segregation.
26. Greenberg 1991.
27. Greenberg 1991, citing Heckler 1985. For African American males, homicide victim rates run 6.6 times the white male rate.
28. Born and Purcell (2006) caution against false comfort with localism, suggesting careful analysis of such things as use of chemicals and pesticides, directions of federal subsidies, and transportation costs.
29. Poppendieck 2010, 12, referring to the NCLB Act (No Child Left Behind). Also Cooper and Holmes 2006.
30. Marmor and Mashaw 1992. Lanchester 2014.
31. Buenker 1973, vii–vii.
32. Ibid.

1. Cities as Political Targets

1. Maciag 2013.
2. For an insider's scholarly view see Orlebecke 1990.
3. Ferguson and Johnson 2012. According to the *Report of the State Budget Crisis Task Force*, July 17, 2012, states and localities pay more than 90 percent of the cost of elementary and secondary schooling, spend in excess of $200 billion each year for health care, fund almost three-quarters of the nation's public infrastructure, and employ six workers for every one employed by the federal government.
4. Also see works by Raymond Williams and Leo Marx.
5. Glaeser 2011, 56ff.
6. Center City District and Central Philadelphia Development Corporation 2007. Emphasis in original.
7. MacDonald 2012.
8. Eshelman 2009.
9. Clavel, Forester, and Goldsmith 1980.
10. O'Connor 1973, 9.
11. Kennedy 2013.
12. Krugman 2012.
13. Peck 2012, 629.
14. Severe racial gaps persist. See Goldsmith and Blakely 2010; Logan 2013; Glaeser and Vigdor 2012.
15. Goldsmith and Derian 1979.
16. Clavel 2010.
17. On the special nature of this period see Goldsmith and Blakely 2010; Noah 2012; Galbraith 2000; Wilson 2012.
18. Judis 2000, cited in Packer 2011.
19. Sugrue 2012.
20. Freeman 2012, chap. 1.
21. Martin 2013.

22. Martin 2010.

23. Kruse 2012.

24. Powell (1971) writes, "The fundamental premise [is] that business and the enterprise system are in deep trouble, and the hour is late."

25. Packer 2011, 26.

26. Galambos and van Van Ee 2001 (Document 1147; November 8, 1954), http://www.snopes.com/politics/quotes/ike.asp.

27. Wilson 2012 refers to the 1950s and 1960s.

28. Pizzigati 2011, citing Hacker and Pierson 2011.

29. Hacker and Pierson 2011.

30. Counterpart left-wing think tanks are rare and poorly funded.

31. Lowndes (2008, 4) rejects the "backlash" thesis of Phillips (1969) and Edsall and Edsall (1991).

32. Theodore 2011.

33. Gans 1990.

34. Fox News 2013.

35. Mitt Romney sunk his presidential campaign in 2014 by saying 47 percent of the electorate pay no taxes, irresponsibly depending on federal aid. Actually, only 14.4 percent don't pay income taxes, about two-thirds of them elderly, nearly all of them very poor. See http://www.taxpolicycenter.org/taxtopics/federal-taxes-households.cfm.

36. White and White (1962) held that American intellectuals from ear y on held negative attitudes toward cities.

37. Angotti 2006. Moynihan also advised President Lyndon Johnson.

38. Manville 2012.

39. Peck (2006) cautions against "attributing decisive and singular causal agency to the hired intellectuals of the conservative think tanks" but says they "have been prominent *narrators* of this transformation . . . and . . . active *agents* in this process." Also see Peck 2010, Mitchell 2006, and Peck 2013.

40. O'Connor 2008, 334. Thirty-six of fifty-two of the institute's experts (current fellows and *City Journal* contributing editors) are New York City–based.

41. O'Connor 2008, 333.

42. Moody 2007, 16.

43. O'Connor 2008.

44. O'Connor 2008.

45. Furchtott-Roth 2012.

46. Sennett 1970.

47. O'Connor 2008.

48. From December 2011 speeches and ABC News, collected on the *Daily Show with Jon Stewart* (Stewart 2011).

49. Ryan spoke to conservative Bill Bennett on his *Morning in America* in early March 2014. Coates 2014; Edwards 2014.

50. Clark and van Slyke 2005.

51. Paul Weyrich, cited in Powell 2003. Weyrich participated in the founding of the Heritage Foundation in 1973, the Moral Majority, and the Free Congress Foundation, as well as the American Legislative Exchange Council, discussed below.

52. Macek 2006, viii, xvi, 147.

53. Macek 2006, 156–159. The five sentences were vacated, and the city under Mayor de Blasio paid $41 million to settle.

54. Kleine 2013. Also Turberville 2013. Meanwhile, banks made great sums at Detroit's expense (Walsh 2014).

55. See alec.org and alecexposed.org. Also see Pilkington and Goldenberg 2013; Potter 2013.

56. Rizzo 2012.
57. Alberta 2009.
58. Manik-Perlman 2012.
59. Data for 2010. Memphis challenged the Tennessee law in federal court (Locker 2012).
60. A broader challenge in southern states came with the Supreme Court's June 2013 *Shelby v. Holder* decision invalidating Section 4 of the 1965 Voting Rights Act, thus releasing states from federal scrutiny.
61. Goldsmith 2015.
62. Paragraph and this note from Goldsmith 2015. In March 2014 police killed homeless James Boyd (a white thirty-eight-year-old) in Albuquerque, where police have shot thirty-five persons in the last five years, with twenty-two deaths, and the city has so far paid $23 million in court judgments of police misconduct. See abqjournal.com/apd-under-fire. No national records exist of police killings, circumstances, and victims. The NAACP and *USA Today* items are reported by Jaeah Lee, "Exactly How Often Do Police Shoot Unarmed Black Men?," *Mother Jones*, August 15, 2014.
63. Paragraph virtually in its entirety from Goldsmith 2015.
64. Causing some prominent corporations to withdraw from ALEC.

2. Cities as Budget-Cutting Targets

1. Galbraith 2000; Wilson 2012.
2. Schwartz 2014. See Harrison and Bluestone 1988.
3. Piketty and Saez 2012; Edelman 2012; Hacker and Pierson 2011.
4. Piketty 2014, 2–3.
5. Stiglitz interview (2012a). Also Stiglitz book (2012b).
6. Roberts 2006; Simon and Luce 1978. Also see Orlebecke 1990, 196, quoting a memo from Simon to Ford warning that by providing even partial guarantees the federal government "would become enmeshed in the politics of thousands of political subdivisions."
7. State Budget Crisis Task Force 2012.
8. Capodilupo 2002.
9. Grants of large federal sums for schools, health care, transportation, and sometimes housing, supposedly to allow local governments to pursue goals flexibly and efficiently; but such grants also make oversight difficult and thus may permit even very strong local biases to continue.
10. Goldsmith and Jacobs 1982.
11. Goldsmith and Jacobs 1982.
12. Stegman 1993.
13. Orlebecke 1990, 198.
14. Kucinich was subsequently a U.S. representative, serving from 1997 to 2013.
15. Following elections of Reagan, Margaret Thatcher in Britain, and Helmut Kohl in Germany, such policies spread across the globe via the Washington Consensus, Structural Adjustment, etc. Although the Congress did not act, Reagan proposed enterprise zones, an idea imported from Thatcher's anticity policy in Britain, which would have cut minimum wages, gutted occupational safety standards, and relaxed various neighborhood protections in the poorest zones of cities. Goldsmith 1982.
16. Rohe and Galster 2014, 5.
17. Glickman 1980; Goldsmith and Derian 1979.
18. Rohe and Galster 2014, 6. Constant 2012 dollars.
19. Greenberg 1991.
20. Scruggs-Leftwich 2006, 212. Also Goldsmith and Derian 1979; Glickman 1980.
21. Scruggs-Leftwich 2006, 212.

22. Schott 2012.

23. Goetz 2013, 178.

24. ASCE 2013.

25. Lyman 2014.

26. Dadayan 2012.

27. Hoene and Pagano 2011.

28. Calculations by Peck 2012, figure 4, p. 642.

29. Peck 2012, 644.

30. Cooper 2012.

31. Lyman and Walsh 2013.

32. Peck 2012, 634.

33. Harvey (2007) has thus analyzed a much longer historical period for several developed countries, focusing on Barron Haussmann's rebuilding of Paris.

34. Notably, Newt Gingrich and Jeb Bush proposed *extending* bankruptcy options to states, which presumably would require a constitutional amendment. See Bush and Gingrich 2011 and Peck 2013.

35. Maciag 2013. In Michigan, seven cities and school districts have state-appointed emergency managers, and three more have signed consent agreements.

36. Nadeau 2012.

37. Dadayan 2012.

38. Nocera 2012.

39. Robin Hahnel and Martin Hart-Landsberg are professors at Portland State University and Lewis and Clark College. Theriault 2013.

40. Reed 2012.

41. Baker 2012. Farm bills traditionally passed easily with bipartisan support, including food stamps.

42. The rhetorical omissions of all four candidates also included the world's highest incarceration rate, the erosion of civil liberties, threats to separation of church and state, and climate change. Pollitt 2012.

43. Marcuse 2011.

44. Peck 2012, 632.

45. Markusen 2015.

3. Troubled City Schools

1. Data for 2009 from the National Center for Education Statistics (NCES) of the Institute of Education Sciences, U.S. Department of Education, table 69. Unless otherwise noted, statistics are from NCES.

2. Carnevale, Smith, and Strohl 2010. Correlations of earnings, health, skills, and schooling involve complex paths of causation.

3. National Center for Public Policy 2008; Hatami 2006, chap. 6; Sable, Garofano, and Hoffman 2007. On lifetime earnings, Levin and Holmes 2005.

4. The term "dropout factory" originates with Balfanz and Legters (2004).

5. Tavernise 2012b, citing Bailey and Dynarski 2011.

6. Swanson 2009.

7. Schemo 2006b.

8. Otterman 2011b, reporting on NYSED data released June 14.

9. The examples omit twenty-eight of the largest fifty cities.

10. Madden 2014, Carnevale, Smith, and Strohl 2010.

11. Kozol 2012. Also see Kozol 2005.

12. Personal communication from M. Goldsmith, March 1989. Pedro Noguera (2008) documents these kinds of obstacles from his life as a city child, his children's experiences, and his work as a teacher and school researcher.

13. Diane Ravitch, once a strong supporter of NCLB, found that from 1998 to 2007 there were no gains in eighth-grade reading and virtually no improvements in other areas. NCLB comes out in practice as one more inappropriate, too simple response to a complex problem. See Ravitch 2007.

14. Denby 2012.

15. Poor children in rural districts, which may be predominantly white, are often similarly isolated and held back.

16. Orfield, Kucsera, and Siegel-Hawley 2012, 20–21.

17. Noguera and Weingarten 2011. Many school reformers—such as those in the Coalition of Essential Schools—argue that "excellent" suburban schools also need drastic change. But by standard measures of success, the massive problems reside mainly in city schools. Noguera is professor of education at New York University, and Weingarten president, National Federation of Teachers.

18. On tenure see Rothstein 2014.

19. Nancy Zimpher, SUNY chancellor, says we've reached a "crisis point" for teacher education. "We've got to do something radically different than the organizational structure and the intellectual and academic structure that we have today." Bakeman 2012.

20. Thernstrom and Thernstrom 2003, 7.

21. For an example of poorly supported anti-Obama rage see Garner 2010.

22. Alter 2010. See also Ravitch's review (2011) of the antiunion, anti-teacher movie *Waiting for Superman*. On Gates's multimillion-dollar advocacy see Dillon 2011a.

23. Thernstrom and Thernstrom 2003, 5.

24. Thernstrom and Thernstrom 2003, 4.

25. "Dr. Bill Cosby Speaks at the 50th Anniversary Commemoration of the *Brown v. Topeka Board of Education* Supreme Court Decision, May 22, 2004," EBSCO Host Connection. See Cosby 2004.

26. The Thernstroms paint on a broader canvas, claiming that middle-class suburban black children suffer from similar cultural liabilities—watching too much TV, having too few books in the house, studying much less than their white and especially Asian counterparts. Thernstrom and Thernstrom 2003, 142–145.

27. Tatum (1997) offers disturbing evidence on the pressure minority children feel to resist school. Also McWhorter 2000 and Cross 1991.

28. Noguera 2008. Paul Tough (2012) notes a "hidden power of character."

29. Kirp 2012. On slight increase in interdistrict enrollment in federally funded magnet schools see Siegel-Hawley and Frankenberg 2012.

30. Wilson 2009. Wilson points out that white Americans tend to distort and exaggerate the cultural elements.

31. Wilson 2009.

32. Ryan 2010.

33. America's Promise Alliance 2009.

34. *Indymedia.us* 2009; Russo 2011; Saviola 2010. After eight years serving as the Chicago schools' chief, Duncan moved on to become U.S. secretary of education.

35. Joravsky 2004.

36. Ahmed-Ullah, Chase, and Secter 2013.

37. According to a study of twenty-two primary schools and fourteen high schools reformed between 1997 and 2000. Consortium on Chicago School Research 2012.

38. Bruck 2007.

39. Hancock 2007.

40. Diane Ravitch, quoted in Hancock 2007.

41. The grand summary appears in Stone 1998. Other project books include Henig et al. 1999, Portz, Stein, and Jones 1999, and Stone et al. 2001. Portz, Stein, and Jones 1999 offers rich detail on governance in the three cities.

42. The theoretical basis of this work lies in the concept of "regime theory." See Stone 1993, Fainstein 1995, Lauria and Whelan 1995, and Clavel 1995.

43. Boston School Committee chairperson Louise Day Hicks opposed busing with ROAR (Restore Our Alienated Rights) in the 1960s.

44. Schemo 2007.

45. Bowles and Gintis 1976.

46. The binary theoretical distinction between only two classes can easily be transformed to provide a gradient. See Vietorisz 1980.

47. Cassidy 2010, quoting the blogger TED.

48. Behrent 2011. Also see Behrent 2009.

49. Darling-Hammond 2007.

50. See exchange of letters between Deborah Meier and Diane Ravitch in *Education Week* (Meier and Ravitch 2010), http://blogs.edweek.org/edweek/Bridging-Differences/.

51. Similarly, more experienced flight attendants, who are paid more, can also avoid the worst route assignments.

52. Karabel 2007. Dissenting views by Carter 1991 and McWhorter 2000.

53. Brawley 2010.

54. Frug 1999.

55. On club goods and city space see Webster 2007 and Warner 2011.

56. Tondro 1991.

57. Political economists say *re*produce, to distinguish the (re)production of human workers (who enter the labor market) from the production of goods and services (which are traded in other markets).

58. Luke Delvin graduated high school in 2009. Delvin 2011.

59. See Massey and Denton 1993, Orfield 2001, Logan 2000, and Goldsmith and Blakely 2010.

60. U.S. Department of Education, National Center for Education Statistics 2015.

61. U.S. Department of Education, Office for Civil Rights 2014a. With 18 percent of pre-K enrollment, black children constitute 48 percent of those suspended out of school more than once.

62. Orfield 2001. Residential segregation afflicts Asian Americans, Native American Indians, and various subgroups as well, but for schools even more than for housing, the main metropolitan divisions are still white, Hispanic, and black.

63. *Zelman v. Simmons-Harris*, 536 U.S. 639 (2002).

64. This chapter focuses on metropolitan area segregation, but rural racial segregation remains profound. In Wilcox County, Alabama, for example, where 72 percent of the population is black, of the twenty-two hundred students in the public school system, at most ten are white. Barry 2007.

65. *Zelman v. Simmons-Harris*, 536 U.S. 639 (2002).

66. Orfield, Kucsera, and Siegel-Hawley 2012, 75.

67. Census tract populations average about four thousand. Maps produced by the Social Science Data Analysis Network (SSDAN) at the University of Michigan (*CensusScope*). For reactions to SSDAN maps see Denvir 2011. Segregation here is measured by the dissimilarity index, which varies from zero to one hundred and tells what portion of the population would have to move to make racial proportions the same in each district.

68. For Los Angeles, the Dissimilarity Index equals 67.8; Buffalo, 73.2; Milwaukee, 81.5.

69. U.S. Department of Education, Office for Civil Rights 2014a; Rich 2014b.

70. Gootman 2006.

71. Dillon 2006b.

72. Orfield and Eaton 1996.

73. Freedman (2011) reports that "over the last half-century, the number of Catholic schools has fallen to 7,000 from about 13,000, and their enrollment to barely two million children from more than five million. A disproportionate share of the damage has come in big cities." Of non–public school enrollments, still more than 40 percent are in Catholic schools and more than 13 percent in nonsectarian schools. U.S. Department of Education, National Center for Education Statistics 2013.

74. The Court overturned *Plessy* with a unanimous vote in *Brown v. Board of Education* in 1954. Arkansas's governor in 1957 provoked President Eisenhower into sending paratroopers to Little Rock to protect schoolchildren from mob violence.

75. As Orfield and Eaton (1996) point out, the words form a chilling "parallel with the Nazi anthem, 'Deutschland über alles.'" Did the future chief justice mean to suggest that integrationists were behaving like Nazis? See reference to *Columbus Board of Education v. Penick* in Davis 1984 and Rosen 1999.

76. *Parents Involved in Community Schools v. Seattle School District No. 1*, 551 U.S. 701 (2007).

77. Kirp 2007. As late as 2005, successful cross-boundary school integration functioned voluntarily also in Milwaukee and Saint Louis, where at the program's peak, thirteen thousand city students attended suburban schools (despite strong opposition from former governor John Ashcroft). Kozol 2005. As of spring 2007, the Saint Louis Public Schools were unaccredited. Under state law, in order for an unaccredited district to send students to an accredited district, the sending district must pay the tuition in the receiving district of each student it sends. See Gay 2007 and Hampel 2007.

78. Kirp 2007, 4–5.

79. "The nation's large program of compensatory education, Title I, has had great difficulty achieving gains in schools where poverty is highly concentrated. When school districts return to neighborhood schools, white students tend to sit next to middle class students but black and Latino students are likely to be next to impoverished students." Orfield and Yun 1999. Also see Orfield, Kucsera, and Siegel-Hawley 2012.

80. Popular perceptions about *international* mixing in suburban high schools see melting pots everywhere, with whites in the mix, e.g., Dillon 2006a. Orfield and Yun (1999) point out that "all racial groups except whites experience considerable diversity in their schools but whites are remaining in overwhelmingly white schools even in regions with very large non-white enrollments." Orfield, Kucsera, and Siegel-Hawley (2012) count schools as integrated when three ethnic groups each have enrollments 10 percent or higher.

4. Options for City Schools

1. Meier and Ravitch 2010 (blog on *Education Week*).

2. Fliegel 1994.

3. SEED may be free for students, of whom three-quarters are low-income, but the school is costly. Though the school was started with only private funding, the DC government now contributes 94 percent of its budget: $10,000 per student for day school operations and $25,000 per student for boarding, with some additional funds from Title I and private sources. Feldman 2010.

4. Bacon 2014.

5. Tough 2009; Hanson 2013.

6. KIPP operates about one hundred schools in twenty states. Other high-expectation, non-profit charter chains for students from poor families include Green Dot, with sixteen schools in

Los Angeles, and Achievement First, with about twenty schools in Connecticut and New York. Philanthropic funding supports all these schools, reports Dillon 2011b. The group of New York schools called Success Academy drew $72 million in public funds in 2013, supplemented by $22 million in donations. Taylor 2015.

7. Bacon 2014.

8. Lafer 2014.

9. Campaign for Fiscal Equity 2009.

10. Driehaus 2007. About 4,000 charter schools have been opened nationwide, 328 of them in Ohio. In 2007 the new governor and attorney general, both Democrats, seized on the state's report card, which gave more than half the charters grades of D or F. Dillon 2007.

11. See Carnoy 2011.

12. New American Foundation 2014.

13. Hanson 2013 reports that the Harlem Children's Zone spends around $16,000/student/year despite enrolling very few special-needs students, compared to New York City's $14,452, with many special-needs students. The richest 10 percent of New York State school districts average $28,754.

14. Parental demands for compensatory programs for children with special needs cross over into the suburbs. In Westport, Connecticut, a fabulously wealthy town on Long Island Sound, a father says he has spent more than $100,000 suing the school district for denying funds to enroll his daughter, who has a digestive disorder, in a private school. In Hamilton County, Tennessee, the school district feared bills of $10 million annually for other students, so it spent $2.2 million "to avoid having to reimburse [a family] the $60,000 cost of providing their autistic son . . . with one-on-one" support. Cowan 2005.

15. Witte 2000. By 2000, ninety-one private schools enrolled eight thousand students in Milwaukee, 70 percent in religious schools, with vouchers up to $5,100.

16. Lubienski and Lubienski 2006.

17. Lubienski and Lubienski 2006. Unfortunately, all these judgments and ratings are based on test scores; there are alternatives. It is possible, for example, that conservative Christian schools are not as concerned by national test scores as they are by other criteria and subject matter. The Coalition of Essential Schools, to take a very different example, stresses graduation by exhibition and gives less emphasis to standardized test, yet its schools, many of them public schools, have successful students. Nevertheless, the discussion continues here with comparative test scores!

18. Richtel 2000.

19. Goldstein 2011a. Also see Russakoff 2015.

20. Wickham 2011.

21. Welsh-Huggins 2011.

22. Turner, Nichols, and Comey 2012. Earlier analysis of Chicago results over seven years often seemed to show no academic improvement, but as Richard Kahlenberg (2001) says, "Moving to Opportunity was more like moving to mediocrity," to neighborhoods with troubled schools and high minority populations. See also Sanbonmatsu et al. 2007.

23. In Hastings-on-Hudson, long reputed to be an "integrated suburb," where enrollments are 2 percent black, 8 percent Hispanic, 8 percent Asian, and 82 percent white, the white graduation rate is 98 percent, and the overall graduation rate is 96 percent. In Shaker Heights, an intentionally integrated suburb with 38 percent of its enrollment white, the overall graduation rate is 96 percent. These figures are for 2008–2009 (NCES).

24. Tatum 1997 discusses a special METCO program to reduce alienation and isolation. Most similar programs have been challenged in court.

25. Harvard University 1997.

26. Vietorisz, Goldsmith, and Mier 1975.

27. Quercia and Galster (2000, 160; emphasis added) offer a more general discussion of the importance of mutual support.

28. McIntosh 1990. Men play top roles without discomfort, as do whites, McIntosh points out. Gender *does* play a role, of course, but one that is sidestepped for this analysis.

29. Quoting Kai Ting, in Lee 1991.

30. Kai Ting's story is real-life fiction, chronicled in Lee 1991. Brown's autobiography appeared in 1965; Jennings's biography was written by *Wall Street Journal* reporter Ron Suskind (1998).

31. Jonathan Kozol (1991) reported on Mott Haven long ago; school conditions are still very poor.

32. College graduates comprise 14.6 percent of adult residents in the Bronx. In New Jersey cities the figures are lower: Camden 5.4 percent, Newark 9 percent, and Trenton 9.2 percent. The figure is 12.2 percent in Bridgeport, Connecticut.

33. Thanks to Rolf Pendal, who invited me to lecture on these topics at Cornell University, fall semester 2012. See Logan 2000. The Census Bureau has public education financing reports available for every year since 1992, including information on local tax revenue, at http://www.census.gov/govs/www/school.html.

34. Darling-Hammond 2010b.

35. Inside Schools (http://insideschools.org/elementary/gifted-a-other-options), July 24, 2015.

36. Phillips 2012.

37. Sources on Finland: Sahlberg 2012a, 2012b; OECD 2011; Välijärvi 2012; Darling-Hammond 2010b, Darling-Hammond 2010a; Partanen 2011. The PISA countries include all members of the Organisation of European Co-operation and Development plus eleven others.

38. One minor exception: Macao's coefficient of variation in reading is slightly lower.

39. PISA results from 2009 show the *city* of Shanghai first but Finland still right at the top, as it has been every year since the PISA assessments began, in 2000. Note that Chinese cities, like cities throughout the world except for the United States, are more privileged than their suburbs.

40. The coefficient of variation is the standard deviation divided by the mean. The smaller the SD, the narrower the dispersion of scores. For the familiar normal distribution, a tall narrow bell curve shows little dispersion of scores (a small SD), while a low broad bell curve shows much dispersion (a high SD).

41. Linda Darling-Hammond 2010a, 165.

42. O'Sullivan 2014.

43. John H. Gilbert, professor emeritus at North Carolina State University, quoted in Finder 2005.

44. Finder 2005.

45. McCrummen 2011.

46. Darling-Hammond 2010a, 166.

47. Sahlberg 2009, 10, quoted by Darling-Hammond, 2010a, 168.

48. Partanen 2011.

49. Rich 2014a.

50. Partanen 2011.

51. Lerner 2014.

52. Partanen 2011.

53. Darling-Hammond 2010a, citing Buchberger and Buchberger 2003.

54. Partanen 2011.

55. Sahlberg 2009.

56. Partanen 2011.

57. Hungry Birds 2012.

58. Sahlberg 2007.

59. Chapters 1, 3, and 5 of Hacsi 2002 analyze studies to ask whether more money makes schools better. The Thernstroms argue otherwise with flawed logic and oversimplified evidence.

See Schrag 2003b. For a forty-five-year timeline of school-financing changes in California, beginning in 1968 with the California Supreme Court case *Serrano v. Priest*, 5 Cal.3d 584 (1971), challenging property tax funding of schools and ending in 2013 with Governor Jerry Brown's budget using the Local Control Funding Formula, see http://embed.verite.co/timeline/?source=0AnZDmy tGK63SdEJhSFR2MkdTNk94ZHRsa0poYjNxcmc&font=Bevan-PotanoSans&maptype=toner& lang=en&width=1000&height=700.

60. Hacsi 2002, quoting the court and related studies, p. 184.

61. Hacsi 2002, 185. The promise of K–12 school funding from state lotteries has not been met. New York raised 5.3 percent of its total public school funding, *including higher education*, from lotteries in 2006; California, 1.6 percent; other states had figures in between. Stodghill and Nixon 2007.

62. Marshall 2007. Unfortunately, this conclusion allowed Governor Arnold Schwarzenegger to postpone more funding until after "critical school reform," and also tended to conflate problem (largely urban) schools and districts with well-functioning (suburban) ones.

63. Schrag 2003a, 98, citing Grissmer et al. 2000.

64. See the introductory chapter of the 158-page comprehensive report by leading education researchers, released by PACE. Hatami 2006.

65. Improvements may be expected as a result of state funding resulting from Proposition 98, discussed below.

66. The school district was released from federal court order to desegregate in February 2007.

67. "In *Rodriguez* . . . the Burger Court reversed *Brown vs. Board* . . . , finding education not to be a fundamental right guaranteed by the constitution, and therefore that cross-district inequalities of funding did not violate any constitutional provision." Hacsi 2002, 186. Since the *Rodriguez v. San Antonio ISD* chill, most school financing appeals have come to state courts, but the conservative majority on the Roberts Court continued the attack on affirmative action with *Parents Involved in Community Schools v. Seattle School District No. 1*, 551 U.S. 701 (2007), to disallow the use of race as "the sole determining factor" in student assignment in *in-district* voluntary racial integration in Seattle and Louisville.

68. Coles 2000.

69. Carey 2004. The disparities vary by state. Half the states spend more in rich districts, and thirty-one spend more in primarily white districts.

70. Reported by the Education Trust in 2004. New York courts have since required the state to spend more on New York City schools, but disputes remain unresolved.

71. Goldsmith and Blakely 2010, 110–111.

72. *Milliken v. Bradley*, 418 U.S. 717 (1974).

73. Schrag 2003a.

74. U.S. Department of Education 2014b.

75. Heuer and Stullich 2011, exhibit 5, p. 18. The American Recovery and Reinvestment Act of 2009 forced school districts to reveal the inequalities.

76. See chap. 1 in Schrag 2003a.

77. Schrag 2003a, 56–57, quoting Roza and Miles 2000.

78. Quoted in Schrag 2003a, 98.

79. Schrag 2003a, 127, quoting Hunter 2000.

80. Schrag 2003a, 111–125. For commentary on *Abbott* see ibid., 115. See 52NJ473 and 20Cal3d25.

81. Lerner 2014; Hu 2006. In early 2008 the governor, major city mayors, and suburban legislators reopened the issue, considering proposals to shift some funding from the poorest districts, which receive half of all state aid. Chen 2008.

82. Russakoff 2015. Even $100 million doesn't buy so much these days. The building of one new high school in Chicago cost more than $80 million.

83. The governor tried to defund the state educational program but was rebuffed by the state Supreme Court; http://www.ontheissues.org/governor/Chris_Christie_Education.htm.

84. Fensterwald and Frey 2015. School funding from the state rose to $68.4 billion for fiscal 2015, including $7.9 billion for community colleges.

85. For a timeline from *Serrano* in 1968 to LCFF in 2013, see http://embed.verite.co/timeline/?source=0AnZDmytGK63SdEJhSFR2MkdTNk94ZHRsa0poYjNxcmc&font=Bevan-PotanoSans&maptype=toner&lang=en&width=1000&height=700.

86. In 2011, funding in the *average* district came 57 percent from the state, 29 percent from property taxes and other local sources, and 14 percent from the federal government. Weston 2011.

87. Ed Source, http://edsource.org/2014/latest-but-outdated-ed-week-survey-ranks-california-50th-in-per-pupil-spending/56196.

5. The Paradox of Plenty

1. This chapter's title is borrowed from sociologist and nutritionist Marion Nestle, the Paulette Goddard Professor of Nutrition, Food Studies, and Public Health at New York University.

2. Lustig 2013.

3. *Reversing the Epidemic: The New York City Obesity Task Force Plan to Prevent and Control Obesity*, New York City Obesity Task Force, 2012.

4. Annual subsidies for farms and ranches amount to more than $15 billion, and in 1995–2011 totaled $277.3 billion, three-quarters going to 10 percent of enterprises. See EWG 2012.

5. Coutts and Kawachi 2006. Latest such damages, from poisoned water.

6. Lustig 2013, 29.

7. And also in isolated poor rural areas.

8. Zedlewski, Waxman, and Gundersen 2012, 5.

9. Whitman, Shah, and Benjamins 2011, table 6–3, pp. 134–135. A recent survey of cause-specific health outcomes for children in 1992 and 2002 *not* focused on Chicago (Silver et al. 2011) finds distressed cities fare much worse.

10. Whitman, Shah, and Benjamins 2011, 140–141. Diabetes prevalence is highest among Puerto Ricans (p. 53). Neighborhoods of color: Humboldt Park, West Town, North Lawndale, Roseland, Albany Park, and Uptown. White: Norwood Park and West Ridge.

11. Whitman, Shah, and Benjamins 2011, table 3–7, p. 54.

12. Whitman, Shah, and Benjamins 2011, 138–139. NP = 21 percent, WR = 22 percent, Chicago = 22 percent.

13. Whitman Shah, and Benjamins 2011, 55. Forty percent of respondents did not understand the nutritional guidelines.

14. A ten-year HOPE VI project estimated at $500 million aims to replace all 267 low-income units at the Hunters View project and add 530 new condos and rentals at market rate. Some 150 families were displaced in 2010.

15. Corburn 2009, 108–110.

16. Yeh and Katz 2006, 106–125, at 110. Also see Short, Guthman, and Raskin 2007 on San Francisco food deserts. The median size of a supermarket nationally in 2010 was 46,000 square feet—down slightly from a peak of 48,750 in 2006—carrying 38,718 items. Food Marketing Institute 2013.

17. Hillier 2014; Cummins, Flint, and Matthews 2014.

18. Raja, Ma, and Yadav 2008 on Buffalo. In Oakland, CA, small stores carry a variety of foods, of varying quality and affordability, some serving specific ethnic populations, small "food oases" (Short, Guthman, and Raskin 2007).

19. Clifton 2004. Data for study: interviews with low-income families, Austin, TX (Yeh and Katz 2006, 111).

20. Rural food deserts have low incomes, limited automobiles, and no public transportation (Gershon 2012). Auto-share systems that provide relatively inexpensive short-term use of cars, ideal for grocery trips, rarely serve the poor.

21. Farley et al. 2009—a study of fresh versus unhealthy foods in a Louisiana community.

22. Mexican workers in New York City's Korean-owned neighborhood stores (Ness 2005).

23. Doussard 2013.

24. Rabin 2011, reporting on Renee Y. Hsia et al., in *Journal of the AMA*, a study financed by the R. W. Johnson Foundation.

25. Nestle 2007, 385–393.

26. Personal communication, Anna C. Read, December 2012; Tuttle 2012; Ghorayshi 2012; Martin 2007.

27. Cited in New York State and New York City reports: Ruberto and Spence 2011.

28. Cited in New York City report: http://www.cdc.gov/diabetes/pubs/pdf/ndfs_20.1.pdf.

29. Cited in New York City report: Raufman et al. 2009.

30. U.S. Department of Agriculture, Economic Research Service—Supplemental Nutrition Assistance Program (SNAP) Data System. "Time Series Data."

31. U.S. Department of Agriculture, Economic Research Service 2012. The USDA stopped using "hunger" in 2007. Poppendieck 2010, 161–189.

32. 26 percent and 24 percent, respectively. Potamites and Gordon 2010. Data for study: USDA school nutrition dietary assessment, 2005.

33. Benbow, Wang, and Whitman 1998; Hogue et al. 2013 on LA.

34. Poppendieck 2010, 161–162.

35. Yeh and Katz 2006, 113.

36. Rosner 1995, 4 and 14.

37. Derrick 2001 on New York City.

38. Donofrio 2007.

39. Donofrio 2007. In Vienna, land use and food planning came together: Hochhausl 2012.

40. Brawley 2011.

41. Sen 1982.

42. Spirn 1984, 242.

43. "Every three and a half days we are losing a farm to subdivisions, commercial and industrial real estate." Nationally, around one million acres of farmland are lost annually, the equivalent of a Vermont every five years. In thirty years, Long Island has lost a quarter of its farmland, down to thirty-four thousand acres, only 3 percent of Long Island. "Concrete is the last crop" (Stony Brook University 2012).

44. Clancy 2004.

45. Boarnet 2006; Kaufman 2004.

46. This individual/collective distinction is *not* the same as that between reform and revolution. Marx and Engels, the authors of the *Communist Manifesto*, theorized and strategized on the two intertwined processes: the revolutionary overthrow of the capitalist system (a structural change whose likelihood they overestimated); and reforms like reducing the workday from twelve hours or more to the now standard eight hours, to improve life and empower workers (which they actively advocated). Like other major nineteenth-century theorists, these advocates of deep structural change did not ignore but incorporated reform.

47. Simon 2006, 143; Wallis 2004.

48. Harris 2012.

49. Tavernise 2012a.

50. Harris 2012.

51. Lustig 2013, 23, and 229ff.

52. Nestle 2007, 367, 370.

53. New York City 2012.

54. San Francisco Department of Public Health 2004. Such recommendations would move toward the Finnish school circumstances, described in the previous chapter. But of course Finland is a nation state, with power to change many things affecting its communities.

55. Harper et al. 2009, 6.

56. Meter 2009, cited in Harper et al. 2009, 6.

57. Black 2009, cited in Harper et al. 2009, 6.

58. Harper et al. 2009, 48.

59. U.S. Census: $582 billion in 2010, 13.1 percent.

60. Hoynes, Miller, and Simon 2012; $2,563 in 2008.

61. In Rome, with 150,000 students, "70 percent of all food served at school cafeterias is organic . . . from 400 Italian organic farms. . . . Each meal costs about 5 euros (or $6.40), but this is subsidized. . . . Rome [charges] families only 2 euros per meal (or $2.60)." Poor families are further subsidized (Paolocci 2010).

62. Center for Science in the Public Interest 2013; Poppendieck 2010, 3, 9; U.S. Department of Agriculture, Food and Nutrition Service 2015b.

63. Poppendieck 2010, 3–5. The cost to the USDA was "close to $11 billion in fiscal 2007."

64. Seversen and May 2002, quoted by Poppendieck 2010, 4.

65. Leib et al. 2012.

66. Zedlewski, Waxman, and Gundersen 2012.

67. Zedlewski, Waxman, and Gundersen 2012, 3.

68. Center on Budget and Policy Priorities, 2014; Zedlewski, Waxman, and Gundersen 2012.

69. U.S. Department of Agriculture, Food and Nutrition Service 2014 and 2015a.

70. America's Second Harvest merged with Foodchain in 2001.

71. Feedingamerica.org.

72. Nestle 2007, 361 (emphasis added).

73. Lustig 2013, 241.

74. R. Gershon, personal communication, 2013.

75. York 2010; Warner 2010; Poppendieck 1998.

76. Simon 2006, 311, 318.

77. Bellisari 2008; Ulijaszek 2002.

78. Nestle 2007.

79. Parker-Pope 2009, citing research by David Kessler.

80. David Kessler, pediatrician and former Food and Drug Administration head, investigates parallels of tobacco industry manipulation of nicotine with food industry fine-tuning of salt, sugar, and fats. Kessler 2009.

81. Simon 2013.

82. Nestle 2007.

83. A similar attempt failed in Congress. Nestle 2007, 221, 226.

84. Nestle 2007, 360.

85. Simon 2013.

86. Quoted by Simon 2013, 19–20.

87. Fang 2015.

88. CDC 2015.

89. CDC 2015, using data from the Federal Trade Commission.

90. Reported in CDC 2015.

91. Simon 2006, 121.

92. Seversen and May 2002; Nixon 2012.

93. Poppendieck 2010, 72.

94. Poppendieck 2010, 79–83.

95. The 2012 reforms institute a long-sought conservative shift, gradually increasing the "full-price" cost of the nutritious NSLP lunch, reducing the subsidy by forty-five cents a meal. Poppendieck 2010, 16–17. Center for Science in the Public Interest 2013.

96. Poppendieck 2010, 3, 16–17.

97. Yee 2012.

98. Katz 2012.

99. Amaral 2012.

100. Attkisson 2012.

101. For a listing of changed land-use laws enabling urban farming, for example, in Kansas City, San Francisco, Seattle, and Chattanooga, as well as a listing of obstacles to change, see Leib et al. 2012, table 4–1, p. 50, and table 4–2, pp. 53–54.

102. https://199.230.52.49/resources/multimedia/syllabi.

103. Morales 2011 and http://www.community-food.org/.

104. Corburn 2009, 110–114, quote on 113.

105. Leib et al. 2012, 70.

106. Raja et al. 2014.

107. Wekerle 2004.

108. Harper et al. 2009, appendix D, 54–56.

109. Leib et al. 2012.

110. Dahlberg 1994.

111. Hillier 2014.

112. Dig Deep Farms and Produce 2013.

113. Just Food 2013.

114. Guzzardi 2011.

115. Source: Urban Farmers in Chicago, *Green for All*, quoted from Leib et al. 2012, 60.

116. Pollan 2008.

117. Smith 2010.

118. Smith 2010.

119. See the Healthy Stores website of the Johns Hopkins Center for Human Nutrition: http://healthystores.org/.

120. Owens 2010.

121. Scharper 2012.

122. See http://www.toronto.ca/health/tfpc/index.htm.

123. Poppendieck 2010, 93–94.

124. Poppendieck 2010, 3.

125. For discussion of some of the early reform work see Cooper and Holmes 2006.

126. Stone 2009.

127. The National Farm to School Network, based at the Urban & Environmental Policy Institute at Occidental College, http://www.farmtoschool.org/. See Stone 2009.

128. Riverside City population close to 350,000; Riverside County more than 2.2 million.

129. Stone 2009.

130. Stone 2009.

131. Duenwald 2002.

132. Knupfer 2013, 190.

133. R. Gershon, personal communication.

134. Yee 2014.

135. Leib et al. 2012, 7–8.

136. Leib et al. 2012, 7–8.

137. Strom 2012.

138. Leib et al. 2012, 11.

139. Stiglitz 2015.
140. Nestle 2007.

6. Drugs, Prisons, and Neighborhoods

1. Portions of this chapter appeared in Goldsmith 2011.
2. Goode 2012.
3. In 2013 only 32 percent of male inmates in state and federal prisons were non-Hispanic whites. When not otherwise noted, statistics come from publications of the Bureau of Justice Statistics (BJS).
4. Gottschalk (2006) gives a nuanced, historical interpretation of the rise of the "carceral state" and argues that the drug war was not "the primary engine" of growth. Also see Gottschalk 2012a.
5. In drafts, Eisenhower tied three institutions together: the military, industry, and the Congress. He removed the Congress from the delivered version, hoping not to provoke legislative discord.
6. Probation and parole peaked in 2007, declining by 6.9 percent by 2013.
7. Gottschalk (2006, 2012b.) acknowledges bias in the drug war but argues that the focus on race obscures class and other determinants of prisoner growth. Stuntz (2011) attributes prison growth to the Rockefeller drug laws and other that followed, zero-tolerance policing, and sentence mandates. See also Gopnik 2012. Many prisoners either await trial unable to afford bail (about five hundred thousand, more than a fifth of all prisoners) or are rearrested on (often petty) probation and parole violations.
8. Gottschalk 2006, 30.
9. Presidents Bill Clinton and George W. Bush and Senator Patrick Leahy all used the term. Caulkins et al. 2005, 3.
10. The firm and repeated opposition to legalization contrasts sharply with the book's many other proposals, which are in line with proposals made by advocates of legalization. For an enthusiastic review see Gottschalk 2012a.
11. Emphasis added. The Global Commission on Drug Policy (2014) included former U.S. secretary of state George Shultz, former Federal Reserve chair Paul Volcker, seven former national presidents or prime ministers, and former UN Secretary-General Kofi Annan. Supporting documents come from the UN Office on Drugs and Crime; commissioned studies by the European Union; case studies on Switzerland, the United Kingdom, the Netherlands, and Portugal; and comparative studies among U.S. states. On opposition to the Global Commission see DuPont 2011. For numerous research citations in line with Global Commission findings see Drug War Facts 2015.
12. Gottschalk 2012b. The term "civil death," or *civiliter mortuus*, comes down in the law from the ancient concept of banishment. It captures these losses of rights of citizenship.
13. Although the bulk of the drug war and its negative effects hit cities, the war also targets disenfranchised rural poor men and women, mostly white. The battle against meth takes place mostly in rural areas of midwestern states (Missouri the early peak). Federal Judge Mark Bennett in conservative northern Iowa overcame his reluctance to speak publicly against the war after having sentenced 1,092 persons to long prison terms for nonviolent crimes, forced to do so by congressionally imposed sentence mandates. Bennett 2012.
14. Robert Mier, commissioner of economic development in Harold Washington's administration in Chicago, argued that race and racism had profound effects on *all* city planning activity in U.S. cities. Mier 1994, 235–239.
15. Szalavitz 2011.
16. Swendsen et al. 2012.
17. U.S. Department of Health and Human Services 2011.

18. Survey data on addicts and alcoholics were last available for 2005.

19. In response to criticism, the New York police chief claimed stop-and-frisk was the only option for keeping the streets safe. Forman and Stutz (2012) note neighborhood-friendly and effective options. The city ended the vigorous arrest policy late in 2014 with drastically lowered marijuana penalties.

20. Owens (2011) argues that, contrary to popular beliefs, Prohibition did *not* lead to increased rates of homicide, concluding that "the American experience of alcohol prohibition provides no compelling evidence that legalizing modern drug markets would reduce violent crime.'

21. All such figures are rough estimates. Kleiman, Caulkins, and Hawken (2011) estimated $260 billion. Later reports (e.g., UNDOC 2015) give higher rough estimates, given increasing drug use (and population) worldwide. Kilmer et al. (2015) report that cocaine use in the United States declined approximately 50 percent from 2006 to 2010, while marijuana consumption increased about 30 percent.

22. Kilmer et al. (2015). Earlier, Caulkins et al. (2005) noted sixteen million users in 2001 and $65 billion in sales. Kleiman, Caulkins, and Hawken (2011) estimated $60 billion (p. 121) and $65 billion (173, 175). As the number of users has increased (UNDOC 2015), the value may be higher. In 2005, estimates for drug monies moving south across the U.S.-Mexico border ran between $8 billion and $24 billion.

23. U.S. Office of National Drug Control Policy 2011, ix. About two-thirds of the total is due to lost productivity.

24. Miron and Waldock (2010, 1) estimate that ending law enforcement, interdiction, and international supply disruption would save the federal government $15.6 billion and state and local governments $25.7 billion per year. They also estimate that taxing drug use could generate $46.7 billion in revenue. Also see Becker, Murphy, and Grossman 2006.

25. Kearney et al. 2014.

26. The DEA has grown to employ almost five thousand special agents. more than ninety-nine hundred employees altogether, and its budget has increased twenty-seven-fold, to more than $2 billion a year.

27. National Research Council 2014, 118–121.

28. National Research Council 2014, 128–129.

29. Until the 1980s, juvenile courts "aimed to treat criminal behavior, not punish it." Then, "juvenile courts became increasingly punitive." Despite their immaturity and frequent inability to understand cause and effect (or the Miranda warning), "more than 200,000 youth under 18 are tried as adults each year." In 2005, the Supreme Court abolished the death penalty for juveniles, but they are still sentenced to life imprisonment without parole (Aviv 2012).

30. Seventy-seven of the one hundred were in Florida (Liptak 2009). A *mandatory* sentence of life without parole for teen murder was ruled unconstitutional by the Supreme Court in June 2012.

31. Bobo and Johnson 2004.

32. Miron and Waldock 2010.

33. Many possession arrests involve police suspicion (unprovable) of marketing.

34. Rockefeller also refused to work for a peaceful resolution to the rebellion in Attica Prison in 1971. In the end, twenty-nine prisoners and ten guards were killed, four other dying in subsequent days under "uncertain circumstances" (Bandele 2011).

35. Justice Mapping Center 2012. Also see Kearney et al. 2014.

36. Data for 2003. Eric Cadora and Charles Swarts of the Justice Mapping Center developed the maps with Laura Kurgan at Columbia University's Spatial Information Design Lab (Macintyre 2007).

37. As quoted in Wilgoren 2007.

38. American Civil Liberties Union 2009.

39. Yardley 2009.

40. Martin and Rashidian 2012.

41. Archibold 2012.

42. Miles 2013.

43. Falco 1996, 120–121.

44. Falco 1996, 123.

45. Falco 1996.

46. Cabañas 2014.

47. Taylor 2012. U.S. agencies sometimes proudly advertise involvement in Colombia, Peru, Mexico, and elsewhere. The Drug Enforcement Administration (DEA) has been involved in killings of innocent persons while attempting to interdict shipments of cocaine in several Latin American republics. After operations that killed villagers in May and on July 27 and 31, 2012, DEA agents assisted Honduran air force fighter pilots to shoot down two small planes flown from a town on the coast of Venezuela. The planes were destroyed at sea. No one knows who or how many were killed (Cave and Thompson 2012; Shanker 2012).

48. Carrie Nation (1846–1911) opposed tobacco and alcohol. Amid her radical activity, which led to arrests in Oklahoma, Kansas, Missouri, and Arkansas, she was highly successful as a touring lecturer.

49. Falco 1996, 120–121. "Today the perceived link between foreigners and drugs still prompts the U.S. government to use diplomacy, coercion, money, and even military force to try to stop drugs from entering the country."

50. Kleber, quoted in Ryzik 2007. Either Nixon was ignorant of the facts, lied twice, or the White House chief of staff lied: "[President Nixon] emphasized that you have to face the fact that the whole problem is really the blacks. The key is to devise a system that recognizes this while appearing not to" (Haldeman 1994, 53, cited in Baum 1996).

51. In the eyes of many authorities, young black men are more likely to threaten the community and less reformable. Zatz 2000, 518.

52. The Justice Department at first applied the law only to those arrested after its passage but then, in July 2011, agreed it should apply to anyone sentenced after the change.

53. Zatz 2000, 507.

54. Starting point: population percentages 2010 Census: white 72.4 percent, black 12.6 percent, Hispanic origin 16.3 percent, Native American 0.9 percent, Asian 4.8 percent.

55. Zatz 2000, 538.

56. Alexander 2010, 100.

57. Bonczar (2003) assumes stable incarceration rates. Also Guerino, Harrison, and Sabol 2011. *These numbers do* not *include prisoners in local jails, which omits more than one-quarter of the total.*

58. National Research Council 2014, 64–65.

59. Gottschalk (2012b) points out that even if only whites were counted, the United States would still have the highest incarceration rate in the world.

60. Compared to 22 percent in 1965 (Brame et al. 2012).

61. On national disproportions, see Pettit and Western 2004, Bonczar 2003, Bonczar and Beck 1997.

62. Institute on Women 2009.

63. Mauer 2013. Also see Beck and Harrison 2005, 11; Blanchette and Brown 2006; and U.S. Department of Justice, Bureau of Justice Statistics 2003; The much lower prison rates for women presumably result from a complex set of sources, all related to gender and society.

64. Mauer 2013.

65. Associated Press 2007.

66. In 2011 Texas abolished its scandalous Youth Commission and Juvenile Probation Commission, replacing them with the Juvenile Justice Department; rates of youth detention have

declined markedly. In the United States, youth of color constitute only 32 percent of the juvenile population, but they make up 58 percent of the youth held in juvenile facilities (Children's Defense Fund 2012).

67. Galbraith 2004; Bright 2003, 6. Although many expect that the poor commit more crimes of the sort that lead to arrests, does the absence of defense lawyers make any such conclusion suspect?

68. Greenhouse 2004. The U.S. Supreme Court later disallowed the policy.

69. Bark 2007.

70. Professor Bill Quigley, quoted in Templeton 2007.

71. Wacquant 2002; Wacquant 2010, 77.

72. Other scholars, including Harvard sociologist Orlando Patterson (2007), see the current system on its own as "a means of controlling young black men." Also see Brown University economist Glenn Loury (2008), and Cole 1999.

73. Alexander 2010, 103–119.

74. The most reliable information comes from the annual National Survey on Drug Use and Health, conducted since 1988 by the Research Triangle Institute (U.S. Department of Health and Human Services 2011).

75. Mauer 2006, 166. Also see Zimring 2011.

76. Gwynne 2012. Zimring (2011) concludes that other police practices, not stop-and-frisk, have lowered New York's crime rates. But because many whites believe that low-income people are more prone to crime, and because race is closely associated with income (or social class), whites may assume that profiling is a more efficient (less expensive) way to catch "bad guys." Blow 2014.

77. Collum (2010) writes about New Jersey troopers seeking Trooper of the Year awards via stops of drivers with brown skin. Regarding the movie *The Hurricane* (1999) see "The Truths of 'Hurricane' are Complex" (Purdy 2000). Dennis W. Archer, when Detroit mayor, remembered his own police gunpoint stop fifteen years earlier, when he was president of the state bar association (Meredith 1999).

78. Staples (2009) cites Pager 2007. The Bureau of Justice study found police *stops* of autos in 2002 not racially biased (Smith and Durose 2006, 2).

79. Durose, Langan, and Levin 2001. Neuspiel (1996) also reports higher mortality and morbidity among black mothers than white. Chasnoff, Landress, and Barrett (1990) report higher cocaine use by black women (7.5 versus 1.8 percent) and higher cannabinoids use by white women (14.4 versus 6 percent).

80. Zatz 2000, 522.

81. Goldensohn and Levy 2014.

82. Zatz 2000, 527.

83. National Gang Center 2012.

84. Kulish 2007.

85. Mauer 2009, 2006.

86. PRRAC 2011.

87. McElrath et al. 2005.

88. Leiber and Fox 2005.

89. Younge 2007. Reed Walters, the Jena district attorney, defended his attempted murder charge, saying Louisiana statutes provided him no way of objecting to students putting nooses on schoolyard trees, but he had to charge five students with attempted murder when, unprovoked, they attacked one student (Walters 2007). Following large civil rights protests, the then seventeen-year-old plea-bargained a battery charge.

90. Moore 2007a. Many authority bias problems may often be made manifest in drug sweeps.

91. Durose, Langan, and Levin 2001. Hispanic felons are included in both demographic groups, so no separate statistic is available. Sentencing bias is not restricted to drug cases. In murder cases, what matters most is the race of the victim. Once charged, those who kill whites (as

opposed to blacks) are much more likely to receive a death sentence. See Liptak 2008. Much earlier data, from the 1980s, show blacks four times as likely as whites to get the death penalty in Georgia (Baldus, Pulaski, and Woodworth 1983, 709). Also in Georgia in the 1980s, "more than 20 percent of black defendants convicted of murdering white victims received the death penalty, compared with eight percent of whites who killed other whites and one percent of blacks who killed other blacks" (Glater 2007).

92. Druznid.org, quoted in Meierhoefer 1992, 20.

93. Source: Haney and Zimbardo 1998, 718, emphasis added. "Minor reforms under Governor Pataki in 2005 and 2004 made a small segment of the Rockefeller Drug Law prisoner population eligible to apply for re-sentencing. There are still thousands of people in prison in New York because of the Rockefeller laws, which carry draconian mandatory minimum sentences for drug offenses" (Drug Policy Alliance 2005).

94. United States Courts 2012.

95. According to the Bureau of Justice Statistics, drug trafficking now carries the highest conviction rates in state courts. In 2004 such courts convicted 71 percent of the 283,000 arrested for drug trafficking, compared to 68 percent of the 12,000 arrested for murder.

96. As Cole (1999, 161), quoted by Alexander (2010, 128), writes: "The Court has imposed early insurmountable barriers to persons challenging race discrimination at all stages of the criminal justice system." Alexander (2010, 139; also see chap. 3, *passim*), writes: "The Supreme Court has now closed the courthouse doors to claims of racial bias at every stage of the criminal justice process, from stops and searches to plea bargaining and sentencing. The system of mass incarceration is now, for all practical purposes, thoroughly immune from claims of racial bias."

97. The main sources for this section are in the list in Caulkins et al. 2005. Other sources are Travis and Waul 2003; Haney and Zimbardo 1998, 716; the Adoption and Safe Families Act of 1997; Mauer and Chesney-Lind 2002; Fellner and Mauer 1998, 8; Saxe et al. 2001; Lee 2005; and the Bureau of Justice Statistics. Election statistics from Census Bureau.

98. Goffman 2014.

99. On the relationship of violent crime to other aspects of neighborhood crime see Raleigh and Galster 2012.

100. Even during the New York City crack epidemic, three-fourths of all drug-related murders resulted not from drug use but from trafficking issues such as territorial disputes or theft from rival dealers, debt collection, and employee discipline (Goldstein and Brownstein 1987). Nationally, nearly two-thirds of drug-related murders involve marketing disputes rather than violence by drugged-up users or victims or by addicts to support a habit (Caulkins et al. 2005, 10).

101. The Los Angeles Police Department, however, is said to concede turf to drug dealers as long as they keep down violence and keep their business on commercial terms. *Economist* 2007.

102. Venkatesh 2002, 205–206. On this sort of violence also see Hayden 2004.

103. Salisbury 2012. The Census Bureau's figure is $70 billion.

104. These matters are discussed in a series of articles collected in Boston and Ross 1997.

105. McFadden 1992.

106. La'Shay 2012.

107. On kids playing, Census Bureau data cited in Roberts 2007 for New York, Urbina 2007 for Philadelphia, and Ricard 2009 for Washington, DC.

108. Lee and Wildeman 2013, 43.

109. George et al. 2007.

110. Nearly the entire increase between 1986 and 1995 resulted from drug offenses. See U.S. Department of Justice, Bureau of Justice Statistics 2003; Women in Prison Project 2004. Minor changes reduced somewhat the severity of the New York State laws in 2004 and 2005, but still, according to Donna Lieberman, head of the New York Civil Liberties Union, "They're unfair, unjust and cruel . . . and . . . they destroy lives rather than rehabilitate them. They are enforced with blatant racial and ethnic bias." Matthews 2007.

111. U.S. Senate Appropriations Committee 2000.

112. Ella Baker Center 2015.

113. Haskins 2013, 9, 13. The 7 percent and 25.1 percent for black kids contrast with 4 percent and 0.9 percent for white kids.

114. Data are limited, as studies of prisoner families have focused on white male inmates. Several households are typically affected by a single black or Latino arrest; many more grandmothers are recruited as caregivers. All the service providers Barai (2006) talked to in her Chicago interviews said they were severely underfunded and could not provide needed services for clients or expand services to outreach to meet the true need. Booker (2006) noted how lack of funding for rehab programs (halfway houses, etc.) leads to high recidivism.

115. Travis and Waul 2003, ix–x; Lee 2005, 84.

116. Haskins 2014. The data pertain to children living in cities with populations over two hundred thousand.

117. Children's Defense Fund 2012.

118. Ziedenberg 2011, 7.

119. Ziedenberg 2011, 5.

120. Statistics in this section mainly from reports issued by the Bureau of Justice Statistics, but also the following sources: Institute for Criminal Policy Research, various dates; and Drug War Facts, 2007, 2015.

121. Moore 2007b. See Sentencing Project 2005.

122. *New York Times* editorial, October 19, 2010, "Their Debt Is Paid," citing a Sentencing Project study.

123. Gray 2012, citing the Sentencing Project; Mock 2012.

124. When last reported, in the late 1990s, in seven states one-quarter of black men were *permanently* disenfranchised. Fellner and Mauer 1998.

125. Mock 2012.

126. Passed in 1996, this amendment was still in effect in March 2013. By the end of 2011, however, "13 states had opted out . . . and 26 states had modified the ban, leaving only 12 states fully implementing the ban." McCarty et al. 2012.

127. Pollack et al. 2002, 258.

128. Caulkins et al. 2005, 24.

129. Blumstein and Nakamura 2012; also 2010.

130. Ortiz and Briggs 2003, 47. Bennett was the first director of the Office of National Drug Control Policy, 1981–1991.

131. Hart 2014; also 2013.

132. Levitt and Venkatesh 2000, 755; Hayden 2004.

133. Levitt and Venkatesh 2000; Venkatesh 2002, 2008.

134. Levitt and Venkatesh 2000, 786.

135. Levitt and Venkatesh 2000, 786.

7. Drug-War Politics

1. California Secretary of State, "Official Voter Information Guide Prop 47."

2. Chokshi 2014.

3. Mitchell 2015. Without congressional approval, which is highly unlikely, the White House can only experiment.

4. More generally, as Harvey (2012, 56) points out, "any small unpaid bill (a license fee or water bill, for example) can become a lien on a property," which may result in extortionate fees or loss of property.

5. Blumenson and Nilsen 1998b, 63. The value of asset forfeitures had risen to $1.8 billion in 2010.

6. Blumenson and Nilsen 1998b, 89. Thornburgh was attorney general 1988–1991.

7. Blumenson and Nilsen 1998b. In October 2009, the Supreme Court heard arguments in a Chicago case (*Alvarez v. Smith*) on citizens' difficulties in contesting property seizures, later declaring the case moot, since the authorities had returned most of the seized property.

8. Blumenson and Nilsen 1998a.

9. The benefits are doubtful. See Hooks et al. 2004.

10. "[Governor Gray] Davis got a huge boost when the guards endorsed him in 1998, showering him with more than $3 million during his years in office." Martin and Podger 2004.

11. Rothfeld 2008.

12. In response to challenges, some states have begun to adjust their population-counting rules.

13. Nationwide, "between 1980 and 1990, prisoners accounted for 5 percent of the growth in rural populations." Wagner 2009 (prison cells in 2003); Parenti 1999 (rural population growth). The overall prison population in 2010 declined for the first time since 1971, a possible result of recessionary cost-cutting, producing a new attitude toward incarceration.

14. In a June 25, 2007, advertisement in the *Nation*, Common Sense for Drug Policy listed big winners from the drug war.

15. Clifford and Silver-Greenberg 2014.

16. Center for Constitutional Rights 2009.

17. Clifford and Silver-Greenberg 2014; Williams 2015.

18. The executive of American Apparel Inc., an Alabama manufacturer of military uniforms, says his firm pays nine dollars an hour on average plus medical insurance, retirement contributions, and paid vacations. Competing with Unicor is tough. Fox 2012.

19. Shapiro 2011; Montague 2001.

20. Dolnick 2012, about the Bo Robinson center in New Jersey.

21. In California 89 percent of "private" prisoners are people of color, versus 75 percent in public prisons. In Texas the figures are 71 percent and 66 percent, and in Arizona, 65 percent and 60 percent. Wade 2012.

22. McFadden 1997.

23. Riggs Bank in Washington, DC, was finally exposed, paying $41 million in fines, and then falling into bankruptcy, for having enabled Chilean dictator Augusto Pinochet to deposit millions illegally under false names. Pinochet worked with Riggs through his notorious CIA-related director of secret police, Manuel Contreras. Rohter 2004; O'Hara 2005.

24. Aberdeen professor, secretary of the International Cannabinoid Research Society, quoted by Robichaux 2001.

25. Barthwell (2006), a pharmaceuticals consultant, challenges the concept of "medical marijuana," doubting "quality, safety, and efficacy."

26. Seth DiStefano (2009), a field organizer and lobbyist for the ACLU in West Virginia, notes "pressure from an industry looking to expand its market and profit margins." Because "drug testing constitutes a search under the Fourth Amendment and may only be done constitutionally under certain circumstances . . . West Virginia has seen the steady creep of proposals that seek to expand the number of citizens [including schoolchildren] who would be mandated by law to provide a sample of their urine for random government inspection."

27. Quoted in Norment 1989.

28. See Caulkins et al. (2005, 27–28) for the Rand Corp. drug research team's list of the reasons for voters and politicians to ignore the truth about the drug war.

29. Riggs (2013) attributes higher-potency marijuana to prohibition.

30. Technically, for economists, their demand is inelastic with respect to regulation.

31. The elasticity of violence with respect to drug price (or drug shortages) appears to be negative; large drug-import seizures, causing temporary reductions in supply and pushing up the price, are said to cause problems on the street.

32. Global Commission on Drug Policy 2014.

33. Lucas 2009.

34. As a theory of crime prevention, "broken windows" finds little support. Harcourt 2001; Sridhar 2006.

35. Thanks to Jonathan Wellemeyer for suggesting this formulation.

36. Korte 2009.

37. U.S. Office of the President 2012, table 3, p. 17.

38. Douglas 2014. Banks remain reluctant, and dealers remain burdened with large quantities of cash. According to the ranking Republican member of the Senate's Judiciary Committee, Chuck Grassley: "Marijuana trafficking is illegal under federal law, and it's illegal for banks to deal with marijuana sale proceeds under federal law. Only Congress can change these laws. The administration can't change the law with a memo." Quoted in Douglas 2014.

39. Elders wondered about legalization as an alternative to drug-war mayhem. "Baer suppressed a large quantity of heroin he deemed seized without probable cause, until attacks by the media, Senator Dole and President Clinton led him to reverse his ruling," and "Weld found his nomination to be Ambassador to Mexico hijacked by Senator Jesse Helms on grounds that Weld had supported proposals to allow the medical use of marijuana" (Blumenson and Nilsen 1998b).

40. Booker quote from Moran 2007. Schmoke from Chideya 2007.

41. Wickham 2007.

42. LEAP has "more than 150,000 supporters including police, judges, prosecutors, prison wardens, FBI and DEA agents, and civilian supporters of drug policy reform" (http://www.leap.cc/about/who-we-are/).

43. Kelly 2007. Kelly does not mention gun sales or the NRA, but see "The NRA's Senate," editorial, *New York Times*, July 2, 2007, on Senate committee approval for even stronger Tiahrt amendment language. Tiahrt spoke for the gun lobby, mainly financed by gun manufacturers, which opposes nearly any restriction that might cut into gun sales, whips up opposition to troublesome candidates for Congress, and makes massive campaign contributions.

44. Radio broadcast transcript from *Democracy Now!*, March 30, 2009, emphasis added. Also see Stamper and Beavers 2014.

45. LaMarche 2007. LaMarche was president and CEO of the education-oriented Atlantic Philanthropies from 2007 to 2011. She also wrote that "from 1988 to 1990, the nightly news was engaged in a war against crack mothers—who were all but definitionally black."

46. McKinley 2012.

47. Guerino, Harrison, and Sabol 2012, data in appendix table 23.

48. Gilmore 2007 explores the vast, violent, and racist California prison system. In 2014 the courts allowed California more time to reduce the overcrowding.

49. LaMarche 2007.

50. Butler 1995, 2009.

51. Jarecki 2012.

52. Ferri, Davoli, and Perucci 2006; Inciardi and Harrison 2000.

53. The Vancouver program is seen by proponents as a public health necessity, but others object to the use of public funds.

54. The pharmaceutical industry prefers electronic tracking of sales, which is not effective. Rob Bovett, the district attorney for Lincoln County, Oregon, and the principal author of state anti-meth legislation, blames the industry for resisting a simple fix to "kill the meth monster" (Bovett 2010). Mexico has banned pseudoephedrine entirely, reducing the potency of imports from Mexico.

55. Meanwhile, the Mexican branch of the U.S. *war* on drugs has led to tens of thousands of murders and in many places a collapse of public order.

56. Motel 2014.

57. From thirty-five blocks in some of Brooklyn's poorest neighborhoods, researchers discovered that so many went to prison each year that New York State would spend more than a million dollars on the residents of *each block*. In one block it was $5 million (Gonnerman 2004). Such huge

public spending to imprison residents of poor city blocks occurs across the nation. Maps are available online at the *Justice Atlas of Sentencing and Corrections*, http://www.justiceatlas.org/.

Democracy, Inequality, Urban Policy

Epigraph: Shapiro 2013.

1. Ayres and Edlin (2011) propose a tax to limit after-tax incomes to thirty-six times the median!

2. Powell 2011, quoting Jonathan Lange, a labor organizer affiliated with the Industrial Areas Foundation. Bloomberg signed similar legislation in 2002, to give a living wage to fifty thousand home health workers and nine thousand working in child care.

3. Calculated from the chart in Leonhardt 2012, with data from the Tax Policy Center.

4. Their state and local tax deduction ranges from $4 to $70 on average for taxpayers earning up to $50,000, but it is $5,166 for taxpayers earning more than $200,000. Hanlon 2011.

5. Top *marginal rates* exceeded 90 percent.

6. Tax rate charts from Emmanuel Saez and Thomas Piketty, median incomes from the U.S. Census, and tax breaks from the Tax Policy Center. The three rates were 34.2 percent, 33.6 percent, and 30.4 percent.

7. Parrott et al. 2012, 15.

8. Barro 2014.

9. National Partnership for Women and Families 2015.

10. Reich and Jacobs 2014; Reich, Jacobs, and Deitz 2014.

11. Quote from T. Williams (2014) citing analysis by the Federal Reserve Bank of Cleveland in Hartley 2013, who takes a positive view of gentrification. After Boston, cities with the highest gentrification pressures on low-income neighborhoods are Seattle, New York, San Francisco, Washington, Atlanta, Chicago, and Portland.

12. New York City, Office of the Mayor 2014; Institute of Human Development 2015.

13. Meyerson (2014) adds de Blasio, "Minneapolis's Betsy Hodges, Seattle's Ed Murray, Boston's Martin Walsh, Santa Fe's Javier Gonzales, and many more."

14. T.N. (Los Angeles), the *Economist*, February 1, 2013. By recognizing that "Latinos are among the worst victims of the terrible public schools in many parts of the United States," Republicans might craft "a 21st-century version of the American dream."

15. Fry 2014.

16. The San Francisco proposition failed because of a technicality requiring a larger majority.

17. Keller 2014.

18. Travis, Western, and Redburn 2014, 102–103.

19. Marcuse 2011, blog no. 51.

20. Rosenbaum 2013.

21. Associated Press Election Research Group, George Mason University.

22. Nichols 2011. For evident reasons, Nichols also lists Abraham Lincoln.

23. Appelbaum and Gebeloff 2012.

24. Appelbaum and Gebeloff 2012.

25. It is not so odd in (old) Europe. In Italy, for example, nearly everyone knows and acknowledges that Communist and Socialist governments (and their other-named successors) provide the very best municipal governments, in cities like (Red) Bologna and Modena.

26. Nichols 2011.

27. Nichols 2011.

REFERENCES

Ahmed-Ullah, N., J. Chase, and B. Secter. 2013. "CPS Approves Largest School Closure in Chicago's History." *Chicago Tribune*, May 23.

Alameda County Community Food Bank. 2012. "Facts about Hunger."

Alberta, T. J. 2009. "Census Nominee Rules Out Statistical Sampling in 2010." *Wall Street Journal*, May 15.

Alexander, M. 2010. *The New Jim Crow: Mass Incarceration in the Age of Colorblindness*. New York: New Press.

Alter, J. 2010. "A Case of Senioritis: Gates Tackles Education's Two-Headed Monster." *Newsweek*, December 6.

Alvaredo, F., A. B. Atkinson, T. Piketty, and E. Saez. 2013. "The Top 1 Percent in International and Historical Perspective." *Journal of Economic Perspectives* 27, no. 3 (Summer): 3–20.

Amaral, B. 2012. "Political Food Fight over School Lunches." *Watertown (NY) Daily Times*, October 7.

American Civil Liberties Union. 2009. "Bush Administration Deals Eleventh Hour Blow to Scientific Freedom." January 12.

America's Promise Alliance. 2009. *Cities in Crisis 2009: Closing the Graduation Gap*.

Anderson, E. 2010. *The Imperative of Integration*. Princeton, NJ: Princeton University Press.

Andrade, F. G., and C. F. Mellen. 2012. *Breaking the Taboo*. Film. XiveTV. December 7.

Angotti, T. 2006. "Apocalyptic Anti-urbanism: Mike Davis and His Planet of Slums." *International Journal of Urban and Regional Research* 30, no. 4: 961–967.

Appelbaum, B., and R. Gebeloff. 2012. "Even Critics of Safety Net Increasingly Depend on It." *New York Times*, February 11.

Archibold, R. C. 2012. "U.S. Remains Opposed to Drug Legalization, Biden Tells Region." *New York Times*, March 5.

ASCE (American Society of Civil Engineers). 2013. *2013 Report Card for America's Infrastructure*. March.

Associated Press. 2007. "Census: More Blacks, Latinos Live in Cells Than in Dorms." September 27.

Atkinson, A. B. 2007. "The Distribution of Top Incomes in the United Kingdom, 1908–2000." In *Top Incomes over the Twentieth Century: A Contrast between Continental European and English-Speaking Countries*, edited by A. B. Atkinson and T. Piketty, chap. 4. Oxford: Oxford University Press. Series updated by the same author (2012–2015, Methodological Notes).

Attkisson, S. 2012. "Video Protests Govt. Calorie Limits in School Lunches." *CBS This Morning*, September 26.

August, M. 2014. "Speculating Social Housing: Mixed-Income Public Housing Redevelopment in Toronto's Regent Park and Don Mount Court." Unpublished PhD thesis, University of Toronto.

Aviv, R. 2012. "No Remorse." Annals of Justice. *New Yorker*, January 2.

Ayres, I., and A. S. Edlin. 2011. "Don't Tax the Rich, Tax Inequality Itself." Op-ed. *New York Times*, December 18.

Bachhuber, J., and S. Smith. 2006. "HUD, 'The No. 1 Worst in the United States.'" *Village Voice*, June 27.

Bacon, D. 2014. "Rocketship to Profits." Black Agenda Report. October 8.

Bailey, M., and S. Dynarski. 2011. "Gains and Gaps: Changing Inequality in U.S. College Entry and Completion." NBER Working Paper 17633. December.

Bakeman, J. 2012. "Teacher Education at 'Crisis Point.'" *Ithaca (NY) Journal*, November 16.

Baker, D., G. Pryce, G. Giovannoni, and A. J. Thompson. 2003. "The Therapeutic Potential of Cannabis." *Lancet Neurology* 2, no. 5: 291–298.

Baker, K. 2012. "Republicans to Cities: Drop Dead." Sunday Review. *New York Times*, October 6.

Baldus, D. C., C. Pulaski, and G. Woodworth. 1983. "Comparative Review of Death Sentences: An Empirical Study of the Georgia Experience." *Journal of Criminal Law and Criminology* 74: 661–673.

Balfanz, R., and N. Legters. 2004. *Locating the Dropout Crisis*. Report 70. Johns Hopkins University. September.

Bandele, A. 2011. "After the Attica Uprising." *Nation*, September 9.

Barai, N. 2006. "Substance Abuse Referral Networks, Access to Social Services, and Getting off Drugs: Meeting the Needs of Recovering Women." Unpublished honors thesis, Cornell University.

Bark, E. 2007. "'Breaking Point': Drama, Politics and Gang Warfare behind Bars." Television Review. *New York Times*, October 6.

Barro, J. 2014. "Four States Vote to Raise Minimum Wage." *New York Times*, November 3.

Barry, D. 2007. "Legacy of School Segregation Endures, Separate but Legal." *New York Times*, September 30.

Barthwell, A. 2006. "From Mockery to Medicine." Global Drug Policy.

Baum, D. 1996. *Smoke and Mirrors: The War on Drugs and the Politics of Failure*. Boston: Little, Brown.

Beck, A. J., and P. M. Harrison. 2005. "Prison and Jail Inmates at Midyear 2004." *Bureau of Justice Statistics Bulletin*, April 24.

Becker, G. S., K. M. Murphy, and M. Grossman. 2006. "The Market for Illegal Goods: The Case of Drugs." *Journal of Political Economy* 114 (February): 38–60.

Behrent, M. 2009. "Reclaiming Our Freedom to Teach: Education Reform in the Obama Era." *Harvard Educational Review*. Summer.

———. 2011. "The War on Teachers: A First-Hand Account." *Alternatives Internationales*, March 17.

Bellisari, A. 2008. "Evolutionary Origins of Obesity." *Obesity Reviews* 9, no. 2: 165–180.

Benbow, N., Y. Wang, and S. Whitman. 1998. "The Big Cities Health Inventory, 1997." *Journal for Community Health* 23, no. 6 (December): 471–489.

Benner, C., and M. Pastor. 2010. *Just Growth: Inclusion and Prosperity in America's Metropolitan Regions*. New York: Routledge.

Bennett, M. 2012. "How Mandatory Minimum Sentences Forced Me to Send More Than 1,000 Non-violent Drug Offenders to Federal Prison." *Nation*, November 12.

Bischoff, K., and S. F. Reardon. 2013. "Residential Segregation by Income, 1970–2009." Report for the American Communities Project of Brown University. October 16.

Black, J. 2009. "The Economics of Local Food: All You Can Eat." *Wall Street Journal*, September 8.

Blanchette, K., and S. L. Brown. 2006. *The Assessment and Treatment of Women Offenders: An Integrative Perspective*. New York: Wiley & Sons.

Blow, C. 2014. "Crime and Punishment." Op-ed. *New York Times*, December 1.

Blumenson, E., and E. Nilsen. 1998a. "The Drug War's Hidden Agenda." *Nation*, March 9.

———. 1998b. "Policing for Profit: The Drug War's Hidden Economic Agenda." *University of Chicago Law Review* 65, no. 35: 35–114.

Blumenthal, M. 2009. *Republican Gomorrah: Inside the Movement That Shattered the Party*. New York: Nation Books.

Blumstein, A., and K. Nakamura. 2010. "'Redemption' in an Era of Widespread Criminal Background Checks." *National Institute of Justice Journal*, no. 263. http://nij.gov/journals/263/Pages/redemption.aspx.

———. 2012. "Paying a Price, Long after the Crime." Op-ed. *New York Times*, January 9.

Boarnet, M. G. 2006. "Planning's Role in Building Healthy Cities." *Journal of the American Planning Association* 72:5–9.

Bobo, L. D., and D. Johnson. 2004. "A Taste for Punishment: Black and White Americans' Views on the Death Penalty and the War on Drugs." *Du Bois Review* 1, no. 1: 151–180.

Bonczar, T. P. 2003. "Prevalence of Imprisonment in the U.S. Population, 1974–2001." *Bureau of Justice Statistics Special Report*. August.

Bonczar, T. P., and A. J. Beck. 1997. *Lifetime Likelihood of Going to State or Federal Prison*. Bureau of Justice Statistics Special Report. March.

Booker, C. 2006. "Newark Mayor: Black Leaders Must Innovate." National Public Radio, August 8.

Born, B., and M. Purcell. 2006. "Avoiding the Local Trap: Scale and Food Systems in Planning Research." *Journal of Planning Education and Research* 26, no. 2 (December): 195–207.

Boston, T., and C. Ross, eds. 1997. *The Inner City: Urban Poverty and Economic Development in the Next Century*. New Brunswick, NJ: Transaction.

Bovett, R. 2010. "How to Kill the Meth Monster." Op-ed. *New York Times*, November 15.

Bowles, S., and H. Gintis. 1976. *Schooling in Capitalist America: Educational Reform and the Contradictions of Economic Life*. New York: Basic Books.

Brame, R., M. G. Turner, R. Paternoster, and S. D. Bushway. 2012. "Cumulative Prevalence of Arrests from Ages 8 to 23 in a National Sample." *Pediatrics* 129, no. 1: 21–27.

Brawley, A. 2010. "Columbus, Ohio: White City?" *CityForward* (blog), April 12. http://cityforward.wordpress.com/2010/04/12/columbus-ohio-white-city/.

———. 2011. "Asparagus, Beet, Carrot: The History, Relocation, and Significance of the Chicago Wholesale Produce Market in the Region's Food System." Unpublished MRP thesis, Cornell University.

Bright, S. B. 2003. "The Accused Get What the System Doesn't Pay For: Poor Legal Representation for People Who Can't Afford Lawyers." In *Prison Nation: The Warehousing of America's Poor*, edited by Tara Herivel and Paul Wright, 6–22. New York: Routledge.

Brody, L. 2014. "A Mad Rush to Eroll Preschoolers." *Wall Street Journal*, August 3.

Brown, C. 1965. *Manchild in the Promised Land*. New York: Macmillan.

Bruck, C. 2007. "Fault Lines." *New Yorker*, May 21.

Buchberger, F., and I. Buchberger. 2003. "Problem Solving Capacity of a Teacher Education System as a Condition of Success? An Analysis of the 'Finnish Case.'" In *Education Policy Analysis in a Comparative Perspective*, edited by F. Buchberger and S. Berghammer, 222–237. Linz, Austria: Trauner.

Buenker, J. D. 1973. *Urban Liberalism and Progressive Reform*. New York: Scribner's.

Burge, K. 2012. "Study Finds Inequities in Schools' Zone Plans." *Boston Globe*, October 1.

Bush, J., and N. Gingrich. 2011. "Better Off Bankrupt: States Need a New Way to Deal with Budget Crises." Op-ed. *Los Angeles Times*, January 27.

Butler, P. 1995. "Racially Based Jury Nullification." *Yale Law Journal* 105, no. 3 (December): 677–725.

———. 2009. *Let's Get Free: A Hip-Hop Theory of Justice*. New York: New Press.

Cabañas, M. 2014. "The Global Drug Trade and the War on Drugs in the Americas: A Historical Review." *Latin American Perspectives* 41, no. 2: 232–235.

California Dropout Research Project. 2014. City Profiles—for 2009/2010.

Campaign for Fiscal Equity. 2009. *Maxed Out: New York City School Overcrowding Crisis*. New York Campaign for Fiscal Equity. May.

Capodilupo, L. 2002. "Municipal Assistance Corporation for the City of New York (MAC): User's Guide to the Mac Archive." Archive on Municipal Finance and Leadership. April.

Carey, K. 2004. "The Funding Gap 2004: Many States Still Shortchange Low-Income and Minority Students." Education Trust. October.

Carnevale, A. P., N. Smith, and J. Strohl. 2010. "Help Wanted: Projections of Jobs and Education Requirements through 2018." Georgetown University Center on Education and the Workforce.

Carnoy, M. 2011. "As Higher Education Expands, Is It Contributing to Greater Inequality?" *National Institute Economic Review* 215 (January): R34–R47.

Carter, S. A. 1991. *Reflections of an Affirmative Action Baby.* New York: Basic Books.

Casella, J., and J. Ridgeway. 2012. "New York's Black Sites." *Nation,* July 30 / August 6.

Cassidy, J. 2010. "What Good Is Wall Street?" *New Yorker,* November 29.

Castells, M. 1977. *The Urban Question: A Marxist Approach.* Cambridge, MA: MIT Press.

———. 1983. *The City and the Grassroots: A Cross-Cultural Theory of Urban Social Movements.* Berkeley: University of California Press.

Caulkins, J. P., P. Reuter, M. Iguchi, and J. Chiesa. 2005. "How Goes the 'War on Drugs'? An Assessment of U.S. Drug Problems and Policy." Rand Corp.

Cave, D., and G. Thompson. 2012. "U.S. Rethinks a Drug War after Deaths in Honduras." *New York Times,* October 12.

CDC (Centers for Disease Control and Prevention). 2015. "Nutrition Advertising Targeting Children." Public Health Law Program. http://www.cdc.gov/phlp/winnable/advertising_children.html.

Center City District and Central Philadelphia Development Corporation. 2007. *Center City: Planning for Growth, 2007–2012.* April.

Center on Budget and Policy Priorities. 2014. "Introduction to the Supplemental Nutrition Assistance Program." June 4.

Center for Constitutional Rights. 2009. "Corporate Exploitation and the Prison System." Fact sheet.

Center for Science in the Public Interest. 2013. "The Dollars and Cents of the New School Meal Regulations."

Chasnoff, J., H. Landress, and M. Barrett. 1990. "The Prevalence of Illicit-Drug or Alcohol Use during Pregnancy and Discrepancies in Mandatory Reporting in Pinellas County, Florida." *New England Journal of Medicine* 322 (April 26): 1202–1206.

Chen, D. W. 2008. "New Jersey Panel Approves School Financing Plan." *New York Times,* January 4.

Chicago Public Building Commission. 2012. "2012 Chicago Public School Openings." Board meeting presentation. September 11.

Chideya, F. 2007. "Drugs . . . Legalize It?" National Public Radio. August 15.

Children's Defense Fund, Juvenile Justice. 2012. http://www.childrensdefense.org/policy-priorities/juvenile-justice/.

Chokshi, N. 2014. "California Voters Seem Ready to End the State's 'Tough on Crime' Era." *Washington Post,* October 31.

Clancy, K. 2004. "Potential Contributions of Planning to Community Food Systems." *Journal of Planning Education and Research* 23, no. 4: 435–438.

Clark, J., and T. van Slyke. 2005. "Making Connections." *In These Times,* April 14.

Clavel, P. 1986. *The Progressive City.* Brunswick, NJ: Rutgers University Press.

———. 1995. "Regimes, Planning and Progressive Coalitions in Cities." *Planning Theory* 14:44–64.

———. 2010. *Activists in City Hall: The Progressive Response to the Reagan Era in Boston and Chicago*. Ithaca, NY: Cornell University Press.

Clavel, P., J. Forester, and W. W. Goldsmith, eds. 1980. *Urban and Regional Planning in an Age of Austerity*. New York: Pergamon Press.

Clifford, S., and J. Silver-Greenberg. 2014. "Orange Is the New Green." *New York Times*, June 27.

Clifton, K. J. 2004. "Mobility Strategies and Food Shopping for Low-Income Families: A Case Study." *Journal of Planning Education and Research* 23, no. 4 (June): 402–413.

Coates, T-N. 2014. "The Secret Lives of Inner-City Black Males." *Atlantic*, March 18.

Cole, D. 1999. *No Equal Justice: Race and Class in the American Criminal Justice System*. New York: New Press.

Coleman-Jensen, A., M. Nord, M. Andrews, and S. Carlson. 2012. "Household Food Security in the United States in 2011." ERR-141, U.S. Department of Agriculture Economic Research Service. September.

Coles, R. 2000. *Lives of Moral Leadership*. New York: Random House.

Collum, J. 2010. *The Black Dragon: Racial Profiling Exposed*. Sun River, MT: Jigsaw Press.

Consortium on Chicago School Research. 2012. "Turning Around Low-Performing Schools in Chicago." University of Chicago.

Cooper, A., and L. M. Holmes. 2006. *Lunch Lessons: Changing the Way We Feed Our Children*. New York: William Morrow.

Cooper, M. 2012. "Budget Woes Prompt Erosion of Public Jobs, with a Heavy Toll in Silicon Valley." *New York Times*, February 18.

Corburn, J. 2009. *Toward the Healthy City: People, Places, and the Politics of Urban Planning*. Cambridge, MA: MIT Press.

Cosby, B. 2004. Address at the NAACP. Washington, DC. May 17.

Coutts, A., and I. Kawachi. 2006. "The Urban Social Environment and Its Effects on Health." In *Cities and the Health of the Public*, edited by Nicholas Freudenberg and David Vlahov, 49–53. Nashville: Vanderbilt University Press.

Cowan, A. L. 2005. "Amid Affluence, a Struggle over Special Education." *New York Times*, April 24.

Cross, W. E., Jr. 1991. *Shades of Black: Diversity in African-American Identity*. Philadelphia: Temple University Press.

Cummins, S., E. Flint, and S. Matthews. 2014. "New Neighborhood Grocery Store Increased Awareness of Food Access but Did Not Alter Dietary Habits or Obesity." *Health Affairs* 33, no. 2: 283–291.

Dadayan, L. 2012. "State and Local Government Jobs Continue to Decline in Most States." Data Alert, Nelson A. Rockefeller Institute of Government. February 17.

Dahl, R. 1961. *Who Governs? Democracy and Power in an American City*. New Haven, CT: Yale University Press.

Dahlberg, K. A. 1994. "Food Policy Councils: The Experience of Five Cities and One County." Joint Meeting of the Agriculture, Food, and Human Values Society and the Society for the Study of Food and Society. Tucson, AZ, June 11.

Darling-Hammond, L. 2007. "Evaluating 'No Child Left Behind.'" *Nation*, May 21.

———. 2010a. "The Finnish Success Story." In *The Flat World of Education: How America's Commitment to Equity Will Determine Our Future*, 164–173. New York: Teachers College Press.

———. 2010b. "Steady Work: How Countries Build a Strong Teaching and Learning System." In *The Flat World and Education: How America's Commitment to Equity Will Determine Our Future*, 163–193. New York: Teachers College Press.

Davis, S. 1984. "Justice Rehnquist's Equal Protection Clause: An Interim Analysis." *University of Nebraska Law Review* 63:288–313.

Delvin, L. 2011. Letter to the Editor. *New York Times*, March 16.

Democracy Now! 2015. The War and Peace Report. National Public Radio, June 5.

Denby, D. 2012. "Public Defender: Dane Ravitch Takes on a Movement." *New Yorker*, November 19.

Denvir, D. 2011. "Five Myths about the 10 Most Segregated Metro Areas." *Salon*, April 3.

Derrick, P. 2001. *Tunneling to the Future: The Story of the Great Subway Expansion That Saved New York*. New York: NYU Press.

Dig Deep Farms and Produce. 2013. http://www.digdeepcsa.com/.

Dillon, S. 2006a. "In Schools across U.S., the Melting Pot Overflows." *New York Times*, August 27.

———. 2006b. "Law to Segregate Omaha Schools Divides Nebraska." *New York Times*, April 15.

———. 2007. "Ohio Goes after Charter Schools That Are Failing." *New York Times*, November 8.

———. 2011a. "Behind Grass-Roots Schools Advocacy, Bill Gates." *New York Times*, May 22.

———. 2011b. "Charter School Champion Shifts Focus." *New York Times*, March 26.

DiStefano, S. D. 2009. "Testing for Drugs and Profits." Op-ed. *Charleston (WV) Gazette*, October 6.

Dolnick, S. 2012. "At a Halfway House, Bedlam Reigns." *New York Times*, June 17.

Donofrio, G. A. 2007. "Feeding the City." *Gastronomica: The Journal of Food and Culture* 7, no. 4 (Fall): 30–41.

Douglas, D. 2014. "Obama Administration Clears Banks to Accept Funds from Legal Marijuana Dealers." *Washington Post*, February 14.

Doussard, M. 2013. *Degraded Work: The Struggle at the Bottom of the Labor Market*. Minneapolis: University of Minnesota Press.

Driehaus, B. 2007. "Ohio Experiment Survives Cuts by Becoming a Charter School." *New York Times*, June 13.

Drug Policy Alliance. 2005. eNewsletter. November 17.

Drug War Facts. 2007. "Common Sense for Drug Policy." November.

———. 2015. Get the Facts: Drug War Facts.org. http://www.drugwarfacts.org/cms/#sthash.BK3RypLq.dpbs.

Duenwald, M. 2002. "An 'Eat More' Message for a Fattened America." *New York Times*, February 19.

Duncan, G., and R. J. Murnane, eds. *Whither Opportunity? Rising Inequality, Schools, and Children's Life Chances*. New York: Russell Sage Foundation, 2011.

DuPont. 2011. "Commentary: Global Commission on Drug Policy Offers Reckless, Vague Drug Legalization Proposal; Current Drug Policy Should Be Improved through Innovative Linkage of Prevention, Treatment and the Criminal Justice System." Institute for Behavior and Health, July 12, 2011. Revised October 26

Durose, M., P. Langan, and D. Levin. 2001. "Felony Sentences in State Courts." Bureau of Justice Statistics, October 1.

Economist. 2007. "Living with Cockroaches: City Gangs." United States. August 4.

Edelman, P. 2012. So Rich, So Poor: Why It's So Hard to End Poverty in America. New York: New Press.

Edsall, T. B. 2012. The Age of Austerity: How Scarcity Will Remake American Politics. New York: Doubleday.

Edsall, T. B., and M. D. Edsall. 1991. Chain Reaction: The Impact of Race, Rights, and Taxes on American Politics. New York: Norton.

Edwards, D. 2014. "Paul Ryan Cites 'White Nationalist' to Blame Poverty on Lazy Men in 'Inner Cities.'" Rawstory.com.

Ella Baker Center. 2015. Report on Economic Hardships for Families of Inmates. August.

Eshelman, R. S. 2009. "Philadelphia Rising." Nation, March 30.

EWG (Environmental Working Group). 2012. Farm Subsidies. "The United States Summary Information." http://farm.ewg.org/region.php?fips=00000.

Fainstein, S. 1995. "Politics, Economics, and Planning: Why Urban Regimes Matter." Planning Theory 14:34–43.

Falco, M. 1996. "U.S. Drug Policy: Addicted to Failure." Foreign Policy, no. 102 (Spring): 120–121.

Fang, Lee. 2015. "With These Hires, Congress Becomes Even More Like a Corporation." Nation, March 11.

Farley, T., J. Rice, J. N. Bodor, D. A. Cohen, R. N. Bluthenthal, and D. Rose. 2009. "Measuring the Food Environment, Shelf Space of Fruits, Vegetables, and Snack Foods in the U.S." Journal of Urban Health, Bulletin of the New York Academy of Medicine 86, no. 5: 672–682.

Feldman, S. 2010. "Meet SEED, D.C.'s One-of-a-Kind Public Boarding School." Greater Greater Washington (blog), October 22.

Fellner, J., and M. Mauer. 1998. Losing the Vote: The Impact of Felony Disenfranchisement Laws in the United States. Sentencing Project.

Fensterwald, J., and S. Frey. 2015. "Budget Deal Confirms Record K–12 Spending." EdSource, June 16. http://edsource.org/2015/budget-deal-confirms-record-k-12-spending/8159.

Ferguson, T., and R. A. Johnson. 2012. "Municipal Bankruptcy: The Lessons of California." Op-ed. Los Angeles Times, July 31.

Ferri, M., M. Davoli, and C. Perucci. 2006. "Heroin Maintenance Treatment." Journal of Substance Abuse Treatment 30, no. 1: 63–72.

Finder, A. 2005. "As Test Scores Jump, Raleigh Credits Integration by Income." New York Times, September 25.

Fliegel, S. 1994. "Debbie Meier and the Dawn of Central Park East." City Journal, Winter. http://www.city-journal.org/story.php?id=1414.

Food Marketing Institute. 2013. "Supermarket Facts: Industry Overview."

Food Runners San Francisco. 2015. "About Food Runners." http://www.foodrunners.org/about/.

Forman, N., Jr., and T. Stutz. 2012. "Beyond Stop-and-Frisk." Op-ed. New York Times, April 19.

Fox, E. J. 2012. "Factory Owners: Federal Prisoners Stealing Our Business." CNN Money, August 14.

Fox News. 2013. "Star Parker: War on Poverty Brings Poverty into the Suburbs." August 21. http://www.urbancure.org/mbarticle.asp?id=364&t=Star-Parker-War-on-poverty-brings-poverty-into-the-suburbs.

Freedman, S.G. 2011. "As Catholic Schools Close in Major Cities, the Need Only Grows." *New York Times*, June 3.

Freeman, J. B. 2012. *American Empire: The Rise of a Global Power, the Democratic Revolution at Home, 1945–2000*. New York: Viking.

Freudenberg, N., S. Galea, and D. Vlahov. 2006. *Cities and the Health of the Public*. Nashville: Vanderbilt University Press.

Frug, G. E. 1999. *City Making: Building Communities without Building Walls*. Princeton, NJ: Princeton University Press.

Fry, Richard. 2014. "U.S. High School Dropout Rate Reaches Record Low." Pew Research Center, October 2.

Furchtott-Roth, D. 2012. "A Big Gap Means There Is Room to Move Up." *New York Times*, October 18.

Gafni, M. 2010. "Feds Bust Suspected Ecstasy Drug Ring Centered around Bay Area Rap Label Founded by Mac Dre." *Oakland Tribune*, updated April 25.

Galambos, L., and D. van Van Ee, eds. 2001. *The Papers of Dwight David Eisenhower: The Presidency; Keeping the Peace*. Vol. 18. Baltimore: Johns Hopkins University Press.

Galbraith, J. K. 2000. *Created Unequal: The Crisis in American Pay*. Chicago: University of Chicago Press.

Galbraith, S. M. 2004. "So Tell Me Why Do Women Need Something Different?" *Journal of Religion & Spirituality in Social Thought* 23, nos. 1–2: 197–212.

Gallagher, J. 2004. "New York Ranking 'Number One' Again." *Ithaca (NY) Journal*, October 11.

Gans, H. 1990. "Deconstructing the Underclass." *Journal of the American Planning Association* 56, no. 3: 271–278.

Garner, D. 2010. "Obama's Linda Darling-Hammond and Her Failed School." *Education News*, April 16.

Gay, M. 2007. "State Takes Control of Troubled Public Schools in St. Louis." *New York Times*, March 23.

George, S., R. Hoist, H. Jung, R. LaLonde, and R. Varghese. 2007. "Incarcerated Women, Their Children, and the Nexus with Foster Care." Final Report to National Institute of Justice. November.

Gershon, R. 2012. Co-op Extension Report. Ithaca, NY.

Ghorayshi, A. 2012. "Too Big to Chug: How Our Sodas Got So Huge." *Mother Jones*, June 25.

Gilmore, R. 2007. *Golden Gulag: Prisons, Surplus, Crisis, and Opposition in Globalizing California*. Berkeley: University of California Press.

Glaeser, E. 2011. *Triumph of the City*. New York: Macmillan.

Glaeser, E., and J. Vigdor. 2012. "The End of the Segregated Century." Manhattan Institute Civic Report No. 66.

Glater, J. D. 2007. "Race Gap: Crime vs. Punishment." *New York Times*, October 7.

Glaze, L. E., and D. Kaeble. 2014. "Correctional Populations in the United States, 2013." Bureau of Justice Statistics, Office of Justice Programs, U.S. Department of Justice. December 19. http://www.bjs.gov/index.cfm?ty=pbdetail&iid=5177.

Glickman, N. J. 1980. *The Urban Impacts of Federal Policies*. Baltimore: Johns Hopkins University Press.

Global Commission on Drug Policy. 2014. *Taking Control: Pathways to Drug Policies That Work*. September.

Goetz, E. G. 2013. *New Deal Ruins: Race, Economic Justice, and Public Housing Policy*. Ithaca, NY: Cornell University Press.

Goffman, Alice. 2014. *On the Run: Fugitive Life in an American City*. Chicago: University of Chicago Press.

Goldensohn, R., and R. Levy. 2014. "When It's a Crime to Have a Baby." *Nation*, December 29.

Goldin, C., and R. A. Margo. 1992. "The Great Compression: The Wage Structure in the United States at Mid-century." *Quarterly Journal of Economics* 107 (February): 1–34.

Goldsmith, W. W. 1982. "Bringing the Third World Home." *Working Papers for a New Society* 9 (March/April): 24–30.

——. 2003. "The Invisibility of Color, or 'I Thought This Was a Course on Writing!'" In *Local Knowledges, Local Practices*, edited by J. Monroe, 116–126. Pittsburgh: University of Pittsburgh Press.

——. 2011. "The Drug War and Inner-City Neighborhoods." In *Oxford Handbook of Urban Economics and Planning*, edited by N. Brooks, K. Donaghy, and G. Knaap, 248–276. New York: Oxford University Press.

——. 2015. "The Drug War, Prisons, and Police Killings of Black Men." *Progressive Planning*, Spring.

Goldsmith, W. W., and E. J. Blakely. 2010. *Separate Societies: Poverty and Inequality in U.S. Cities*. 2nd ed. Philadelphia: Temple University Press. First published in 1992.

Goldsmith, W. W., and M. J. Derian. 1979. "Toward a National Urban Policy—Critical Reviews—Is There an Urban Policy?" *Journal of Regional Science* 19:93–103.

Goldsmith, W. W., and H. M. Jacobs. 1982. "The Improbability of Urban Policy: The Case of the United States." *Journal of the American Planning Association* 48, no. 1: 53–66.

Goldstein, D. 2011a. "$1 Million Survey on Newark Public School Reform Proves Inconclusive." *Dana Goldstein* (blog), January 6.

——. 2011b. "Should All Kids Go to College?" *Nation*, July 15.

Goldstein, P., and H. H. Brownstein. 1987. "Drug Related Crime Analysis—Homicide." New York State Division of Criminal Justice Services.

Gonnerman, J. 2004. "Million-Dollar Blocks: The Neighborhood Costs of America's Prison Boom." *Village Voice*, November 16.

Goode, E. 2012. "Fighting a Drawn-Out Battle against Solitary Confinement." *New York Times*, March 31.

Gootman, E. 2006. "Dip in Blacks and Hispanics at Top Schools." *New York Times*, August 18.

Gopnik, A. 2012. "The Caging of America." *New Yorker*, January 30.

Gottschalk, M. 2006. *The Prison and the Gallows: The Politics of Mass Incarceration in America*. Cambridge: Cambridge University Press.

———. 2012a. "Kicking the Habit." *New Republic*, February 13.

———. 2012b. "What's Race Got to Do with It? Penal Reform and the Future of the Carceral State and American Politics." Presentation at Cornell University, October 19.

Gray, K. 2012. "Banned from Voting Booths: Ex-convicts." *Salon*, October 22.

Greenberg, M. 1991. "American Cities: Good and Bad News about Public Health." *Bulletin of the New York Academy of Medicine* 67, no. 1 (January–February): 17–21.

Greenhouse, L. 2004. "Race-Based Prison Policy Is under Justices' Scrutiny." *New York Times*, November 3.

Grissmer, D., A. Flanagan, J. Kawsata, and S. Williamson. 2000. "Improving Student Achievement: What State NAEP Test Scores Tell Us." Rand Corp.

Guerino, P., P. M. Harrison, and W. J. Sabol. 2011. "Prisoners in 2010." Bureau of Justice Statistics, revised February 9.

Guzzardi, W. 2011. "Fresh Moves Mobile Grocery Store: An Innovative Solution to Food Deserts." *Huffington Post*, August 16.

Gwynne, K. 2012. "Courts Expose Stop-and-Frisk as Racist, Unconstitutional NYPD Harassment Strategy." *Alternet*, May 28.

Hacker, J. S., and P. Pierson. 2011. *Winner-Take-All Politics: How Washington Made the Rich Richer—and Turned Its Back on the Middle Class*. New York: Simon & Schuster.

Hacsi, T. A. 2002. *Children as Pawns: The Politics of Educational Reform*. Cambridge, MA: Harvard University Press.

Haldeman, H.R. 1994. *The Haldeman Diaries: Inside the Nixon White House*. New York: G. P. Putnam.

Hampel, P. 2007. "Parents Want City Schools to Pay Clayton Tuition." *St. Louis Post-Dispatch*, November 15.

Hancock, L. 2007. "School's Out." *Nation*, July 9.

Haney, C., and P. Zimbardo. 1998. "The Past and Future of U.S. Prison Policy: Twenty-Five Years after the Stanford Prison Experiment." *American Psychologist* 53, no 7 (July): 709–727.

Hanlon, S. 2011. "Expenditure of the Week: State and Local Tax Deduction " Center for American Progress. February 2.

Hanson D. 2013. "Assessing the Harlem Children's Zone." Discussion paper. Heritage Foundation. March 6.

Harcourt, B. 2001. *Illusion of Order: The False Promise of Broken Windows Policing*. Cambridge, MA: Harvard University Press.

Harper, A., A. Shattuck, E. Holt-Giménez, A. Alkon, and F. Lambrick. 2009. "Food Policy Councils: Lessons Learned." Food First: Institute for Food and Development Policy.

Harris, H. R. 2012. "African American Churches Focus on Being Holy and Healthy." *Washington Post*, June 29.

Harris, P. 2011. "Worlds Apart—the Neighborhoods That Sum Up a Divided America." *Guardian*, September 17.

Harrison, B., and B. Bluestone. 1988. *The Great U-Turn: Corporate Restructuring and the Polarizing of America*. New York: Basic Books.

Hart, C. 2013. *High Price: A Neuroscientist's Journey of Self-Discovery That Challenges Everything You Know about Drugs and Society.* New York: HarperCollins.

———. 2014. "So Man People Benefited from This." Interview of Columbia University professor Carl Hart by Amy Chozick. *New York Times Magazine,* June 29.

Hartley, D. 2013. "Gentrification and Financial Health." Federal Reserve Bank of Cleveland. November 6.

Harvard University. 1997. "METCO Study Finds Broad Support from Parents, Students." *Harvard Gazette,* September 25.

Harvey, D. 2007. *A Brief History of Neoliberalism.* New York: Oxford University Press.

———. 2012. *Rebel Cities: From the Right to the City to the Urban Revolution.* New York: Verso.

Haskins, A. R. 2013. "Mass Imprisonment, Educational Inequality and the Intergenerational Transmission of Disadvantage: Effects of Paternal Incarceration on Children's Educational Outcomes and School Contexts." PhD diss., University of Wisconsin–Madison.

———. 2014. Presentation at the Cornell University Prison Education Program. Ithaca, NY, March 4.

Hatami, H., ed. 2006. *Crucial Issues in California Education 2006: Rekindling Reform.* University of California, Berkeley: Policy Analysis for California Education.

Hayden, T. 2004. *Street Wars: Gangs and the Future of Violence.* New York: New Press.

Heckler, M. M. 1985. "Report of the Secretary's Task Force on Black and Minority Health." U.S. Department of Health and Human Services.

Henig, N. R., R. C. Hula, M. Orr, and D. S. Pedescleaux. 1999. *The Color of School Reform: Race, Politics, and the Challenge of Urban Education.* Princeton, NJ: Princeton University Press.

Heuer, R., and S. Stullich. 2011. "Comparability of State and Local Expenditures among Schools within Districts." U.S. Department of Education.

Hillier, A. 2014. "Evaluating the Impact of a Nonprofit Supermarket on Food Shopping and Eating." Abstract no. 4698. Philadelphia: ACSP Conference.

Hochhausl, S. 2012. "Assisted Autonomy: The Austrian Settlement and Allotment Garden Association." Annual Meeting of the American Association of Geographers, New York City.

Hoene, C. W., and M. A. Pagano. 2011. "City Fiscal Conditions in 2011." Research Brief on America's Cities. National League of Cities. September.

Hogue, C., C. B. Parker, M. Willinger, J. R. Temple Jr., C. M. Bann, R. M. Silver, D. J. Dudley, et al. 2013. "A Population-Based Case-Control Study of Stillbirth: The Relationship of Significant Life Events to the Racial Disparity for African Americans." *American Journal of Epidemiology* 177, no. 8: 755–767.

Hooks, G., C. Mosher, T. Rotolo, and L. Lobao. 2004. "The Prison Industry: Carceral Expansion and Employment in U.S. Counties, 1969–1994." *Social Science Quarterly* 85, no. 1: 37–57.

Howell, W., P. E. Peterson, and M. West. 2007. "What Americans Think about Their Schools: The 2007 'Education Next'—PEPG Survey." *Education Next* 7, no. 4: 12–26.

Hoynes, H. W., D. L. Miller, and D. Simon. 2012. "Income, the Earned Income Tax Credit, and Infant Health." National Bureau of Economic Research. NBER Working Paper No. 18206. July.

Hu, W. 2006. "In New Jersey, System to Help Poorest Schools Faces Criticism." *New York Times*, October 30.

Hungry Birds. 2012. Guest post on Martha Payne, "Here Come the Hungry Birds!" *NeverSeconds* (blog), August 20, and "Hot Potatoes!," August 21.

Hunter, M. A. 2000. "Trying to Bridge the Gaps: Ohio's Search for an Education Finance Remedy." *Journal of Education Finance*, Summer.

Inciardi, J., and L. Harrison. 2000. *Harm Reduction*. New York: Sage.

Indymedia.us. 2009. "Plans to Gut Chicago Public Schools Draws Scores to Protest." January 31.

Institute for Criminal Policy Research (ICPR) at the University of London. Various dates. http://www.prisonstudies.org/. (In 2014 the International Center for Prison Studies merged into ICPR.)

Institute of Human Development. 2015. "Expanding Preschool in New York City—Lifting Poor Children or Middling Families?" University of California, Berkeley. February.

Institute on Women & Criminal Justice. 2009. "Quick Facts: Women and Criminal Justice."

Jarecki, E. 2012. "Voting Out the Drug War." *Nation*, December 3.

Johnston, S., and N. A. Lewis. 2009. "Obama Administration to Stop Raids on Medical Marijuana Distributors." *New York Times*, March 18.

Joravsky, B. 2004. "There Goes Another School." *Chicago Reader*, July 23.

Judis, J. B. 2000. *The Paradox of American Democracy: Elites, Special Interests, and the Betrayal of the Public Trust*. New York: Pantheon Books.

Just Food. 2013. www.justfood.rog.

Justice Mapping Center. 2012. "Justice Atlas of Sentencing and Corrections."

Kahlenberg, R. 2001. *All Together Now: Creating Middle Class Schools through Public School Choice*. Washington, DC: Brookings Institution Press.

Karabel, J. 2007. "The New College Try." *New York Times*, September 24.

Katz, B., and J. Bradley. 2013. *The Metropolitan Revolution: How Cities and Metros Are Fixing Our Broken Politics and Fragile Economy*. Washington: Brookings Institution Press.

Katz, D. 2012. "When Children Reject a Healthy Lunch." *New York Times*, October 11.

Katznelson, I. 1994. *Marxism and the City*. New York: Oxford University Press.

Kaufman, J. L. 2004. "Special Issue: Planning for Community Food Systems." *Journal of Planning Education and Research* 23, no. 4: 335–340.

Kearney, M., B. Harris, E. Jácome, and L. Parker. 2014. *Ten Economic Facts about Crime and Incarceration in the United States*. Hamilton Project. May.

Keller, B. A. 2014. "Letter from Our Editor." Marshall Project, online. November 15.

Kelly, R., 2006. "College Grads See Big Income Boost." CNN, October 25.

Kelly, R. W. 2007. "Washington's Secret Gun Files." Op-ed. *New York Times*, June 16.

Kennedy, G. 2013. "The Fiscal Crisis of the State Revisited." *Parchment in the Fire* (blog), April 11. http://geoffkennedy.org/2013/04/11/the-fiscal-crisis-of-the-state-revisited/.

Kessler, D. 2009. *The End of Overeating: Taking Control of the Insatiable American Appetite*. Emmaus, PA: Rodale.

Kilmer, B., G. Midgette, and C. Saloga. 2015. "Back in the National Spotlight: An Assessment of Recent Changes in Drug Use and Drug Policies in the United States." Center for 21st Century Security and Intelligence. Brookings Institution.

Kirp, D., 2007. "Racists and Robber Barons." *Nation*, July 13.

———. 2012. "Making Schools Work." Op-ed. *New York Times*, May 20.

Kleiman, M., J. P. Caulkins, and A. Hawken. 2011. *Drugs and Drug Policy: What Everyone Needs to Know*. New York: Oxford University Press.

Kleinbard, E. D. 2014. *We Are Better Than This: How Government Should Spend Our Money*. New York: Oxford University Press.

Kleine, R. J. 2013. "Bankruptcy Won't Fix Detroit." *Huffington Post*, July 26.

Knupfer, A. M. 2013. *Food Co-ops in America: Communities, Consumption, and Economic Democracy*. Ithaca, NY: Cornell University Press.

Korte, T. 2009. "New Drug War Strategy Focuses on Weapons and Cash." Associated Press, June 5.

Kozol, J. 1991. *Savage Inequalities: Children in America's Schools*. New York: Crown.

———. 2005. *The Shame of Nation: The Restoration of Apartheid Schooling in America*. New York: Crown.

———. 2012. *Fire in the Ashes: Twenty-Five Years among the Poorest Children in America*. New York: Crown.

Kristof, N. 2011. "Pay Teachers More." *New York Times*, March 13.

Krugman, P. 2012. "The Austerity Agenda." *New York Times*, May 31.

Kruse, K. M. 2012. "For God So Loved the 1 Percent." Op-ed. *New York Times*, January 17.

Kulish, N. 2007. "Europe Fears Meth Foothold Is Expanding." *New York Times*, November 23.

Lafer, G. 2014. "What Happens When Your Teacher Is a Video Game?" *Nation*, September 24.

LaMarche, G. 2007. "After Willie Horton." *Nation*, June 25.

Lanchester, J. 2014. "Money Talks." *New Yorker*, August 4.

Landais, C. 2007. "Les hauts revenus en France 1998–2006: Une explosion des inégalités?" Paris School of Economics Working Paper. Series updated by F. Alvaredo and T. Piketty.

Lankford, H. 1999. "A Descriptive Analysis of the NYS and NYC Teaching Force." *Campaign for Fiscal Equity v. State of New York*, plaintiff's exhibit 1482.

La'Shay, D. 2012. "I Just Wish Guns Were Harder to Come By." National Public Radio, December 20–23.

Lauria, M., and R. K. Whelan. 1995. "Planning Theory and Political Economy: The Need for Reintegration." *Planning Theory* 14: 8–3.

Lee, A. 2005. "Children of Inmates: What Happens to These Unintended Victims?" *Corrections Today* 67: 84–85.

Lee, G. 1991. *China Boy*. New York: Plume.

Lee, H., and C. Wildeman. 2013. "Things Fall Apart: Health Consequences of Mass Imprisonment for African American Women." *Review of Back Political Economy* 40, no. 1 (March): 39–52.

Leib, E. B., et al. 2012. *Good Laws, Good Food: Putting Local Food Policy to Work for Our Communities*. Harvard Law School Food Law and Policy Clinic. July.

Lemann, N. 2011. "Get Out of Town: Has the Celebration of Cities Gone Too Far?" *New Yorker*, June 27.

Leonhardt, D. 2012. "Coming Soon: 'Taxmageddon.'" *New York Times*, April 13.

Lerner, S. 2014. "A Second Chance for the Youngest Americans." *American Prospect*, January 16.

Levin, H., and N. Holmes. 2005. "America's Learning Deficit." *New York Times*, November 7.

Levitt, S., and S. Venkatesh. 2000. "An Economic Analysis of a Drug-Selling Gang's Finances." *Quarterly Journal of Economics*, August: 755–789

Lieber, M. J., and K. C. Fox. 2005. "Race and the Impact of Detention on Juvenile Justice Decision Making." *Crime & Delinquency* 51, no. 4 (October): 470–497.

Liptak, A. 2008. "New Look at Death Sentences and Race." *New York Times*, April 29.

———. 2009. "Justices Weigh Life in Prison for Youths Who Never Killed." *New York Times*, November 8.

Locker, R. 2012. "Memphis Lawsuit Now Goes after State's Voter Photo ID's Law." *Commercial Appeal*, August 8.

Logan, J. R. 2000. "Still a Global City: The Racial and Ethnic Segmentation of New York." In *Globalizing Cities: A New Spatial Order?*, edited by Peter Marcuse and Ronald van Kempen, 158–185. Malden, MA: Blackwell.

———. 2013. "The Persistence of Segregation in the 21st Century Metropolis." *City and Community* 12 (June): 160–168.

Loury, G. C. 2008. *Race, Incarceration, and American Values*. Cambridge, MA: MIT Press.

Lowndes, J. E. 2008. *From the New Deal to the New Right: Race and the Southern Origins of Modern Conservatism*. New Haven, CT: Yale University Press.

Lubienski, C., and S. T. Lubienski. 2006. "Charter, Private, Public Schools and Academic Achievement." National Center for the Study of Privatization in Education, Teachers College, Columbia University.

Lucas, P. 2009. "Business Using Music to Deter Crime and Loitering." *Seattle Times*, July 27.

Lustig, R. H. 2013. *Fat Chance: Beating the Odds against Sugar, Processed Food, Obesity, and Disease*. New York: Hudson Street Press.

Lyman, R. 2014. "Battles Looming over Surpluses in Many States." *New York Times*, February 3.

Lyman, R., and M. W. Walsh. 2013. "Struggling, San Jose Tests a Way to Cut Benefits." *New York Times*, September 23.

MacDonald, T. 2012. "Center City Bounding Back from Recession." *Newsworks*, April 29.

Macek, S. 2006. *Urban Nightmares: The Media, the Right, and the Moral Panic over the City*. Minneapolis: University of Minnesota Press.

Maciag, M. 2013. "How Rare Are Municipal Bankruptcies?" *Governing*, January 24.

Macintyre, L. 2007. "Rap Map." *New Yorker*, January 8.

MacKenzie, E. 1994. *Privatopia: Homeowner Associations and the Rise of Residential Private Government*. New Haven, CT: Yale University Press.

Madden, V. 2014. "Why Poor Students Struggle." Op-ed. *New York Times*, September 22.

Manik-Perlman, T. 2012. "Does PA's New Voter ID Law Impact Groups Differently by Ethnicity?" *Azavea*, August 2.

Manville, M. 2012. "People, Race and Place: American Support for Person- and Place-Based Urban Policy, 1973–2008." *Urban Studies* 49, no. 14 (November): 3101–3119.

Marcuse, P. 2011. "Critical Planning and Other Thoughts—Peter Marcuse's Blog." pmarcuse.wordpress.com.

Markusen, A. 2015. "The High Road Wins." *American Prospect*, Spring.

Marmor, T. R., and J. L. Mashaw. 1992. *America's Misunderstood Welfare State: Persistent Myths, Enduring Realities*. New York: Basic Books.

———. 2011. "How Do You Say 'Economic Security'?" Op-ed. *New York Times*, September 23.

Marshall, C. 2007. "Report Says Public Schools in California Are 'Broken.'" *New York Times*, March 16.

Martin, A. 2007. "Did McDonald's Give in to Temptation?" *New York Times*, July 22.

Martin, A., and N. Rashidian. 2012. "The Colorado Cannabis Factor." *Nation*, October 10.

Martin, I. W. 2008. *The Permanent Tax Revolt: How the Property Tax Transformed American Politics*. Stanford, CA: Stanford University Press.

———. 2010. "Redistributing toward the Rich." *American Journal of Sociology* 116, no. 1 (July): 1–52.

———. 2013. *Rich People's Movements*. New York: Oxford University Press.

Martin, M., and P. J. Podger. 2004. "Prison Guards' Clout Difficult to Challenge." *San Francisco Chronicle*, February 2.

Massey, D. S., and N. A. Denton. 1993. *American Apartheid: Segregation and the Making of the Underclass*. Cambridge, MA: Harvard University Press.

Matthews, C. 2007. "Advocates Seek Reform in 'Unjust' Drug Laws." *Rochester (NY) Democrat & Chronicle*, August 29. Matthews quotes Donna Lieberman, head of the New York Civil Liberties Union.

Mauer, M. 2006. *Race to Incarcerate*. New York: New Press.

———. 2009. *Changing Racial Dynamics of the War on Drugs*. Washington, DC: Sentencing Project. April.

———. 2013. *The Changing Racial Dynamics of Women's Incarceration*. Washington, DC: Sentencing Project.

Mauer, M., and M. Chesney-Lind., eds. 2002. *Invisible Punishment: The Collateral Consequences of Mass Imprisonment*. New York: New Press.

McCarty, M., G. Falk, R. A. Aussenberg, and D. H. Carptenter. 2012. "Drug Testing and Crime-Related Restrictions in TANF, SNAP, and Housing Assistance." Congressional Research Service. August 28.

McCrummen, S. 2011. "Republican School Board in N.C. Backed by Tea Party Abolishes Integration Policy." *Washington Post*, January 12.

McElrath, Y. M., D. C. McBride, E. Ruel, E. M. Harwood, C. J. Vanderwaal, and F. J. Chaloupka. 2005. "Which Substance and What Community? Differences in Juvenile Disposition Severity." *Crime & Delinquency* 51, no. 4 (October): 548–572.

McFadden, R. 1992. "Brooklyn Principal Shot to Death While Looking for Missing Pupil." *New York Times*, December 18.

———. 1997. "Limits on Cash—Transactions Cut Drug-Money Laundering." *New York Times*, March 4.

McIntosh, P. 1990. "White Privilege: Unpacking the Invisible Knapsack." *Independent Schools*, Winter.

McKinley, J. 2012. "Pat Robertson Says Marijuana Use Should Be Legal." *New York Times*, March 8.

McWhorter, J. H. 2000. *Losing the Race: Self-Sabotage in Black America*. New York: Free Press.

Meier, D., and D. Ravitch. 2010. "Bridging Differences." *Education Week* blogs, March 2, March 9, March 11, October 28, and November 2.

Meierhoefer, B. S. 1992. "The General Effect of Mandatory Minimum Prison Terms." Washington, DC: Federal Judicial Center.

Meredith, R. 1999. "Near Detroit, a Familiar Sting in Being a Black Driver." *New York Times*, July 16.

Meter, K. 2009. "Food and Farm Economies: Rural Economics Studies." Crossroads Resource Center, Minneapolis.

Meyerson, H. 2014. "The Revolt of the Cities." *American Prospect*, April/May.

Mier, R. 1975. "Exclusion and Inadequacy Indexes: Labor Market Indicators for Social Planning." Unpublished PhD thesis, Cornell University.

——. 1994. "Some Observations on Race in Planning." *Journal of the American Planning Association* 60:235–239.

Miles, K. 2013. "Aaron Sandusky Sentenced: Marijuana Dispensary Operator Gets 10 Years in Federal Prison." *Huffington Post*, January 9.

Miley, S., 2007. Comment on Monty Neill, "Scrap 'No Child Left Behind'!" *Nation*, July 9.

Miliband, R. 1969. *The State in Capitalist Society*. New York: Basic Books, 1969.

Miron, J. A., and K. Waldock. 2010. "The Budgetary Impact of Ending Drug Prohibition." *Social Science Research Network*, September 27.

Mitchel, J. 2015. "Pell Grants to Be Restored for Prisoners." *Wall Street Journal*, July 27.

Mitchell, K. 2006. " 'Liberating the City: Between New York and New Orleans'—a Response." *Urban Geography* 27, no. 8: 722–728.

Mock, B. 2012. "Florida's Felonious Voting Trap." *Nation*, October 15.

Montague, E. 2001. "Private Prisons: A Sensible Solution." Seattle: Washington Policy Center.

Moody, K. 2007. *From Welfare State to Real Estate: Regime Change in New York City, 1974 to the Present*. New York: New Press.

Moore, S. 2007a. "Reporting While Black." *New York Times*, September 30.

——. 2007b. "Trying to Break Cycle of Prison at Street Level." *New York Times*, November 23.

Morales, A. 2011. "Growing Food *and* Justice: Dismantling Racism through Sustainable Food Systems." Chap. 7 in *Cultivating Food Justice: Race, Class and Sustainability*, edited by A. Alkon and J. Agyeman. Cambridge, MA: MIT Press.

Moran, T. 2007. "Booker Redirects His Anger at the War on Drugs." *New Jersey Star Ledger*, June 24.

Motel, S. 2014. "6 Facts about Marijuana." Pew Research Center, April 7.

Nadeau, J. B. 2012. "Schools Hand In $66.6 Million Budget." *Woonsocket (RI) Call*, August 2.

National Center for Public Policy and Higher Education. 2008. *Measuring Up 2008: National Report Card on Higher Education*.

National Gang Center. 2012. "National Youth Gang Survey Analysis."

National Partnership for Women and Families. 2015. "State and Local Action on Paid Sick Days." www.NationalPartnership.org. July.

National Research Council. 2014. *The Growth of Incarceration in the United States: Exploring Causes and Consequences*. Committee on Causes and Consequences of High Rates of Incarceration, J. Travis, B. Western, and S. Redburn, eds. Committee on

Law and Justice, Division of Behavioral and Social Sciences and Education. Washington, DC: National Academies Press.

Ness, I. 2005. *Immigrants, Unions, and the New U.S. Labor Market*. Philadelphia: Temple University Press.

Nestle, M. 2007. *Food Politics: How the Food Industry Influences Nutrition and Health*. Revised and expanded edition. Berkeley: University of California Press. Originally published in 2002.

Neuspiel, D.R. 1996. "Racism and Perinatal Addiction." *Ethnicity and Disease* 6, nos. 1–2 (Winter–Spring): 47–55.

New American Foundation. 2014. "School Finance." April 21.

New York City, Department of Health and Mental Hygiene. 2012. "Take Care New York." Updated December 18.

New York City, Office of the Mayor. 2014. "Ready to Launch." January.

Newburger, E. C., and A. E. Curry. 1999. "Educational Attainment in the United States." (Update.) Current Population Reports P20–536, 2000.

Nichols, J. 2011. "How Socialists Built America." *Nation*, May 2.

Nixon, R. 2012. "New Guidelines Planned on School Vending Machines." *New York Times*, February 21.

———. 2014. "House Approves Farm Bill, Ending a 2-Year Impasse." *New York Times*, January 29.

Noah, T. 2012. *The Great Divergence: America's Growing Inequality Crisis and What We Can Do about It*. New York: Bloomsbury.

Nocera, J. 2012. "When ALEC Takes Over Your Town." *New York Times*, June 18.

Noguera, P. A. 2008. *The Trouble with Black Boys: . . . And Other Reflections on Race, Equity, and the Future of Public Education*. San Francisco: Jossey-Bass.

Noguera, P., and R. Weingarten. 2011. "Beyond Silver Bullets for American Education." *Nation*, January 10.

Norment, L. 1989. "Charles Rangel: The Front-Line General in the War on Drugs." *Ebony*, March.

O'Brien, M. 2012. "California's Catholic Hierarchy Takes Stand against Illegal-Immigration Dragnet." *Bay Area News Group*, January 30.

O'Connor, A. 2008. "The Privatized City: The Manhattan Institute, the Urban Crisis, and the Conservative Counterrevolution in New York." *Journal of Urban History* 34:333–353.

O'Connor, J. 1973. *Fiscal Crisis of the State*. New York: St. Martin's.

OECD (Organisation for Economic Co-operation and Development). 2011. *Lessons from PISA for the United States*. Strong Performers and Successful Reformers in Education. OECD Publishing.

O'Hara, T. 2005. "Riggs and PNC Reach New Merger Agreement." *Washington Post*, February 11.

O'Hara, T., and K. Day. 2004. "Riggs Bank Hid Assets of Pinochet, Report Says." *Washington Post*, July 15.

Open Hand. 2012. "About Us." http://www.openhand.org/. Programs continued in late 2015.

Orfield, G. 2001. *Schools More Separate: Consequences of a Decade of Resegregation*. Civil Rights Project, Harvard University.

Orfield, G., and S. E. Eaton. 1996. *Dismantling Desegregation: The Quiet Reversal of Brown v. Board of Education*. New York: New Press.

Orfield, G., J. Kucsera, and G. Siegel-Hawley. 2012. *E Pluribus . . . Separation. Deepening Double Segregation for More Students*. Civil Rights Project, Harvard University.

Orfield, G., and J. T. Yun. 1999. *Resegregation in American Schools*. Civil Rights Project, Harvard University.

Orlebecke, C. J. 1990. "Chasing Urban Policy: A Critical Retrospect." Chapter 9 in *The Future of National Urban Policy*, edited by Marshall Kaplan and Franklin H. James. Durham, NC: Duke University Press.

Ortiz, A., and L. Briggs. 2003. "The Culture of Poverty, Crack Babies, and Welfare Cheats: The Making of the 'Healthy White Baby Crisis.'" *Social Text* 21, no. 3: 39–57.

O'Sullivan, J. 2014. "In a First, Washington Supreme Court Finds Legislature in Contempt." *Seattle Times*, September 11.

Otterman, S. 2011a. "College-Readiness Low among State Graduates, Data Show." *New York Times*, June 14.

———. 2011b. "37% of New York Graduates Adequately Prepared for College, Data Show." *New York Times*, June 15.

Owens, D. M. 2010. "Check It Out: Get Your Groceries at the Library." National Public Radio, April 26.

Owens, E. G. 2011. "The (Not So) Roaring '20s." Op-ed. *New York Times*, October 1.

Packer, G. 2011. "The Broken Contract: Inequality and American Decline." *Foreign Affairs* 90, no. 6 (November/December): 20–31.

Pager, D. 2007. *Marked: Race, Crime, and Finding Work in an Era of Mass Incarceration*. Chicago: University of Chicago Press.

Paolocci, F. 2010. "Italian School Lunches Go Organic, Low-Cost, Local." *Globalpost*, September 8.

Parenti, C. 1999. "Lockdown America." *Times Literary Supplement*, no. 5041, 36.

Parker-Pope, T. 2009. "How the Food Makers Captured Our Brains." *New York Times*, June 23.

Parrott, J., F. Mauro, D. D. Kallick, C. Boldiston, B. Kramer, and H.-Y. Shin. 2012. *Pulling Apart: The Continuing Impact of Income Polarization in New York State*. Fiscal Policy Institute Report. November 15.

Partanen, A. 2011. "What Americans Keep Ignoring about Finland's School Success." *Atlantic*, December 29.

Patterson, O. 2007. "Jena, O.J. and the Jailing of Black America." *New York Times*, September, 30.

Peck, J. 2006. "Liberating the City: Between New York and New Orleans." *Urban Geography* 27, no 8: 681–713.

———. 2010. *Constructions of Neoliberal Reason*. Oxford: Oxford University Press.

———. 2012. "Austerity Urbanism." *City: Analysis of Urban Trends, Culture, Theory, Policy, Action* 16, no. 6: 626–655.

———. 2013. "Pushing Austerity: State Failure, Municipal Bankruptcy and the Crises of Fiscal Federalism in the USA." *Cambridge Journal of Regions, Economy and Society*, July 30.

Pettit, B., and B. Western. 2004. "Mass Imprisonment and the Life Course: Race and Class Inequality in U.S. Incarceration." *American Sociological Review* 69 (April): 151–169.

Phillips, A. M. 2012. "As Number of Gifted Children Soars a Fight Brews for Slots in Kindergarten." *New York Times*, April 14.

Phillips, K. 1969. *The Emerging Republican Majority*. New York: Arlington House.

Piketty, T. 2001. *Les hauts revenus en France au XXe siècle: Inégalités et redistributions 1901–1998*. Paris: Grasset.

———. 2007. "Income, Wage and Wealth Inequality in France, 1901–1998." Chap. 3 in *Top Incomes over the Twentieth Century: A Contrast between Continental European and English-Speaking Countries*, edited by A. B. Atkinson and T. Piketty. Oxford: Oxford University Press.

———. 2014. *Capital in the Twenty-First Century*. Cambridge, MA: Harvard University Press.

Piketty, T., and E. Saez. 2007. "Income and Wage Inequality in the United States, 1913–2002." Chap. 5 in *Top Incomes over the Twentieth Century: A Contrast between Continental European and English-Speaking Countries*, edited by A. B. Atkinson and T. Piketty. Oxford: Oxford University Press. Series updated by the same authors.

———. 2012. "Top Incomes and the Great Recession: Recent Evolutions and Policy Implications." Paper presented at the 13th Jacques Polak Annual Research Conference, International Monetary Fund, Washington, DC, November 8–9.

———. 2015. "Income Inequality in the United States, 1913–1998." *Quarterly Journal of Economics* 118 (1), 10–39. *Tables and Figures Updated to 2014 in Excel Format*. June. Table A3.

Pilkington, E., and S. Goldenberg. 2013. "ALEC Facing Funding Crisis from Donor Exodus in Wake of Trayvon Martin Row." *Guardian*, December 3.

Piven, F. 1994. "Reflections on Ralph Miliband." *New Left Review*, no. 206 (July–August): 23–26.

Pizzigati, S. 2011. "Why Greater Equality Strengthens Society." *Nation*, December 26.

Polantzas, N. 1976. "The Capitalist State: A Reply to Miliband and Laclau." *New Left Review*, no. 95 (January–February): 63–83.

Pollack, H., S. Danziger, K. S. Seefeldt, and R. Jayakody. 2002. "Substance Use among Welfare Recipients." *Social Service Review* 76:257–274.

Pollan, M. 2008. "Farmer in Chief." *New York Times Magazine*, October 12.

Pollitt, K. 2012. "Debate This!" *Nation*, October 29.

Poppendieck, J. 1998. *Sweet Charity? Emergency Food and the End of Entitlement*. New York: Viking.

———. 2010. *Free for All: Fixing School Food in America*. Berkeley: University of California Press.

Portz, J., L. Stein, and R. R. Jones. 1999. *City Schools and City Politics: Institutions and Leadership in Pittsburgh, Boston, and St. Louis*. Lawrence: University Press of Kansas.

Potamites, E., and A. Gordon. 2010. *Children's Food Security and Intakes from School Meals: Final Report*. Contractor and Cooperator Report No. 61, USDA, ERS. May.

Potter, W. 2013. "Shining a Light on ALEC's Power to Shape Policy." Moyers & Co. December 11.

Poverty & Race. 2011. "Implicit Bias: A Forum." *Poverty & Race* 20, no. 5 (September/October).

Powell, B. A. 2003. "Framing the Issues: UC Berkeley Professor George Lakoff Tells How Conservatives Use Language to Dominate Politics." NewsCenter. *UC Berkeley News*, October 27.

Powell, L. F., Jr. 1971. "Confidential Memorandum: Attack on American Free Enterprise System." August 23.

Powell, M. 2011. "In Gilded City, a Living Wage Still Stirs Fears." *New York Times*, December 20.

PRRAC (Poverty and Race Research Action Council). 2011. "Implicit Bias: A Forum." *Poverty and Race* 20, no. 5 (September/October).

Purdy, M. 2000. "The Truths of 'Hurricane' Are Complex." Our Towns. *New York Times*, February 13.

Quercia, R., and G. Galster. 2000. "Threshold Effects and Neighborhood Change." *Journal of Planning Education and Research* 20, no. 2: 146–162.

Rabin, R. C. 2011. "Study Finds Fewer Emergency Rooms as Need Rises." *New York Times*, May 18.

Raja, S., C. Ma, and P. Yadav. 2008. "Beyond Food Deserts: Measuring and Mapping Racial Disparities in Neighborhood Food Environments." *Journal of Planning Education and Research* 27, no. 4 (Summer): 469.

Raja, S., D. Pickard, S. Baek, and C. Delgado. 2014. "Rustbelt Radicalism: A Decade of Food Systems Planning in Buffalo, New York." *Journal of Agriculture, Food Systems, and Community Development* 4, no. 4: 173–189.

Raleigh, E., and G. Galster. 2012. "Neighborhood Disinvestment, Abandonment and Crime Dynamics." Paper for presentation at meetings of the Association of Collegiate Schools of Planning, Cincinnati, November.

Raufman J., M. Berger, C. Olson, and B. Kerker. 2009. "Diabetes among New York City Adults." *New York City Vital Signs* 8, no. 5: 1–4.

Ravitch, D. 2007. "Get Congress out of the Classroom." *New York Times*, October 3.

Reed, B. 2012. "The GOP's Welfare Lie." *Nation*, September 5.

Reich, M., and K. Jacobs. 2014. "All Economics Is Local." Op-ed. *New York Times*, March 23.

Reich, M., K. Jacobs, and M. Deitz, eds. 2014. *When Mandates Work Raising Living Standards at the Local Level*. Berkeley: University of California Press.

Ricard, M. 2009. "Idea to Limit Ex-Offenders in Area Roils Community Meeting." *Washington Post*, July 19.

Rich, M. 2014a. "Nation's Wealthy Places Pour Private Money into Public Schools, Study Finds." *New York Times*, October 22.

———. 2014b. "School Data Finds Pattern of Inequality along Racial Lines." *New York Times*, March 21.

Richtel, M. 2000. "Entrepreneur Pushes Plan to Fix California Schools." *New York Times*, April 17.

Riggs, M. 2013. "Obama's War on Pot." *Nation*, October 30.

Rimer, S. 2007. "The High School Kinship of Cristal and Queen." *New York Times*, June 24.

Rizzo, S. 2012. "Some of Christie's Biggest Bills Match Model Legislation from D.C. Group Called ALEC." *New Jersey Star-Ledger*, April 1.

Roberts, D. E. 1991. "Punishing Drug Addicts Who Have Babies: Women of Color, Equality, and the Right of Privacy." *Harvard Law Review* 104:1419–1482.

Roberts, S. 2006. "Infamous 'Drop Dead' Was Never Said by Ford." *New York Times*, December 28.

———. 2007. "Census Reveals Fear over Neighborhoods." *New York Times*, November 1.

Robichaux, M. 2001. "Researchers Aim to Develop Marijuana without the High." *Wall Street Journal*, February 28.

Rohe, W. M., and G. C. Galster. 2014. "The Community Development Block Grant Program Turns 40: Proposals for Program Expansion and Reform." *Housing Policy Debate* 24, no. 1: 3–13.

Rohter, Larry. 2004. "Pinochet Continues to Haunt Chile's Civilian Government." *New York Times*, July 18.

Rosen, J. 1999. "Rehnquist's Choice." Annals of Law. *New Yorker*, January 11.

Rosenbaum, D. 2013. "Ryan Budget Would Slash SNAP Funding by $135 Billion over Ten Years." Center on Budget and Policy Priorities, March 15.

Rosner, D. 1995. *Hives of Sickness: Public Health and Epidemics in New York City*. Brunswick, NJ: Rutgers University Press.

Rothfeld, M. 2008. "Gov. vs. Prison Guards: A Test of Wills." *Los Angeles Times*, September 22.

Rothstein, J. 2014. "Teacher Quality Policy When Supply Matters." *American Economic Review* (forthcoming—June).

Roza, M., and K. H. Miles. 2000. "Policy Inadvertently Robs Poor Schools to Benefit the Rich." *Seattle Post-Intelligencer*, September 24.

Ruberto, R., and M. Spence. 2011. "Adult Diabetes Prevalence in New York State." Diabetes Prevention and Control Program, Bureau of Chronic Disease Prevention and Research, New York State Department of Health.

Ruiz-Tagle, J. 2014. "Bringing Inequality Closer: A Comparative Urban Sociology of Socially Diverse Neighborhoods." Unpublished PhD thesis, University of Illinois at Chicago.

Rumberger, R. W., and S. Rotermund. 2009. "Ethnic and Gender Differences in California High School Graduation Rates." California Dropout Research Project Statistical Brief 11. March.

Russakoff, D. 2015. *The Prize: Who's in Charge of America's Schools?* New York: Houghton Mifflin Harcourt.

Russo, A. 2011. "Board Meeting Protest Update." District 299: The Inside Scoop on CPS. December 15.

Ryan, C. L. 2005. "What It's Worth: Field of Training and Economic Status in 2001." Current Population Reports Series, P70–98. Washington, DC: U.S. Census Bureau. September.

Ryan, J. 2010. *Five Miles Away, a World Apart: One City, Two Schools, and the Story of Educational Opportunity in Modern America*. New York: Oxford University Press.

Ryzik, M. 2007. "Cocaine: Hidden in Plain Sight." *New York Times*, June 10.

Sable, J., A. Garofano, and L. Hoffman. 2007. "Public Elementary and Secondary School Student Enrollment, High School Completions, and Staff from the Common Core of Data: School Year 2005–2006." National Center for Education Statistics, Common Core of Data, U.S. Department of Education.

Saez, E., and M. Veall. 2007. "The Evolution of High Incomes in Canada, 1920–2000." Chap. 6 in *Top Incomes over the Twentieth Century: A Contrast between Continental European and English-Speaking Countries*, edited by A. B. Atkinson and T. Piketty. Oxford: Oxford University Press.

Sahlberg, P. 2007. "Education Policies for Raising Student Learning: The Finnish Approach." *Journal of Education Policy* 22, no. 2: 147–171.

———. 2009. "Educational Change in Finland." In *International Handbook of Educational Change*, edited by A. Hargreaves, M. Fullan, A. Lieberman, and D. Hopkins, 1–28. Dordrecht, Netherlands: Kluwer Academic.

———. 2011. *Finnish Lessons: What Can the World Learn from Educational Change in Finland?* New York: Teachers College Press, Columbia University.

———. 2012a. "How GERM Is Infecting Schools around the World." Pasi Sahlberg blog, June 30. In the *Washington Post*, June 29.

———. 2012b. "What the U.S. Can't Learn from Finland about Ed Reform." *Washington Post* blog Answer Sheet, April 17.

Salisbury, S. 2012. "How to Fund an American Police State." *Nation* online, March 5.

Sanbonmatsu, L., J. Kling, G. Duncan, and J. Brooks-Gunn. 2007. "Neighborhoods and Academic Achievement: Results from the Moving to Opportunity Experiment." National Bureau of Economic Research.

San Francisco and Marin Food Banks. 2011. *Annual Report.* November 10.

San Francisco Department of Public Health. 2004. "Prevention Strategic Plan." February.

Saviola, S. 2010. "Despite Protests, Chicago Public Schools Continue with Closings." *Columbia Chronicle*, March 1.

Saxe, L., C. K. Kadushin, A. Beveridge, D. Livert, E. Tighe, D. Rindskopf, J. Ford, and A. Brodsky. 2001. "The Visibility of Illicit Drugs: Implications for Community-Based Drug Control Strategies." *American Journal of Public Health* 91, no. 12 (December): 1987–1984.

Scharper, J. 2012. "Baltimore Program Connects Farms and Corner Stores: Pilot Designed to Improve Residents' Eating Habits." *Baltimore Sun*, August 8.

Schemo, D. J. 2006a. "It Takes More Than Schools to Close Achievement Gap." *New York Times*, August 9.

———. 2006b. "Most Students in Big Cities Lag Badly in Basic Science." *New York Times*, November 16.

———. 2007. "Failing Schools Strain to Meet U.S. Standard." *New York Times*, October 16.

Schott, L. 2012. "Policy Basics: An Introduction to TANF." Center on Budget and Policy Priorities. December 4.

Schrag, P. 2003a. *Final Test: The Battle for Adequacy in America's Schools*. New York: New Press.

———. 2003b. "How the Other Half Learns." *Nation*, November 10.

Schwartz, H. 2007. "Summer Lunch Crunch." *Nation*, June 25.

Schwartz, N. D. 2014. "The Middle Class Is Steadily Eroding: Just Ask the Business World." *New York Times*, February 3.

Scruggs-Leftwich, Y. 2006. *Consensus and Compromise: Creating the First National Urban Policy*. Lanham, MD: University Press of America.

Sen, A. 1982. *Poverty and Famines: An Essay on Entitlements and Deprivation*. Oxford: Clarendon Press.

Sennett, R. 1970. *The Uses of Disorder: Personal Identity and City Life*. New York: Knopf.

Sentencing Project. 2005. *Prison Town: The Real Cost of Prisons Project*. Washington, DC.

Seversen, K., and M. May. 2002. "Growing Up Too Fat: Kids Suffer Adult Ailments as More Become Dangerously Obese." *San Francisco Chronicle*, May 12.

Shane, S. 2012. "The Opiate of Exceptionalism." *New York Times*, October 21.

Shanker, T. 2012. "Lessons of Iraq Help U.S. Fight a Drug War in Honduras." *New York Times*, May 5.

Shapiro, D. 2011. *Banking on Bondage: Private Prisons and Mass Incarceration*. American Civil Liberties Union.

Shapiro, F. 2013. "Quotable Harvard: An Expert's Pick of Choice Harvard Words." *Harvard Magazine*, March–April.

Sharkey, P. 2013. *Stuck in Place: Urban Neighborhoods and the End of Progress toward Racial Equality*. Chicago: University of Chicago Press.

Short, A., J. Guthman, and S. Raskin. 2007. "Food Deserts, Oases, or Mirages? Small Markets and Community Food Security in the San Francisco Bay Area." *Journal of Planning Education and Research* 26, no. 3 (March): 352–364.

Siegel-Hawley, G., and E. Frankenberg. 2012. "Reviving Magnet Schools." UCLA Civil Rights Project. February.

Silver, D., T. Mijanovich, J. Uyei, F. Kapadia, and B. C. Weitzman. 2011. "Lifting Boats without Closing Gaps: Child Health Outcomes in Distressed U.S. Cities from 1992–2002." *American Journal of Public Health* 101, no. 2: 278–284.

Simon, M. 2006. *Appetite for Profit: How the Food Industry Undermines Our Health and How to Fight Back*. New York: Nation Books.

———. 2013. *And Now a Word from Our Sponsors: Are America's Nutrition Professionals in the Pocket of Big Food?* Eat Drink Politics. January.

Simon, W. E., and C. B. Luce. 1978. *A Time for Truth*. New York: Reader's Digest Press.

Simpson, G. R. 2004. "Riggs Bank Had Longstanding Link to the CIA." *Wall Street Journal*, December 31.

Smith, E. L., and M. R. Durose. 2006. "Characteristics of Drivers Stopped by Police, 2002." Bureau of Justice Statistics Special Report. June.

Smith, P. 2010. "Baltimore Gets One of the Country's First Food Czars." *GOOD*, July 1.

Solidarity against Austerity. 2013. "Portland's Austerity Resistance Movement Sparks Changes to City Budget." July 1.

Spirn, A. W. 1984. *The Granite Garden: Urban Nature and Human Design*. New York: Basic Books.

Sridhar, C. R. 2006. "Broken Windows and Zero Tolerance: Policing Urban Crimes." *Economic and Political Weekly* 41, no. 19: 1841–1843.

Stamper, N. 2009. *Breaking Rank: A Top Cop's Expos of the Dark Side of American Policing*. New York: Nation Books.

Stamper, N., and E. Beavers. 2014. "Congress: Stop Militarizing Law Enforcement: Commentary." *Roll Call*, October 9.

Staples, B. 2009. "Even Now, There's Risk in 'Driving While Black.'" *New York Times*, June 15.

State Budget Crisis Task Force. 2012. *Report of the State Budget Crisis Task Force*. http://www.statebudgetcrisis.org/wpcms/.

Stegman, M. A. 1993. "National Urban Policy Revisited." *North Carolina Law Review* 71, no. 5: 1737–1777.

Stephens-Davidowitz, S. 2014. "The Geography of Fame." Op-ed. *New York Times*, March 22.

Stewart, J. 2011. *The Daily Show with Jon Stewart*. Comedy Central. December 13.

Stiglitz, J. 2012a. "Economist Joseph Stiglitz on Income Inequality in the U.S." American Public Media. Interview by Kai Ryssdal. *Marketplace*, June 6.

———. 2012b. *The Price of Inequality: How Today's Divided Society Endangers Our Future*. New York: Norton.

———. 2015. "Greece, the Sacrificial Lamb." Sunday Review. *New York Times*, July 26.

Stodghill, R., and R. Nixon. 2007. "For Schools, Lottery Payoffs Fall Short of Promises." *New York Times*, October 7.

Stone, C. N. 1993. "Urban Regimes and the Capacity to Govern: A Political Economy Approach." *Journal of Urban Affairs* 15, no. 1: 1–28.

———. 1998. *Changing Urban Education*. Lawrence: University Press of Kansas.

Stone, C. N., J. R. Henig, B. D. Jones, and C. Pierannunzi. 2001. *Building Civic Capacity: The Politics of Reforming Urban Schools*. Lawrence: University Press of Kansas.

Stone, M. K. 2009. "It's Lunchtime at School: What in Health Is Going on Here?" In *Smart by Nature: Schooling for Sustainability*, 19–60. Healdsburg, CA: Watershed Media.

Stony Brook University. 2012. "Rise of the Young Farmer." Stony Brook, NY.

Storper, M. 2011. Review of *Triumph of the City*, by Edward Glaeser. *Journal of Economic Geography* 11:1079–1082.

Strom, S. 2012. "Judge Rules Restaurant Law Stifles Ohio Cities." *New York Times*, June 12.

Stuntz, W. J. 2011. *The Collapse of American Criminal Justice*. Cambridge, MA: Belknap Press of Harvard University Press.

Substance Abuse and Mental Health Services Administration. 2008. *Results from the 2007 National Survey on Drug Use and Health: National Findings*. NSDUH Series H-34, HHS Publication No. (SMA) 08-4343. Rockville, MD: Substance Abuse and Mental Health Services Administration.

———. 2014. *Results from the 2013 National Survey on Drug Use and Health: Summary of National Findings*. NSDUH Series H-48, HHS Publication No. (SMA) 14-4863. Rockville, MD: Substance Abuse and Mental Health Services Administration.

Sugrue, T. J. 2012. "Empire and Revolution." *Nation*, October 15.

Suskind, R. 1998. *A Hope in the Unseen: An American Odyssey from the Inner City to the Ivy League*. New York: Broadway Books.

Swanson, C. B. 2009. *Cities in Crisis 2009: Closing the Graduation Gap*. Editorial Projects in Education Research Center.

Swendsen, J., M. Burstein, B. Case, K. P. Conway, L. Dierker, J. He, and K. R. Merikangas. 2012. "Use and Abuse of Alcohol and Illicit Drugs in U.S. Adolescents: Results of National Comorbidity Survey—Adolescent Supplement." *Archives of General Psychiatry* 69 no. 4: 390–398.

Szalavitz, M. 2011. "Study: Whites More Likely to Abuse Drugs Than Blacks." *Time*, November 7.

Tatum, B. D. 1997. *Why Are All the Black Kids Sitting Together in the Cafeteria? And Other Conversations about Race*. New York: Basic Books.

Tavernise, S. 2012a."Door to Door in the Heartland, Preaching Healthy Living." Science Times. *New York Times*, September 11.

——. 2012b. "Education Gap Grows between Rich and Poor." *New York Times*, February 9.

——. 2012c. "Obesity in Young Is Seen as Falling in Several Cities." *New York Times*, December 10.

Taylor, A. 2012. "Mexico's Drug War: 50,000 Dead in 6 Years." *Atlantic*, May 17.

Taylor, K. 2015. "At Charters, High Scores and Polarizing Tactics." *New York Times*, April 7.

Templeton, R. 2007. "Locked up in New Orleans." *Nation*, September 10.

Theodore, N. 2011. "The Everyday Violence of Urban Neoliberalism: An Interview." D. Hugill and P. Brogan. May 4.

Theriault, D. C. 2013. "Fritz Drops Political Nuke with 'No' Vote on City Budget." *Portland (OR) Mercury*, May 29.

Thernstrom, A., and S. Thernstrom. 2003. *No Excuses: Closing the Racial Gap in Learning*. New York: Simon & Schuster.

Tondro, T. 1991. *Connecticut Land Use Regulation*. Hartford: University of Connecticut School of Law Press [1978].

Tough, P. 2009. *Whatever It Takes: Geoffrey Canada's Quest to Change Harlem and America*. New York: Mariner Books.

——. 2012. *How Children Succeed: Grit, Curiosity, and the Hidden Power of Character*. New York: Houghton Mifflin Harcourt.

Travis, J., and M. Waul. 2003. *Prisoners Once Removed: The Impact of Incarceration and Reentry on Children, Families, and Communities*. Washington, DC: Urban Institute Press.

Travis, J., B. Western, and S. Redburn, eds. 2014. *The Growth of Incarceration in the United States*. Committee on Causes and Consequences of High Rates of Incarceration. National Research Council. Washington, DC: National Academies Press.

Tucker, J. 2011. "State's High School Dropout Rate Almost 20 Percent." *San Francisco Chronicle*, August 12.

Turberville, W. C. 2013. "The Detroit Bankruptcy." *Demos*, November.

Turner, M., A. Nichols, and J. Comey. 2012. *Benefits of Living in High-Opportunity Neighborhoods*. Urban Institute. September.

Tuttle, B. 2012. "Dollar Menu Double Down: McDonald's Pumps Up $1 Selections." *Time*, December 4.

Ulijaszek, S. J. 2002. "Human Eating Behavior in an Evolutionary Ecological Context." *Proceedings in Nutritional Sociology* 61, no. 4: 517–526.

Urbina, J. 2007. "New Mayor's Top Task: Fight a Wave of Crime." *New York Times*, November 23.

UNDOC (United Nations Office on Drugs and Crime) 2010. *World Drug Report 2010*.

——. 2015. *World Drug Report 2015*.

United States Courts. 2012. "Federal District Court Workload Increases in Fiscal Year 2011." Judiciary News. March 12.

U.S. Congressional Research Service. 2012. *The Senate Agriculture Committee's 2012 Farm Bill (S. 3240): A Side-by-Side Comparison with Current Law*. Ralph M. Chite, coordinator. 7–5700 R42552. Washington, DC. May 30.

U.S. Department of Agriculture, Dietary Guidelines Advisory Committee. 2000. *Report of the Dietary Guidelines Advisory Committee on the Dietary Guidelines for Americans, 2000*.

U.S. Department of Agriculture, Economic Research Service (ERS). 2012. "Definitions of Food Security." September 4.

U.S. Department of Agriculture, Economic Research Service—Supplemental Nutrition Assistance Program (SNAP) Data System. "Time Series Data."

U.S. Department of Agriculture, Food and Nutrition Service. 2014. "Nutrition Program Facts." April.

———. 2015a. "Farmers' Market Nutrition Program." May.

———. 2015b. School Breakfast Program. "Fact Sheet."

U.S. Department of Education, National Center for Education Statistics. 2012. *Numbers and Types of Public Elementary and Secondary Schools from the Common Core of Data: School Year 2010–11*. October.

———. 2013. *Characteristics of Private Schools in the United States: Results from the 2011–12 Private School Universe Survey*.

———. 2015. "Status Dropout Rates." *The Condition of Education 2015* (NCES 2015–144). https://nces.ed.gov/programs/coe/indicator_coj.asp. April.

U.S. Department of Education, Office for Civil Rights (OCR). 2014a. Data Snapshot: School Discipline. March.

———. 2014b. Data Snapshot: Teacher and Counselor Equity. March.

U.S. Department of Health and Human Services (HSS). 2011. "Results from the 2010 National Survey on Drug Use and Health: Summary of National Findings." Substance Abuse and Mental Health Services Administration. September.

———. 2014. "Results from the 2013 National Survey on Drug Use and Health: Summary of National Findings." NSDUH series H-48, HHS publication no. (SMA) 14-4863.

U.S. Department of Justice. Bureau of Justice Statistics. 2003. "Lifetime Likelihood of Going to State or Federal Prison."

U.S. Office of the President. 2012. *FY 2013 Budget and Performance Summary: Companion to National Drug Control Strategy*. April.

U.S. Senate Appropriations Committee. 2000. Subcommittee on the Departments of Commerce, Justice, State, and the Judiciary and Related Agencies, Appropriations for 2001, Part 6: Department of Justice, 698–699. March 2, 15–15, 22–23.

Välijärvi, J. 2012. "The History and Present of the Finnish Educational System." Sino-Finnish Seminar on Education Systems. Shanghai, May 31–June 2.

Välijärvi, J., P. Kupari, P. Linnakylä, P. Reinikainen, S. Sulkunen, J. Törnroos, and I. Afrrman. 2003. *The Finnish Success in PISA—and Some Reasons behind It*. Institute for Educational Research, University of Jyväskylä.

Veall, M. 2010. "Top Income Shares in Canada: Updates and Extensions." McMaster University, Department of Economics, mimeo.

——. 2012. "Top Income Shares in Canada: Recent Trends and Policy Implications." *Canadian Journal of Economics* 45, no. 4: 1247–1272. Series updated by author.

Venkatesh, S. 2002. *American Project: The Rise and Fall of a Modern Ghetto*. Cambridge, MA: Harvard University Press.

——. 2006. *Off the Books: The Underground Economy of the Urban Poor*. Cambridge, MA: Harvard University Press.

——. S. 2008. *Gang Leader for a Day: A Rogue Sociologist Takes to the Streets*. New York: Penguin.

Vietorisz, T. 1980. "The Hieroglyph of Production." Epilogue to *Growth, Profits, and Property: Essays in the Revival of Political Economy*, edited by E. Nell, 303–312. New York: Cambridge University Press.

Vietorisz, T., W. Goldsmith, and R. Mier. 1975. *Poverty Strategies: A Comparison of Latin America and the United States*. Los Angeles: School of Architecture and Urban Planning, University of California.

Wacquant, L. 2002. "From Slavery to Mass Incarceration: Rethinking the 'Race Question' in the US." *New Left Review* 13 (January–February).

——. 2010. "Class, Race and Hyperincarceration in Revanchist America." *Daedalus*, Summer.

Wade, L. 2012. "The Number of People in Private Prisons Has Grown by 1,664% in the Last 19 Years." *Policymic*, February.

Wagner, P. 2009. "Importing Constituents." Prison Policy Initiative Database. October 22.

Wallis, C. 2004. "Lessons from the [Obesity] Summit." *Time*, June 5.

Walsh, M. W. 2014. "Judge Disallows Plan by Detroit to Pay Off Banks." *DealBook*, January 16.

Walters, R. 2007. "Justice in Jena." *New York Times*, September 26.

Warner, M. 2010. "Feeding America One Snickers at a Time: Mars' Ridiculous Anti-hunger Promotion." *Moneywatch*, August 16.

Warner, M. E. 2011. "Club Goods and Local Government: Questions for Planners." *Journal of the American Planning Association* 77, no. 2: 155–166.

Webster, C. 2007. "Property Rights, Public Space and Urban Design." *Town Planning Review* 78, no. 1 (January): 81–101.

Wekerle, G. R. 2004. "Food Justice Movements: Policy, Planning, and Networks." *Journal of Planning Education and Research* 23, no. 4 (June): 378–386.

Welsh-Huggins, A. 2011. "Kelley Williams-Bolar, Mom Arrested for Faking Address to Send Children to Better Schools, Has Pardon Rejected by Parole Board." *Huffington Post*, September 2.

Weston, M. 2011. "Financing California's Public Schools." Public Policy Institute of California. November. http://www.ppic.org/main/publication_show.asp?i=1001.

White, M., and L. White. 1962. *The Intellectual versus the City, from Thomas Jefferson to Frank Lloyd Wright*. Cambridge, MA: Harvard University Press.

Whitman, S., A. M. Shah, and M. R. Benjamins. 2011. *Urban Health: Combating Disparities with Local Data*. New York: Oxford University Press.

Wickham, D. 2007. "One Democratic Candidate's Courageous Stand on Drugs." *Ithaca (NY) Journal*, May 10.

——. 2011. "Ohio Forced Desperate Mother's Hand." *USA Today*, January 31.

Wilgoren, D. 2007. "Bush Says Drug Policy Working." *Washington Post*, December 11.

Wilkinson, R. G., and K. Pickett. 2010. *The Spirit Level: Why Greater Equality Makes Societies Stronger*. New York: Bloomsbury.

Williams, P. 2014. "Drop Dead, Detroit!" *New Yorker*, January 27.

Williams, T. 2014. "Cities Mobilize to Help Those Threatened by Gentrification." *New York Times*, March 3.

——. 2015. "The High Cost of Calling the Imprisoned." *New York Times*, March 31.

Wilson, W. J. 2009. *More Than Just Race: Being Black and Poor in the Inner City*. New York: Norton.

——. 2012. "The Great Disparity." Reviews of *The Great Divergence*, by T. Noah, and *Coming Apart*, by C. Murray. *Nation*, July 30, 27–32.

Winerip, M. 2011. "For Detroit Schools, Hope for the Hopeless." *New York Times*, March 14.

Witte, J. F. 2000. *The Market Approach to Education: An Analysis of America's First Voucher Program*. Princeton, NJ: Princeton University Press.

Women in Prison Project. 2004. "Women Prisoners and Substance Abuse Fact Sheet." From Drug War Facts. March.

Yardley, W. 2009. "Some Find Hope for a Shift in Drug Policy." *New York Times*, February 15.

Yee, V. 2012. "No Appetite for Good-for-You School Lunches." *New York Times*, October 6.

——. 2014. "Co-ops Find They Aren't to Every Taste." *New York Times*, February 12.

Yeh, M-C, and D. L. Katz. 2006. "Food, Nutrition, and the Health of Urban Populations." In *Cities and the Health of the Public*, edited by Nicholas Freudenberg, David Vlahov, and Sandro Galea, 106–127. Nashville: Vanderbilt University Press.

YoRaps. 2012. "Mac Dre's Thizz Entertainment Releases Official Statement about DEA Drug Bust." April 26.

York, E. B. 2010. "How Feeding America Became the Go-to Cause for Marketers." *Advertising Age*, May 3.

Young, R. 2013. "Rebellious Cities." *Monthly Review* 65, no. 7 (December).

Younge, G. 2007. "Jena is America." *Nation*, October 8.

Zatz, M. S. 2000. "The Convergence of Race, Ethnicity, Gender, and Class on Court Decision Making: Looking toward the 21st Century." *Criminal Justice* 33:503–552 (3rd vol. by the Office of Justice Programs, National Institute of Justice).

Zedlewski, S., E. Waxman, and C. Gundersen. 2012. "SNAP's Role in the Great Recession and Beyond." Urban Institute. July.

Ziedenberg, J. 2011. "You're an Adult Now." National Institute of Corrections. December.

Zimring, F. E. 2011. *The City That Became Safe: New York's Lessons for Urban Crime and Its Control*. New York: Oxford University Press.

Index

Note: Page numbers in *italics* indicate figures; those with a *t* indicate tables.